D1226273

THE SONG OF THE MACHINE

THE SONG OF THE MACHINE

From Disco to DJs to Techno, a Graphic Novel of Electronic Music

David Blot & Mathias Cousin

Foreword by Daft Punk

**Translated from the French
by Joseph Laredo**

Editorial coordination by Benoit Pierre of Enormous Comics,
Jean-Marie Delbès, Laurent Cousin and David Blot

BLACK DOG
& LEVENTHAL
PUBLISHERS
NEW YORK

Copyright © Éditions Allia, Paris, 2016

English language translation copyright © 2019 by Black Dog & Leventhal Publishers, an imprint of Perseus Books, LLC, a subsidiary of Hachette Book Group, Inc.

Translated from the French by Joseph Laredo

Cover design by Kirk Damer

Cover copyright © 2019 by Hachette Book Group, Inc.

Hachette Book Group supports the right to free expression and the value of copyright. The purpose of copyright is to encourage writers and artists to produce the creative works that enrich our culture.

The scanning, uploading, and distribution of this book without permission is a theft of the author's intellectual property. If you would like permission to use material from the book (other than for review purposes), please contact permissions@hbgusa.com. Thank you for your support of the author's rights.

Black Dog & Leventhal Publishers
Hachette Book Group
1290 Avenue of the Americas
New York, NY 10104
www.hachettebookgroup.com
www.blackdogandleventhal.com

Originally published in 2000, and updated in 2016, by Éditions Allia, France.

First U.S. edition: October 2019

Black Dog & Leventhal Publishers is an imprint of Perseus Books, LLC, a subsidiary of Hachette Book Group, Inc. The Black Dog & Leventhal Publishers name and logo are trademarks of Hachette Book Group, Inc.

The publisher is not responsible for websites (or their content) that are not owned by the publisher.

The Hachette Speakers Bureau provides a wide range of authors for speaking events. To find out more, go to www.HachetteSpeakersBureau.com or call (866) 376-6591.

Print book interior design by Katie Benezra and Clea Chmela.

LCCN: 2019937391

ISBNs: 978-0-316-52617-3 (paper over board), 978-0-316-52624-1 (ebook), 978-0-7624-9517-7 (ebook), 978-0-7624-9516-0 (ebook)

Printed in China

1010

10 9 8 7 6 5 4 3 2 1

CONTENTS

INTRODUCTION TO THE
ENGLISH EDITION

When Mathias and I first had the idea around 1996 of telling the story of house music, we had practically nothing to go on. There were no David Mancuso compilations (and we still hadn't met him yet). There weren't mountains of books on the subject (only a handful), no websites with any kind of real information. It was before the time of YouTube and Wikipedia. There weren't even any films or documentaries; *Maestro* and *24 Hour Party People* had yet to be made. In fact, it was the very lack of sources and the difficulty of tracking down the information, especially from Paris, that spurred us on to tell the story of a genre of music that was, at that time, totally unacknowledged in France.

This book was originally published as two volumes. Volume 1 of *The Song of the Machine*, which comprised the first six chapters of this book, was published in France in 2000, but we'd been working on it on and off—being young and naturally lazy—for several years before that. In this first part, Mathias and I were writing about things we'd never actually experienced. We'd never been to The Hacienda, we were just babies when The Loft first opened its doors, and we were still in grade school when The Garage closed theirs forever.

Volume 2 (chapters 7 through 10) was published three years later. This part of the book reflects the time that Mathias and I lived through, from the first raves in 1990 to the French Touch phenomenon ten years later. Whereas in Volume 1 we wanted to tell the story of the origins of house music, staying as close as we could to the truth that we knew and uncovered through our research (and when our relationship to it seemed too far away, as in the Detroit chapter, we changed the names), in Volume 2, nearly all the characters you'll read about here are fictional, based on people we met or stories we heard during those years we were involved in the scene. For example, the character Stanley Rose (chapter 9) is loosely based on Lil Louis, but it's absolutely not Lil Louis. Jim, the French DJ in Chapter 10, is a compilation character based loosely on Laurent Garnier, Dimitri from Paris, and François Kevorkian. But it's none of them exclusively. It's Jim.

The Song of the Machine is by no means a history book. It's a comic book. A graphic novel. An art form in and of itself, which, much like house music, is an art form that has taken decades to be recognized as such. We hope that it is a thoughtful and entertaining book, but it doesn't pretend to be "the truth." How can it be? Thirty years later, people are still arguing about the origin of the word "house."

So here it is, finally in English, *The Song of the Machine*: a comic book done by two young French guys in Paris, dreaming about clubs in New York and Chicago. Hope you enjoy this book as much as we enjoyed the music.

DAVID BLOT, 2019, PARIS

Thanks to François Capuron,
Guy Delcourt, Paul Hahn @ Daft Arts,
Cedric Hervet, Shoichi Kajino,
Pierre Le-Tan, Maxime Marion, New Order,
Daft Punk, and Romain Tassinari.

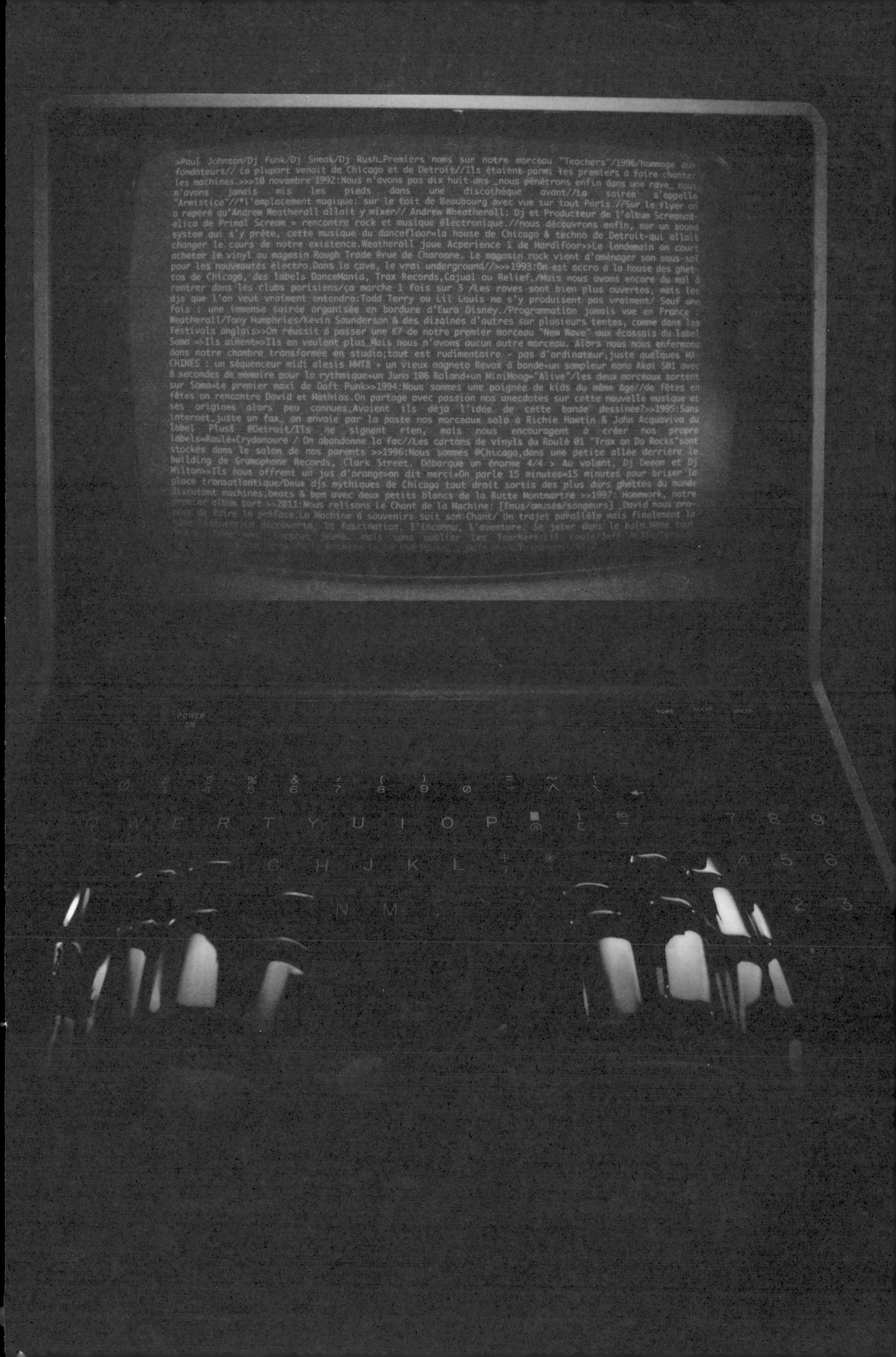
>Paul Johnson/Dj Funk/Dj Sneak/Dj Rush_Premiers noms sur notre morceau "Teachers"/1996/hommage aux
fondateurs// La plupart venait de Chicago et de Detroit//Ils étaient parmi les premiers à faire chanter
les machines.>>>10 novembre 1992:Nous n'avons pas dix huit ans _nous pénétrons enfin dans une rave_ nous
n'avons jamais mis les pieds dans une discothèque avant//La soirée s'appelle
"Armistice"//*l'emplacement magique: sur le toit de Beaubourg avec vue sur tout Paris //Sur le flyer on
a repéré qu'Andrew Weatherall allait y mixer// Andrew Wheatherall: Dj et Producteur de l'album Screamad-
elica de Primal Scream = rencontre rock et musique électronique.//nous découvrons enfin, sur un sound
system qui s'y prête, cette musique du dancefloor=la house de Chicago & techno de Detroit-qui allait
changer le cours de notre existence.Weatherall joue Acperience 1 de Hardlfoor>>Le lendemain on court
acheter le vinyl au magasin Rough Trade @rue de Charonne. Le magasin rock vient d'aménager son sous-sol
pour les nouveautés électro.Dans la cave, le vrai underground//>>>1993:On est accro à la house des ghettos de Chicago, des labels DanceMania, Trax Records,Cajual ou Relief./Mais nous avons encore du mal à
rentrer dans les clubs parisiens/ça marche 1 fois sur 3 /Les raves sont bien plus ouvertes, mais les
djs que l'on veut vraiment entendre:Todd Terry ou Lil Louis ne s'y produisent pas vraiment/ Sauf une
fois : une immense soirée organisée en bordure d'Euro Disney./Programmation jamais vue en France :
Weatherall/Tony Humphries/Kevin Saunderson & des dizaines d'autres sur plusieurs tentes, comme dans les
festivals anglais>>On réussit à passer une K7 de notre premier morceau "New Wave" aux écossais du label
Soma =>Ils aiment=>Ils en veulent plus_Mais nous n'avons aucun autre morceau. Alors nous nous enfermons
dans notre chambre transformée en studio;tout est rudimentaire - pas d'ordinateur,juste quelques MA-
CHINES : un séquenceur midi alesis MMT8 + un vieux magneto Revox à bande+un sampleur mono Akai S01 avec
8 secondes de mémoire pour la rythmique+un Juno 106 Roland+un MiniMoog="Alive"/les deux morceaux sortent
sur Soma=Le premier maxi de Daft Punk>>1994:Nous sommes une poignée de kids du même âge//de fêtes en
fêtes on rencontre David et Mathias.On partage avec passion nos anecdotes sur cette nouvelle musique et
ses origines alors peu connues_Avaient ils déjà l'idée de cette bande dessinée?>>1995:Sans
internet_juste un fax_ on envoie par la poste nos morceaux solo à Richie Hawtin & John Acquaviva du
label Plus8 @Detroit/Ils ne signent rien, mais nous encouragent à créer nos propre
labels=Roulé+Crydamoure / On abandonne la fac//Les cartons de vinyls du Roulé 01 "Trax on Da Rocks"sont
stockés dans le salon de nos parents >>1996:Nous sommes @Chicago,dans une petite allée derrière le
building de Gramophone Records, Clark Street. Débarque un énorme 4/4 > Au volant, Dj Deeon et Dj
Milton>>Ils nous offrent un jus d'orange>on dit merci+On parle 15 minutes=15 minutes pour briser la
glace transatlantique/Deux djs mythiques de Chicago tout droit sortis des plus durs ghettos du monde
discutant machines,beats & bpm avec deux petits blancs de la Butte Montmartre >>1997: Homework, notre
premier album sort >>2011:Nous relisons le Chant de la Machine: [Emus/amusés/songeurs] _David nous pro-
pose de faire la préface.La Machine à souvenirs suit son Chant/ Un trajet parallèle mais finalement la
la découverte, la fascination, l'inconnu, l'aventure. Se jeter dans le bain.

> Paul Johnson / DJ Funk / DJ Sneak / DJ Rush… The first names in our *Teachers* track, our / 1996 / homage to the founding fathers of house// Most of them were from Chicago and Detroit // They were the first to make machines sing. >>> November 10, 1992: We're still underage, but we finally manage to get into a rave. We've never even set foot in a disco before// The gig is called "Armistice" // The location is incredible: the roof of the Pompidou Centre in Paris, looking out over the entire city // According to the flyer, the mixer is Andrew Weatherall // Andrew Weatherall! DJ and producer of Primal Scream's *Screamadelica*—a part rock, part electronic music album // That's how we finally got to hear these new kinds of dance music, Chicago house and Detroit techno—and on a sound system that was just made for it. It was an experience that changed our lives. Weatherall played "Acperience 1" by Hardfloor // The next morning we were running to Rough Trade on the Rue de Charonne to buy the LP. Rough Trade specialized in rock, but it had just done up its basement to cater to the new craze for electronic music. Underground music underground // >>> 1993: We're addicted to house from Chicago on labels like Trax, Cajual, and Relief. / The Dance Mania series—but we're still getting kicked out of Paris clubs / We only get in a third of the time / Raves are a lot easier, but the DJs we really wanted to hear, like Todd Terry and Lil Louis, didn't do them much / Except once: a massive gig near Disneyland Paris (Euro Disney back then). The program was like no other we'd ever seen: Weatherall / Tony Humphries / Kevin Saunderson, and dozens of others, on different stages, like at a music festival >> We manage to persuade a Scottish guy from Soma Recordings => to listen to a cassette of our first recording, "The New Wave" => He likes it. He wants more. But we don't have any more. So we lock ourselves away in the back bedroom we've turned into a studio. Everything is basic—no computers, just a few machines: an Alesis MMT-8 MIDI sequencer, an old Revox reel-to-reel, an Akai S01 mono sampler with eight seconds of sample memory, a Roland Juno-106 synthesizer, a Minimoog…The result is "Alive" / That and "The New Wave" are released by Soma as Daft Punk's first EP >> 1994: We're still just kids // a bunch of kids around the same age, moving from gig to gig. We meet up with David and Mathias. We excitedly exchange stories about how we got into this new style of music and where it came from, which no one really knew. Maybe they already had this comic idea? >> 1995: We still don't have the internet; only a fax machine. We post our tracks to Richie Hawtin and John Acquaviva of Plus8 in Detroit / They don't take them, but they encourage us to set up our own labels = Roulé + Crydamoure. / We quit college // Boxes of LPs of Roulé's first album, *Trax on Da Rocks*—are piled up in our parents' living room >> 1996: We're in Chicago, in a little alley behind Gramophone Records on Clark Street. A huge four-by-four pulls up > At the wheel is DJ Deeon, beside him DJ Milton >> They offer us an orange juice > We say thank you and talk for fifteen minutes = which is what it takes to break the transatlantic ice / two iconic DJs from Chicago, straight out of one of the world's toughest neighborhoods, talking machines, beats, and BPM with two little white guys from the smart part of Paris >> 1997: *Homework*, our first album, is released >> 2011: We reread *The Song of the Machine* (touching, amusing, thought-provoking), and David asks us to do the preface. The Memory Machine cranks out its own song = a similar refrain and ultimately the same story: discovery, fascination, fear of the unknown, adventure. Jumping in at the deep end, even though you're still young. Still a teenager. Because you're young. But not forgetting our Teachers: Lil Louis / Jeff Mills / Derrick Carter / Armando / *The Song of the Machine* in the house.

Daft Punk, Spring 2011∎

CHAPTER 1

PRIME TIME

BEFORE THE MACHINE

Cleo Brown
Boogie Woogie — 1935

Fats Domino
The Fat Man — 1949

Ruth Brown
5-10-15 Hours — 1952

"Big Mama" Thornton
Hound Dog — 1953

Bill Doggett
Honky Tonk — 1956

The Exciters
Tell Him — 1962

Wilbert Harrison
Let's Work Together
(1962 & 1969 versions) — 1962

Martha and the Vandellas
Heat Wave — 1963

The Crystals
Da Doo Ron Ron — 1963

The Four Pennies
When the Boy's Happy,
(The Girl's Happy Too) — 1963

Sam Cooke
Live at the Harlem Square Club (LP) — 1963

Jackie Wilson and LaVern Baker
Think Twice (Version X) — 1964

Otis Redding and The Bar-Kays
Try a Little Tenderness (Live at UpBeat) — 1967

Archie Bell and The Drells
Tighten Up — 1968

Hollywood Jills
He Makes Me So Mad — 1968

Diana Ross and The Supremes
He's My Sunny Boy — 1968

Eddie Holman
I Surrender — 1969

Sly and The Family Stone
Thank You
(Falettinme Be Mice Elf Agin) — 1969

Isaac Hayes
Hyperbolicsyllabicsesquedalymistic — 1969

The Chi-Lites
Stoned out of My Mind — 1973

Bobby Womack
Across 110th Street — 1973

Shuggie Otis
Inspiration Information (LP) — 1974

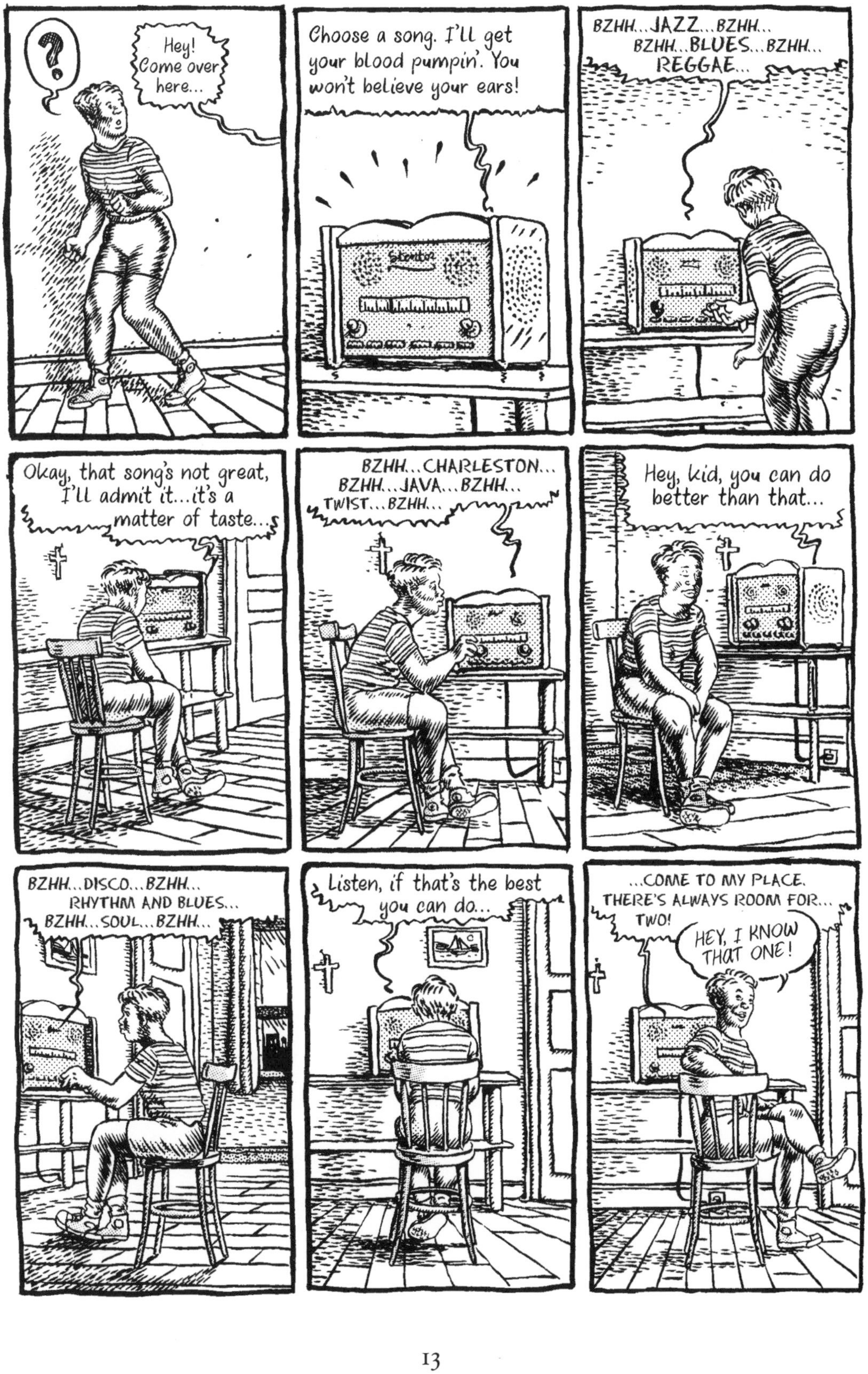
?
Hey! Come over here...
Choose a song. I'll get your blood pumpin'. You won't believe your ears!
BZHH...JAZZ...BZHH... BZHH...BLUES...BZHH... REGGAE...
Okay, that song's not great, I'll admit it...it's a matter of taste...
BZHH...CHARLESTON... BZHH...JAVA...BZHH... TWIST...BZHH...
Hey, kid, you can do better than that...
BZHH...DISCO...BZHH... RHYTHM AND BLUES... BZHH...SOUL...BZHH...
Listen, if that's the best you can do...
...COME TO MY PLACE. THERE'S ALWAYS ROOM FOR... TWO!
HEY, I KNOW THAT ONE!

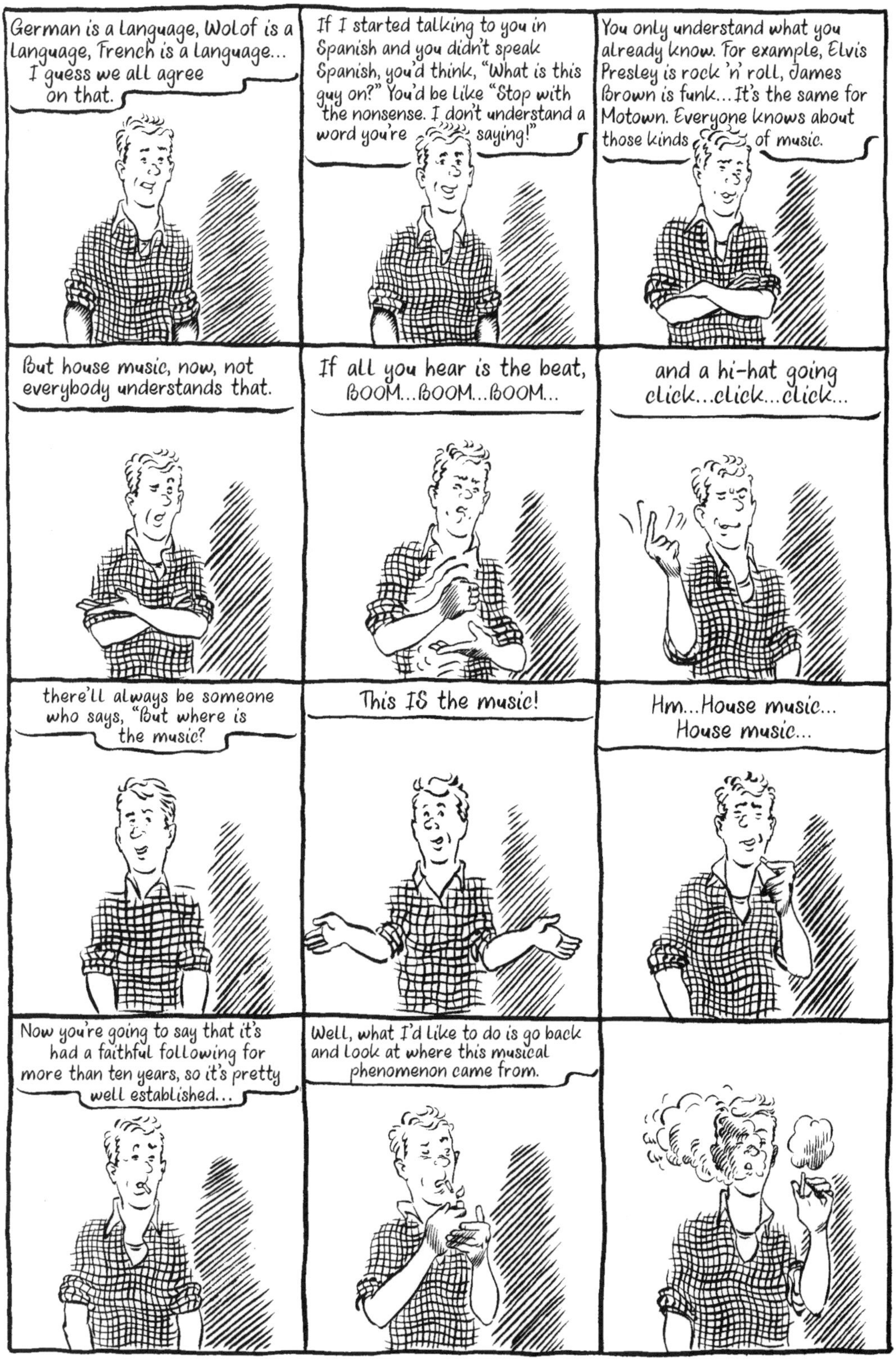
German is a language, Wolof is a language, French is a language... I guess we all agree on that.
If I started talking to you in Spanish and you didn't speak Spanish, you'd think, "What is this guy on?" You'd be like "Stop with the nonsense. I don't understand a word you're saying!"
You only understand what you already know. For example, Elvis Presley is rock 'n' roll, James Brown is funk... It's the same for Motown. Everyone knows about those kinds of music.
But house music, now, not everybody understands that.
If all you hear is the beat, BOOM...BOOM...BOOM...
and a hi-hat going click...click...click...
there'll always be someone who says, "But where is the music?
This IS the music!
Hm...House music... House music...
Now you're going to say that it's had a faithful following for more than ten years, so it's pretty well established...
Well, what I'd like to do is go back and look at where this musical phenomenon came from.

PROLOGUE

Weeelll...here we go! **House music,** right? But what exactly is it? And where did it come from? From disco? Or from the actual places where disco was played: discotheques, clubs, nightclubs...? Are we talking about the history of a dance-the "disco dance"-or about the disk jockeys themselves? In fact, for most people, disco *is* a dance, with clearly defined steps-a kind of ritual to be learned, just like rock and roll, the jerk, the twist, or the tango used to be. Etymologically speaking, the word "disco" comes from the French "discothèque," meaning a place where discs are stored. In fact, the world's first discotheque was in Rue de la Huchette in Paris, although it was really just a bar that was open late.

As a genre, disco didn't just appear overnight, in 1978; and the clubs didn't have to wait for John Travolta's on-screen gyrations to start a chain reaction, either. Disco, house, and techno had roots that stretched way back, and in many directions. To Jamaica in the 1940s, where sound systems were first set up outdoors. To Europe and the United States, where the postwar spread of affordable record players saw the start of teenage house parties-those impromptu get-togethers where a turntable could stand in for an entire band. For the over-eighteens, clubs like Whisky a Go Go on Sunset Boulevard and later Castel and Chez Régine in Paris started opening around 1960. If France had taken the lead initially, England now took over, with clubs that were a little more hip playing The Beatles, Twiggy, etc. Then it was back to New York, where the celebrity nightclub Arthur-founded in 1965 by Sybil Christopher, actor Richard Burton's ex-wife-became a runaway success when it opened its doors to the general public. And it was home to one of the world's first disk jockeys-Terry Noel, who became the prototype of the unpredictable superstar DJ. Early visitors to Arthur can remember a physical altercation between Terry and John Wayne (yes, the movie star!), who insisted on hearing his favorite 45. If Terry had not refused to play it, Wayne might have become the first cowboy DJ in history!

The end of the sixties saw this first wave of discotheques fizzle out. The hippies weren't exactly into dancing, and would've rather been out in the fresh air than inside a smoky club anyway. Only the jet-setters continued to frequent upmarket and exclusive nightclubs. After the Stonewall riots in New York in 1969, which asserted LGBTQ+ rights, a second type of club established itself alongside—and sometimes in combination with—the jet set club: the gay club.

This was the start of an explosion of New York clubs, and the list of names—some of them French—makes for magical reading. There were Shepheard's, L'Oursin, but also...

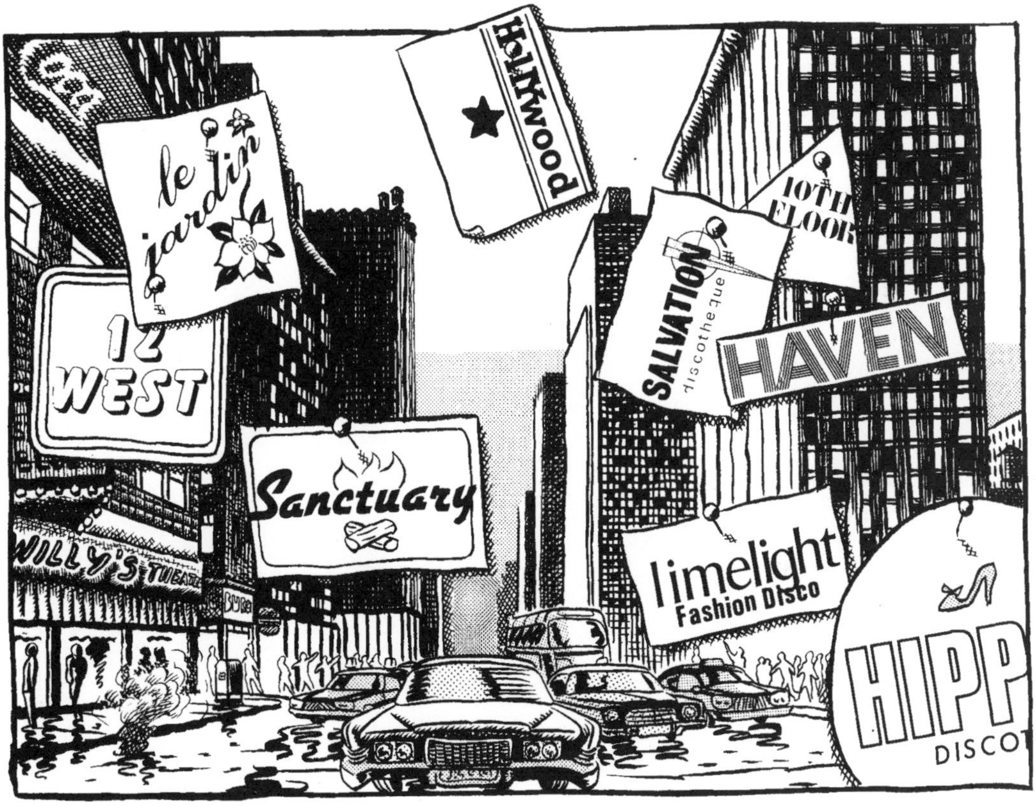
le jardin
Hollywood
10TH FLOOR
SALVATION discotheque
HAVEN
12 WEST
Sanctuary
WILLY'S THEATRE
limelight Fashion Disco
HIPP DISCO

Among the key DJs of that period were Michael Capella, Francis Grasso, and David Rodriguez. And although there wasn't yet any disco music as such, these guys were laying its foundations by mixing rock, R & B, jazz, and Latin music. Hey, we even managed to track down a few classic tracks Bobby DJ Guttadaro used to play at the Zodiac Club in the late sixties:

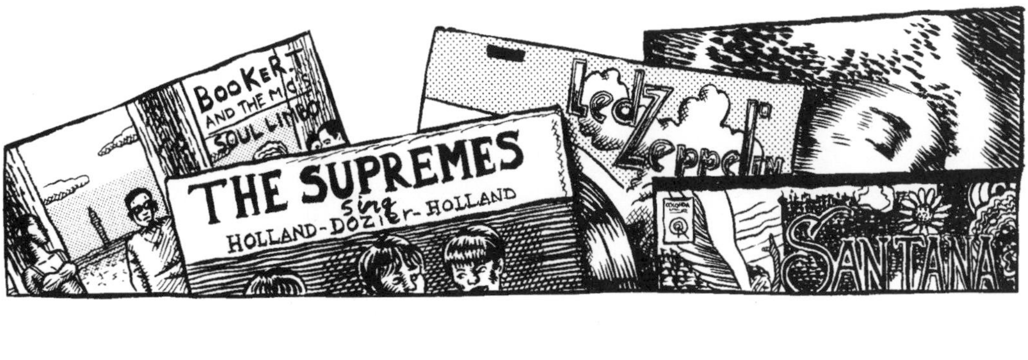
BOOKER T AND THE MG'S SOUL LIMBO
THE SUPREMES sing HOLLAND-DOZIER-HOLLAND
Led Zeppelin
SANTANA

In the Early 70s,

one club stood out—and it would change everything. The Loft, on the corner of Broadway and Bleecker Street in Lower Manhattan, opened its doors in 1971. Interestingly, it wasn't a club at all; it really was a loft. And it was the home of DJ and party organizer David Mancuso.

71/72
THE LOFT
CARD MEMBER
N° 262
F. Welch

Bleecker Street

The Loft regulars

It all started at The Loft

The amazing story of house music starts right here, with the couple hundred people who got together every weekend at The Loft. You had to have a membership card—and it wasn't easy to get one. You had to be as nuts about music as Mancuso himself—oh, and it helped if you were gay. Blacks, whites, and Latinos all danced to the best sound system in the city. It was the first time a nightclub had boasted such mind-blowing sound quality. It was all-enveloping, the bass so plush that dancers would just abandon themselves to it.

The only way Mancuso could get around the authorities was to maintain that it was a private party, which meant he couldn't sell alcohol. No problem! Drugs made up for that. Since The Loft wasn't officially a club, Mancuso could close whenever he felt like it. The parties would go on for hours and the later you arrived, the better.

David Mancuso was the first (and ultimate) cult DJ, and he kept The Loft concept going as he moved from apartment to apartment—from Loft to Loft—despite constant clashes with the authorities. In 1979, he escaped prosecution thanks to...his socks! Indicted for organizing parties

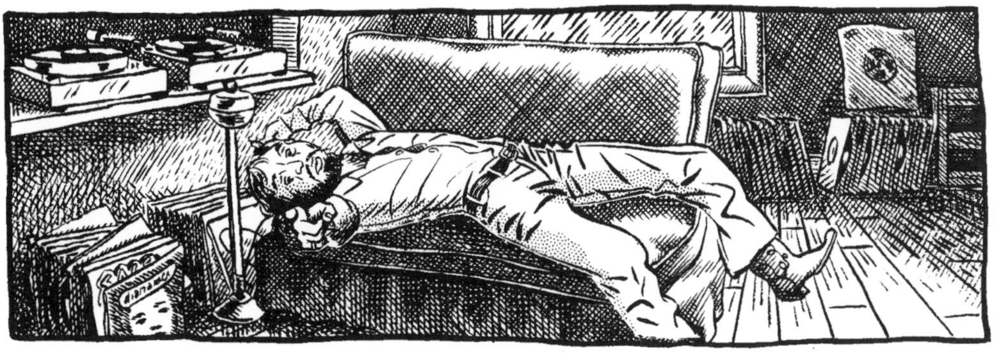

on a commercial basis (a good enough reason to shut down this den of iniquity), Mancuso called his friend Mel Cheren, who saved him by testifying: "Your Honor, do you really think a man who puts on odd socks every morning without even noticing could run any kind of business?"

Mancuso was exonerated!

Pioneer number 2: Nicky Siano:

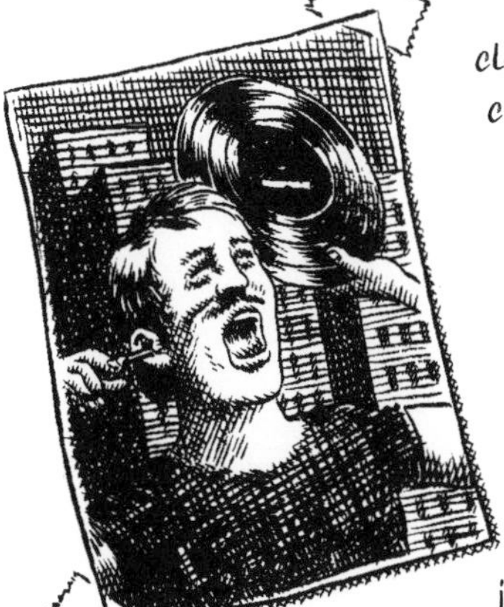

At fourteen, Siano starts going to clubs. At sixteen he gets a membership card for The Loft. A year later, in 1971, he takes advantage of its summer closure to open The Gallery, which is a rip-roaring success, attracting artists such as Grace Jones and Loleatta Holloway early on.

Nicky Siano is also the first DJ to be recognized by the recording industry, which is just beginning to realize that DJs can make or break a singer's career.

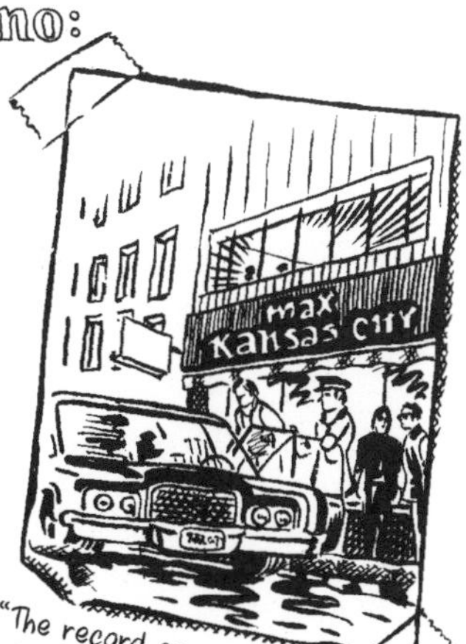
max
Kansas city

"The record companies even picked me up in a limo to go hear their new releases."

ONES TO WATCH

Ten years later, they would be the movers and shakers of house music, but back in 1969, fifteen-year-old Frankie Knuckles had only just met Larry Levan (also fifteen). Three years later, they both landed a job at The Gallery, where Nicky Siano got them to spike every glass of punch with a pinch of acid! Naturally, they also learned how to spin a disk, under Siano's watchful eye.

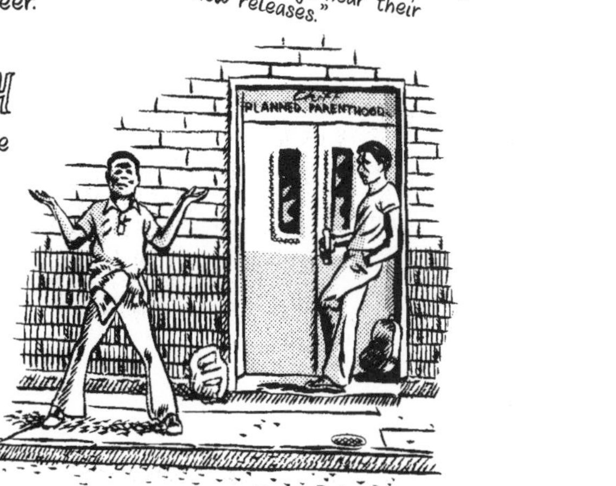
PLANNED PARENTHOOD

And the band played on...

By now, the clubs and the dances (and the drugs!) were well established, but disco music still didn't exist. Well, not officially, anyway. Looking back, it's clear that disco is a development of R & B and soul. With the likes of James Brown, Curtis Mayfield, Isaac Hayes (with "Shaft"), and The Temptations (with their version of the ode to freedom "Papa Was a Rollin' Stone"), R & B moved away from the style of Otis Redding, took on elements of funk, and became more rhythmic and leggy.

In Philadelphia, in 1972,

Kenny Gamble and Leon Huff are the two highest-profile producers.

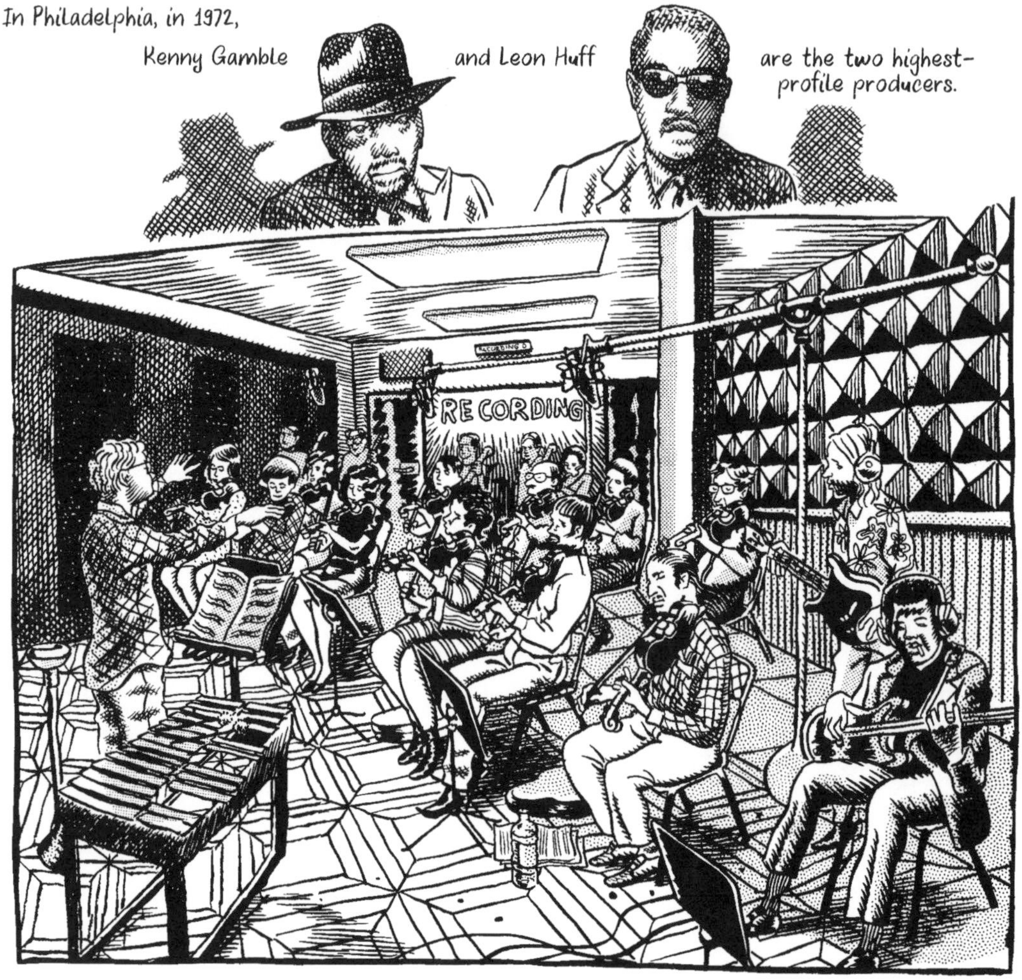
RE CORDING

Their record company is called PIR (Philadelphia International Records) and they've invented the Philly Sound–the precursor of disco, with a rich, full, symphonic style and easily comprehensible lyrics. All of Gamble and Huff's recordings (of Billy Paul, The O'Jays, MFSB, etc.) feature Vince Montana's inspired orchestrations, performed by the finest string players around.

1973 is the "glamour year," when Broadway meets glam rock and disco finally comes into its own.

And it spreads like wildfire!

Every DJ in New York is after "Soul Makossa," an obscure recording by the totally unknown Manu Dibango. Some now regard this as the very first disco number, while others argue that it was "Armed and Extremely Dangerous" by First Choice or Stevie Wonder's smash hit "Superstition."...

It's 1974, and Miami–the gateway to the Caribbean–has become the crucible of the disco industry. Harry Wayne Casey and Richard Finch are producing George McCrae's delicious "Rock Your Baby" and tracks by KC and the Sunshine Band, which top the charts alongside songs by Barry White and Van McCoy. Disco has its first hits.

But even though everyone is listening to it, disco still doesn't have a universal following. Mom and Pop are still doing the twist...

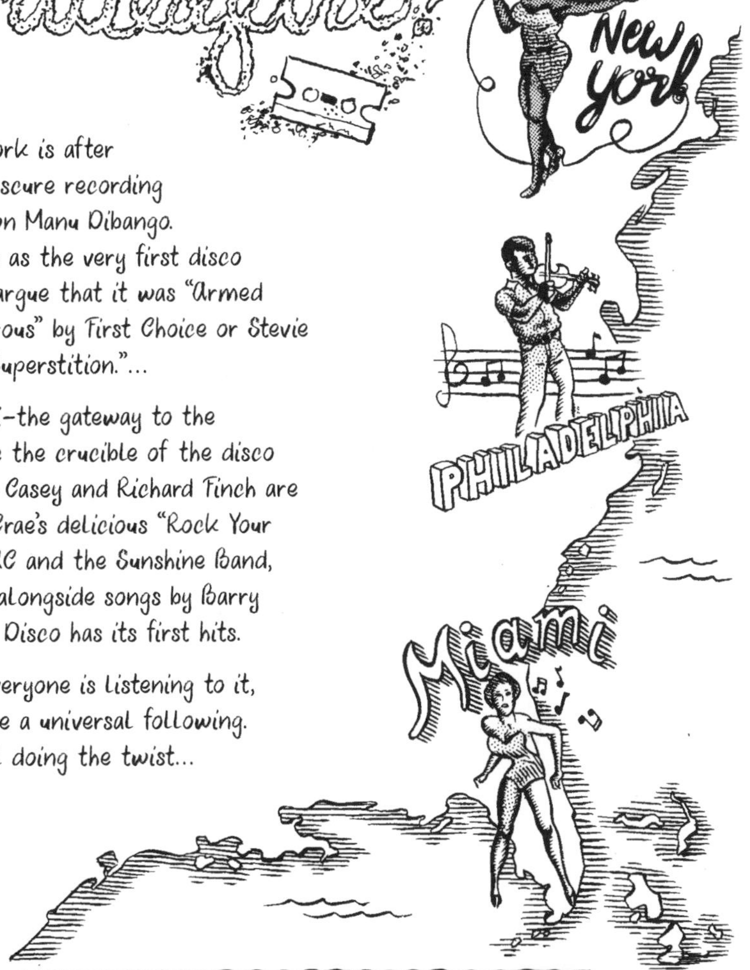
New york
PHILADELPHIA
Miami

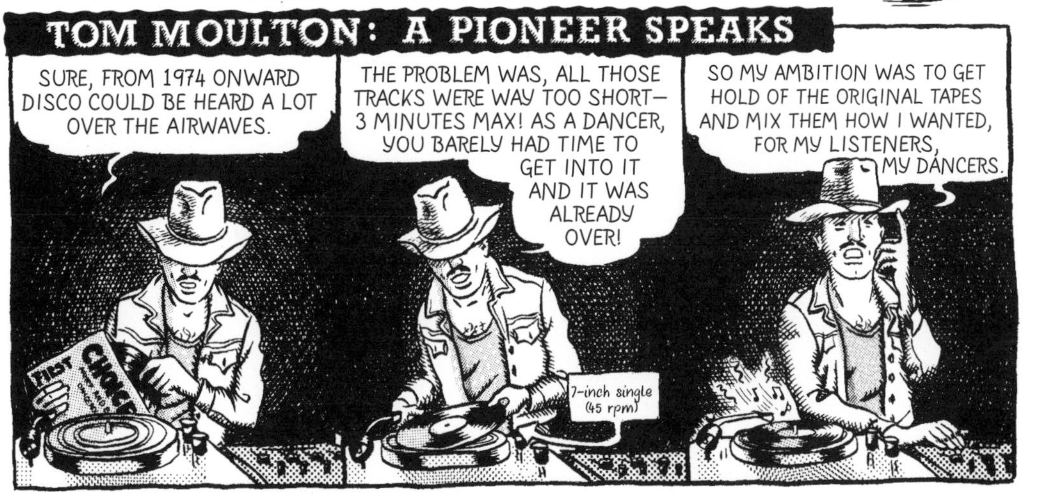
TOM MOULTON: A PIONEER SPEAKS
SURE, FROM 1974 ONWARD DISCO COULD BE HEARD A LOT OVER THE AIRWAVES.
FIRST CHOICE
THE PROBLEM WAS, ALL THOSE TRACKS WERE WAY TOO SHORT— 3 MINUTES MAX! AS A DANCER, YOU BARELY HAD TIME TO GET INTO IT AND IT WAS ALREADY OVER!
7-inch single (45 rpm)
SO MY AMBITION WAS TO GET HOLD OF THE ORIGINAL TAPES AND MIX THEM HOW I WANTED, FOR MY LISTENERS, MY DANCERS.

Quite a guy, that Tom Moulton—a regular ol' disco genius. Did you know, he had all of five inventions to his name: slip-cueing, the break, the medley, the remix, and the twelve-inch single.

While working as a DJ at the Sandpiper in Fire Island, New York, Moulton was unusual in that he would never mix live. Instead, he did his mixing at home and brought the tapes to the club. He admitted he was too fascinated watching the reaction of the dancers to be able to do the mixing there and then.

He ended up with an impressive array of equipment—a proper home studio before its time.

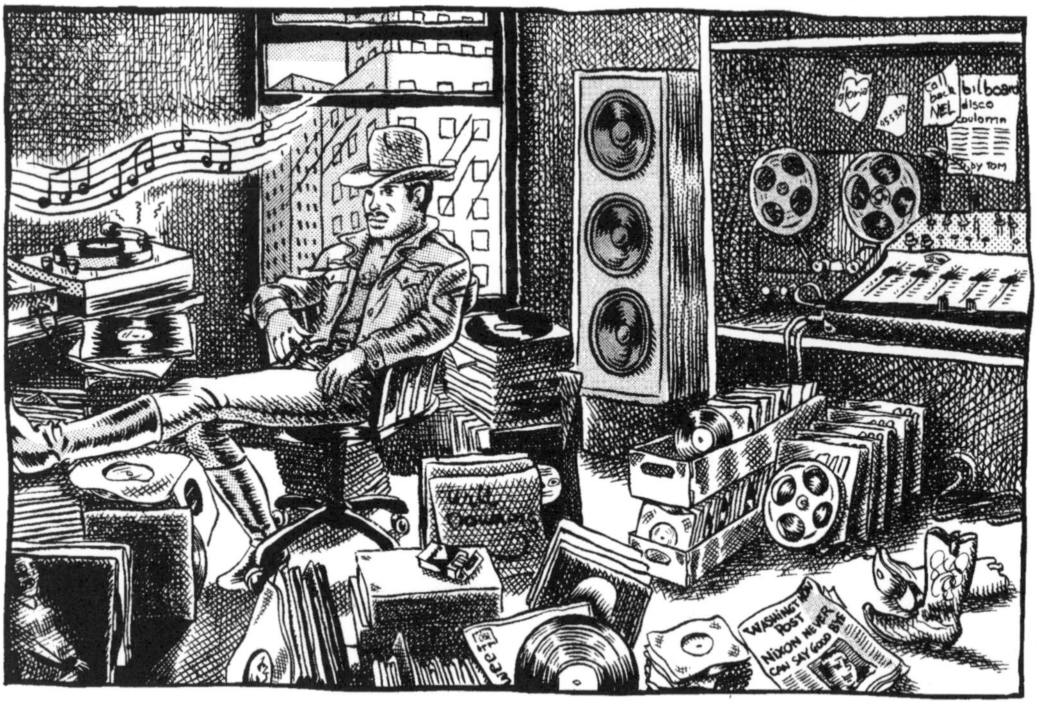
gloria
call back NEL
bilboard disco coulomn
by TOM
WASHINGTON POST
NIXON NEVER CAN SAY GOOD BYE

Thanks to Mel Cheren (the guy who rescued David Mancuso from the jaws of injustice), Moulton got to work on the tapes of a record by Will Downing. It would become the first dance music remix. The idea, which had come from his experience watching dancers, broke the mold of the pop single, extending tracks from three to six or even eight minutes. The insertion of breakdown sections allowed the music to match the flow of the dance floor. As a result, Moulton became the first official recording mixer: between 1973 and 1979, more than a hundred disks were labeled "A Tom Moulton Mix."

Moulton's other key invention came about as a result of pure chance: "I'd just finished a mix of an Al Downing track—this would have been, hang on, '74, that's it—and I had to have a disk ready and pressed within the hour. That was when my assistant, José Rodriguez, told me we'd run out of seven-inch blanks. I said, 'Never mind, go get an LP blank instead; we'll make do with that.' I still remember our faces when we realized the extra dynamic range we'd get by spreading the grooves right out. We had a whole LP side for a six-minute track; the sound would be incredible." Moulton and Rodriguez had just "invented" the twelve-inch single—and were about to drop a bombshell on the music industry at the time. Seven-inch disks were for pop; from now on, disco would be twelve-inch.

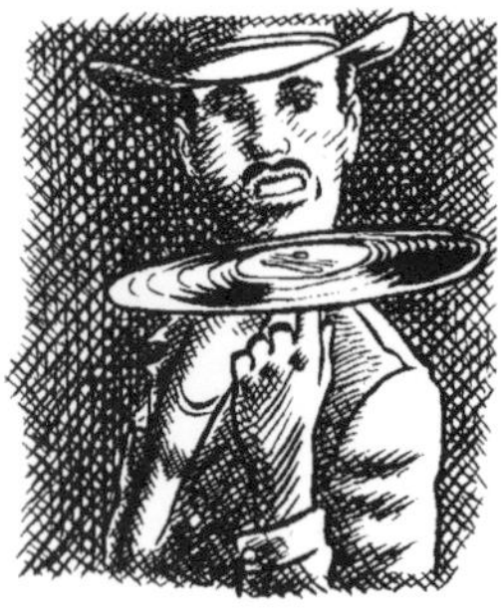

MEANWHILE...

There were, of course, other key players–both DJs and producers–in the disco story, as well as cities other than New York and countries other than the USA. Jamaica, for example, where a whole new vocabulary–from sound systems to dub and MCs–was being invented, as well as new production techniques, which would eventually add to the disco mix.

And then there were the outsiders: those who were neither gay nor jet-setters–or just happened not to live in Manhattan. DJ Kool Herc was born in Jamaica, but settled in the Bronx. He and his buddies were too young to go to clubs, and would never have been allowed in anyway. "Disco was too bourgeois for us." So they stayed where they were. In 1974, when he was playing the projects in Sedgwick Avenue, Kool Herc hit on it. His big idea? To cut 'n' mix James Brown with James Brown, losing everything except the percussion breaks.

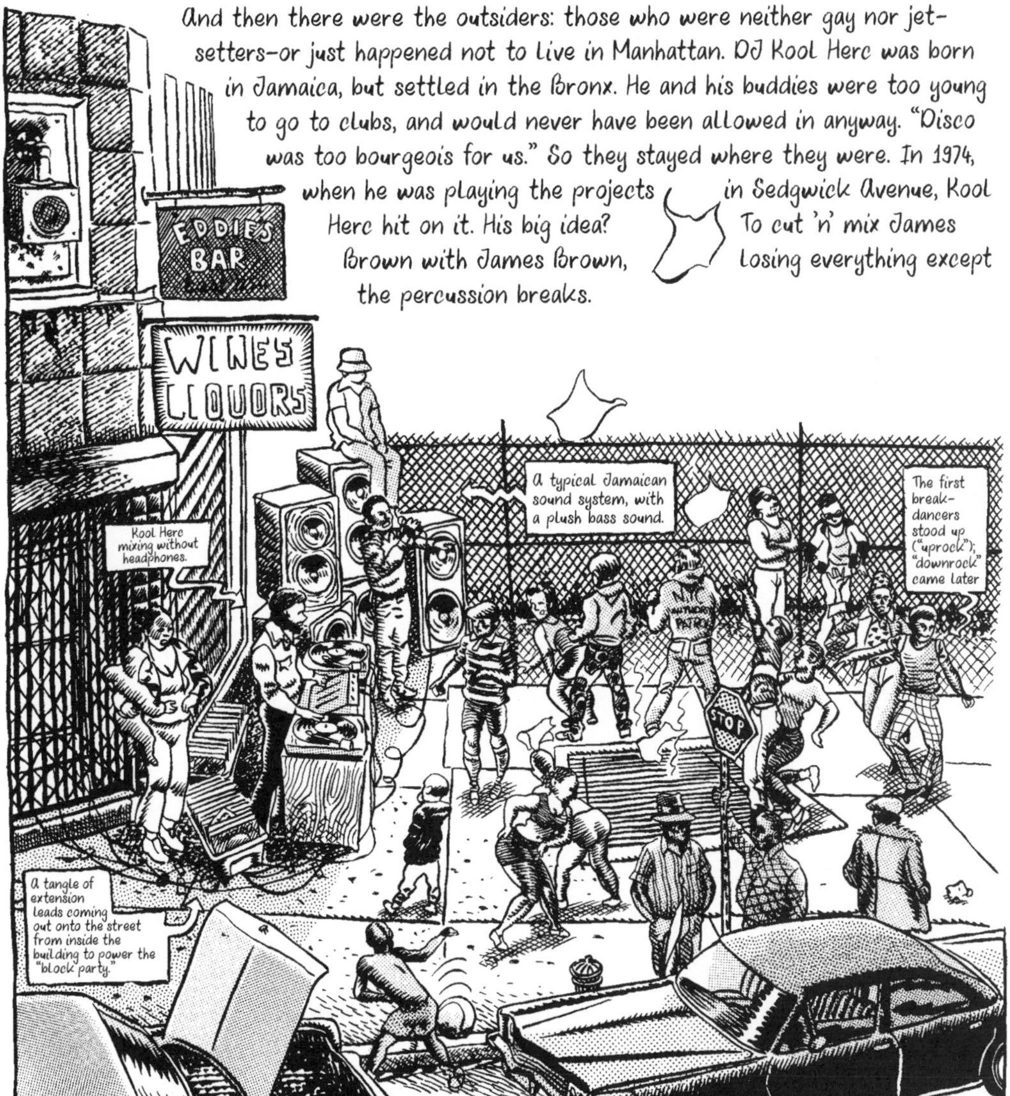
EDDIE'S BAR
WINES LIQUORS
A typical Jamaican sound system, with a plush bass sound.
The first break-dancers stood up ("uprock"); "downrock" came later
Kool Herc mixing without headphones.
STOP
A tangle of extension leads coming out onto the street from inside the building to power the "block party."

Kool Herc would soon join forces with other Bronx kids like Afrika Bambaataa and Grandmaster Flash (the first "scratcher"). Together, they created the whole hip-hop and rap culture. This was an alternative to disco–or, rather, a reaction to it, since its adherents were denied access to the upmarket New York clubs. When disco declined in the eighties, it was rap that gradually took its place. The transition started even before the *Saturday Night Fever* disco bandwagon got going. But that's jumping ahead...

CHAPTER 2

DISCO MANIA

WHEN THE MACHINE GOES WILD

MFSB
Love Is The Message
(A Tom Moulton Mix) — 1973

David Bowie
Young Americans — 1975

Hamilton Bohannon
Bohannon's Beat — 1975

Rose Royce
Car Wash (LP) — 1976

Donna Summer and Giorgio Moroder
I Feel Love — 1977

The Salsoul Orchestra
feat. Loleatta Hollway
Runaway — 1977

Roy Ayers
Running Away — 1977

Chic
The Chic Organization — 1977–1979

Marvin Gaye
Got to Give It Up — 1977

First Choice
Let No Man Put Asunder — 1977

Bee Gees
Night Fever — 1977

The Rolling Stones
Miss You — 1978

Rod Stewart
Da Ya Think I'm Sexy? — 1978

Wabiné
The Martians Visit — 1978

Michael Jackson
Don't Stop 'Til You Get Enough — 1979

Inner Life and Jocelyn Brown
I'm Caught Up
(In A One Night Love Affair) — 1979

Sylvester
I Need Somebody to Love Tonight — 1979

Diana Ross and Chic
Diana (LP) — 1980

Unlimited Touch
I Hear Music in the Streets
(François K. Mix) — 1980

Northend
Tee's Happy (Tee Scott Mix) — 1981

Crashers
Flight to Jamaica — 1981

France Joli
Gonna Get Over You
(François K. and Randy Red Mix) — 1981

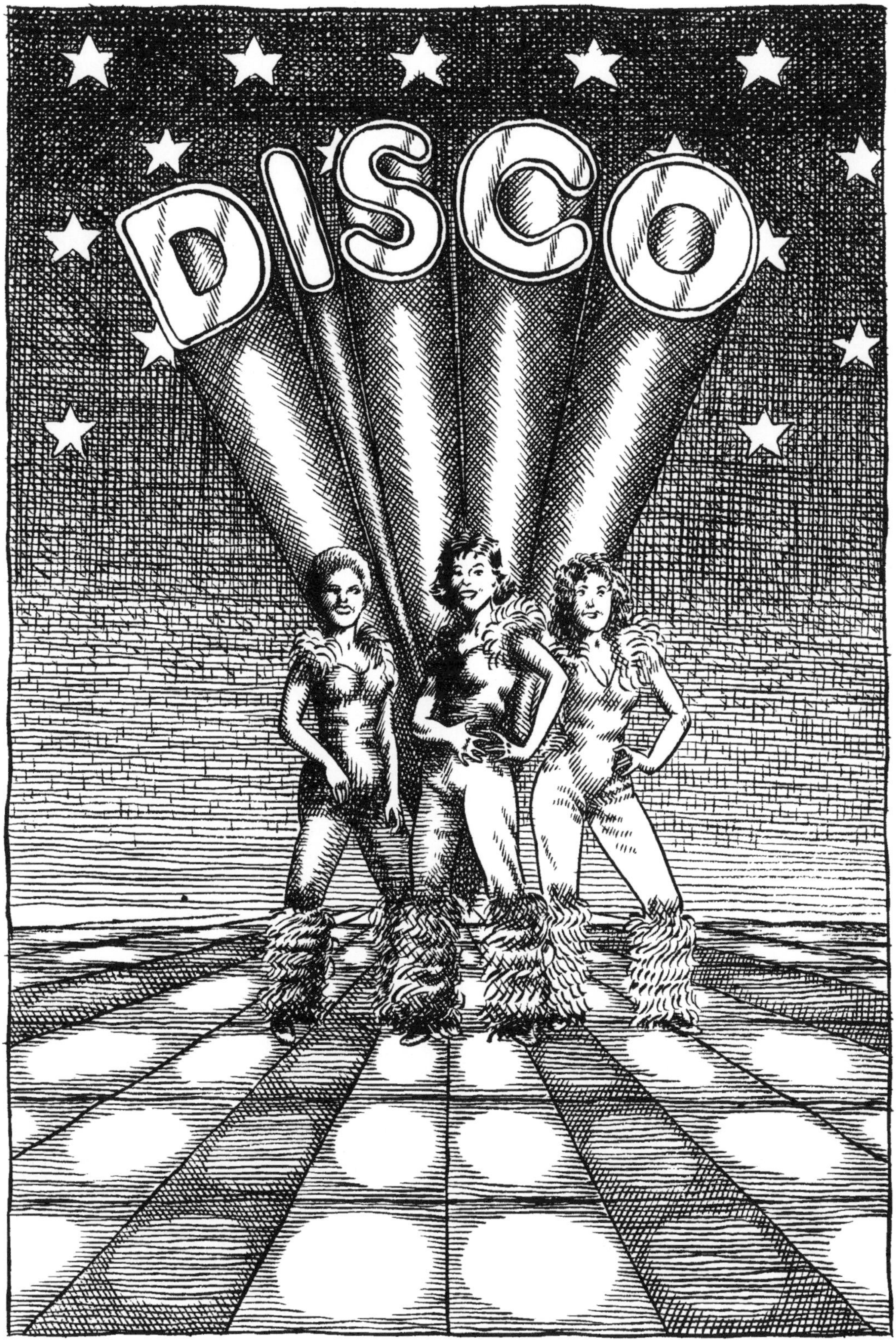
DISCO

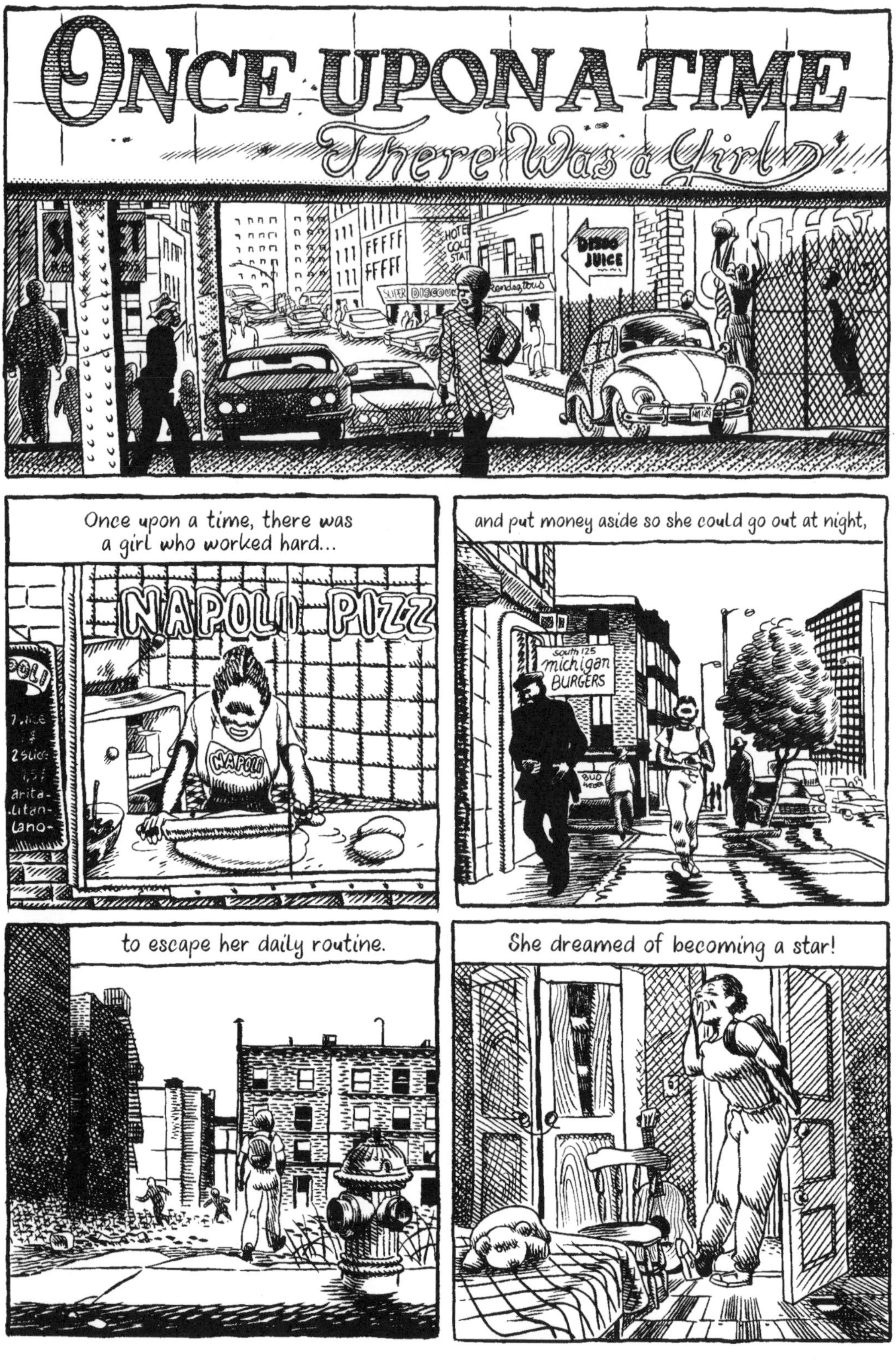
ONCE UPON A TIME
There Was a Girl
DISCO JUICE
SUPER DISCOUN
Once upon a time, there was a girl who worked hard...
NAPOLI PIZZ
NAPOLI
and put money aside so she could go out at night,
south 125 michigan BURGERS
to escape her daily routine.
She dreamed of becoming a star!

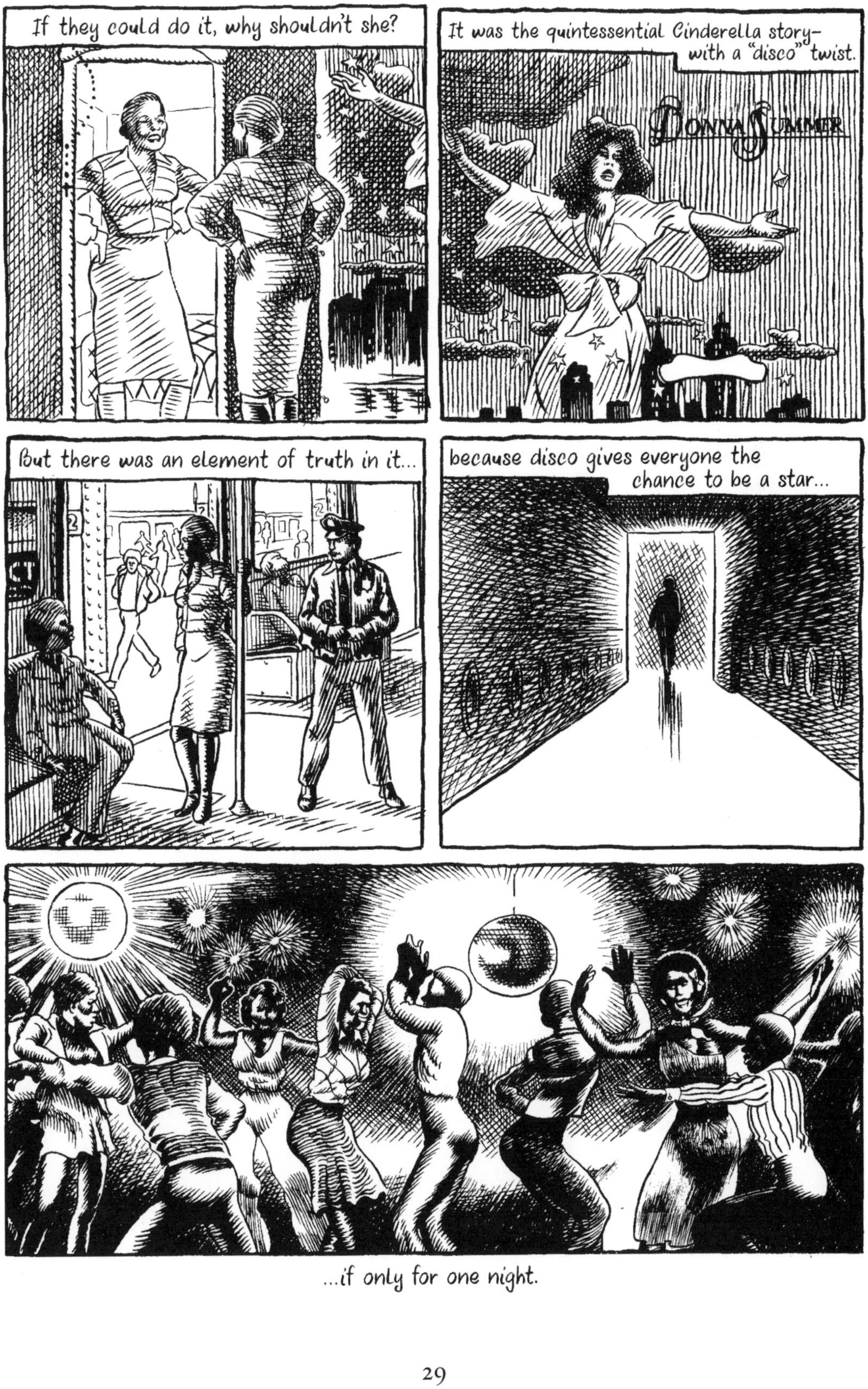
If they could do it, why shouldn't she?
It was the quintessential Cinderella story—with a "disco" twist.
DONNA SUMMER
But there was an element of truth in it...
because disco gives everyone the chance to be a star...

...if only for one night.

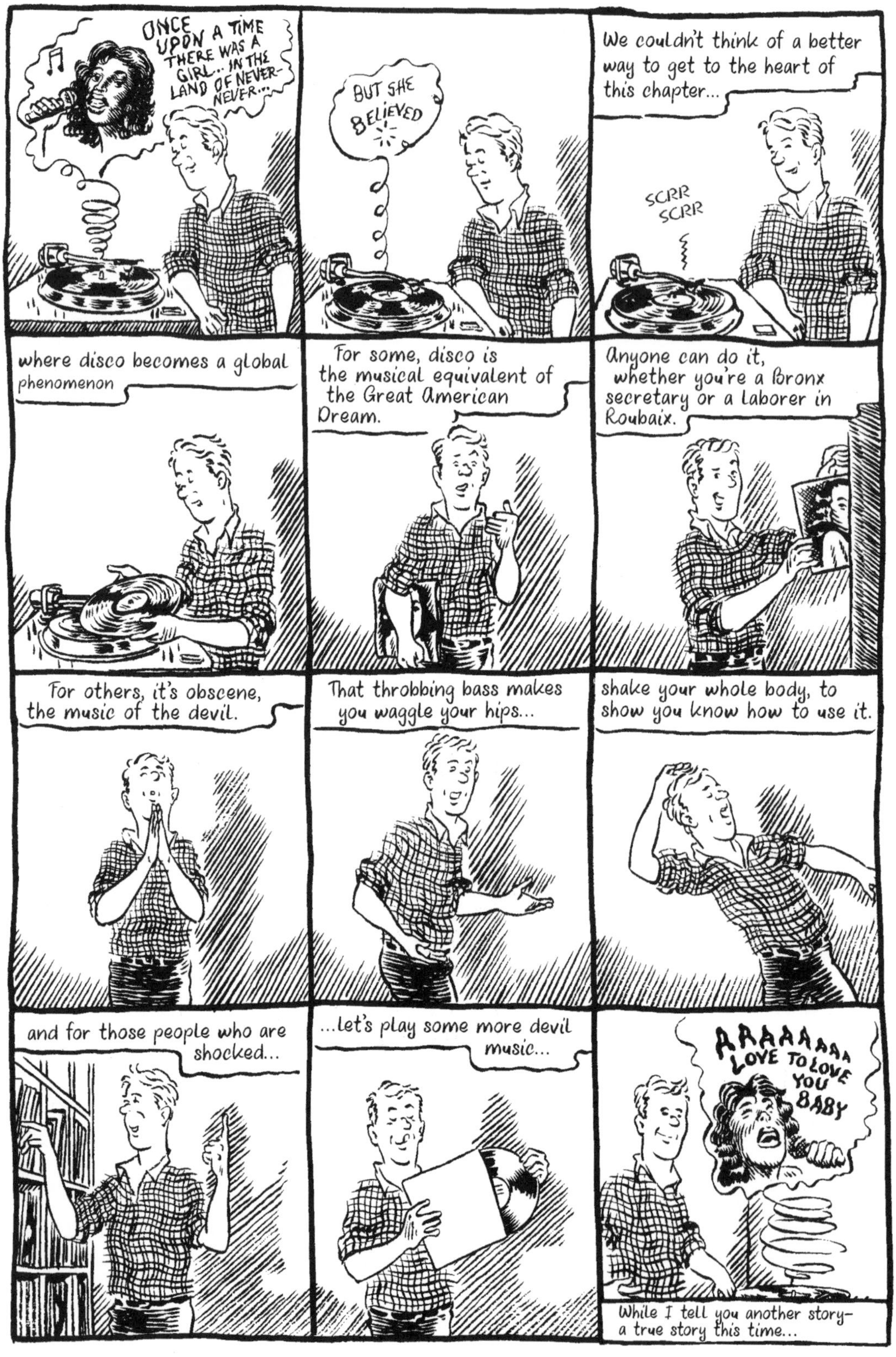
ONCE UPON A TIME THERE WAS A GIRL... IN THE LAND OF NEVER-NEVER...
BUT SHE BELIEVED
We couldn't think of a better way to get to the heart of this chapter...
SCRR SCRR
where disco becomes a global phenomenon
For some, disco is the musical equivalent of the Great American Dream.
Anyone can do it, whether you're a Bronx secretary or a laborer in Roubaix.
For others, it's obscene, the music of the devil.
That throbbing bass makes you waggle your hips...
shake your whole body, to show you know how to use it.
and for those people who are shocked...
...let's play some more devil music...
AAAAAAA LOVE TO LOVE YOU BABY
While I tell you another story– a true story this time...

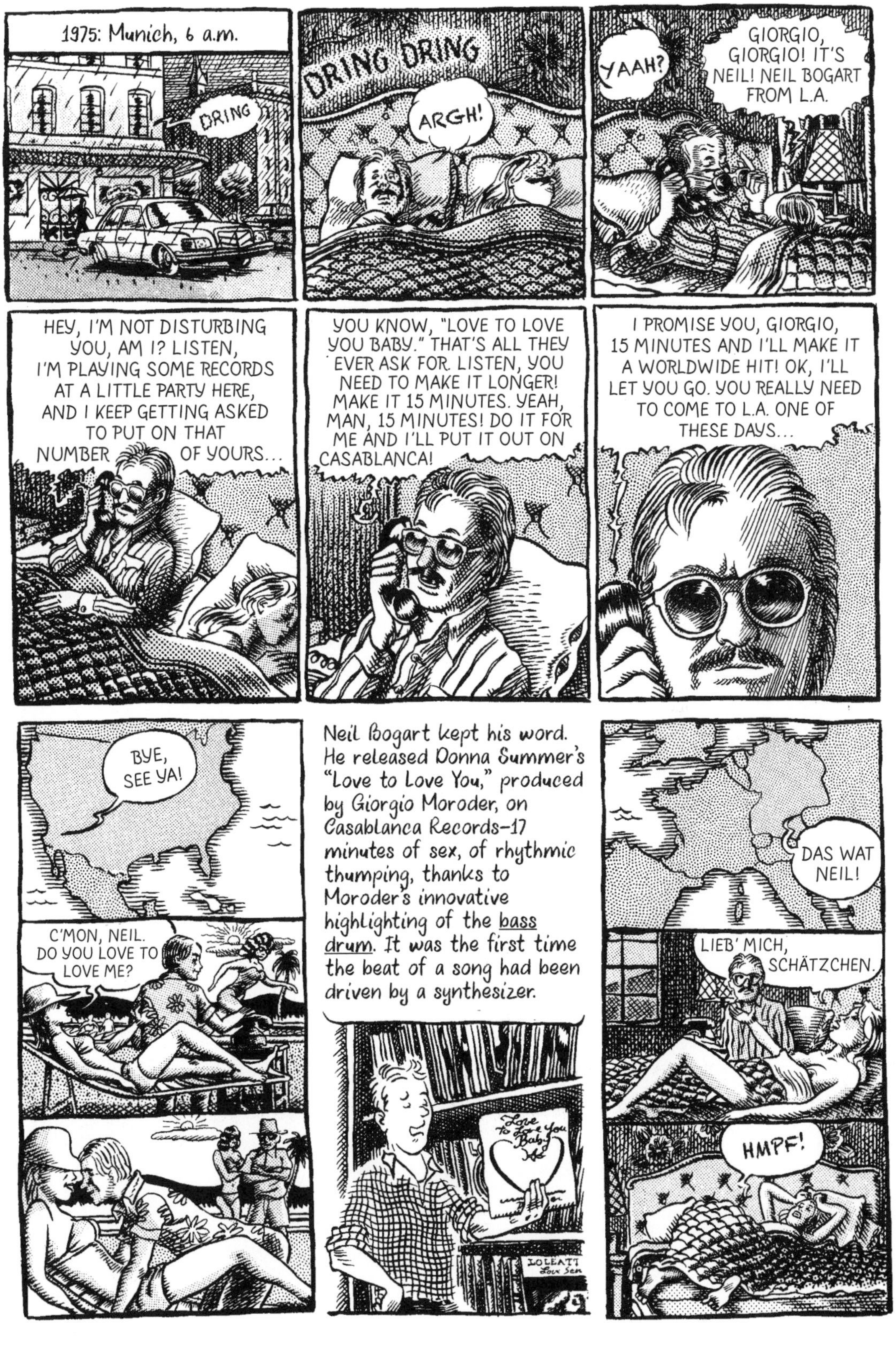

1975: Munich, 6 a.m.
DRING
DRING DRING
ARGH!
YAAH?
GIORGIO, GIORGIO! IT'S NEIL! NEIL BOGART FROM L.A.
HEY, I'M NOT DISTURBING YOU, AM I? LISTEN, I'M PLAYING SOME RECORDS AT A LITTLE PARTY HERE, AND I KEEP GETTING ASKED TO PUT ON THAT NUMBER OF YOURS...
YOU KNOW, "LOVE TO LOVE YOU BABY." THAT'S ALL THEY EVER ASK FOR. LISTEN, YOU NEED TO MAKE IT LONGER! MAKE IT 15 MINUTES. YEAH, MAN, 15 MINUTES! DO IT FOR ME AND I'LL PUT IT OUT ON CASABLANCA!
I PROMISE YOU, GIORGIO, 15 MINUTES AND I'LL MAKE IT A WORLDWIDE HIT! OK, I'LL LET YOU GO. YOU REALLY NEED TO COME TO L.A. ONE OF THESE DAYS...
BYE, SEE YA!
C'MON, NEIL. DO YOU LOVE TO LOVE ME?
Neil Bogart kept his word. He released Donna Summer's "Love to Love You," produced by Giorgio Moroder, on Casablanca Records—17 minutes of sex, of rhythmic thumping, thanks to Moroder's innovative highlighting of the bass drum. It was the first time the beat of a song had been driven by a synthesizer.
Love to Love You Baby
DAS WAT NEIL!
LIEB' MICH, SCHÄTZCHEN.
HMPF!

WHAT IF IT WAS EUROPE that lit the fuse?

Giorgio Moroder and Marc Cerrone—one in Munich, the other in Paris—started listening to Kraftwerk rhythm boxes and decided they could work in dance music. Disco was using more and more technology, and becoming increasingly crude and basic, but so what? In Europe, no one worried about being accused of bad taste. They were only interested in what worked, and they transformed disco into a worldwide genre, turning its American elements into universal clichés.

Here's what a young Frenchman named Jacques Morali had to say:

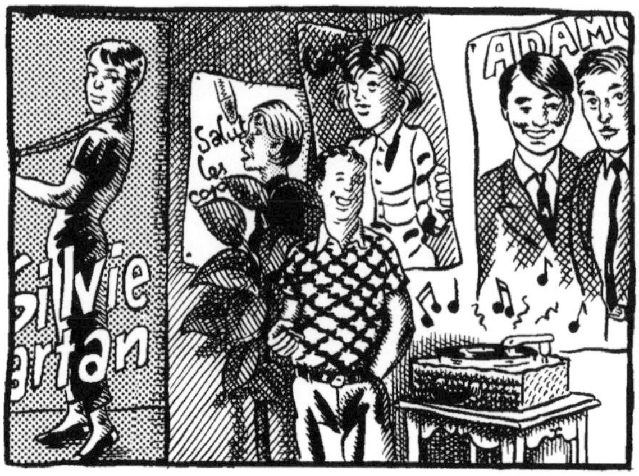
ilvie
rtan

As a teenager in the early sixties I was a big Yé-yé fan—Sylvie Vartan, Claude François...They were my idols. I was living in a small suburb, and I never heard American music.

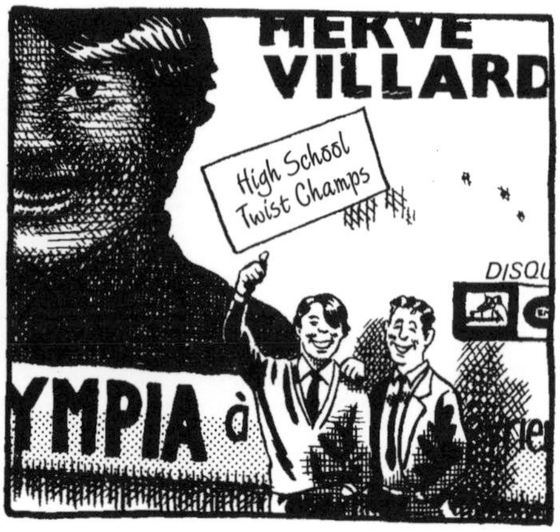
HERVE
VILLARD
High School
Twist Champs
DISQU
YMPIA à

One night, I met the singer Hervé Vilard at Le Fiacre, which was the top gay bar in Paris at the time. We became fast friends, and when his huge hit "Capri, C'est Fini" came out, he took me on as his assistant.

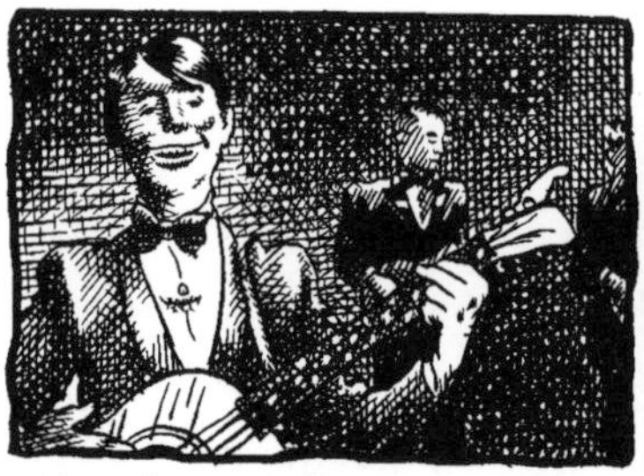

He put on all these airs and graces, but he could be really nasty. He was forever throwing his makeup box at me.

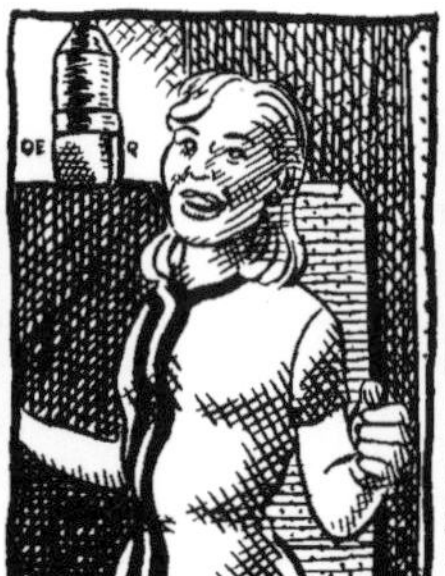

After that, I worked for Michèle Torr

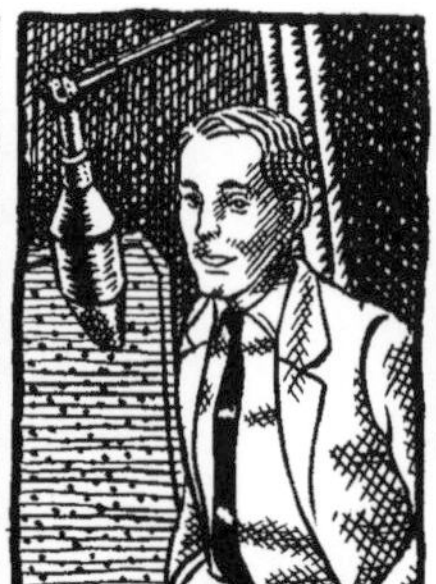

and Christophe.

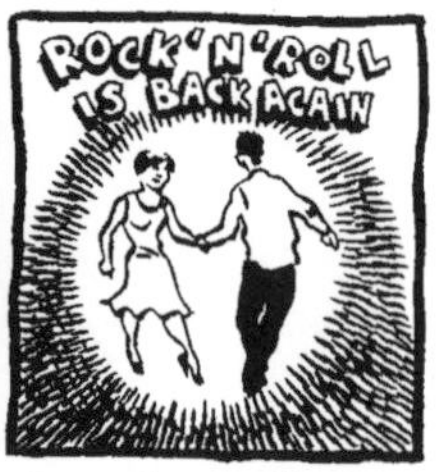
ROCK'N'ROLL
IS BACK AGAIN

I made my first single in 1970. It was a hit. It sold 250,000 copies.

Then, finally, I discovered American music: R & B and Philly soul. In '75 I went to Sigma Studios in Philadelphia, bluffed my way in, and got to work with the Ritchie Family, three girls I put together—and bingo! I hit the jackpot!

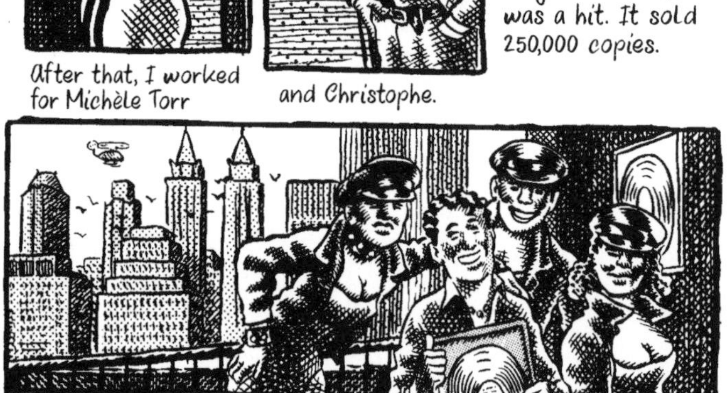
But that was only the beginning...

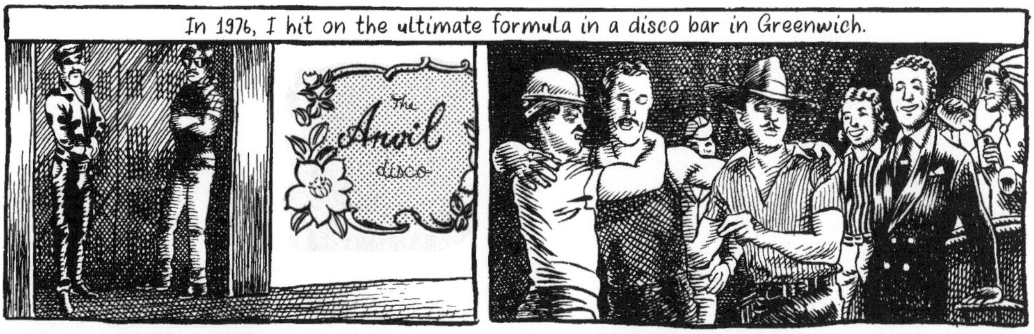
In 1976, I hit on the ultimate formula in a disco bar in Greenwich.
The Anvil disco

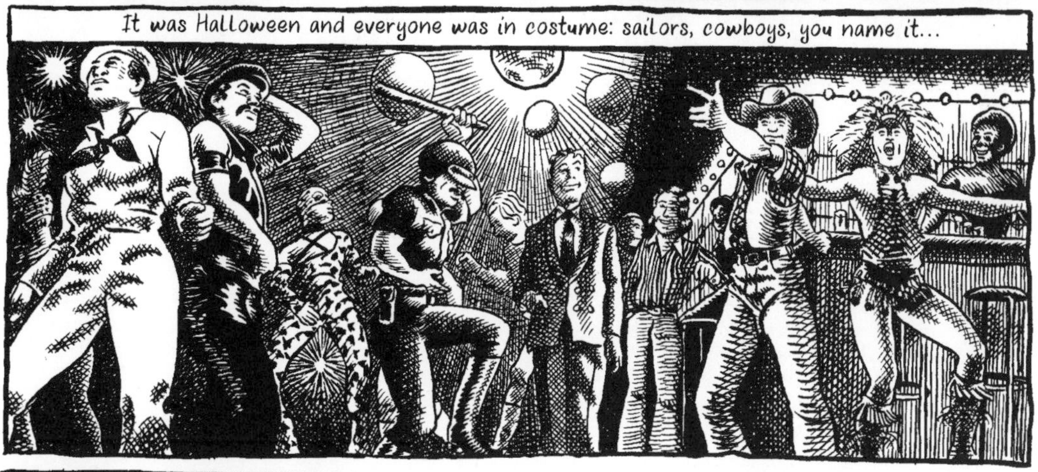
It was Halloween and everyone was in costume: sailors, cowboys, you name it...

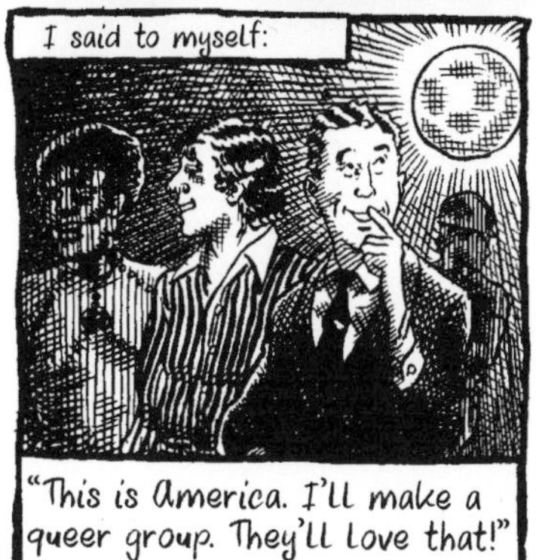
I said to myself:
"This is America. I'll make a queer group. They'll love that!"

Neil Bogart, the boss of Casablanca Records, was all for it. The first Village People album was aimed at the four major gay scenes at the time: San Francisco, Fire Island, Hollywood, and the Village itself. It really was a pure gay album. Remember, I was part of that scene, so there was nothing cynical about it. Initially, we had some success with the group just by targeting discos. That first album sold 150,000 copies.

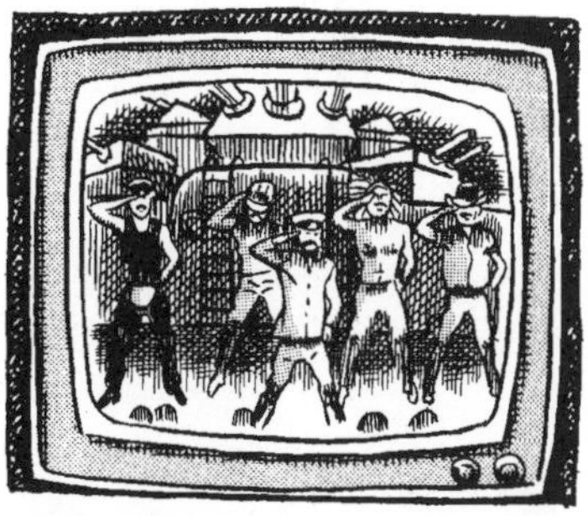

But the gay DJs all refused to play the second album, *Macho Man*, because they felt we were exploiting homosexuals. Nuts! So the reason it sold was that straight people bought it.

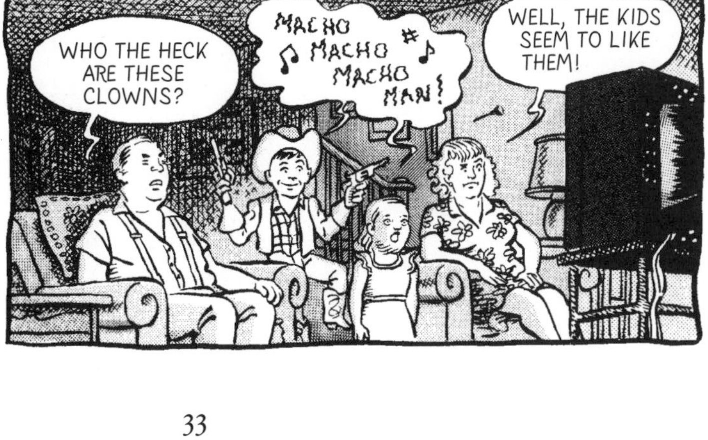
WHO THE HECK ARE THESE CLOWNS?
MACHO MACHO MACHO MAN!
WELL, THE KIDS SEEM TO LIKE THEM!

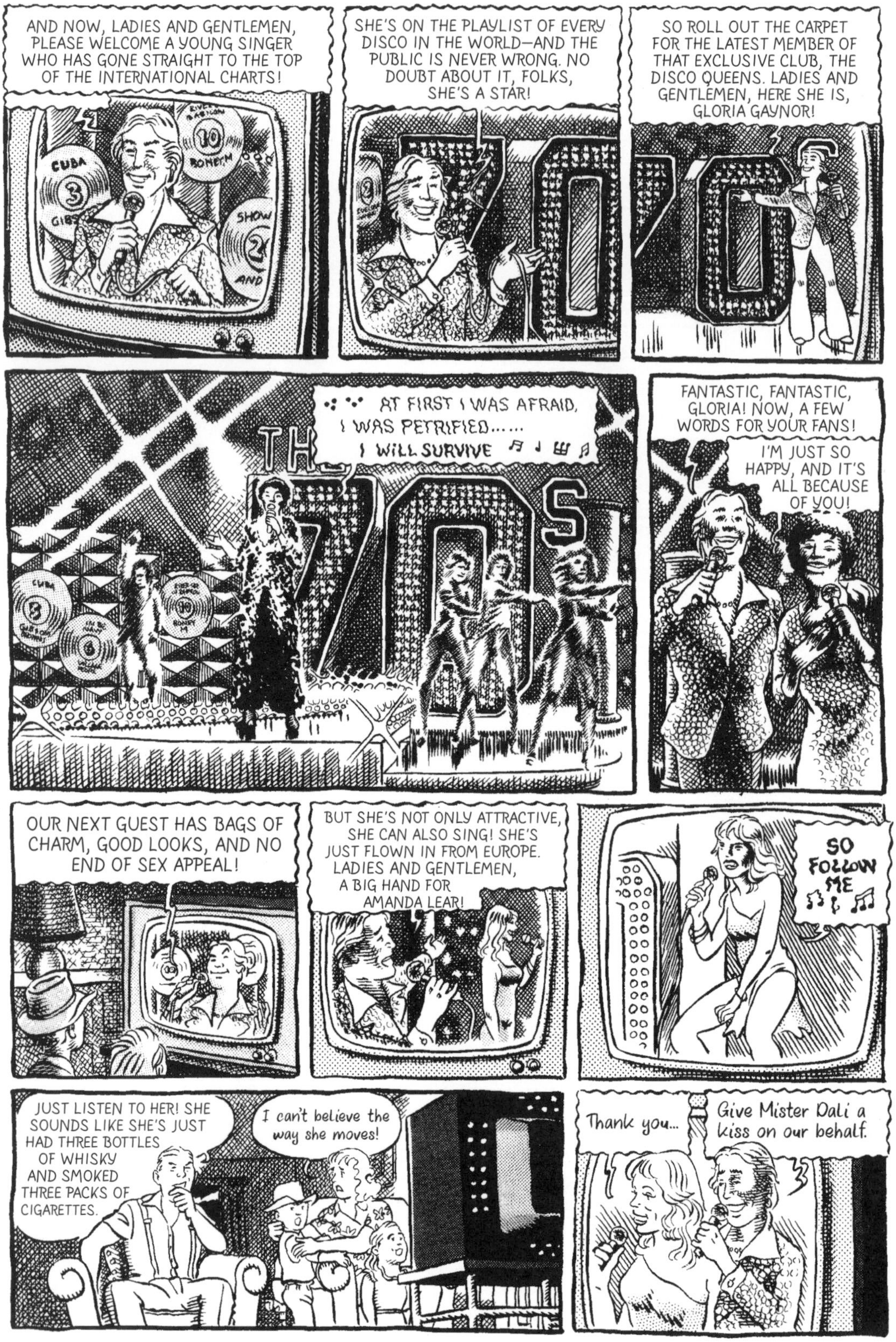

AND NOW, LADIES AND GENTLEMEN, PLEASE WELCOME A YOUNG SINGER WHO HAS GONE STRAIGHT TO THE TOP OF THE INTERNATIONAL CHARTS!
SHE'S ON THE PLAYLIST OF EVERY DISCO IN THE WORLD—AND THE PUBLIC IS NEVER WRONG. NO DOUBT ABOUT IT, FOLKS, SHE'S A STAR!
SO ROLL OUT THE CARPET FOR THE LATEST MEMBER OF THAT EXCLUSIVE CLUB, THE DISCO QUEENS. LADIES AND GENTLEMEN, HERE SHE IS, GLORIA GAYNOR!
AT FIRST I WAS AFRAID, I WAS PETRIFIED...... I WILL SURVIVE
FANTASTIC, FANTASTIC, GLORIA! NOW, A FEW WORDS FOR YOUR FANS!
I'M JUST SO HAPPY, AND IT'S ALL BECAUSE OF YOU!
OUR NEXT GUEST HAS BAGS OF CHARM, GOOD LOOKS, AND NO END OF SEX APPEAL!
BUT SHE'S NOT ONLY ATTRACTIVE, SHE CAN ALSO SING! SHE'S JUST FLOWN IN FROM EUROPE. LADIES AND GENTLEMEN, A BIG HAND FOR AMANDA LEAR!
SO FOLLOW ME
JUST LISTEN TO HER! SHE SOUNDS LIKE SHE'S JUST HAD THREE BOTTLES OF WHISKY AND SMOKED THREE PACKS OF CIGARETTES.
I can't believe the way she moves!
Thank you...
Give Mister Dali a kiss on our behalf.

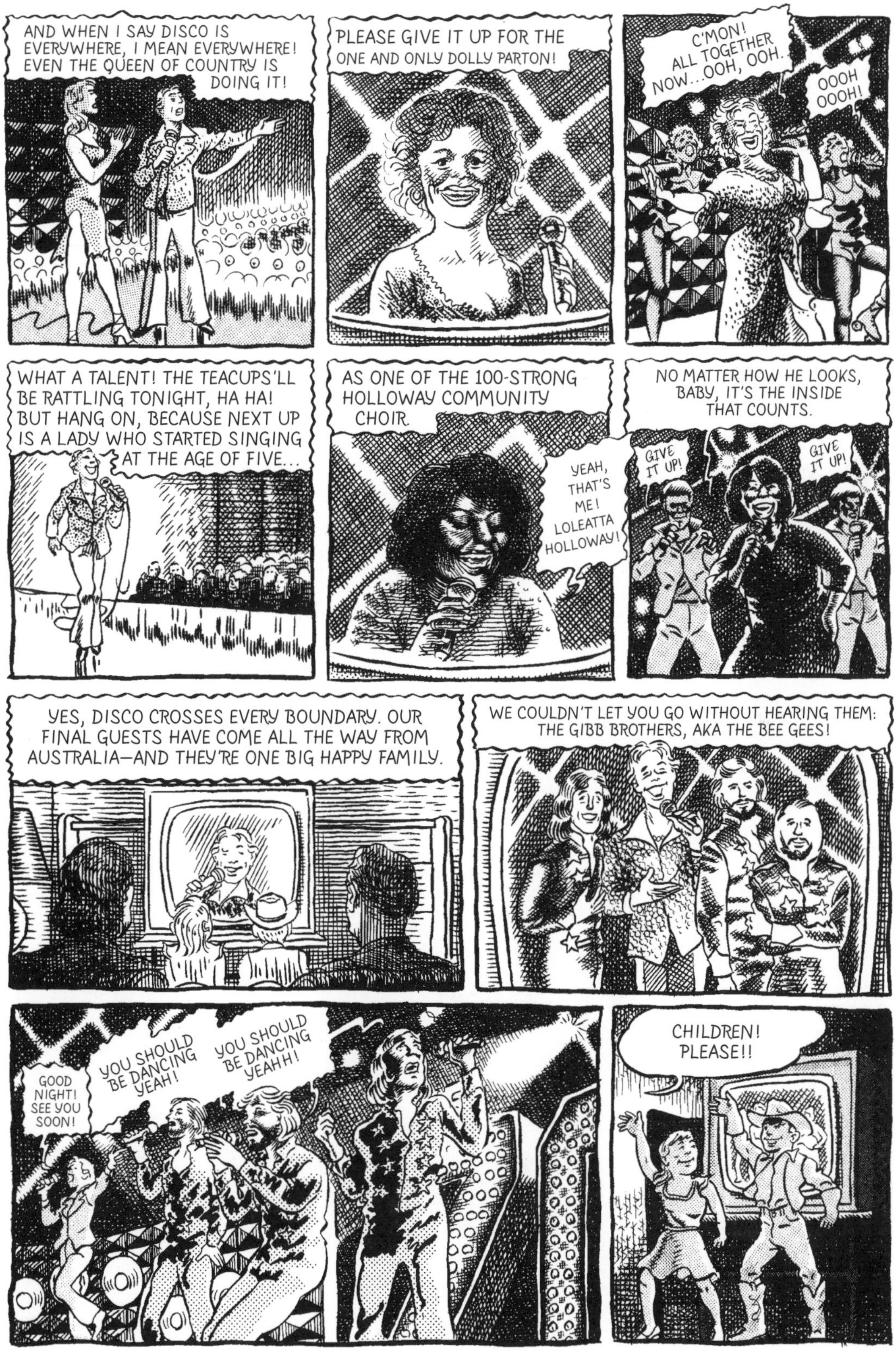
AND WHEN I SAY DISCO IS EVERYWHERE, I MEAN EVERYWHERE! EVEN THE QUEEN OF COUNTRY IS DOING IT!
PLEASE GIVE IT UP FOR THE ONE AND ONLY DOLLY PARTON!
C'MON! ALL TOGETHER NOW...OOH, OOH.
OOOH OOOH!
WHAT A TALENT! THE TEACUPS'LL BE RATTLING TONIGHT, HA HA! BUT HANG ON, BECAUSE NEXT UP IS A LADY WHO STARTED SINGING AT THE AGE OF FIVE...
AS ONE OF THE 100-STRONG HOLLOWAY COMMUNITY CHOIR.
YEAH, THAT'S ME! LOLEATTA HOLLOWAY!
NO MATTER HOW HE LOOKS, BABY, IT'S THE INSIDE THAT COUNTS.
GIVE IT UP!
GIVE IT UP!
YES, DISCO CROSSES EVERY BOUNDARY. OUR FINAL GUESTS HAVE COME ALL THE WAY FROM AUSTRALIA—AND THEY'RE ONE BIG HAPPY FAMILY.
WE COULDN'T LET YOU GO WITHOUT HEARING THEM: THE GIBB BROTHERS, AKA THE BEE GEES!
GOOD NIGHT! SEE YOU SOON!
YOU SHOULD BE DANCING YEAH!
YOU SHOULD BE DANCING YEAHH!
CHILDREN! PLEASE!!

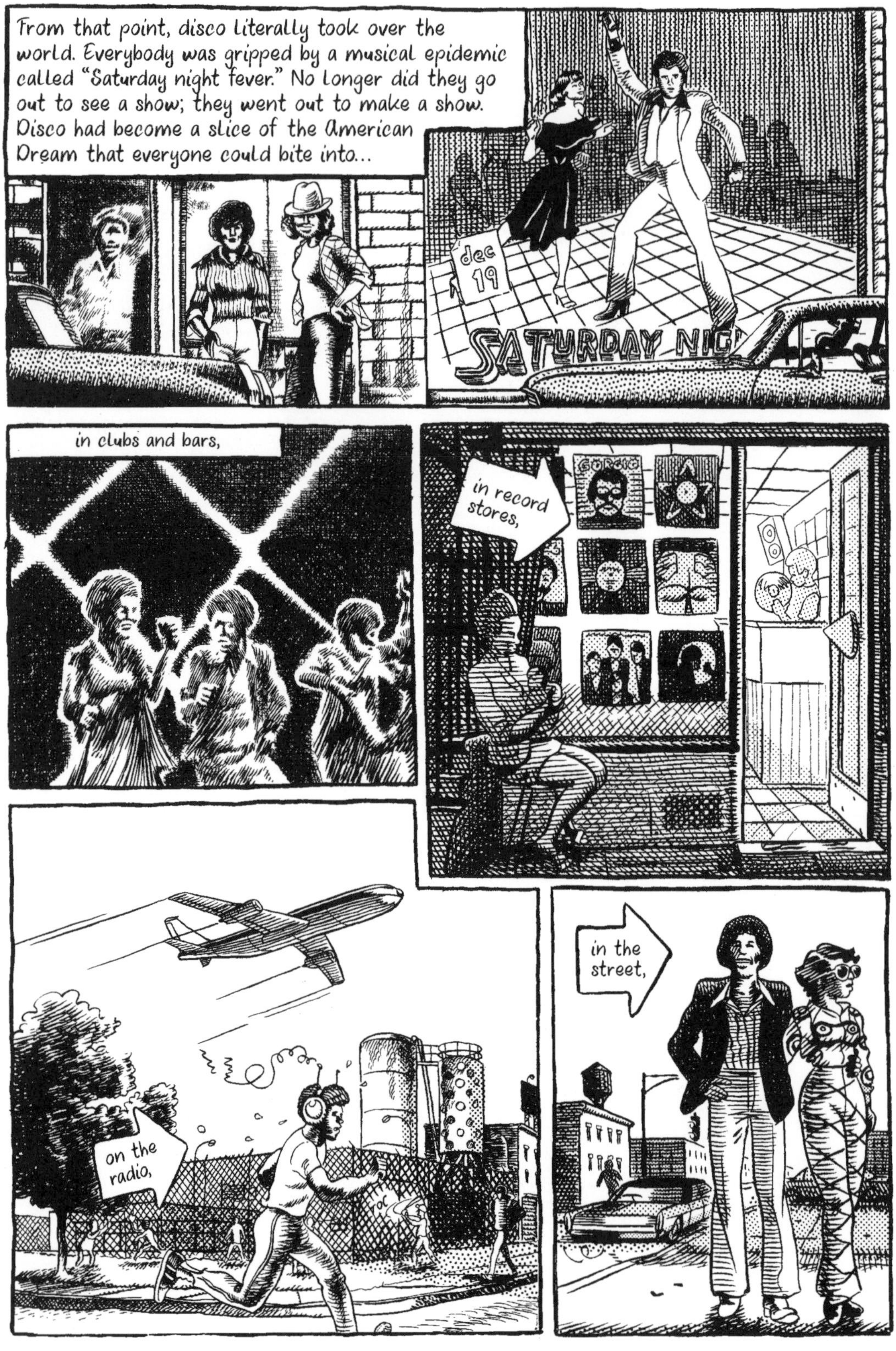
From that point, disco literally took over the world. Everybody was gripped by a musical epidemic called "Saturday night fever." No longer did they go out to see a show; they went out to make a show. Disco had become a slice of the American Dream that everyone could bite into...
dec 19
SATURDAY NIG
in clubs and bars,
in record stores,
on the radio,
in the street,

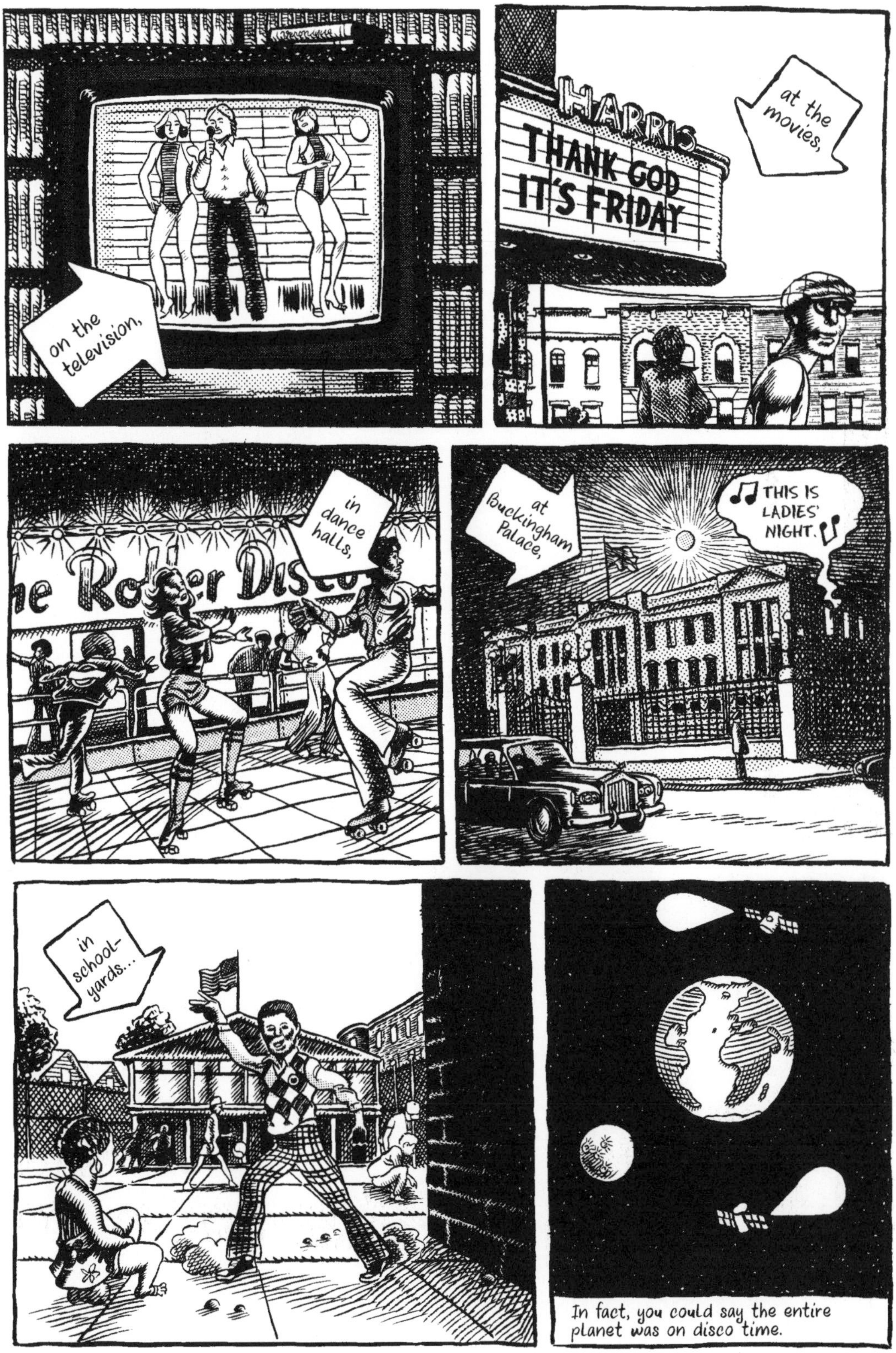
on the television,
HARRIS
THANK GOD IT'S FRIDAY
at the movies,
in dance halls,
at Buckingham Palace,
THIS IS LADIES' NIGHT.
in school-yards...
In fact, you could say the entire planet was on disco time.

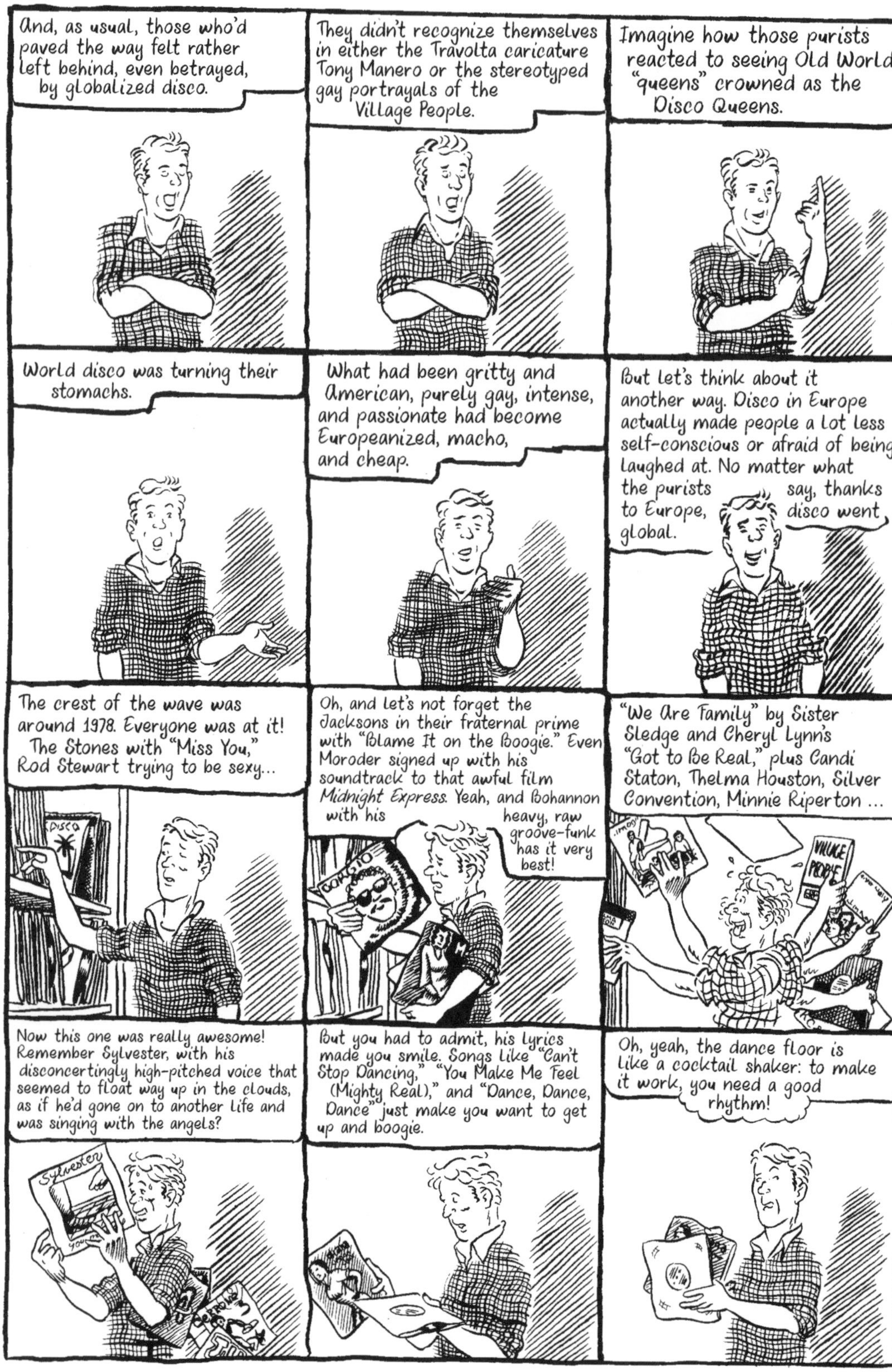
And, as usual, those who'd paved the way felt rather left behind, even betrayed, by globalized disco.
They didn't recognize themselves in either the Travolta caricature Tony Manero or the stereotyped gay portrayals of the Village People.
Imagine how those purists reacted to seeing Old World "queens" crowned as the Disco Queens.
World disco was turning their stomachs.
What had been gritty and American, purely gay, intense, and passionate had become Europeanized, macho, and cheap.
But let's think about it another way. Disco in Europe actually made people a lot less self-conscious or afraid of being laughed at. No matter what the purists say, thanks to Europe, disco went global.
The crest of the wave was around 1978. Everyone was at it! The Stones with "Miss You," Rod Stewart trying to be sexy...
Oh, and let's not forget the Jacksons in their fraternal prime with "Blame It on the Boogie." Even Moroder signed up with his soundtrack to that awful film *Midnight Express*. Yeah, and Bohannon with his heavy, raw groove-funk has it very best!
"We Are Family" by Sister Sledge and Cheryl Lynn's "Got to Be Real," plus Candi Staton, Thelma Houston, Silver Convention, Minnie Riperton ...
Now this one was really awesome! Remember Sylvester, with his disconcertingly high-pitched voice that seemed to float way up in the clouds, as if he'd gone on to another life and was singing with the angels?
Sylvester
But you had to admit, his lyrics made you smile. Songs like "Can't Stop Dancing," "You Make Me Feel (Mighty Real)," and "Dance, Dance, Dance" just make you want to get up and boogie.
Oh, yeah, the dance floor is like a cocktail shaker: to make it work, you need a good rhythm!

Disco Dance to
Good Times by Chic
ATLANTIC RECORD ATL 50 634/ 1979.

One of the all-time greats

The disk

The dancer

Wait a minute! What about Chic—surely the disco group par excellence? We've hardly even mentioned them yet. We're talking about Nile Rodgers (guitar) and Bernard Edwards (bass), who wrote the hit "Good Times." Here's how it goes:

First, it makes you tap your foot,

then the bass loosens your hips,

your arms swing away from your body in time with the   riffs,

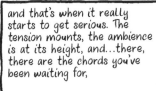

and that's when it really starts to get serious. The tension mounts, the ambience is at its height, and...there, there are the chords you've been waiting for,

#3 ♫

the chords that go straight to your head,

and suddenly you feel weightless, as if your mind and your body have merged...

but, sadly, all good things must come to an end sooner or later.

CRRT Wow!

...man, those guys sure are talented!

Thank you.

No, no, really, your music really gets to me every time I hear it.

HA! HA! HA! HA!

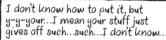

I don't know how to put it, but y-y-your...I mean your stuff just gives off such...such...I don't know...

SUCH GOOD VIBES?

Yeah, that's it! That's exactly it!

LISTEN, IT'S REALLY NOT COMPLICATED. IT'S ALL ABOUT GIVING YOU...

A GOOD TIME.

HMMM... NICE MOVES!

But, seriously, you have a unique talent for getting people to shake their asses!

We just listened to "Good Times." I mean, it gets every single part of your body moving.

LEMME TELL YOU WHAT IT TAKES TO WRITE A GOOD SONG: AU-DA-CI-TY!

NO POINT IN OVER-COMPLICATING THINGS.

Did you say audacity? That's it! If I think about it, while I'm dancing, it makes me want to connect with every part of my partner's body.

THAT'S WHAT YOU NEED TO DANCE LIKE THAT: AUDACITY!

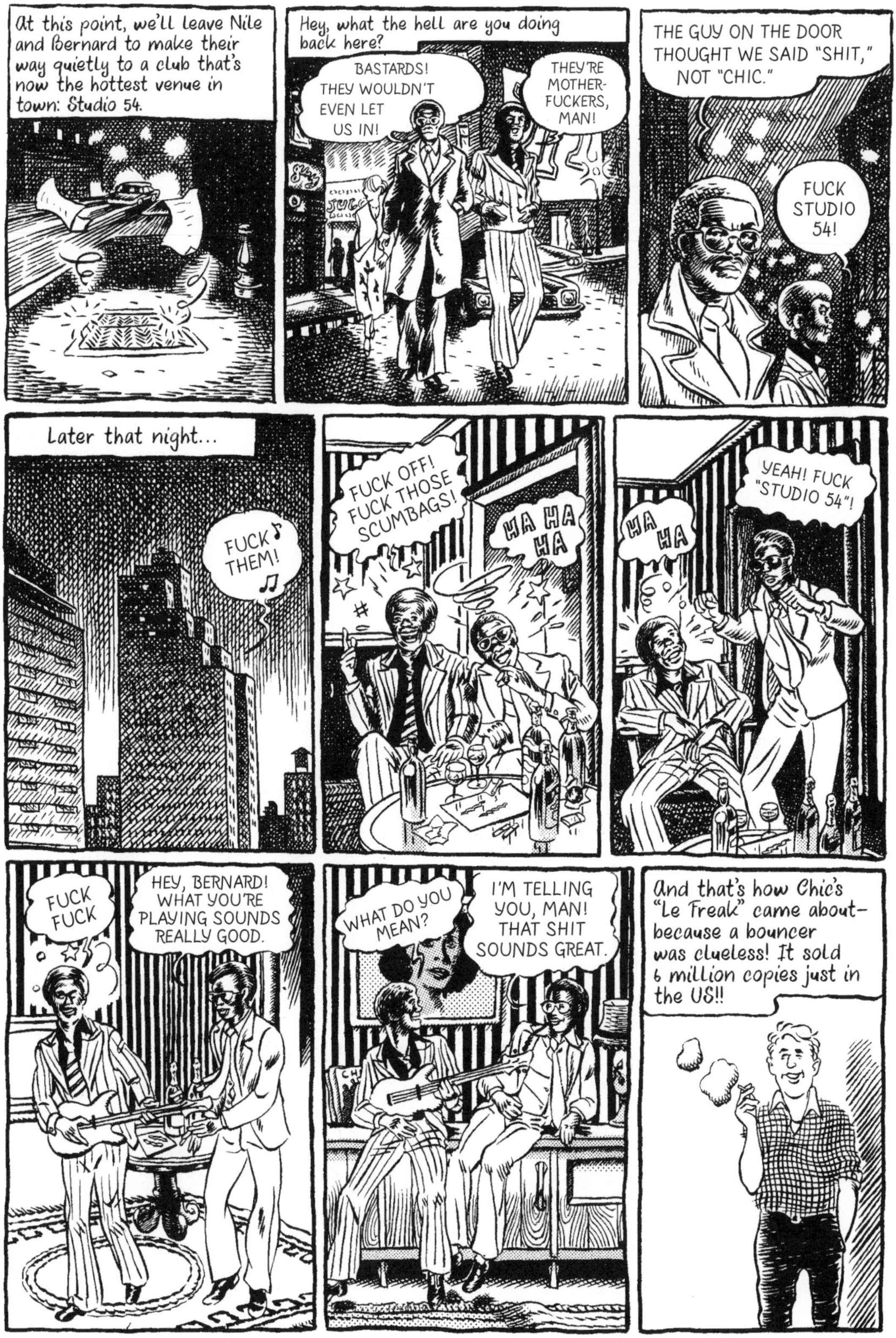
At this point, we'll leave Nile and Bernard to make their way quietly to a club that's now the hottest venue in town: Studio 54.
Hey, what the hell are you doing back here?
BASTARDS! THEY WOULDN'T EVEN LET US IN!
THEY'RE MOTHER-FUCKERS, MAN!
THE GUY ON THE DOOR THOUGHT WE SAID "SHIT," NOT "CHIC."
FUCK STUDIO 54!
Later that night...
FUCK THEM!
FUCK OFF! FUCK THOSE SCUMBAGS!
HA HA HA
HA HA
YEAH! FUCK "STUDIO 54"!
FUCK FUCK
HEY, BERNARD! WHAT YOU'RE PLAYING SOUNDS REALLY GOOD.
WHAT DO YOU MEAN?
I'M TELLING YOU, MAN! THAT SHIT SOUNDS GREAT.
And that's how Chic's "Le Freak" came about—because a bouncer was clueless! It sold 6 million copies just in the US!!

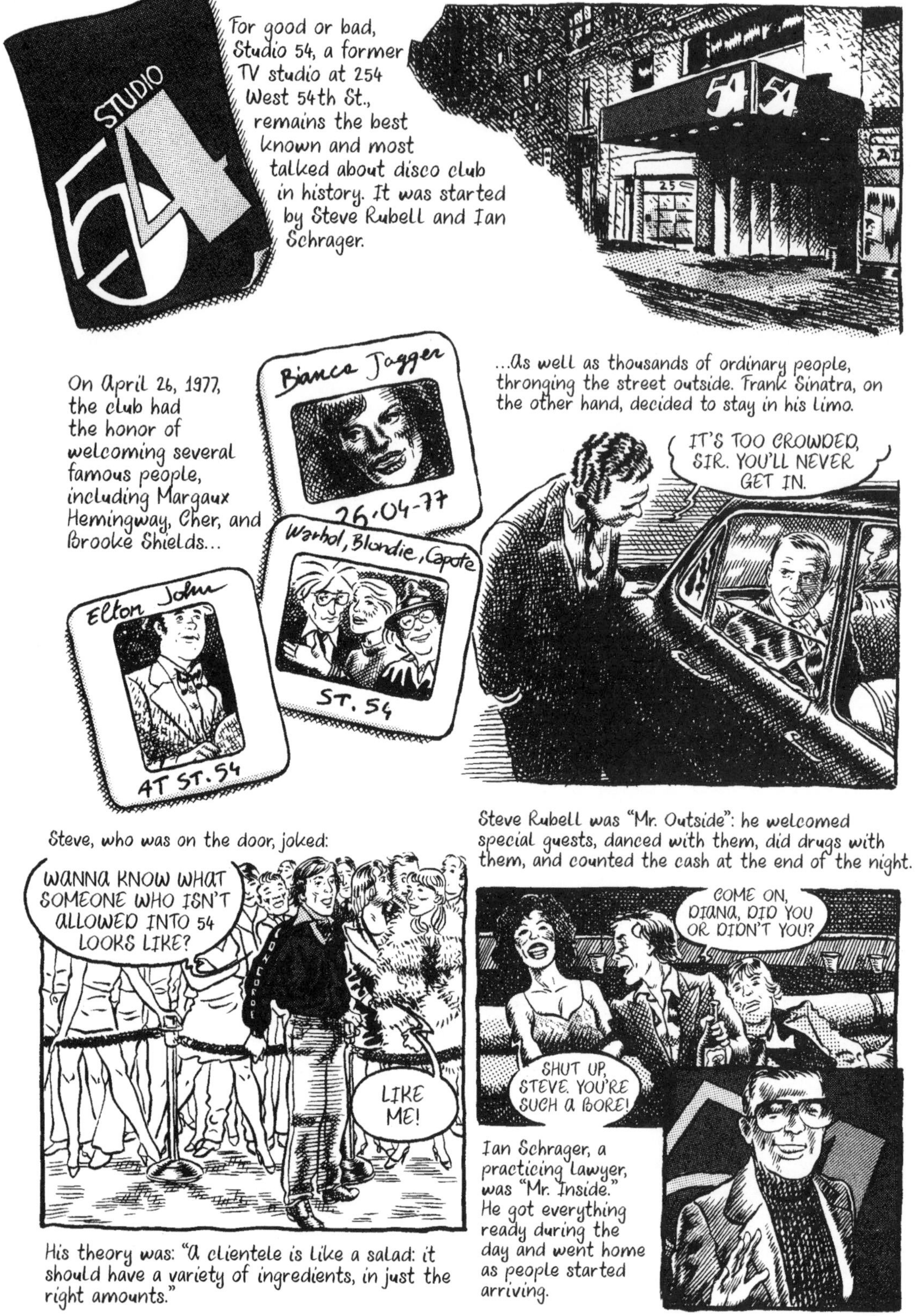
STUDIO 54
For good or bad, Studio 54, a former TV studio at 254 West 54th St., remains the best known and most talked about disco club in history. It was started by Steve Rubell and Ian Schrager.
54 54
On April 26, 1977, the club had the honor of welcoming several famous people, including Margaux Hemingway, Cher, and Brooke Shields...
Bianca Jagger
26.04-77
Warhol, Blondie, Capote
ST. 54
Elton John
AT ST. 54
...as well as thousands of ordinary people, thronging the street outside. Frank Sinatra, on the other hand, decided to stay in his limo.
IT'S TOO CROWDED, SIR. YOU'LL NEVER GET IN.
Steve, who was on the door, joked:
WANNA KNOW WHAT SOMEONE WHO ISN'T ALLOWED INTO 54 LOOKS LIKE?
LIKE ME!
His theory was: "A clientele is like a salad: it should have a variety of ingredients, in just the right amounts."
Steve Rubell was "Mr. Outside": he welcomed special guests, danced with them, did drugs with them, and counted the cash at the end of the night.
COME ON, DIANA, DID YOU OR DIDN'T YOU?
SHUT UP, STEVE. YOU'RE SUCH A BORE!
Ian Schrager, a practicing lawyer, was "Mr. Inside." He got everything ready during the day and went home as people started arriving.

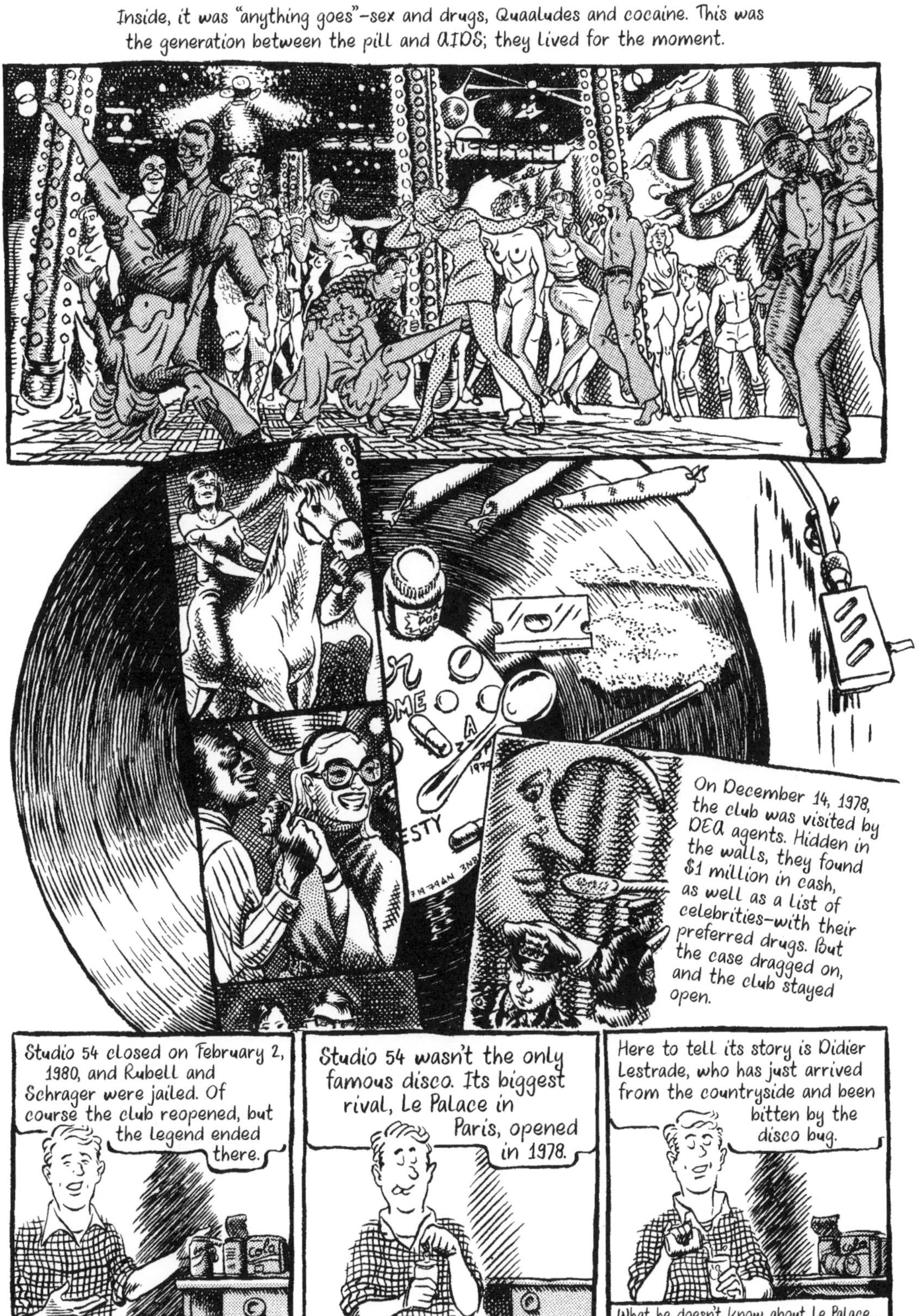
Inside, it was "anything goes"–sex and drugs, Quaaludes and cocaine. This was the generation between the pill and AIDS; they lived for the moment.
On December 14, 1978, the club was visited by DEA agents. Hidden in the walls, they found $1 million in cash, as well as a list of celebrities–with their preferred drugs. But the case dragged on, and the club stayed open.
Studio 54 closed on February 2, 1980, and Rubell and Schrager were jailed. Of course the club reopened, but the legend ended there.
Studio 54 wasn't the only famous disco. Its biggest rival, Le Palace in Paris, opened in 1978.
Here to tell its story is Didier Lestrade, who has just arrived from the countryside and been bitten by the disco bug.
What he doesn't know about Le Palace...

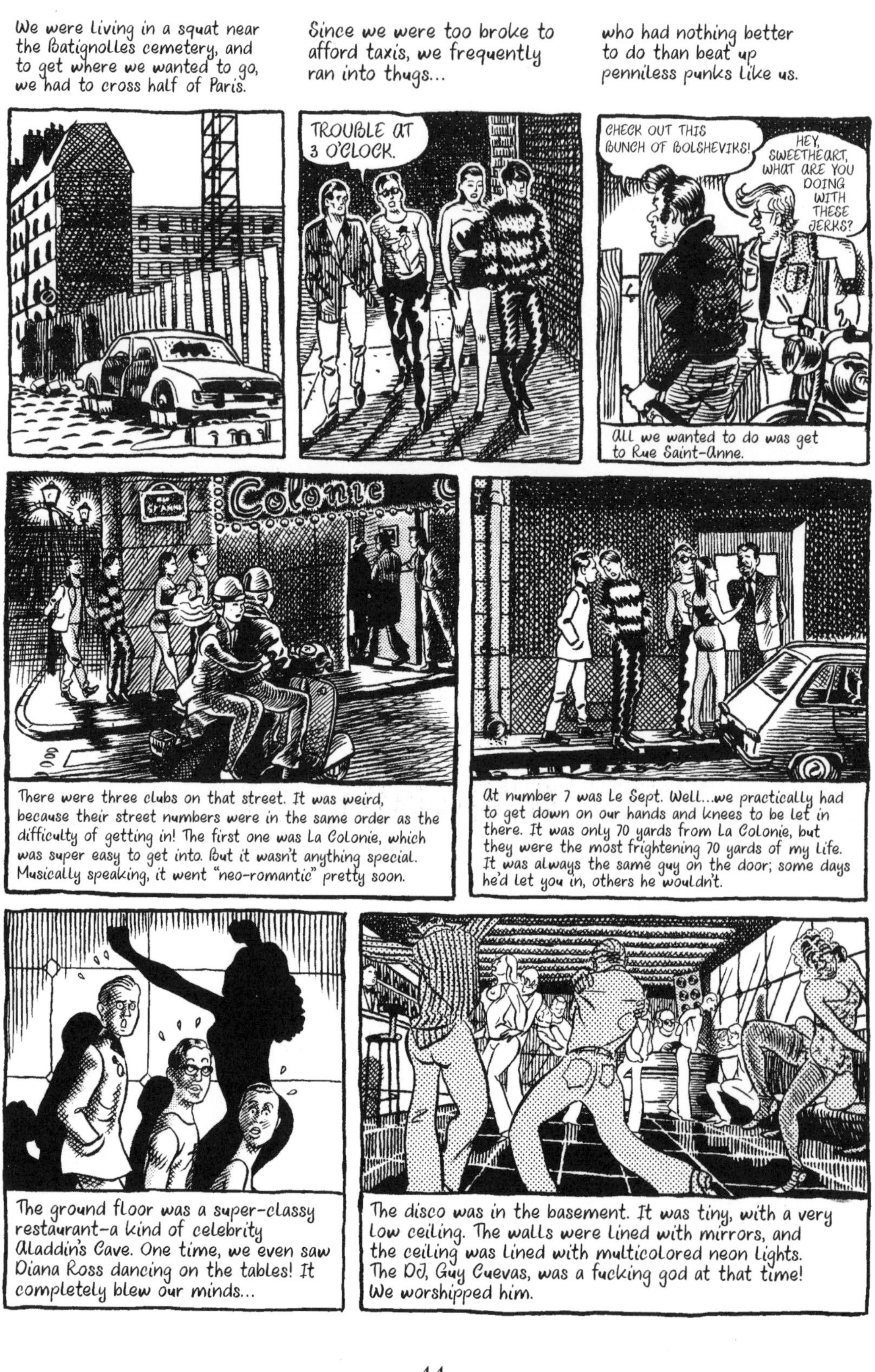
We were living in a squat near the Batignolles cemetery, and to get where we wanted to go, we had to cross half of Paris.
Since we were too broke to afford taxis, we frequently ran into thugs...
TROUBLE AT 3 O'CLOCK.
who had nothing better to do than beat up penniless punks like us.
CHECK OUT THIS BUNCH OF BOLSHEVIKS!
HEY, SWEETHEART, WHAT ARE YOU DOING WITH THESE JERKS?
All we wanted to do was get to Rue Saint-Anne.
Colonie
There were three clubs on that street. It was weird, because their street numbers were in the same order as the difficulty of getting in! The first one was La Colonie, which was super easy to get into. But it wasn't anything special. Musically speaking, it went "neo-romantic" pretty soon.
At number 7 was Le Sept. Well...we practically had to get down on our hands and knees to be let in there. It was only 70 yards from La Colonie, but they were the most frightening 70 yards of my life. It was always the same guy on the door; some days he'd let you in, others he wouldn't.
The ground floor was a super-classy restaurant–a kind of celebrity Aladdin's Cave. One time, we even saw Diana Ross dancing on the tables! It completely blew our minds...
The disco was in the basement. It was tiny, with a very low ceiling. The walls were lined with mirrors, and the ceiling was lined with multicolored neon lights. The DJ, Guy Cuevas, was a fucking god at that time! We worshipped him.

It was the first time we'd ever heard disco in a disco.
Was the mixing good? No idea. We didn't even notice it.
When he played a hit like "Shame" by Evelyn "Champagne" King, all the neon lit us up like a giant flare gun. We'd never seen anything like it!

The idea was to dance all night without ever sitting out—the essential thing being to avoid the waiters and waitresses, because the drinks cost an arm and a leg.

Farther down the street was Le Pimm's, which was the crème de la crème. We never even went there. No point: we'd never get in. It was the only after-hours club in Paris; it stayed open till 4 a.m.

For the jet-setters in those days, the perfect evening out was: (1) go to the opera,

(2) eat out,

(3) hit a club (often Le Sept),

(4) finish off at Le Pimm's—but not until an hour later: they had to go home first to doll themselves up!

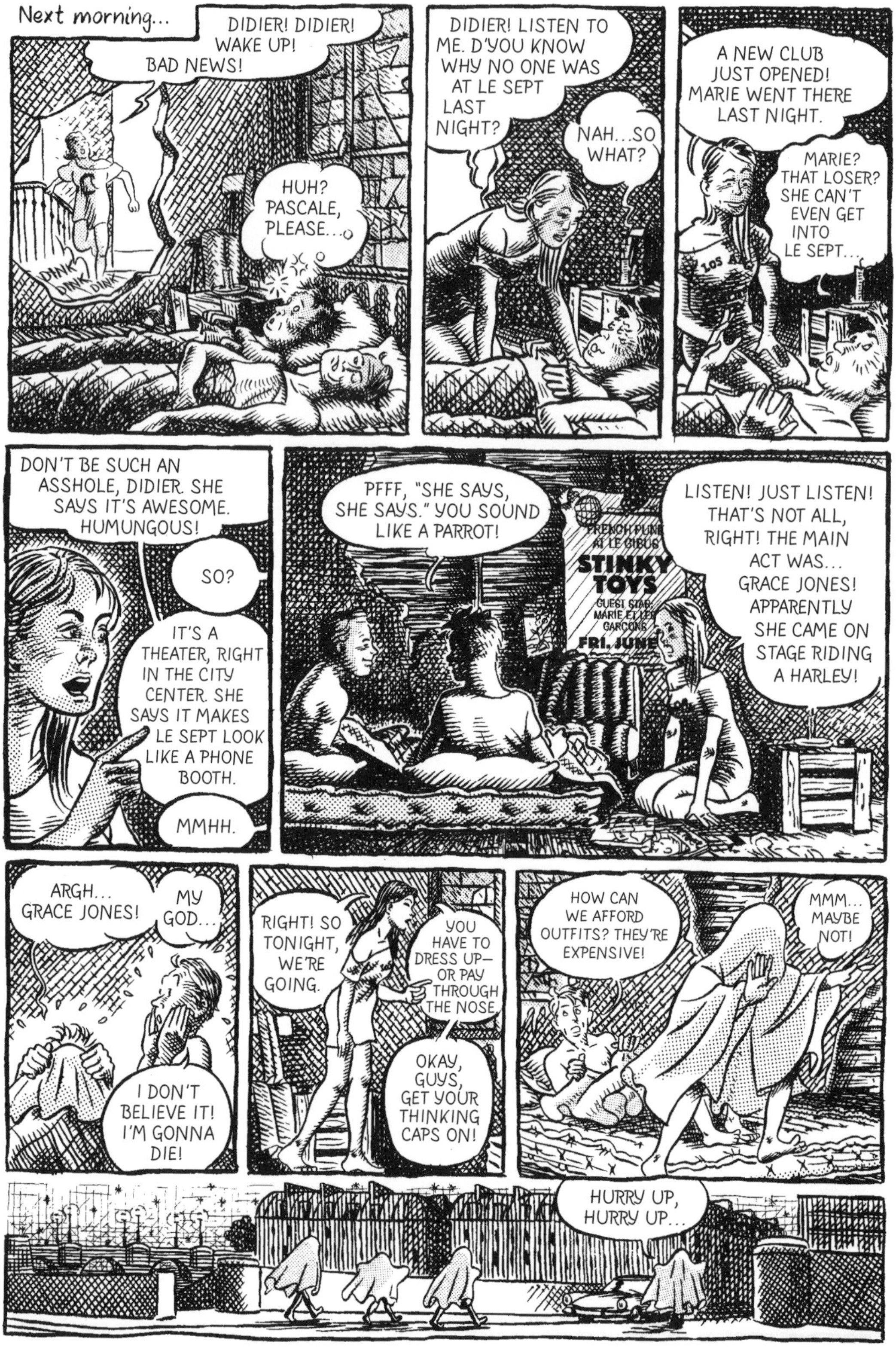

Next morning...
DIDIER! DIDIER! WAKE UP! BAD NEWS!
DINK DINK DINK
HUH? PASCALE, PLEASE...
DIDIER! LISTEN TO ME. D'YOU KNOW WHY NO ONE WAS AT LE SEPT LAST NIGHT?
NAH...SO WHAT?
A NEW CLUB JUST OPENED! MARIE WENT THERE LAST NIGHT.
MARIE? THAT LOSER? SHE CAN'T EVEN GET INTO LE SEPT...
DON'T BE SUCH AN ASSHOLE, DIDIER. SHE SAYS IT'S AWESOME. HUMUNGOUS!
SO?
IT'S A THEATER, RIGHT IN THE CITY CENTER. SHE SAYS IT MAKES LE SEPT LOOK LIKE A PHONE BOOTH.
MMHH.
PFFF, "SHE SAYS, SHE SAYS." YOU SOUND LIKE A PARROT!
STINKY TOYS
FRI. JUNE
LISTEN! JUST LISTEN! THAT'S NOT ALL, RIGHT! THE MAIN ACT WAS... GRACE JONES! APPARENTLY SHE CAME ON STAGE RIDING A HARLEY!
ARGH... GRACE JONES!
MY GOD...
I DON'T BELIEVE IT! I'M GONNA DIE!
RIGHT! SO TONIGHT, WE'RE GOING.
YOU HAVE TO DRESS UP—OR PAY THROUGH THE NOSE.
OKAY, GUYS, GET YOUR THINKING CAPS ON!
HOW CAN WE AFFORD OUTFITS? THEY'RE EXPENSIVE!
MMM... MAYBE NOT!
HURRY UP, HURRY UP...

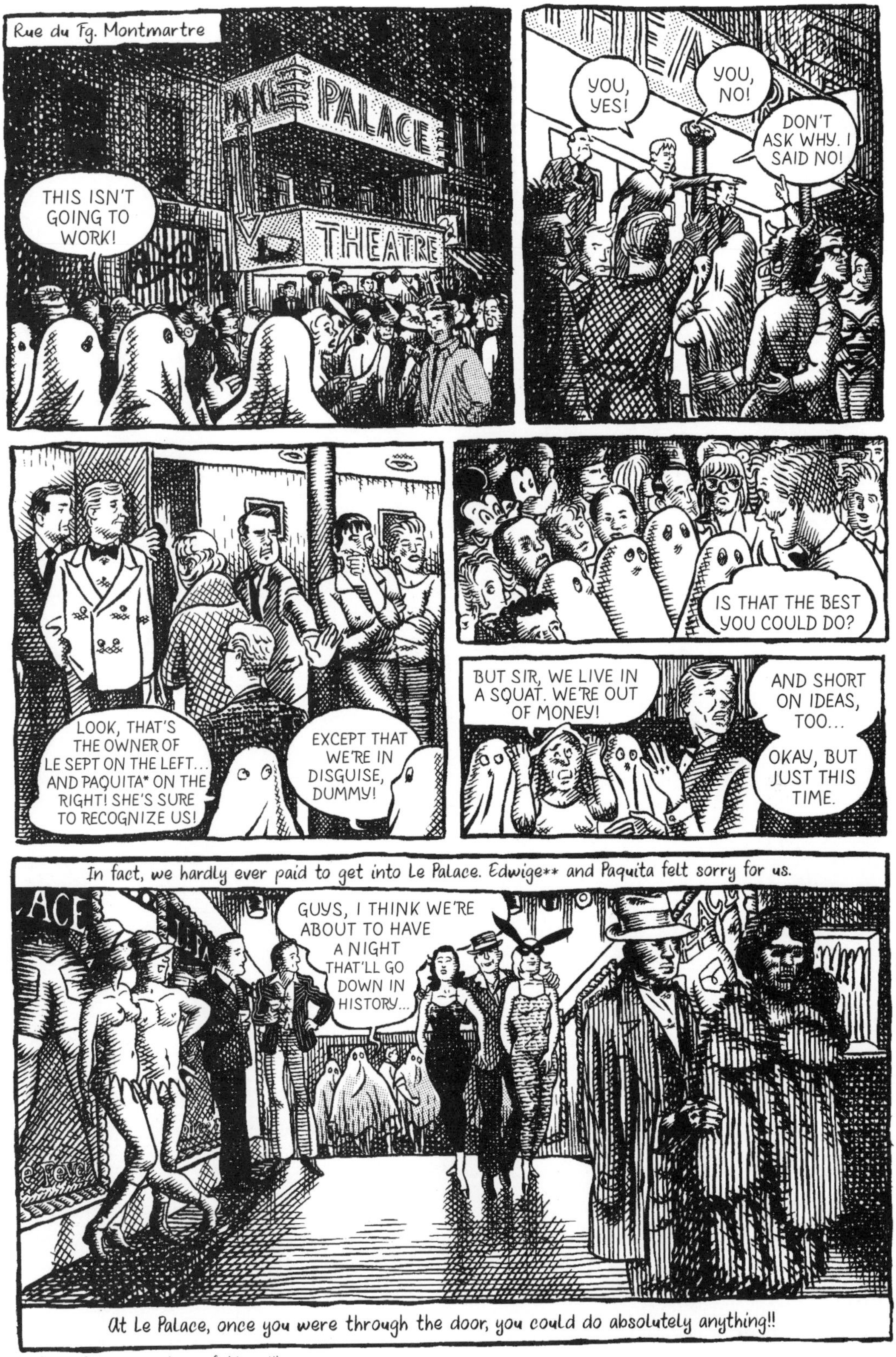
Rue du Fg. Montmartre
PALACE
THEATRE
THIS ISN'T GOING TO WORK!
YOU, YES!
YOU, NO!
DON'T ASK WHY. I SAID NO!
LOOK, THAT'S THE OWNER OF LE SEPT ON THE LEFT... AND PAQUITA* ON THE RIGHT! SHE'S SURE TO RECOGNIZE US!
EXCEPT THAT WE'RE IN DISGUISE, DUMMY!
IS THAT THE BEST YOU COULD DO?
BUT SIR, WE LIVE IN A SQUAT. WE'RE OUT OF MONEY!
AND SHORT ON IDEAS, TOO...
OKAY, BUT JUST THIS TIME.
In fact, we hardly ever paid to get into Le Palace. Edwige** and Paquita felt sorry for us.
GUYS, I THINK WE'RE ABOUT TO HAVE A NIGHT THAT'LL GO DOWN IN HISTORY...
At Le Palace, once you were through the door, you could do absolutely anything!!

* Paquita Paquin: a well-known fashion editor.
** Edwige Belmore, the "Queen of Punk."

Le Palace was at the heart of Parisian nightlife for several years. Supposedly just a nightclub, it went way beyond that and became a way of life, where everyone was part of the show–stars, jet-setters, ordinary Parisians... Disco swept them all up and broke down their inhibitions.

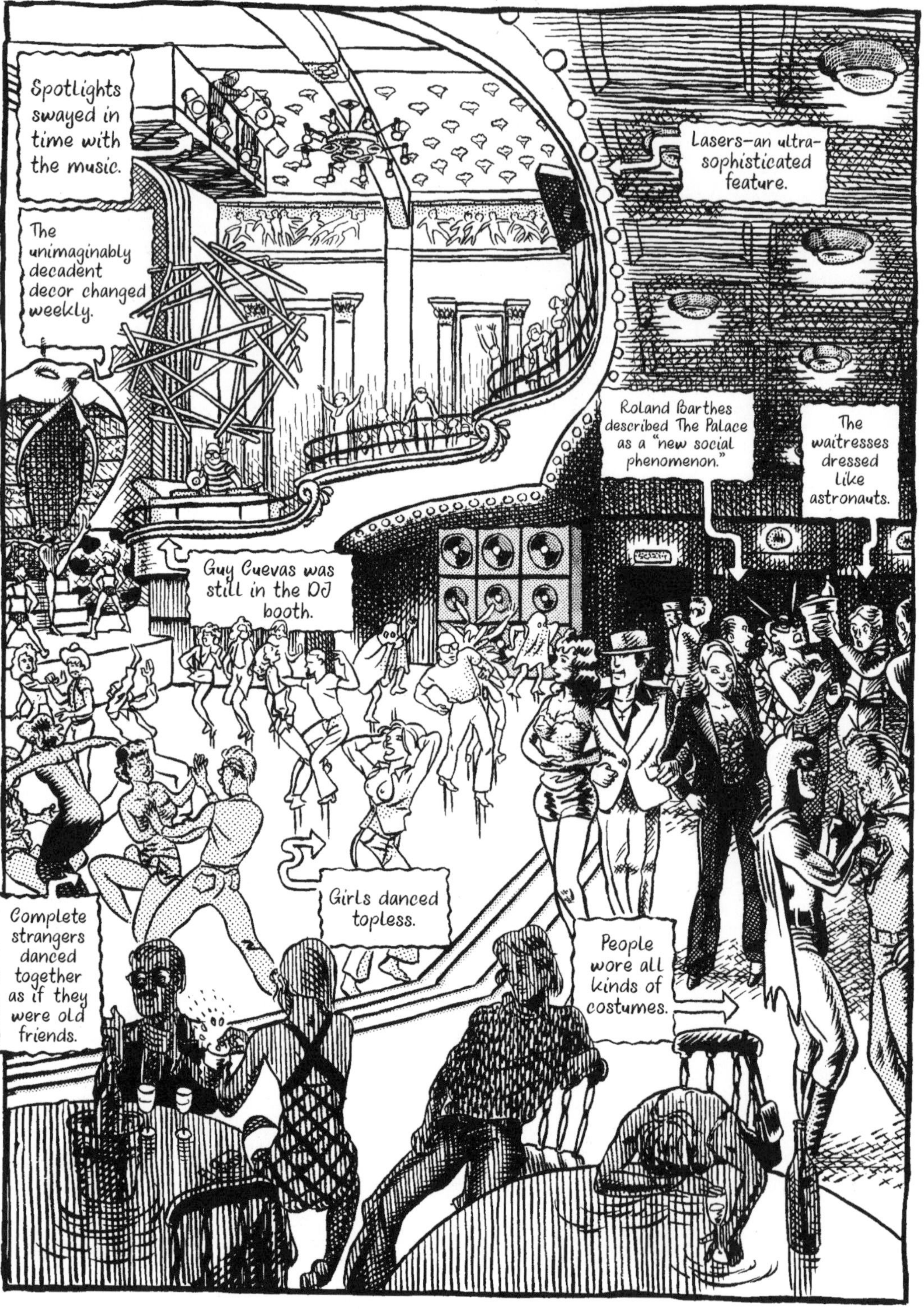

Spotlights swayed in time with the music.
The unimaginably decadent decor changed weekly.
Lasers–an ultra-sophisticated feature.
Roland Barthes described The Palace as a "new social phenomenon."
The waitresses dressed like astronauts.
Guy Cuevas was still in the DJ booth.
Girls danced topless.
Complete strangers danced together as if they were old friends.
People wore all kinds of costumes.

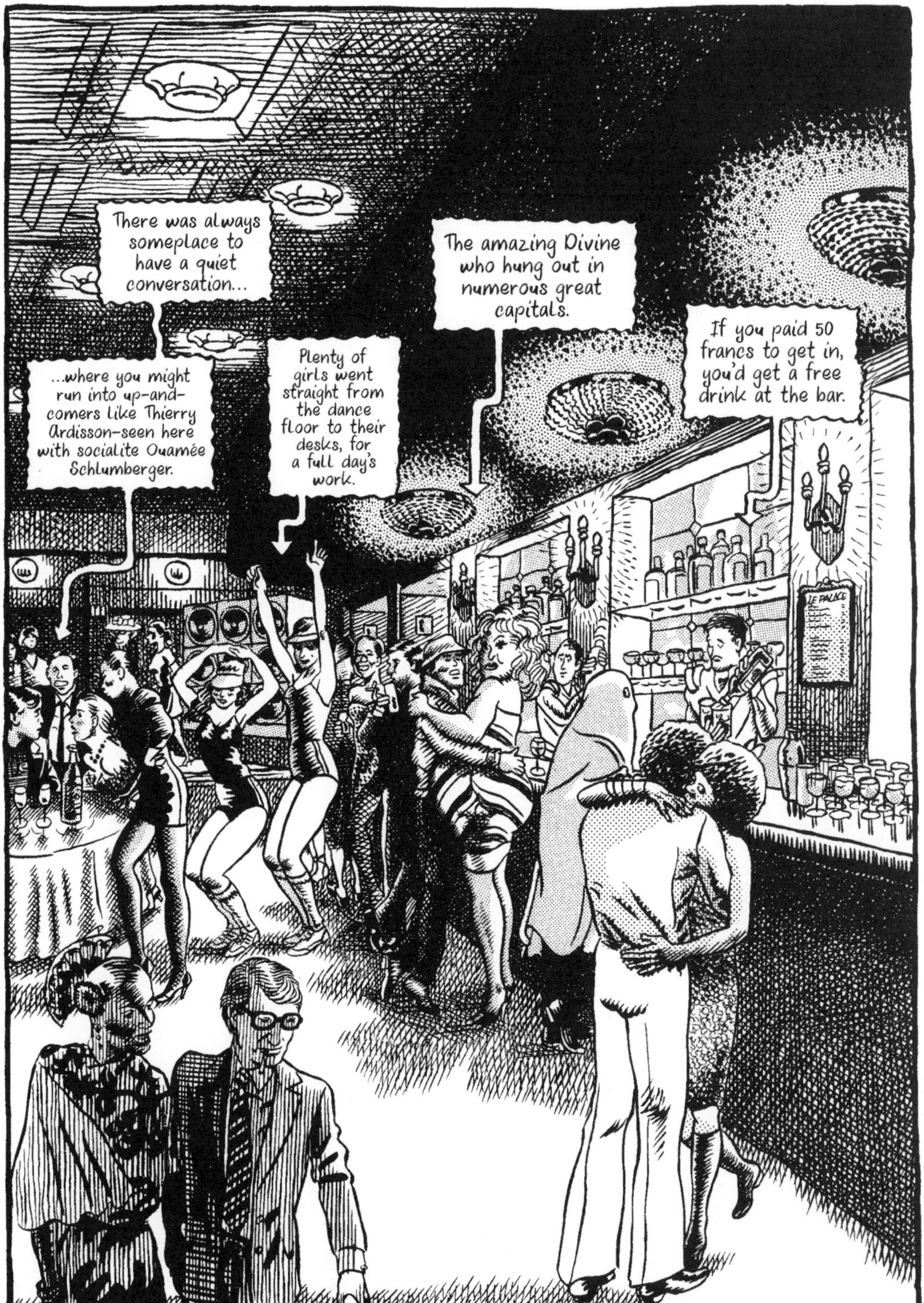
There was always someplace to have a quiet conversation...
...where you might run into up-and-comers like Thierry Ardisson—seen here with socialite Ouamée Schlumberger.
Plenty of girls went straight from the dance floor to their desks, for a full day's work.
The amazing Divine who hung out in numerous great capitals.
If you paid 50 francs to get in, you'd get a free drink at the bar.
LE PALACE

Le Palace was as much a den of iniquity and cocaine-fueled perversion as it was a haven for social anonymity, where everyone could create their own personal approach to life and pleasure.

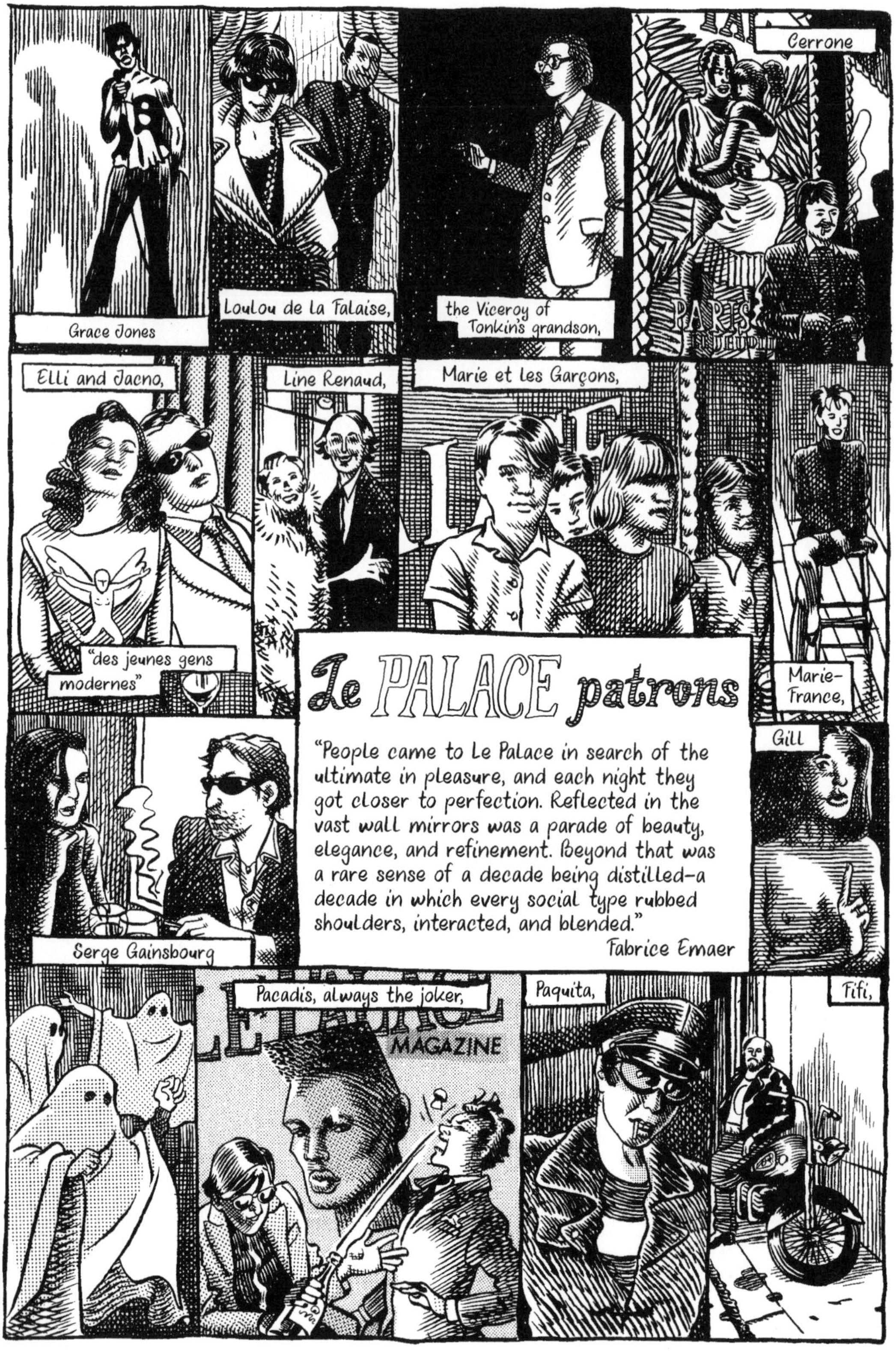

Grace Jones
Loulou de la Falaise,
the Viceroy of Tonkin's grandson,
Cerrone
PARIS
Elli and Jacno,
"des jeunes gens modernes"
Line Renaud,
Marie et les Garçons,
Marie-France,
Le PALACE patrons
"People came to Le Palace in search of the ultimate in pleasure, and each night they got closer to perfection. Reflected in the vast wall mirrors was a parade of beauty, elegance, and refinement. Beyond that was a rare sense of a decade being distilled–a decade in which every social type rubbed shoulders, interacted, and blended."
Fabrice Emaer
Serge Gainsbourg
Gill
Pacadis, always the joker,
MAGAZINE
Paquita,
Fifi,

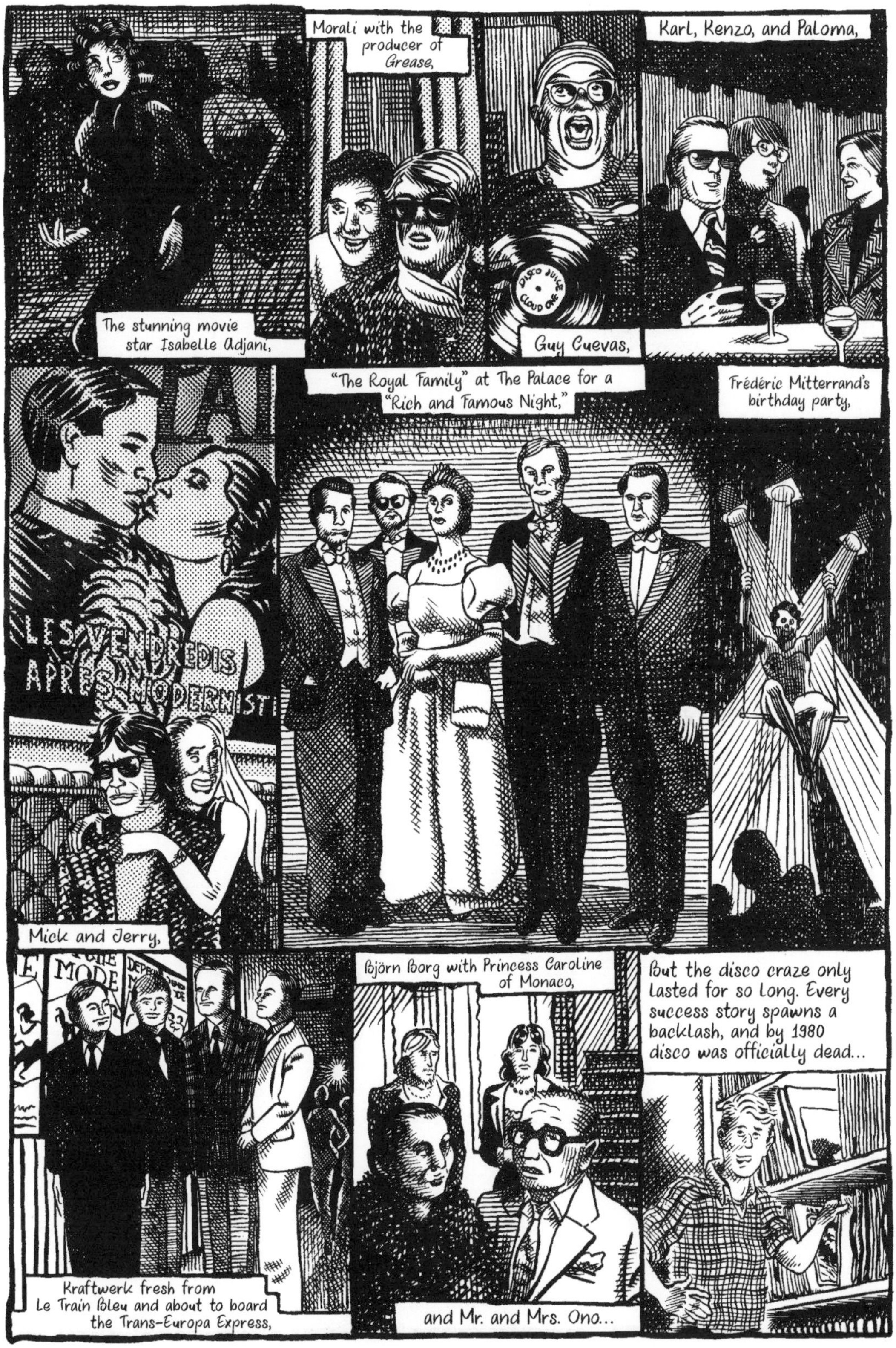
The stunning movie star Isabelle Adjani,
Morali with the producer of *Grease*,
Guy Cuevas,
DISCO JUICE CLOUD ONE
Karl, Kenzo, and Paloma,
LES VENDREDIS APRÈS MODERNISTE
Mick and Jerry,
"The Royal Family" at The Palace for a "Rich and Famous Night,"
Frédéric Mitterrand's birthday party,
MODE
Kraftwerk fresh from Le Train Bleu and about to board the Trans-Europa Express,
Björn Borg with Princess Caroline of Monaco,
and Mr. and Mrs. Ono...
But the disco craze only lasted for so long. Every success story spawns a backlash, and by 1980 disco was officially dead...

The Song of the Machine
Disco goes up in FLAMES!
It had to happen sooner or later, but it came as a shock nonetheless.
July 12, 1979. Popular radio DJ Steve Dahl blew up pallet-loads of disco records in center field at Chicago's famous Comiskey Park. Dubbed "Disco Demolition Night," the high-profile stunt attracted a motley collection of drunk fans, many of whom showed up just for the spectacle. "Burn disco, burn...but this time for real!" was their chilling, violent chant.
Two Victims Testify
"They attacked us from all sides with sticks, and it turned into a massacre. We were mutilated, murdered, burned alive... We lost count of the dead."
MACHINE
14

Blame the PRODUCERS?

What if the record producers were responsible for the demise of disco?

The disco explosion had been phenomenal: not just the music, but the outfits, the lifestyle… Looking back on it, disco was the last mass music movement. Punk, goth, grunge…everything that followed was just an alternative, and certainly not a widespread way of life.

Disco was an international consumer product–and a best-selling one. But it wasn't so much the singers, musicians, and DJs as the people behind them–producers, label managers, club owners–who profited from it. The artists were so naive they let themselves get eaten alive. People did weird things, came up with more and more outlandish concepts: "space disco," for example–did you hear of that one? John Travolta meets Darth Vader!

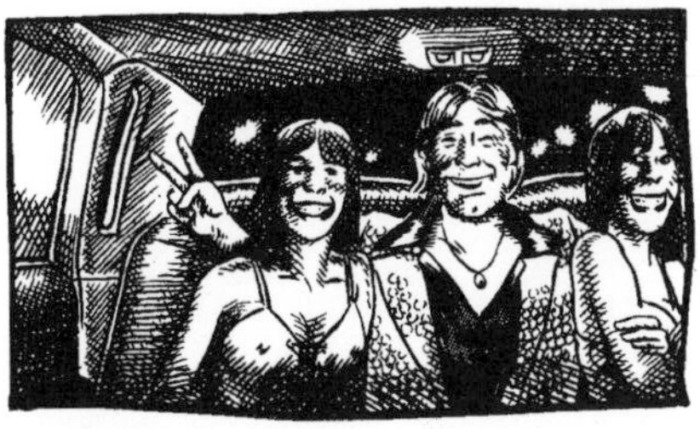

We found the culprit…

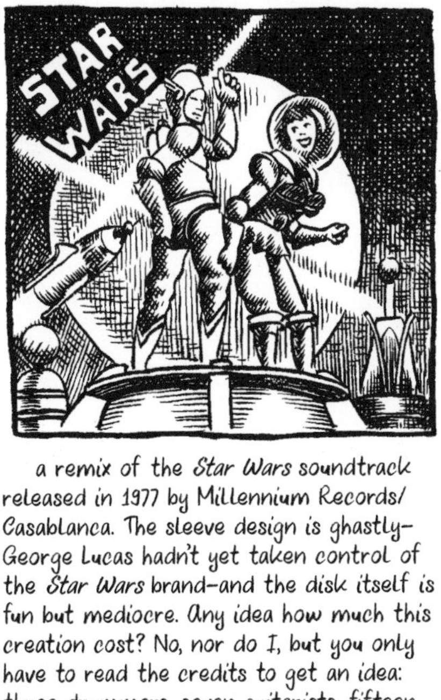
STAR WARS

a remix of the *Star Wars* soundtrack released in 1977 by Millennium Records/Casablanca. The sleeve design is ghastly–George Lucas hadn't yet taken control of the *Star Wars* brand–and the disk itself is fun but mediocre. Any idea how much this creation cost? No, nor do I, but you only have to read the credits to get an idea: three drummers, seven guitarists, fifteen violin players…I could go on: a total of seventy-five musicians, not to mention all the engineers and "special studio tape effects" guys. Disco went broke. Oh, that doesn't mean there weren't any disco hits after 1980, but the machine had already jammed; people had started looking for something else.

Those weird London punks were becoming a sensation, and hip-hop was spreading, making its mark. The people's revenge against the disco jet-setters? But remember how it had all started, in 1971 at The Loft… Hell, doesn't time fly! Disco would be saved by the underground–again. Throughout the eighties, even as it was being universally trashed, traces of it could be found everywhere–from New York's rap to Manchester's new wave to Washington's go-go…all the way to the final stop on our journey, house music. But there had to be a connection: the reincarnation needed a venue. It was called Paradise Garage…

15

CHAPTER 3

LARRY LEVAN
AND PARADISE GARAGE

THE NEW ELIXIR

James Brown
Give It Up & Turn It Loose (Live version) — 1970

Eddie Kendricks
Girl You Need a Change of Mind — 1973

Diana Ross
Love Hangover — 1976

Bumblebee Unlimited
Love Bug (Larry Levan Disco Mix) — 1978

Kraftwerk
The Robots — 1978

Eddy Grant
Living on the Frontline — 1979

Gino Soccio
Dancer — 1979

Loose Joints
Is It All Over My Face? — 1980

Atmosfear
Dancing in Outer Space — 1981

The Clash
Magnificent Dance — 1981

David Byrne and Brian Eno
Jezebel Spirit — 1981

Grace Jones
Pull Up to the Bumper
(Larry Levan Garage Mix) — 1981

Taana Gardner
Heartbeat (Larry Levan Club Mix) — 1981

ESG
Moody — 1981

Class Action
Week End (Larry Levan Mix) — 1981

Tom Tom Club
Genius of Love — 1981

Yazoo
Situation — 1982

Peech Boys
Don't Make Me Wait — 1983

Imagination
Changes (Larry Levan Dub) — 1983

Gwen Guthrie
Padlock (EP) — 1983

Man Friday
Love Honey, Love Heartache — 1986

Fingers Inc.
Mystery of Love — 1986

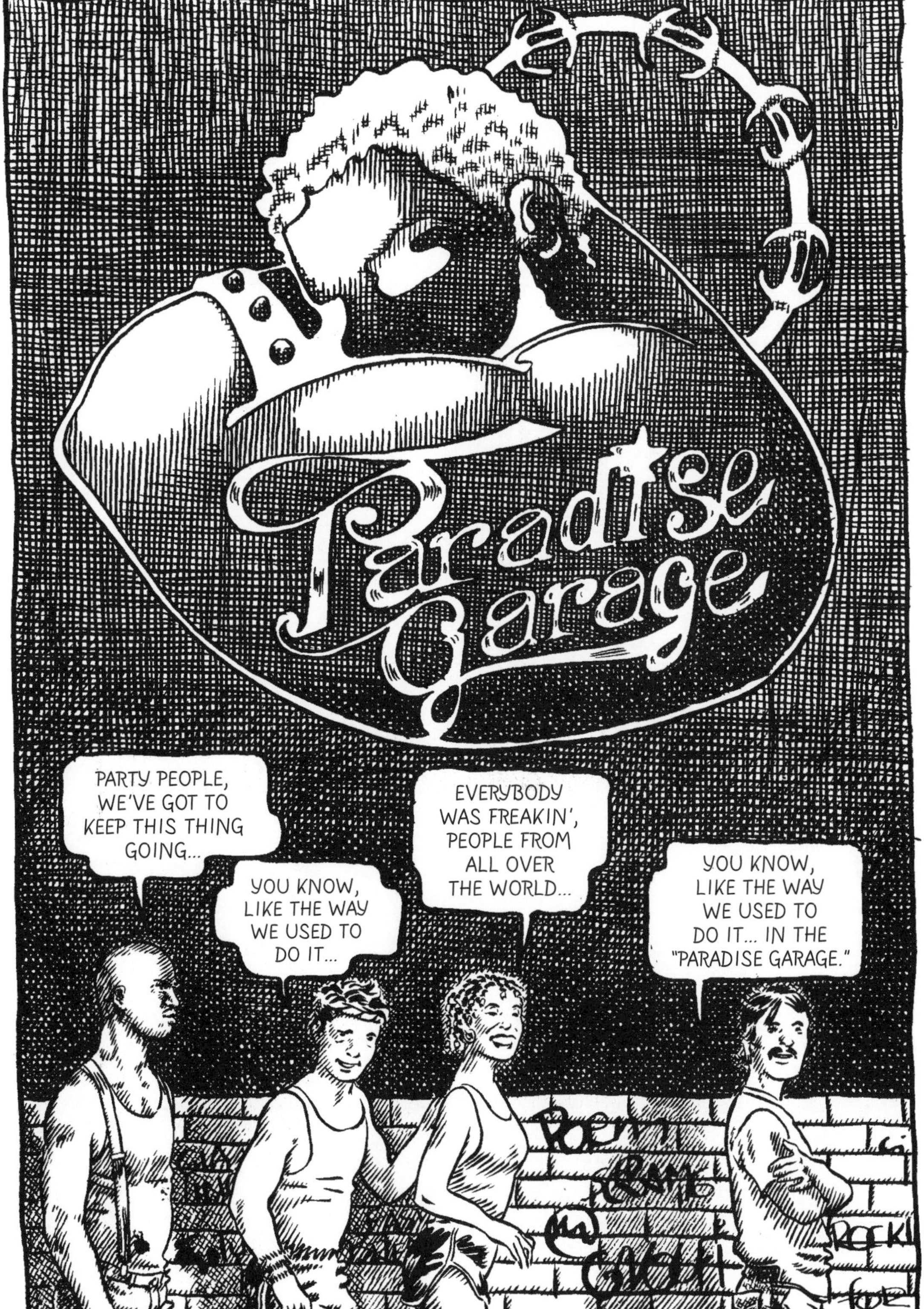
Paradise Garage
PARTY PEOPLE, WE'VE GOT TO KEEP THIS THING GOING...
YOU KNOW, LIKE THE WAY WE USED TO DO IT...
EVERYBODY WAS FREAKIN', PEOPLE FROM ALL OVER THE WORLD...
YOU KNOW, LIKE THE WAY WE USED TO DO IT... IN THE "PARADISE GARAGE."

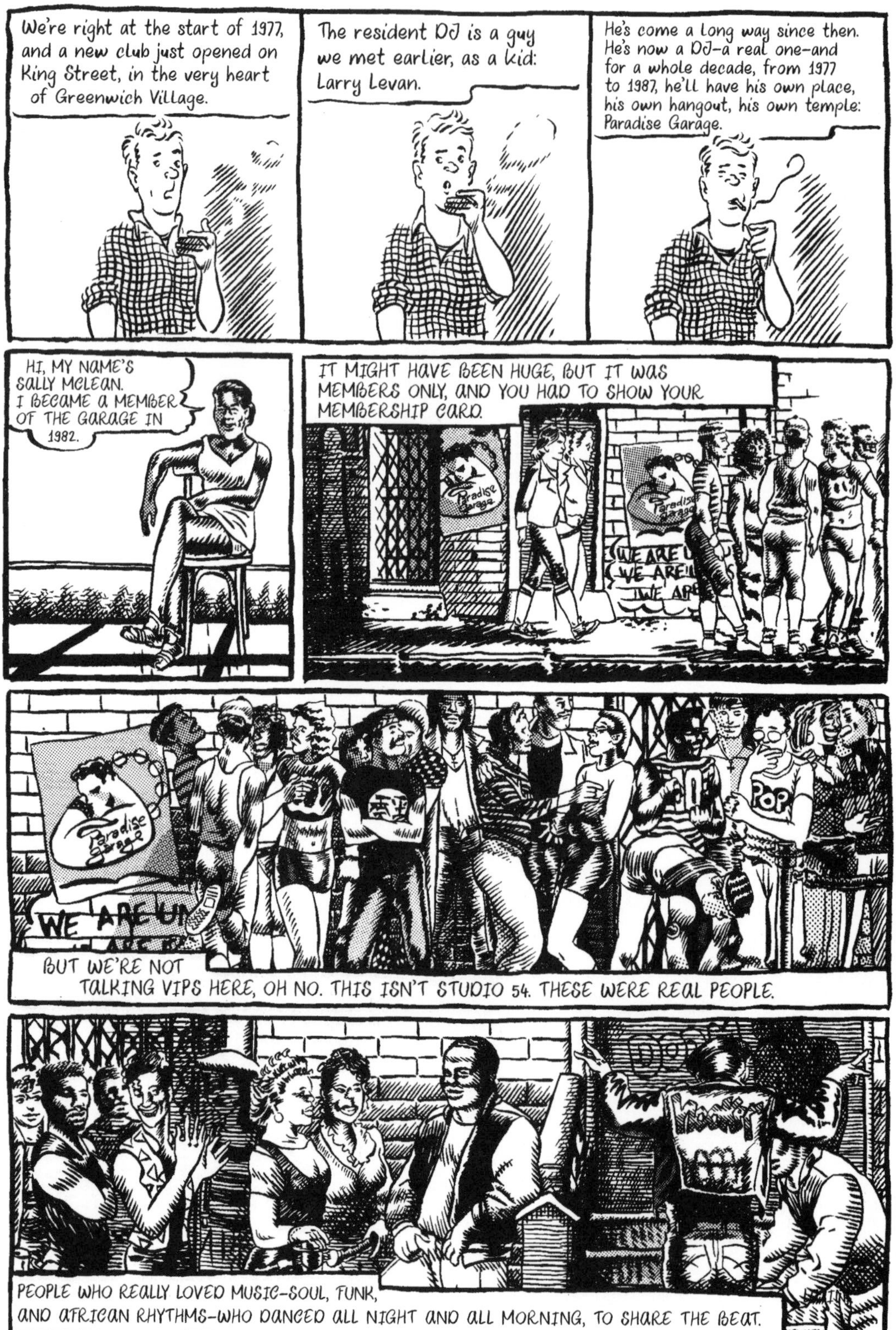
We're right at the start of 1977, and a new club just opened on King Street, in the very heart of Greenwich Village.
The resident DJ is a guy we met earlier, as a kid: Larry Levan.
He's come a long way since then. He's now a DJ–a real one–and for a whole decade, from 1977 to 1987, he'll have his own place, his own hangout, his own temple: Paradise Garage.
HI, MY NAME'S SALLY MCLEAN. I BECAME A MEMBER OF THE GARAGE IN 1982.
IT MIGHT HAVE BEEN HUGE, BUT IT WAS MEMBERS ONLY, AND YOU HAD TO SHOW YOUR MEMBERSHIP CARD.
Paradise Garage
Paradise Garage
Paradise Garage
POP
BUT WE'RE NOT TALKING VIPS HERE, OH NO. THIS ISN'T STUDIO 54. THESE WERE REAL PEOPLE.
PEOPLE WHO REALLY LOVED MUSIC–SOUL, FUNK, AND AFRICAN RHYTHMS–WHO DANCED ALL NIGHT AND ALL MORNING, TO SHARE THE BEAT.

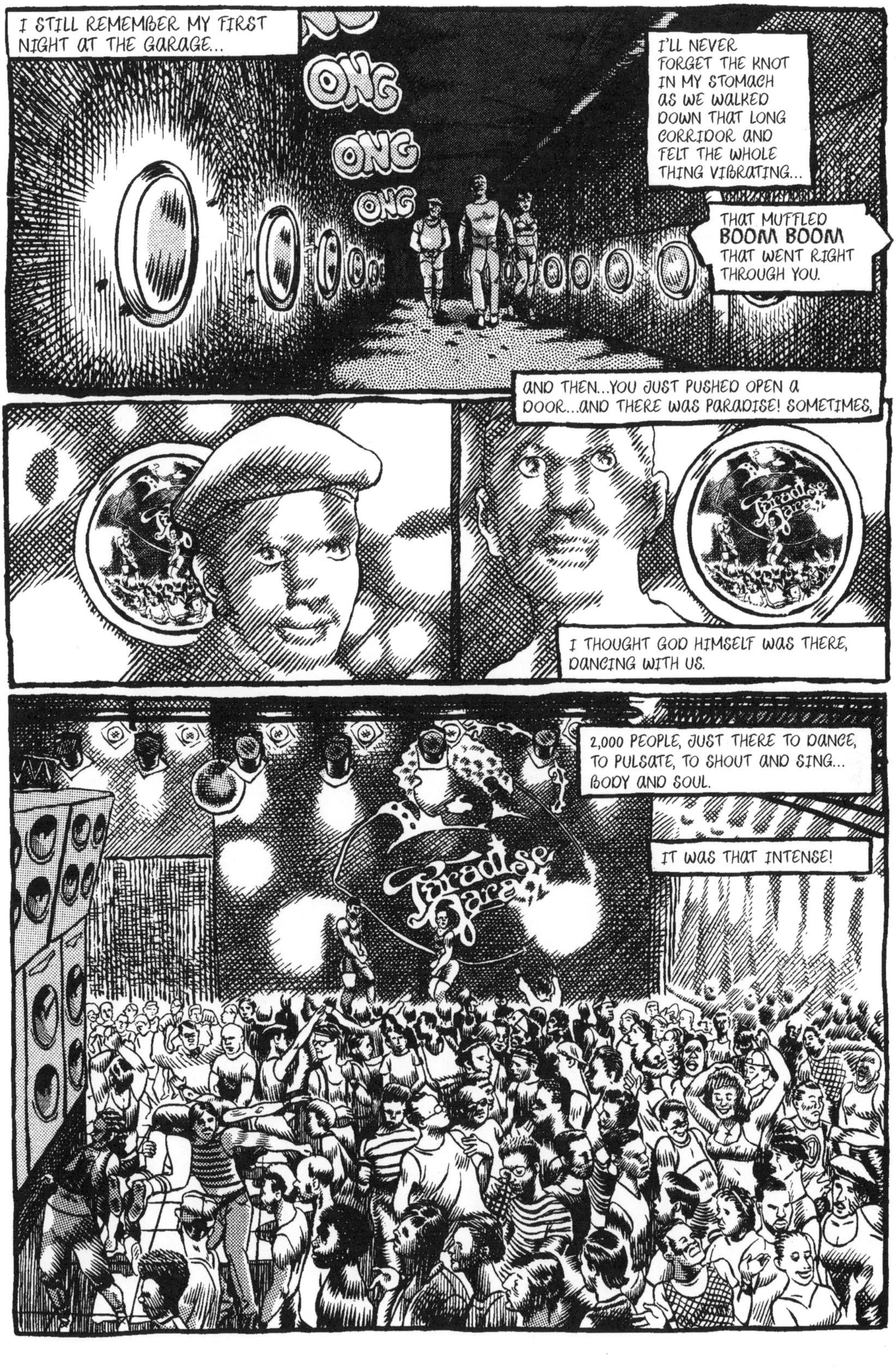
I STILL REMEMBER MY FIRST NIGHT AT THE GARAGE...
ONG
ONG
ONG
I'LL NEVER FORGET THE KNOT IN MY STOMACH AS WE WALKED DOWN THAT LONG CORRIDOR AND FELT THE WHOLE THING VIBRATING...
THAT MUFFLED BOOM BOOM THAT WENT RIGHT THROUGH YOU.
AND THEN...YOU JUST PUSHED OPEN A DOOR...AND THERE WAS PARADISE! SOMETIMES,
I THOUGHT GOD HIMSELF WAS THERE, DANCING WITH US.
2,000 PEOPLE, JUST THERE TO DANCE, TO PULSATE, TO SHOUT AND SING... BODY AND SOUL.
IT WAS THAT INTENSE!
Paradise Garage

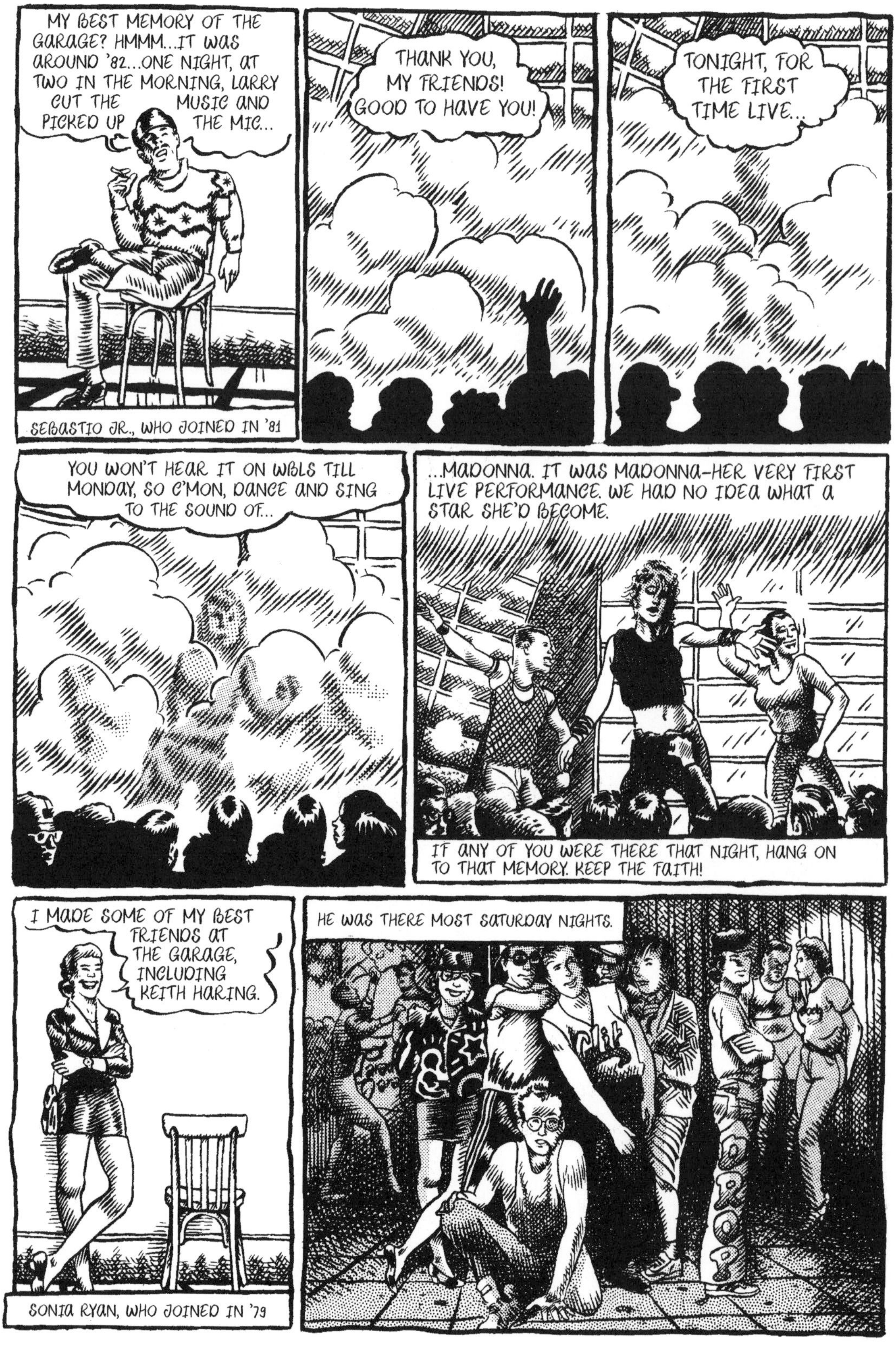
MY BEST MEMORY OF THE GARAGE? HMMM...IT WAS AROUND '82...ONE NIGHT, AT TWO IN THE MORNING, LARRY CUT THE MUSIC AND PICKED UP THE MIC...
SEBASTIO JR., WHO JOINED IN '81
THANK YOU, MY FRIENDS! GOOD TO HAVE YOU!
TONIGHT, FOR THE FIRST TIME LIVE...
YOU WON'T HEAR IT ON WBLS TILL MONDAY, SO C'MON, DANCE AND SING TO THE SOUND OF...
...MADONNA. IT WAS MADONNA–HER VERY FIRST LIVE PERFORMANCE. WE HAD NO IDEA WHAT A STAR SHE'D BECOME.
IF ANY OF YOU WERE THERE THAT NIGHT, HANG ON TO THAT MEMORY. KEEP THE FAITH!
I MADE SOME OF MY BEST FRIENDS AT THE GARAGE, INCLUDING KEITH HARING.
SONIA RYAN, WHO JOINED IN '79
HE WAS THERE MOST SATURDAY NIGHTS.

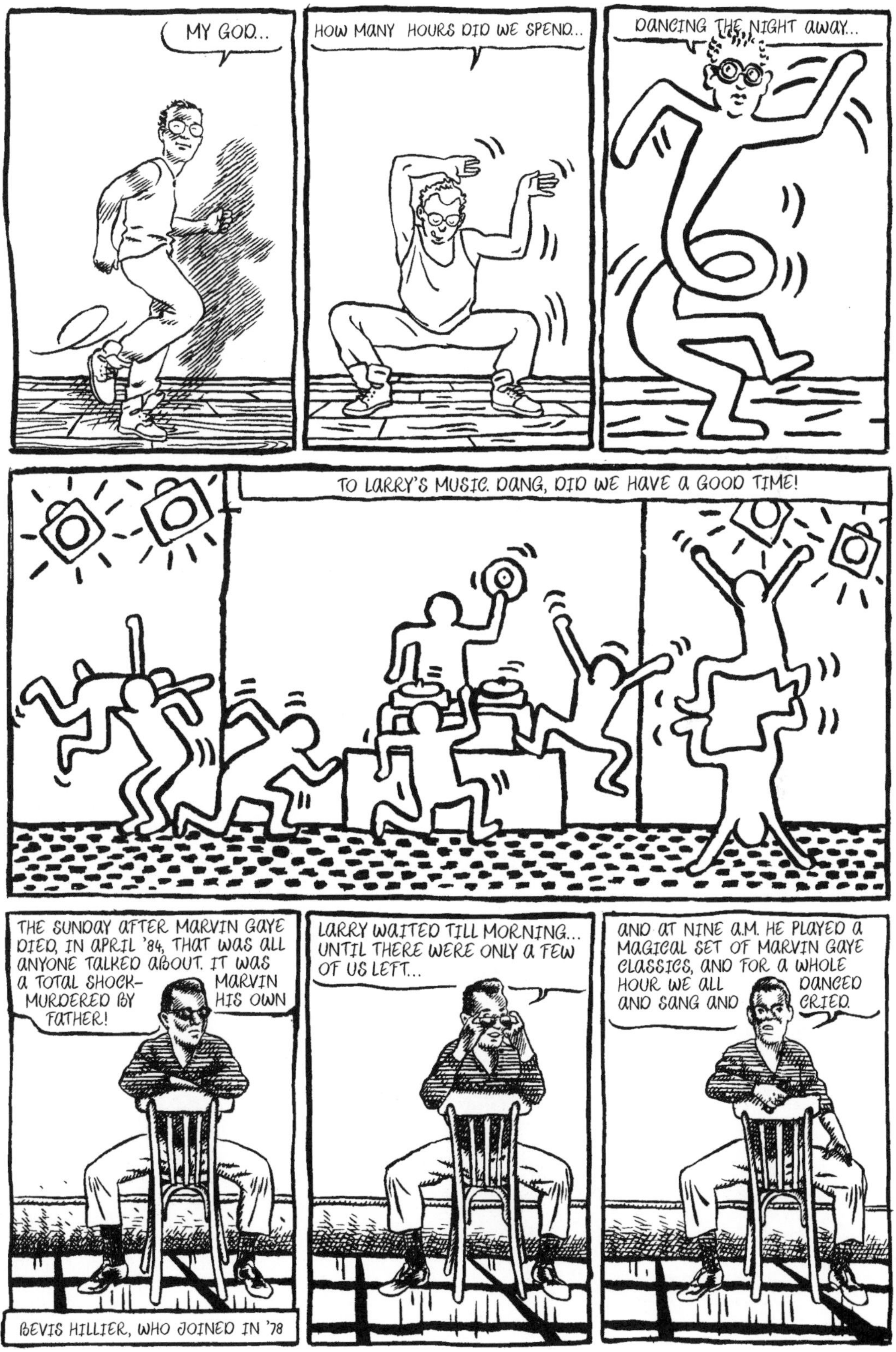
MY GOD...
HOW MANY HOURS DID WE SPEND...
DANCING THE NIGHT AWAY...
TO LARRY'S MUSIC. DANG, DID WE HAVE A GOOD TIME!
THE SUNDAY AFTER MARVIN GAYE DIED, IN APRIL '84, THAT WAS ALL ANYONE TALKED ABOUT. IT WAS A TOTAL SHOCK-- MARVIN MURDERED BY HIS OWN FATHER!
BEVIS HILLIER, WHO JOINED IN '78
LARRY WAITED TILL MORNING... UNTIL THERE WERE ONLY A FEW OF US LEFT...
AND AT NINE A.M. HE PLAYED A MAGICAL SET OF MARVIN GAYE CLASSICS, AND FOR A WHOLE HOUR WE ALL DANCED AND SANG AND CRIED.

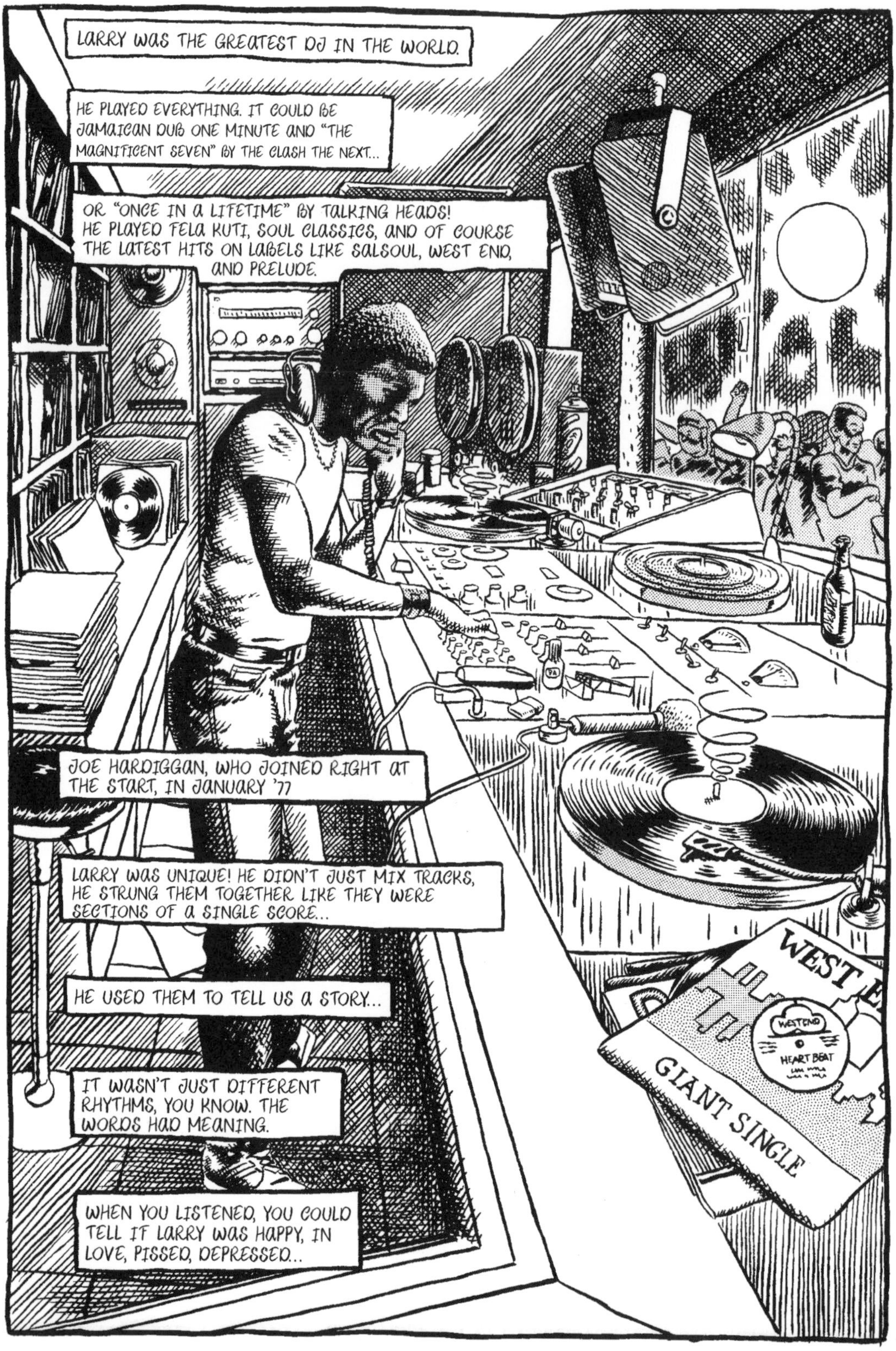
LARRY WAS THE GREATEST DJ IN THE WORLD.
HE PLAYED EVERYTHING. IT COULD BE JAMAICAN DUB ONE MINUTE AND "THE MAGNIFICENT SEVEN" BY THE CLASH THE NEXT...
OR "ONCE IN A LIFETIME" BY TALKING HEADS! HE PLAYED FELA KUTI, SOUL CLASSICS, AND OF COURSE THE LATEST HITS ON LABELS LIKE SALSOUL, WEST END, AND PRELUDE.
JOE HARDIGGAN, WHO JOINED RIGHT AT THE START, IN JANUARY '77
LARRY WAS UNIQUE! HE DIDN'T JUST MIX TRACKS, HE STRUNG THEM TOGETHER LIKE THEY WERE SECTIONS OF A SINGLE SCORE...
HE USED THEM TO TELL US A STORY...
IT WASN'T JUST DIFFERENT RHYTHMS, YOU KNOW. THE WORDS HAD MEANING.
WHEN YOU LISTENED, YOU COULD TELL IF LARRY WAS HAPPY, IN LOVE, PISSED, DEPRESSED...
WEST E
WESTEND
HEART BEAT
GIANT SINGLE

IN '81, HE PLAYED US FOR THE FIRST TIME...

JOSH CURRY, WHO JOINED IN '77

ONE OF HIS GREATEST RECORDS—'CAUSE LARRY WAS ALSO A KICK-ASS PRODUCER, YOU KNOW...

WEST END

HEARTBEAT (PARTY)

TAANA GARDNER

produced by larry levan

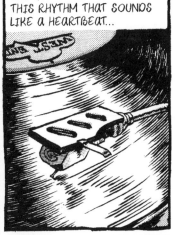

AND IN THE BREAK THERE'S THIS RHYTHM THAT SOUNDS LIKE A HEARTBEAT...

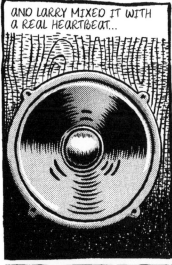

AND LARRY MIXED IT WITH A REAL HEARTBEAT...

AND AT EVERY BEAT THESE RED LIGHTS GOT BRIGHTER AND BRIGHTER...

AND THEN HE SLOWED DOWN THE TRACKS AND STOPPED THE HEARTBEAT...AND THERE WAS THIS DEATHLY SILENCE...

GIVE US MORE!

GIVE US MORE!

SHHH!

SHHH!

LARRY LEVAN WAS A WEIRD GUY, YOU KNOW...

ONE TIME, HA HA HA...

VICKY WELSH, WHO JOINED IN '84

EVERYONE WAS ALREADY DANCING, AND LARRY LOOKED OUT OF HIS BOOTH AND SAW THAT THE DISCO BALLS WERE DIRTY...

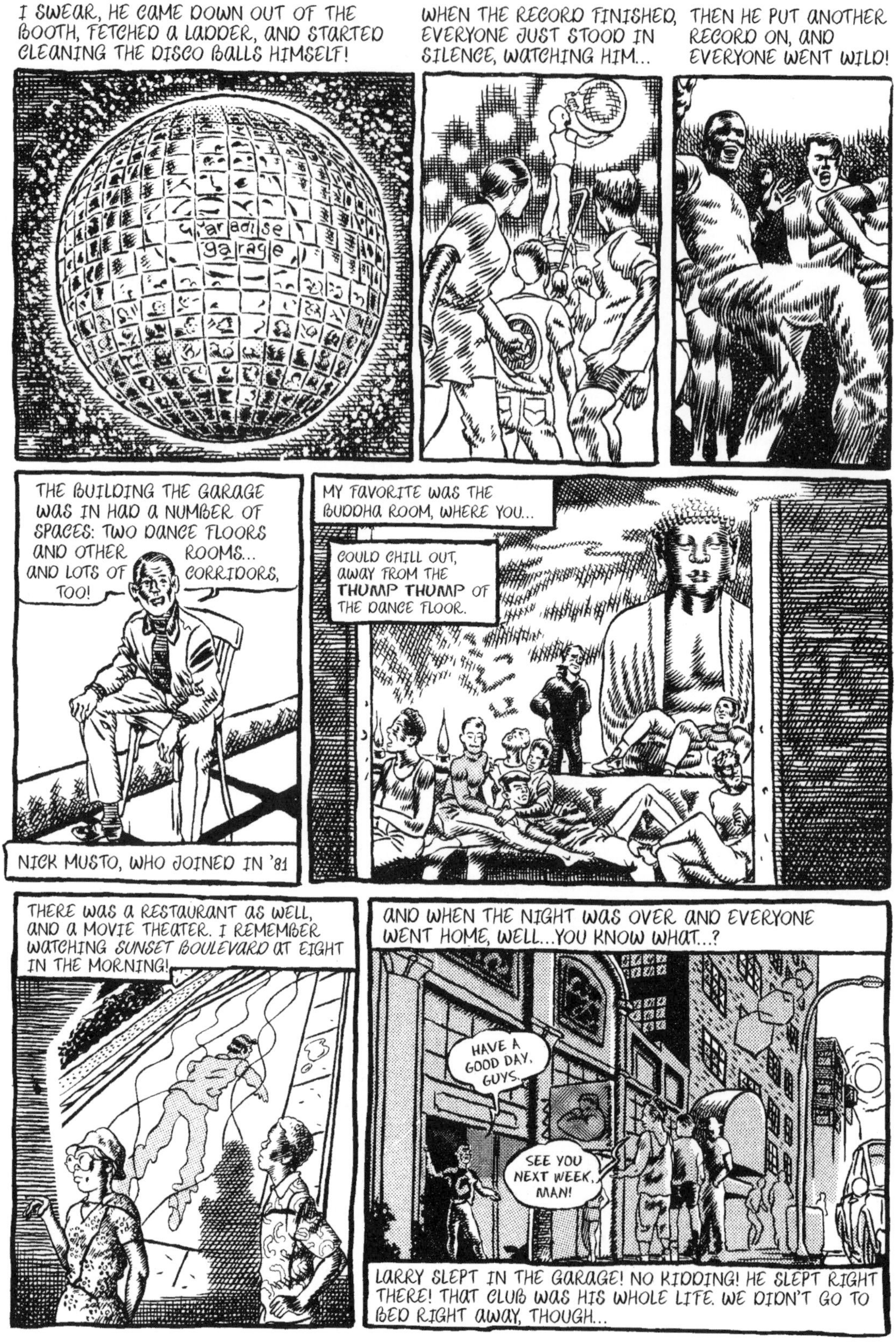
I SWEAR, HE CAME DOWN OUT OF THE BOOTH, FETCHED A LADDER, AND STARTED CLEANING THE DISCO BALLS HIMSELF!
paradise garage
WHEN THE RECORD FINISHED, EVERYONE JUST STOOD IN SILENCE, WATCHING HIM...
THEN HE PUT ANOTHER RECORD ON, AND EVERYONE WENT WILD!
THE BUILDING THE GARAGE WAS IN HAD A NUMBER OF SPACES: TWO DANCE FLOORS AND OTHER ROOMS...
AND LOTS OF CORRIDORS, TOO!
NICK MUSTO, WHO JOINED IN '81
MY FAVORITE WAS THE BUDDHA ROOM, WHERE YOU...
COULD CHILL OUT, AWAY FROM THE THUMP THUMP OF THE DANCE FLOOR.
THERE WAS A RESTAURANT AS WELL, AND A MOVIE THEATER. I REMEMBER WATCHING SUNSET BOULEVARD AT EIGHT IN THE MORNING!
AND WHEN THE NIGHT WAS OVER AND EVERYONE WENT HOME, WELL...YOU KNOW WHAT...?
HAVE A GOOD DAY, GUYS.
SEE YOU NEXT WEEK, MAN!
LARRY SLEPT IN THE GARAGE! NO KIDDING! HE SLEPT RIGHT THERE! THAT CLUB WAS HIS WHOLE LIFE. WE DIDN'T GO TO BED RIGHT AWAY, THOUGH...

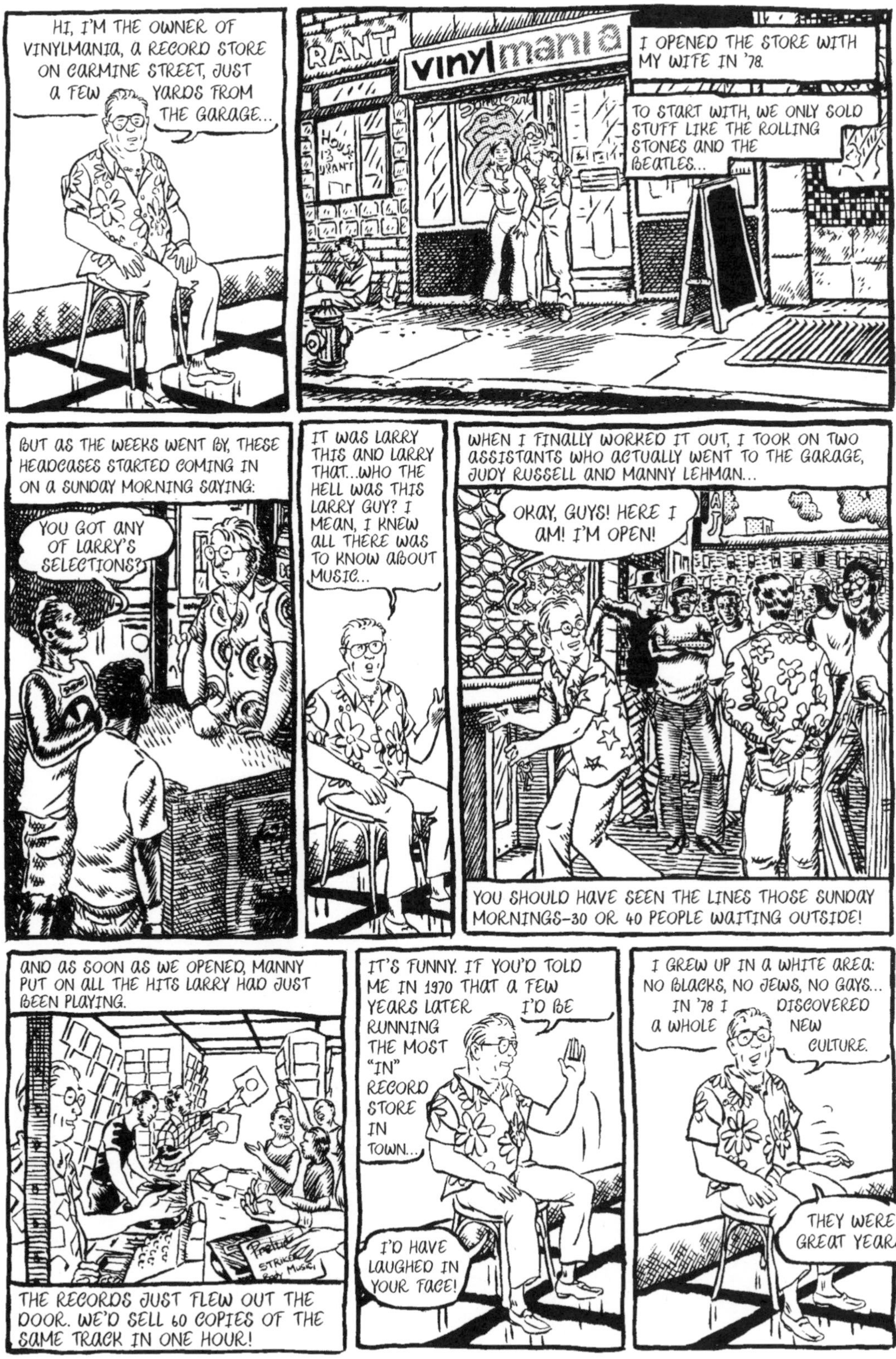
HI, I'M THE OWNER OF VINYLMANIA, A RECORD STORE ON CARMINE STREET, JUST A FEW YARDS FROM THE GARAGE...
vinylmania
I OPENED THE STORE WITH MY WIFE IN '78.
TO START WITH, WE ONLY SOLD STUFF LIKE THE ROLLING STONES AND THE BEATLES...
BUT AS THE WEEKS WENT BY, THESE HEADCASES STARTED COMING IN ON A SUNDAY MORNING SAYING:
YOU GOT ANY OF LARRY'S SELECTIONS?
IT WAS LARRY THIS AND LARRY THAT...WHO THE HELL WAS THIS LARRY GUY? I MEAN, I KNEW ALL THERE WAS TO KNOW ABOUT MUSIC...
WHEN I FINALLY WORKED IT OUT, I TOOK ON TWO ASSISTANTS WHO ACTUALLY WENT TO THE GARAGE, JUDY RUSSELL AND MANNY LEHMAN...
OKAY, GUYS! HERE I AM! I'M OPEN!
YOU SHOULD HAVE SEEN THE LINES THOSE SUNDAY MORNINGS—30 OR 40 PEOPLE WAITING OUTSIDE!
AND AS SOON AS WE OPENED, MANNY PUT ON ALL THE HITS LARRY HAD JUST BEEN PLAYING.
THE RECORDS JUST FLEW OUT THE DOOR. WE'D SELL 60 COPIES OF THE SAME TRACK IN ONE HOUR!
IT'S FUNNY. IF YOU'D TOLD ME IN 1970 THAT A FEW YEARS LATER I'D BE RUNNING THE MOST "IN" RECORD STORE IN TOWN...
I'D HAVE LAUGHED IN YOUR FACE!
I GREW UP IN A WHITE AREA: NO BLACKS, NO JEWS, NO GAYS... IN '78 I DISCOVERED A WHOLE NEW CULTURE.
THEY WERE GREAT YEARS.

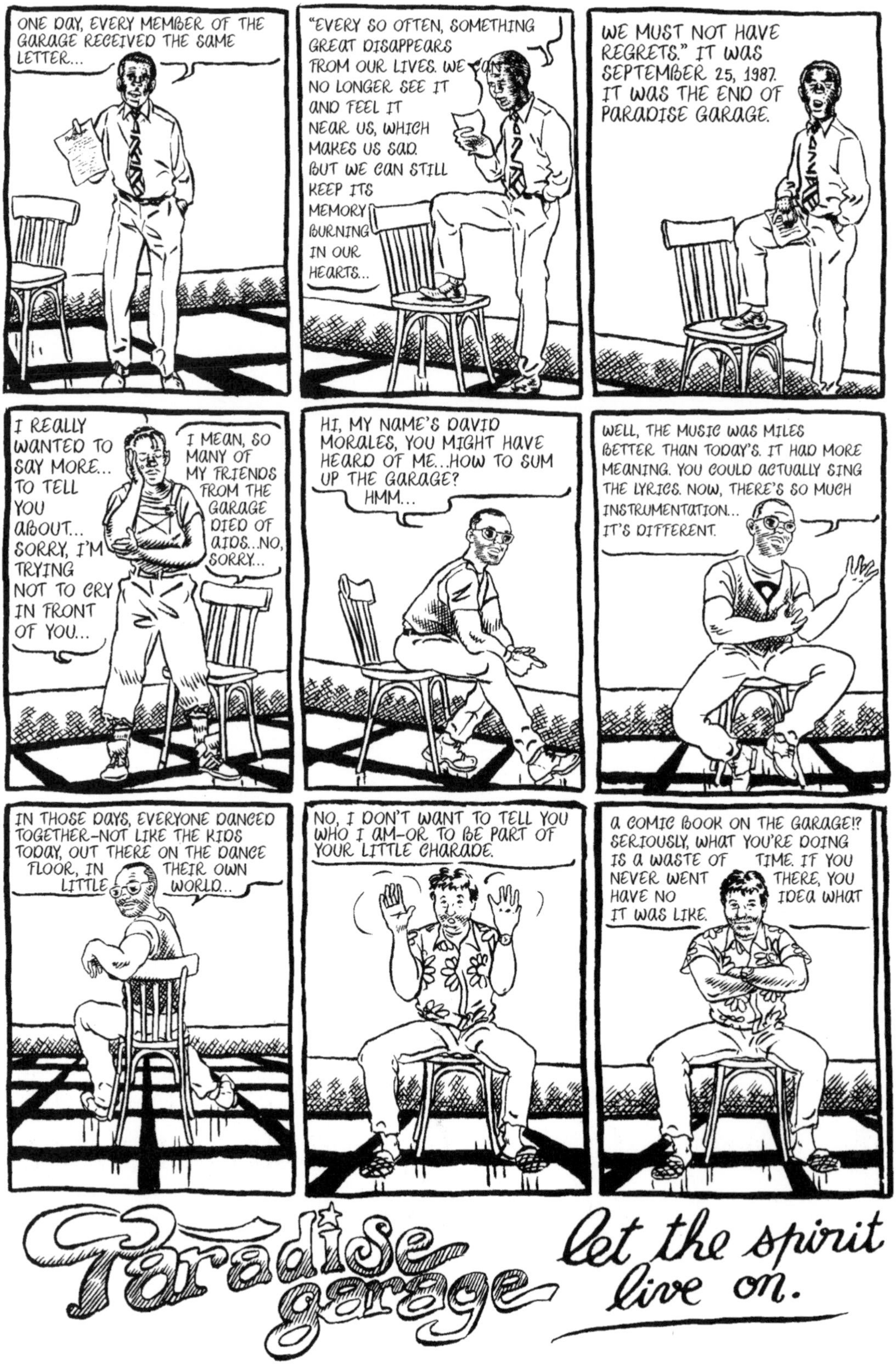
ONE DAY, EVERY MEMBER OF THE GARAGE RECEIVED THE SAME LETTER...
"EVERY SO OFTEN, SOMETHING GREAT DISAPPEARS FROM OUR LIVES. WE CAN NO LONGER SEE IT AND FEEL IT NEAR US, WHICH MAKES US SAD. BUT WE CAN STILL KEEP ITS MEMORY BURNING IN OUR HEARTS...
WE MUST NOT HAVE REGRETS." IT WAS SEPTEMBER 25, 1987. IT WAS THE END OF PARADISE GARAGE.
I REALLY WANTED TO SAY MORE... TO TELL YOU ABOUT... SORRY, I'M TRYING NOT TO CRY IN FRONT OF YOU...
I MEAN, SO MANY OF MY FRIENDS FROM THE GARAGE DIED OF AIDS...NO, SORRY...
HI, MY NAME'S DAVID MORALES, YOU MIGHT HAVE HEARD OF ME...HOW TO SUM UP THE GARAGE? HMM...
WELL, THE MUSIC WAS MILES BETTER THAN TODAY'S. IT HAD MORE MEANING. YOU COULD ACTUALLY SING THE LYRICS. NOW, THERE'S SO MUCH INSTRUMENTATION... IT'S DIFFERENT.
IN THOSE DAYS, EVERYONE DANCED TOGETHER–NOT LIKE THE KIDS TODAY, OUT THERE ON THE DANCE FLOOR, IN THEIR OWN LITTLE WORLD...
NO, I DON'T WANT TO TELL YOU WHO I AM–OR TO BE PART OF YOUR LITTLE CHARADE.
A COMIC BOOK ON THE GARAGE!? SERIOUSLY, WHAT YOU'RE DOING IS A WASTE OF TIME. IF YOU NEVER WENT THERE, YOU HAVE NO IDEA WHAT IT WAS LIKE.
Paradise garage
let the spirit live on.

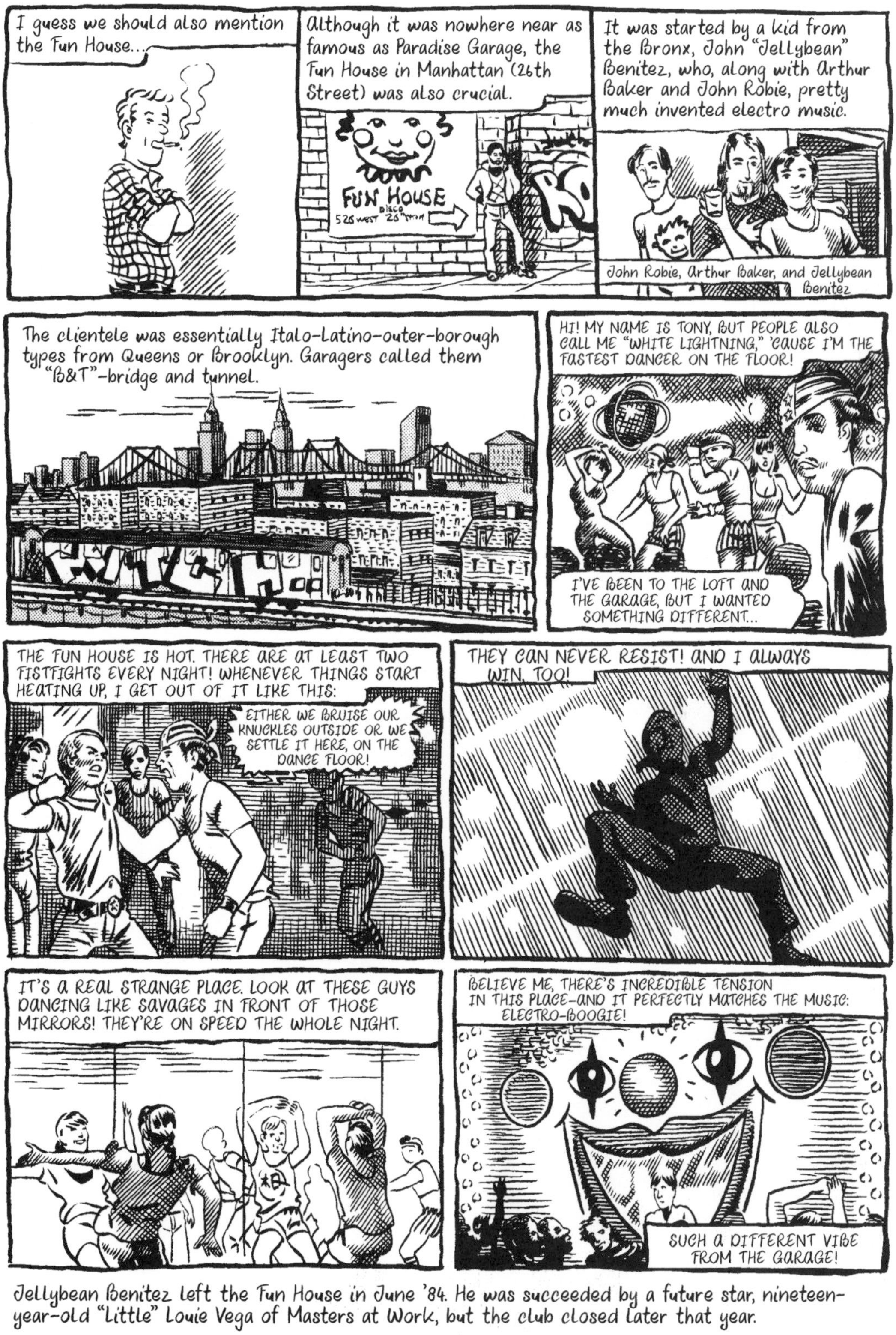
I guess we should also mention the Fun House...
Although it was nowhere near as famous as Paradise Garage, the Fun House in Manhattan (26th Street) was also crucial.
FUN HOUSE
It was started by a kid from the Bronx, John "Jellybean" Benitez, who, along with Arthur Baker and John Robie, pretty much invented electro music.
John Robie, Arthur Baker, and Jellybean Benitez
The clientele was essentially Italo-Latino-outer-borough types from Queens or Brooklyn. Garagers called them "B&T"–bridge and tunnel.
HI! MY NAME IS TONY, BUT PEOPLE ALSO CALL ME "WHITE LIGHTNING," 'CAUSE I'M THE FASTEST DANCER ON THE FLOOR!
I'VE BEEN TO THE LOFT AND THE GARAGE, BUT I WANTED SOMETHING DIFFERENT...
THE FUN HOUSE IS HOT. THERE ARE AT LEAST TWO FISTFIGHTS EVERY NIGHT! WHENEVER THINGS START HEATING UP, I GET OUT OF IT LIKE THIS:
EITHER WE BRUISE OUR KNUCKLES OUTSIDE OR WE SETTLE IT HERE, ON THE DANCE FLOOR!
THEY CAN NEVER RESIST! AND I ALWAYS WIN, TOO!
IT'S A REAL STRANGE PLACE. LOOK AT THESE GUYS DANCING LIKE SAVAGES IN FRONT OF THOSE MIRRORS! THEY'RE ON SPEED THE WHOLE NIGHT.
BELIEVE ME, THERE'S INCREDIBLE TENSION IN THIS PLACE–AND IT PERFECTLY MATCHES THE MUSIC: ELECTRO-BOOGIE!
SUCH A DIFFERENT VIBE FROM THE GARAGE!

Jellybean Benitez left the Fun House in June '84. He was succeeded by a future star, nineteen-year-old "Little" Louie Vega of Masters at Work, but the club closed later that year.

CHAPTER 4

CHICAGO AND HOUSE MUSIC

CHI-TOWN SELECTION

Phuture (DJ Pierre and Co.)
Acid Tracks
(Marshall Jefferson Production) — 1986

Virgo (Adonis and Marshall Jefferson)
Free Yourself — 1986

Mr. Fingers (Larry Heard)
Can U Feel It/Washing Machine — 1986

**Fingers Inc.
(Larry Heard and Robert Owens)**
Bring Down the Walls — 1986

Joe Smooth feat. Anthony Thomas
The Promised Land — 1987

Frankie Knuckles feat. Jamie Principle
Baby Wants to Ride — 1987

Ralphi Rosario
You Used to Hold Me — 1987

Armando
Confusion's Revenge — 1988

Lil Louis
Nyce & Slo (The Luv Bug) — 1990

UBQ Project feat. Kathy Summers
When I Fell N Love — 1991

Kym Sims
Too Blind to See It
(Steve Silk Hurley House Mix) — 1991

Ron Trent
Altered States — 1992

Phuture Scope (DJ Pierre)
Plastic — 1992

Chez Damier
Can You Feel It (Mark Kinchen Dub) — 1992

Mike Dunn
God Made Me Phunky — 1994

Green Velvet
Flash — 1995

Glenn Underground
GU Essentials (EP) — 1995

DJ Sneak
Moon Doggy (EP) — 1995

Felix Da Housecat
Metropolis Present Day?
"Thee Album!" (LP) — 1995

Steve "Silk" Hurley and The Voices of Life
The Word Is Love — 1998

The Don (DJ Pierre)
The Horn Song — 1998

Roy Davis Jr.
Join His Kingdom — 1999

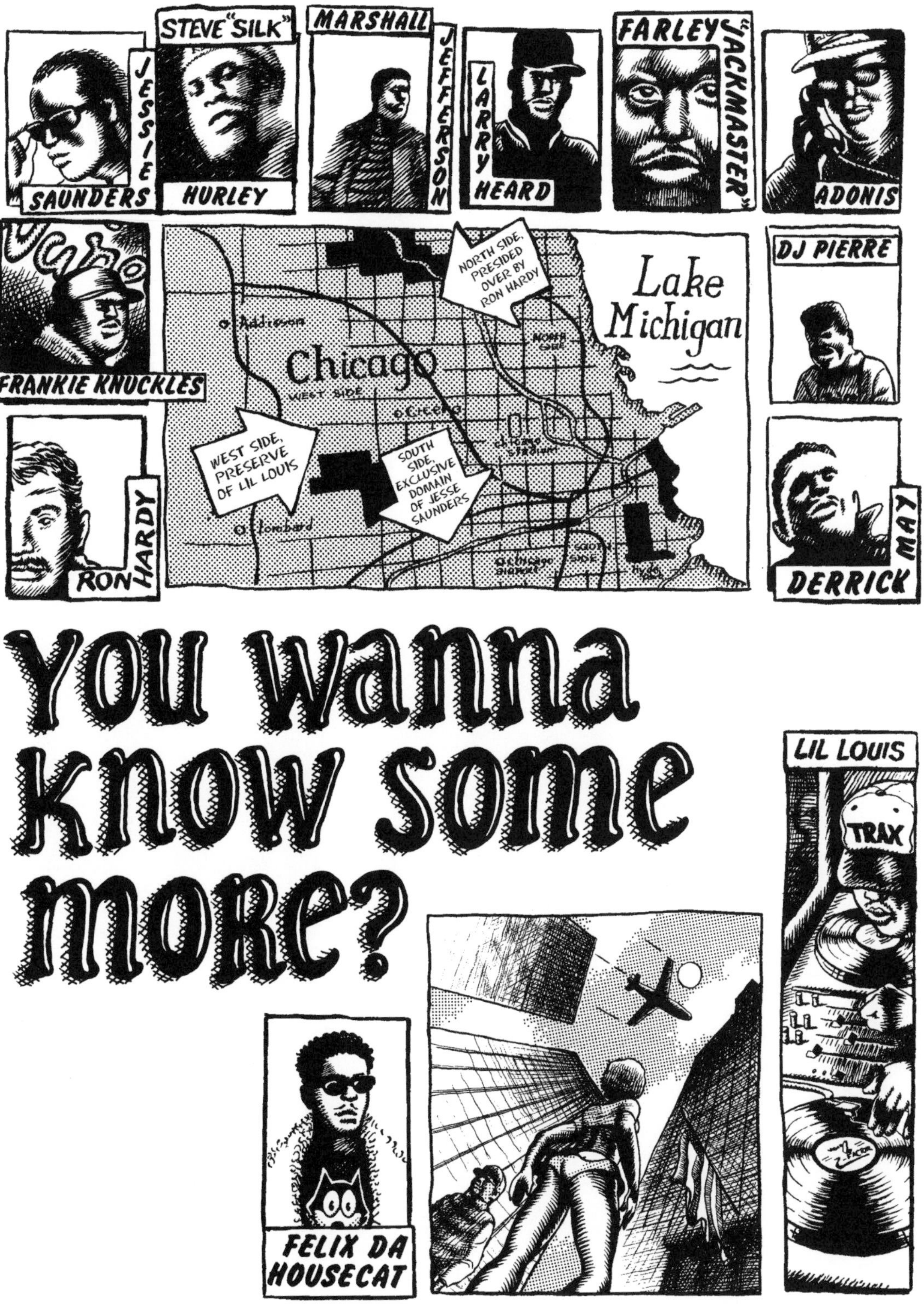
JESSIE SAUNDERS
STEVE "SILK" HURLEY
MARSHALL JEFFERSON
LARRY HEARD
FARLEY "JACKMASTER"
ADONIS
FRANKIE KNUCKLES
Chicago
NORTH SIDE, PRESIDED OVER BY RON HARDY
Lake Michigan
WEST SIDE, PRESERVE OF LIL LOUIS
SOUTH SIDE, EXCLUSIVE DOMAIN OF JESSE SAUNDERS
DJ PIERRE
RON HARDY
DERRICK MAY
You wanna know some more?
LIL LOUIS
TRAX
FELIX DA HOUSECAT

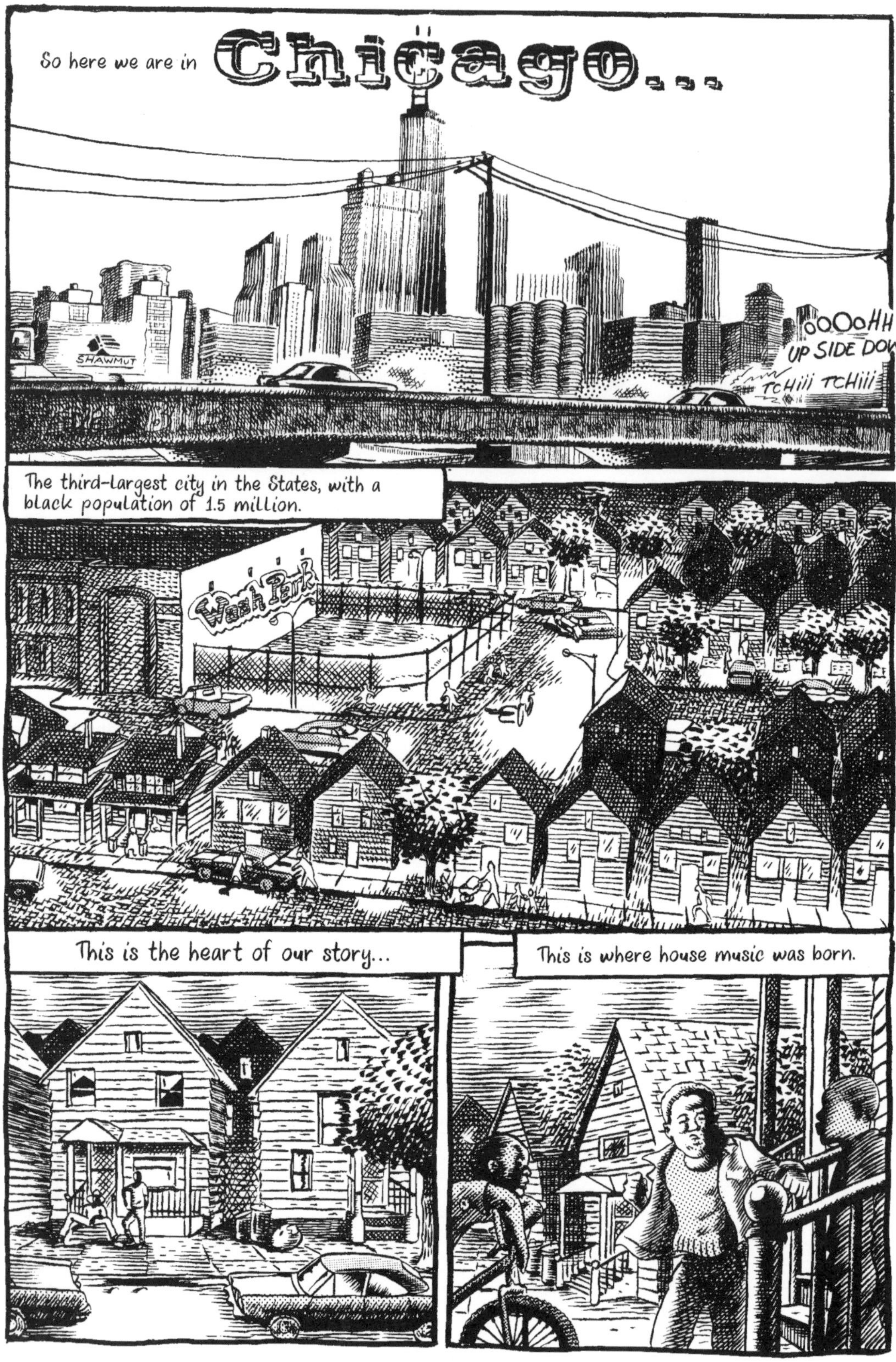
So here we are in Chicago...
SHAWMUT
OOOoHH
UP SIDE DOWN
TCHiii TCHiii
The third-largest city in the States, with a black population of 1.5 million.
Wash Park
This is the heart of our story...
This is where house music was born.

1977:

The storylines interconnect, and what happened in Chicago was directly linked to Larry Levan's Paradise Garage adventure...

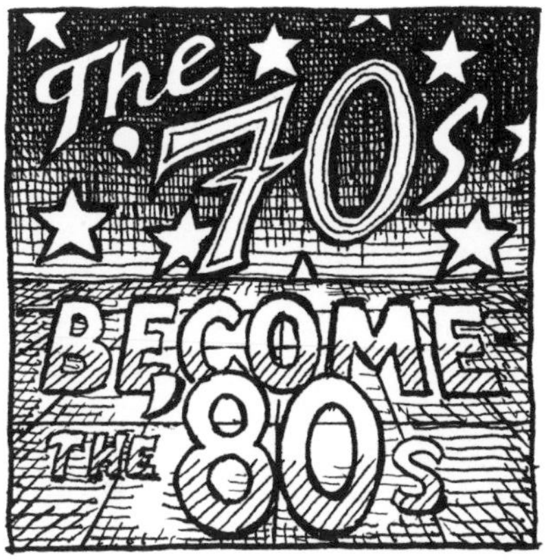
The '70s
Become
the '80s

Remember Frankie Knuckles, who grew up with Larry in the sixties?
Well, right after the Garage opened, a promoter from Chicago, who had just opened his own club, The Warehouse, went to New York to hire Levan...

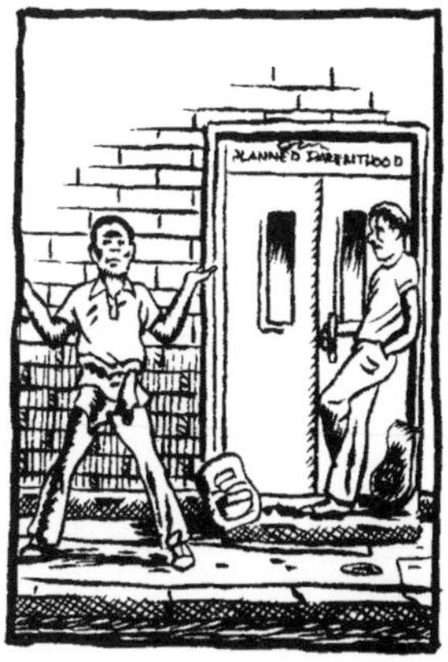

...only to discover that nothing in the world would make Larry leave his Paradise Garage, so it was Larry's buddy Frankie who left for Chicago.

The Warehouse

was phenomenally successful. Chicagoans had never seen a club like it, and to them Knuckles, with all the DJ's skills he'd learned in New York, was a magician, a wizard.

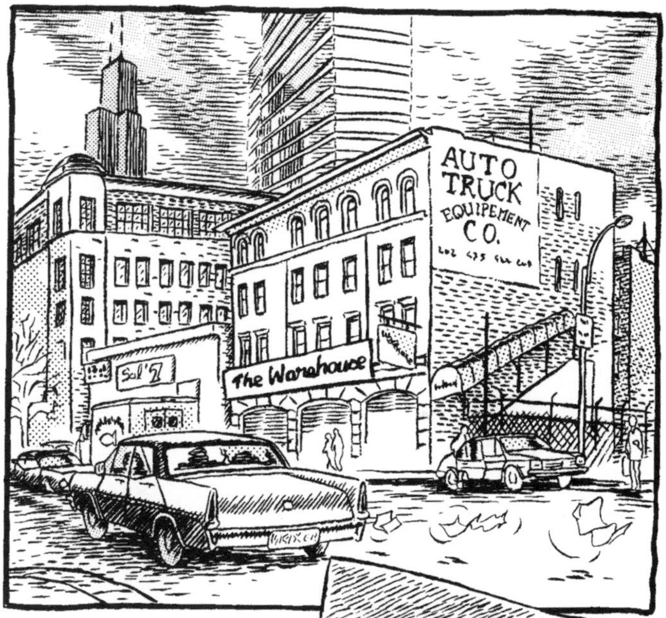
AUTO
TRUCK
EQUIPEMENT
CO.
The Warehouse

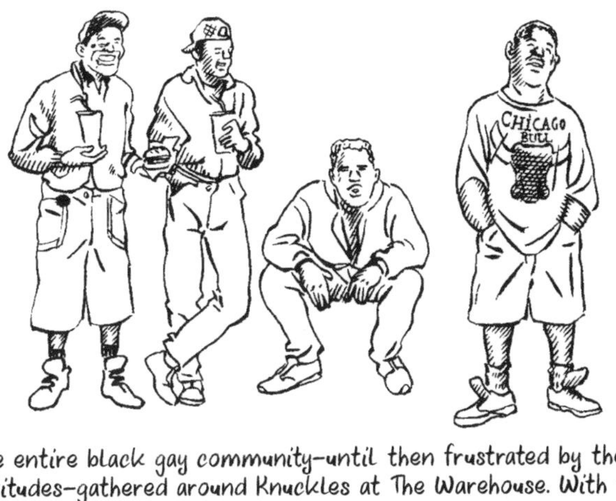
CHICAGO
BULL

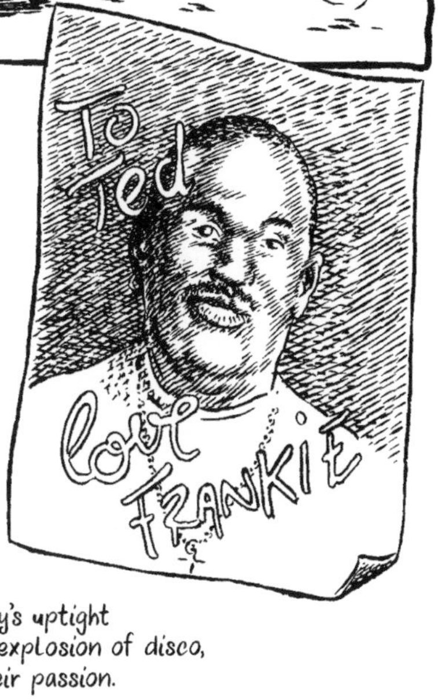
To Ted
love
FRANKIE

The entire black gay community—until then frustrated by the city's uptight attitudes—gathered around Knuckles at The Warehouse. With the explosion of disco, music lovers had at last found a place where they could live their passion.

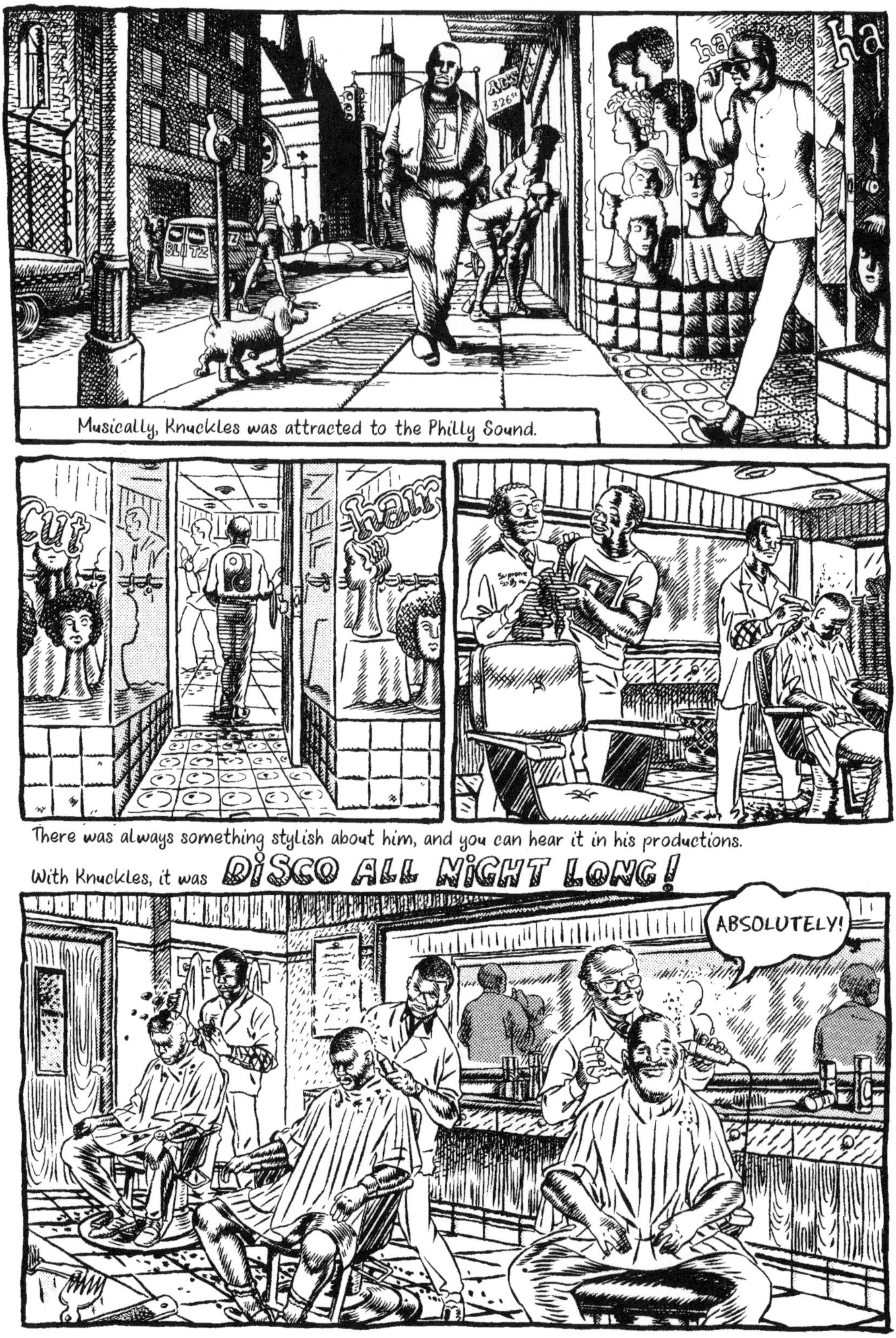
BLITZ
Musically, Knuckles was attracted to the Philly Sound.
cut
hair
There was always something stylish about him, and you can hear it in his productions.
With Knuckles, it was DISCO ALL NIGHT LONG!
ABSOLUTELY!

But when the Disco Sucks! campaign hit the U.S., production took a nosedive.

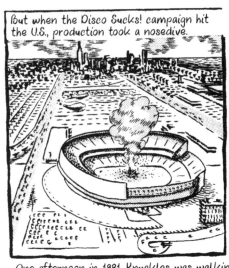

no problem: the tempo slowed and the sound mellowed into funk.

HOWEVER IN CHICAGO

kids didn't want music to be "cool." So Knuckles had to "cheat" by remixing the same numbers with longer breaks.

One afternoon in 1981, Knuckles was walking along a street in Chicago when he saw a sign outside a bar:

WHAT THE HELL IS HOUSE MUSIC?

BUT, FRANKIE, IT'S THE MUSIC YOU PLAY AT THE WAREHOUSE!

Here we play HOUSE MUSIC

Except that in 1981, Knuckles was still playing disco. House music didn't exist—yet it already had a name!

In record stores, disks were being stamped with a new label:

HOUSE
PEECH BOYS
DON'T MAKE ME WAIT

"House" was what kids called The Warehouse...

HEY! YOU COMIN' DOWN?

WHAT FOR?

C'MON, LET'S GO TO THE HOUSE!

And, of course, house was the music you played at home–in the house.

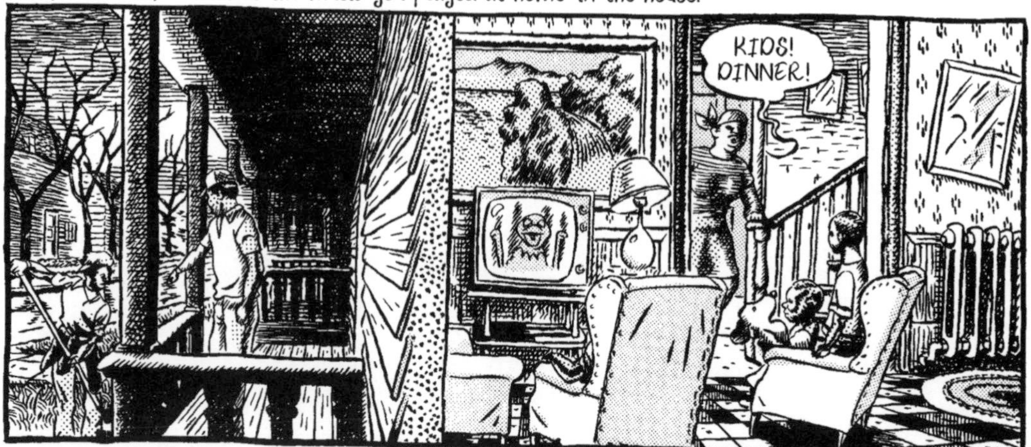
KIDS! DINNER!

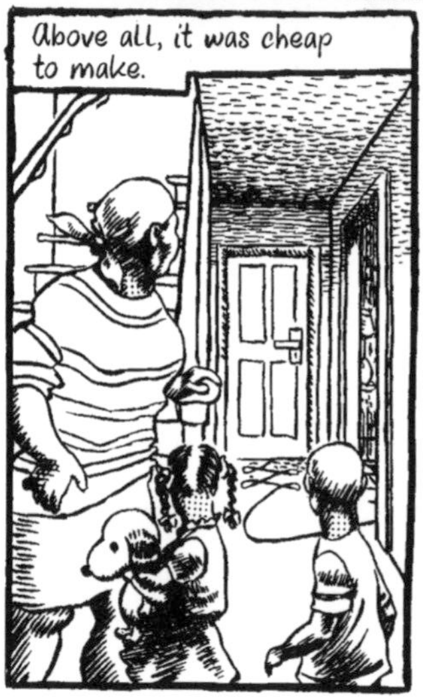
Above all, it was cheap to make.

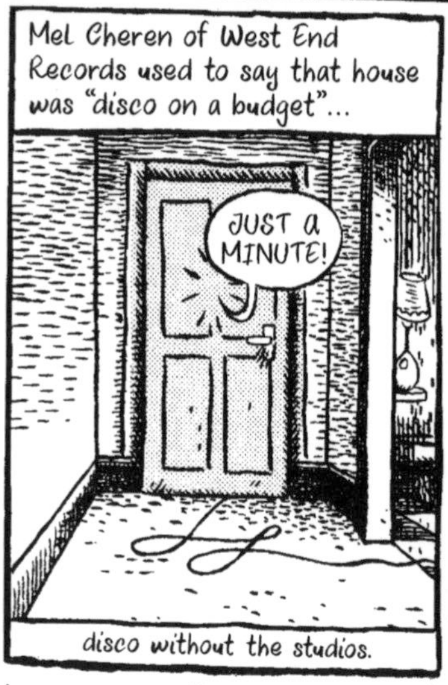
Mel Cheren of West End Records used to say that house was "disco on a budget"...
JUST A MINUTE!
disco without the studios.

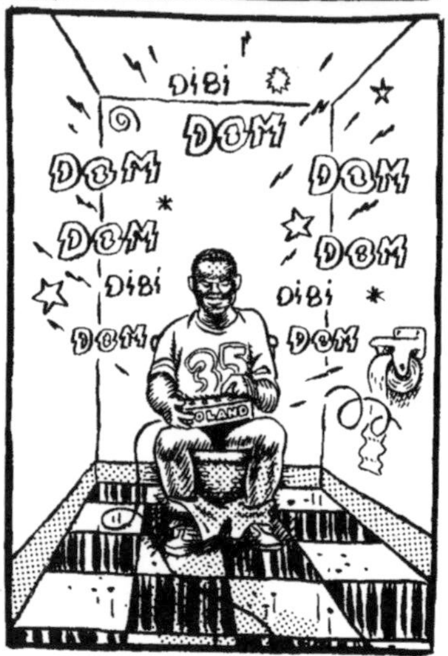
DIBI
DOM
DOM DOM
DOM DOM
DIBI DIBI
DOM DOM
35
ROLAND

You didn't have to have an orchestra anymore; all you needed was two machines:

a ROLAND 303 bass synthesizer...

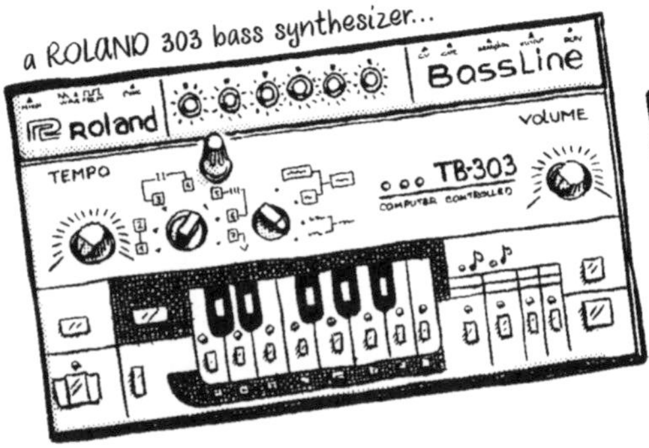
BassLine
Roland
VOLUME
TEMPO
TB-303
COMPUTER CONTROLLED

and a ROLAND 909 drum machine.

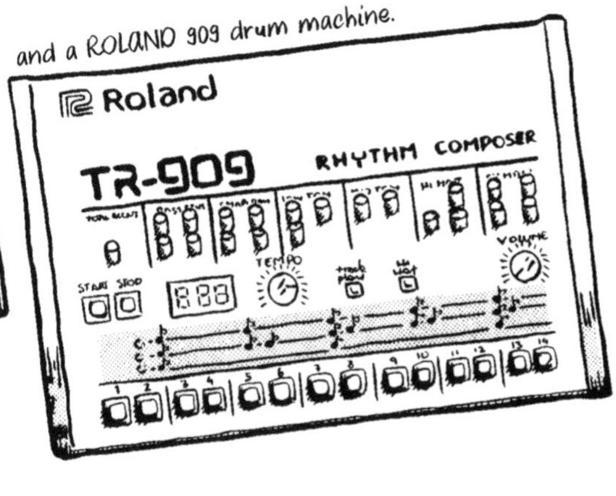
Roland
TR-909
RHYTHM COMPOSER
TEMPO
VOLUME
START STOP

That's how the tracks were made: music without the usual pop structure, but with a dominant rhythm, a groove–just like you could hear at The Warehouse.

In 1983, Knuckles fell out with The Warehouse—too many drugs for his liking. So he left to open his own club, the Power Plant.

Patrons of The Warehouse were distraught. They had to find another Frankie Knuckles! So they went to California and found a guy called Ron Hardy... and then they too opened a new club.

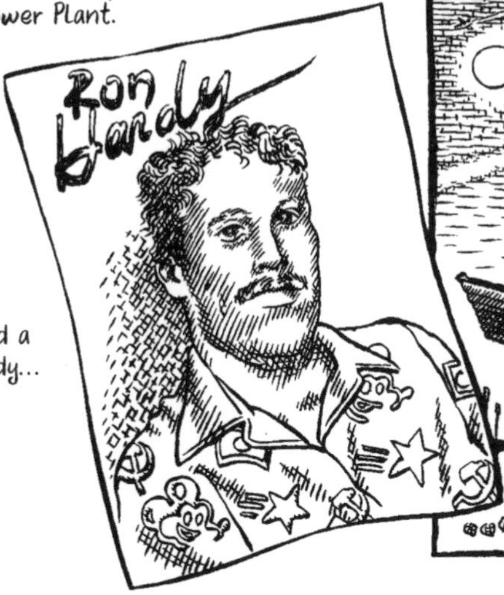

Ron Hardy

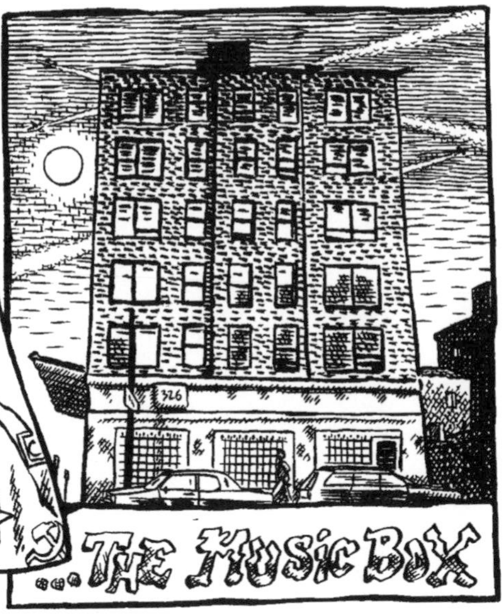

326
...THE MUSIC BOX

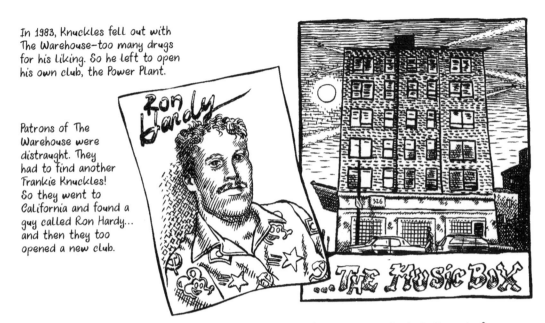

Ron Hardy is another mythical figure in the story of house music. He took the art of mixing even further than Larry Levan, making it more technical and taking bigger risks: such as playing the same track three or four times within an hour, or extending a single track so it lasted half an hour! It was a kind of communion with the public—who were permanently stoned!

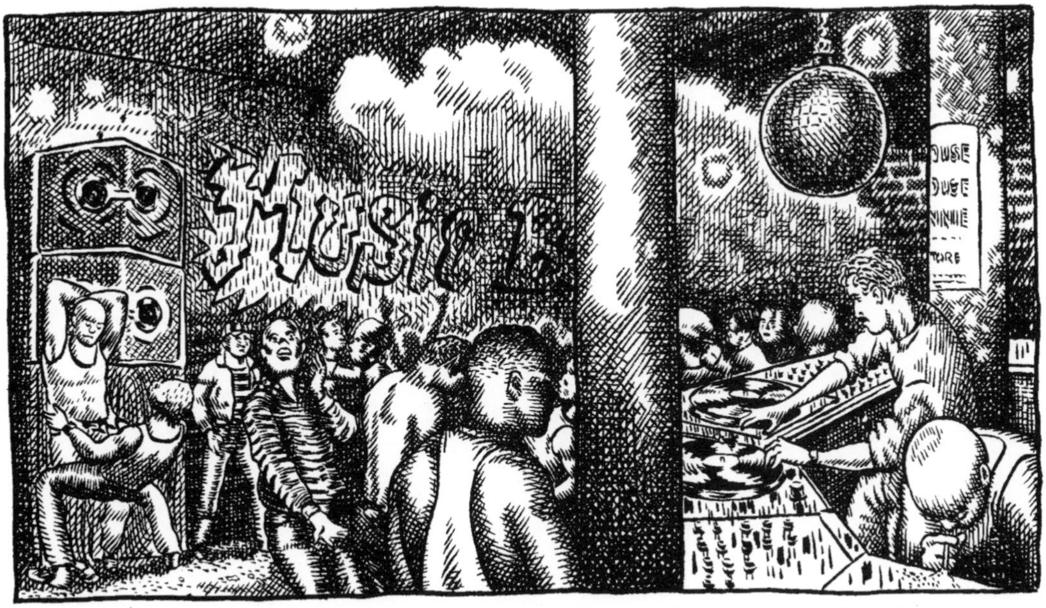

While Knuckles continued the Garage tradition at The Warehouse, Hardy's Music Box was much darker. The music was deafening, and the level of drug use similarly astronomical.

Both Frankie Knuckles and Ron Hardy attracted a swarm of followers, who would leave the club and go home to their Rolands to mix their own tracks, hoping nothing more... than that their DJs would play them.

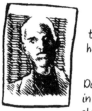

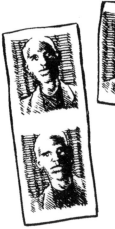

Jamie Principle was the first real producer of house music.

A fan of Depeche Mode, David Bowie, and Prince, in 1983 he wrote two house classics: "Your Love" and "Waiting on My Angel."

B — Your Love — J.M
60
A — WAITING ON MY ANGEL
SONY
MOVE YOUR BODY
A
M. JEFFERSON

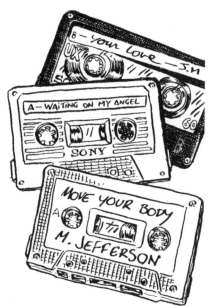

Frankie Knuckles often played them on cassette; the vinyls didn't appear until two or three years later.

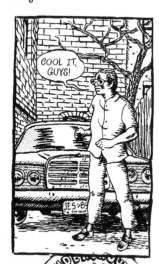

Another pioneer was Marshall Jefferson, who produced two tracks that Ron Hardy played—cementing the link between house music and the clubs.

Officially, the first house music recording to appear on vinyl, in 1984, was Jesse Saunders's "On and On." It was a minor hit, earning Saunders a pocketful of money, which he rapidly squandered on various extravagances. Saunders has often been accused of being more in love with women than he was with music, but then, who am I to say!

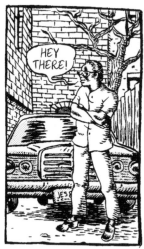

HEY THERE!
WHO ARE THEY TRYING TO IMPRESS?
COOL IT, GUYS!

It was to be the first of many Chicago house classics:

TRAX RECORDS
33RPM
PERSONAL
Jamie Principle
Side A
Epic
LiL LOUIS
STEREO
SIDE A
FRENCH KISS
STEVE SILK HURLEY
produced written by S.L.K
JACK YOUR BODY
this Side
1. Club your body
2. Dub your body
other Side

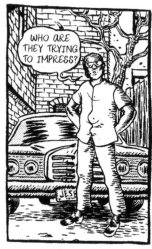

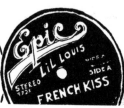

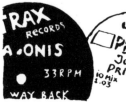

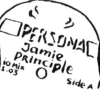

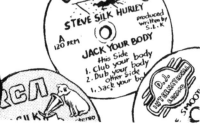

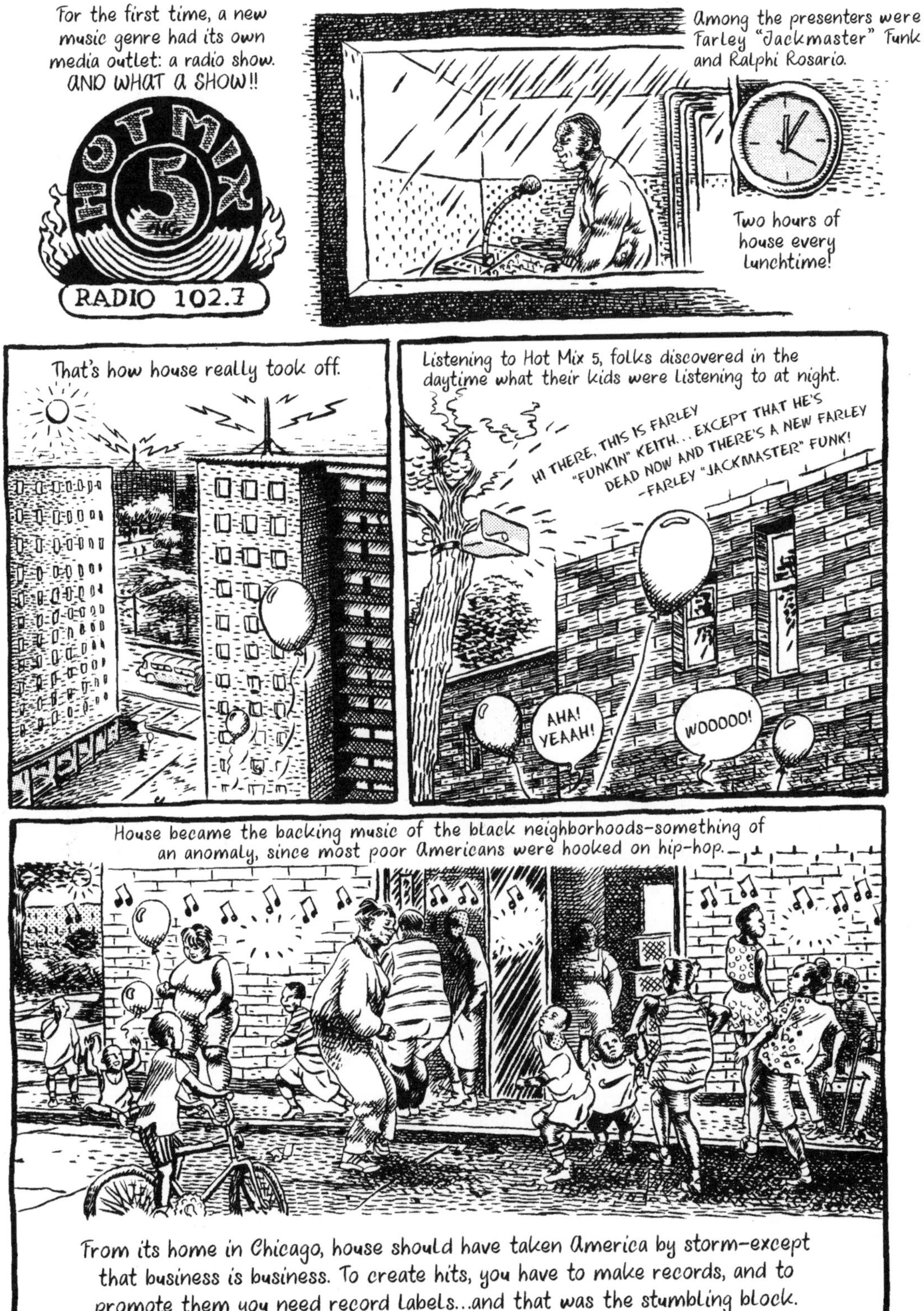

For the first time, a new music genre had its own media outlet: a radio show.
AND WHAT A SHOW!!
HOT MIX 5
RADIO 102.7
Among the presenters were Farley "Jackmaster" Funk and Ralphi Rosario.
Two hours of house every lunchtime!
That's how house really took off.
Listening to Hot Mix 5, folks discovered in the daytime what their kids were listening to at night.
HI THERE, THIS IS FARLEY "FUNKIN" KEITH... EXCEPT THAT HE'S DEAD NOW AND THERE'S A NEW FARLEY -FARLEY "JACKMASTER" FUNK!
AHA! YEAAH!
WOOOOO!
House became the backing music of the black neighborhoods-something of an anomaly, since most poor Americans were hooked on hip-hop.
From its home in Chicago, house should have taken America by storm-except that business is business. To create hits, you have to make records, and to promote them you need record labels...and that was the stumbling block.

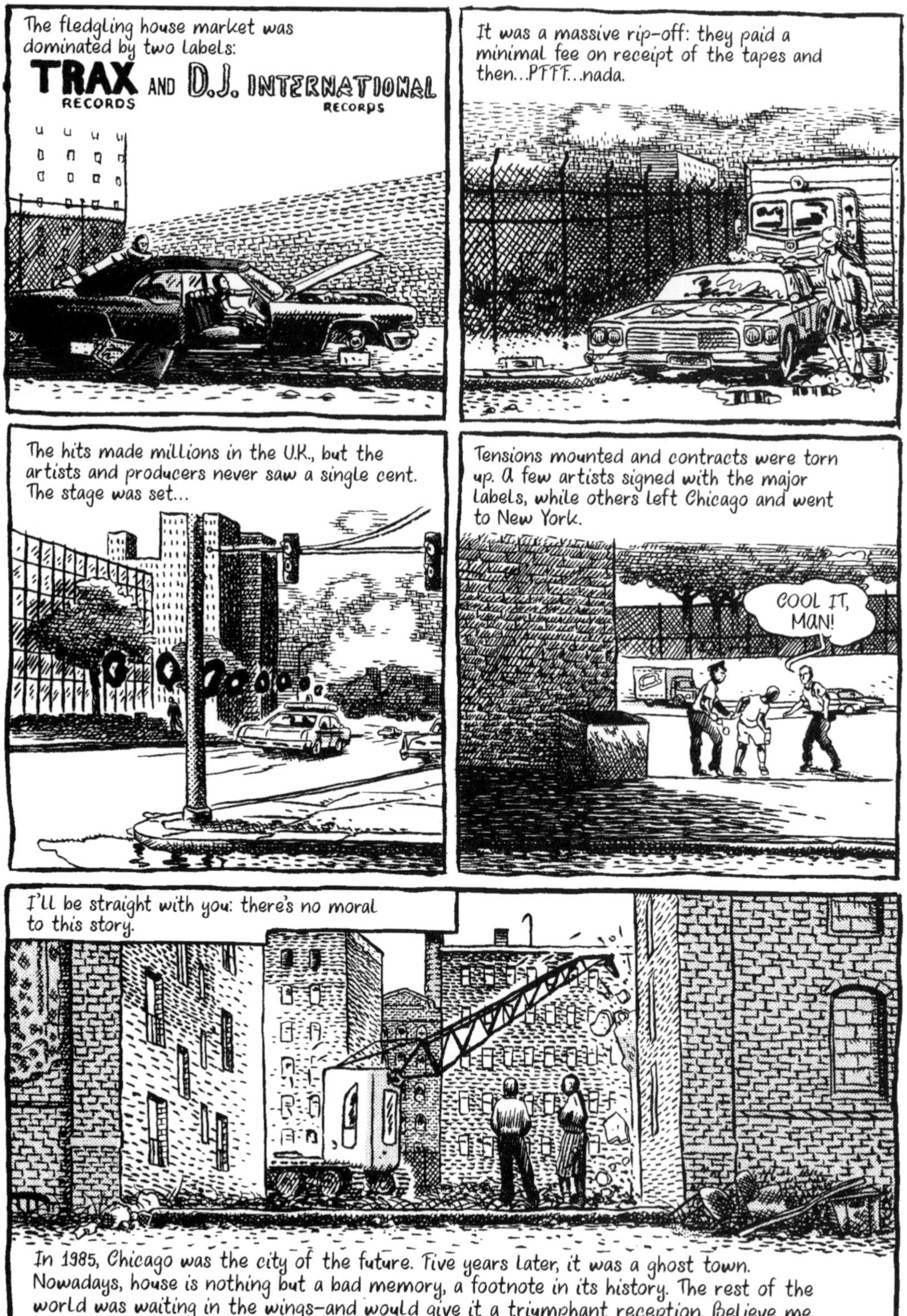
The fledgling house market was dominated by two labels:
TRAX RECORDS AND D.J. INTERNATIONAL RECORDS
It was a massive rip-off: they paid a minimal fee on receipt of the tapes and then...PFFF...nada.
The hits made millions in the U.K., but the artists and producers never saw a single cent. The stage was set...
Tensions mounted and contracts were torn up. A few artists signed with the major labels, while others left Chicago and went to New York.
COOL IT, MAN!
I'll be straight with you: there's no moral to this story.
In 1985, Chicago was the city of the future. Five years later, it was a ghost town. Nowadays, house is nothing but a bad memory, a footnote in its history. The rest of the world was waiting in the wings—and would give it a triumphant reception. Believe me, it really isn't worth being a pioneer.

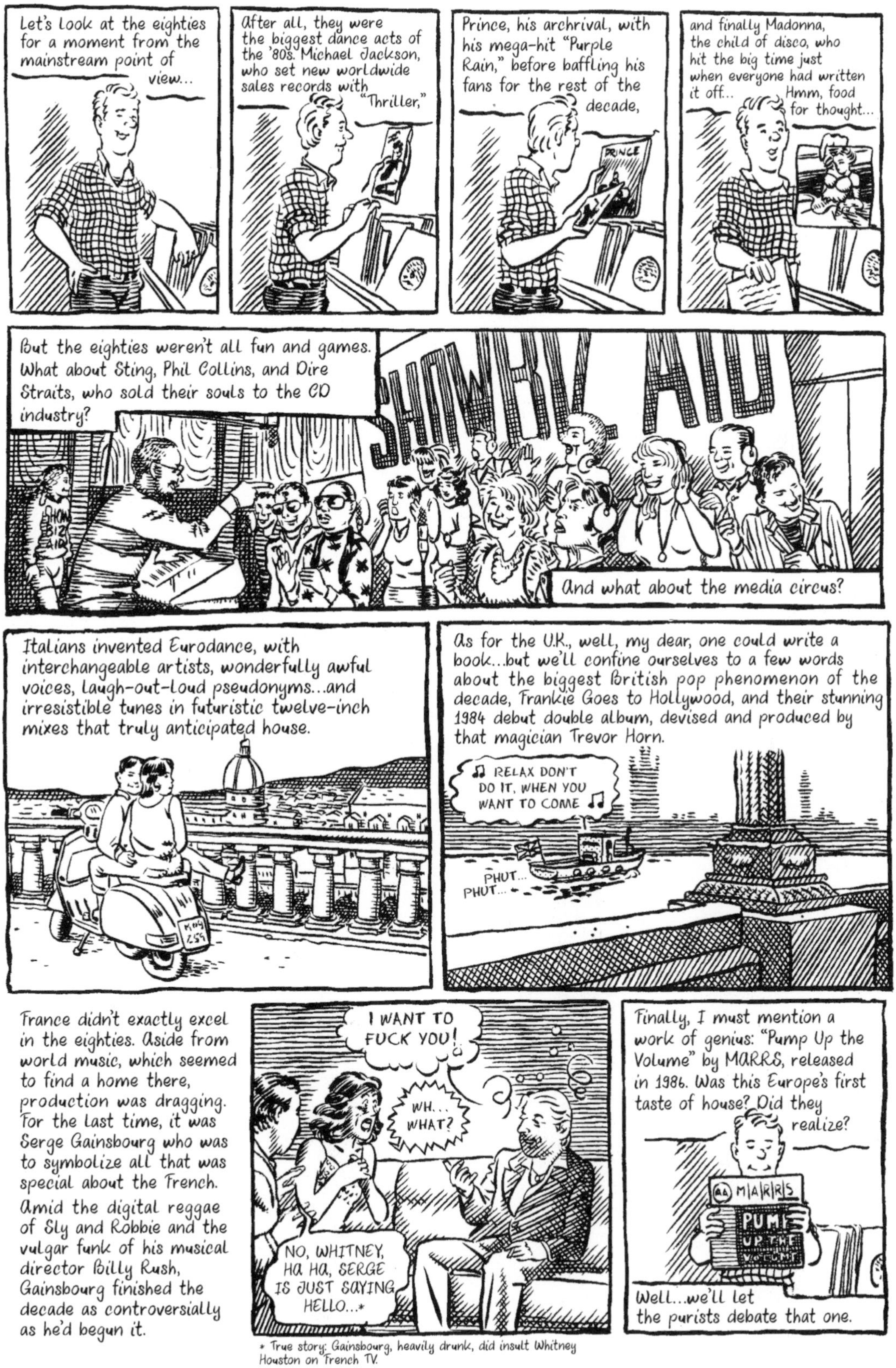

Let's look at the eighties for a moment from the mainstream point of view...
After all, they were the biggest dance acts of the '80s. Michael Jackson, who set new worldwide sales records with "Thriller,"
Prince, his archrival, with his mega-hit "Purple Rain," before baffling his fans for the rest of the decade,
PRINCE
and finally Madonna, the child of disco, who hit the big time just when everyone had written it off...
Hmm, food for thought...
But the eighties weren't all fun and games. What about Sting, Phil Collins, and Dire Straits, who sold their souls to the CD industry?
SHOWBIZ AID
And what about the media circus?
Italians invented Eurodance, with interchangeable artists, wonderfully awful voices, laugh-out-loud pseudonyms...and irresistible tunes in futuristic twelve-inch mixes that truly anticipated house.
As for the U.K., well, my dear, one could write a book...but we'll confine ourselves to a few words about the biggest British pop phenomenon of the decade, Frankie Goes to Hollywood, and their stunning 1984 debut double album, devised and produced by that magician Trevor Horn.
♫ RELAX DON'T DO IT, WHEN YOU WANT TO COME ♫
PHUT... PHUT...
France didn't exactly excel in the eighties. Aside from world music, which seemed to find a home there, production was dragging. For the last time, it was Serge Gainsbourg who was to symbolize all that was special about the French.
Amid the digital reggae of Sly and Robbie and the vulgar funk of his musical director Billy Rush, Gainsbourg finished the decade as controversially as he'd begun it.
I WANT TO FUCK YOU!
WH... WHAT?
NO, WHITNEY, HA HA, SERGE IS JUST SAYING HELLO...*
Finally, I must mention a work of genius: "Pump Up the Volume" by MARRS, released in 1986. Was this Europe's first taste of house? Did they realize?
M|A|R|R|S
PUMP UP THE VOLUME
Well...we'll let the purists debate that one.

* True story: Gainsbourg, heavily drunk, did insult Whitney Houston on French TV.

CHAPTER 5

DETROIT

TECHNO CITY

EXTERNAL INFLUENCES

Parliament
The Clones of Dr. Funkenstein (LP) — 1976

John Carpenter
Assault on Precinct 13 — 1976

Kraftwerk
Trans-Europe Express (LP) — 1977

Giorgio Moroder
Chase — 1978

Human League
Dare (LP) — 1981

Klein + mbo
Dirty Talk — 1982

Depeche Mode
The Sun & the Rainfall — 1982

New Order
Blue Monday — 1983

Divine and Bobby Orlando
Shoot Your Shot — 1983

Casco Presents BWH
Stop — 1983

Cybotron (Juan Atkins)
Clear — 1983

LOCAL HITS

Derrick May
Strings of Life — 1987

Inner City
Paradise (LP) — 1988

Galaxy 2 Galaxy
Hi-Tech Jazz — 1993

Paperclip People (Carl Craig)
Throw — 1994

Robert Hood
Nighttime World (LP) — 1995

Stacey Pullen and Chez Damier
Forever Monna — 1995

Model 500
I Wanna Be There (Juan Atkins Mix) — 1996

Moodymann
Dem Young Sconies — 1997

The Aztec Mystic (DJ Rolando)
Jaguar (Jeff Mills Mix) — 2000

Detroit Grand Pubahs
After School Special — 2001

Octave One
Blackwater (String Instrumental Mix) — 2002

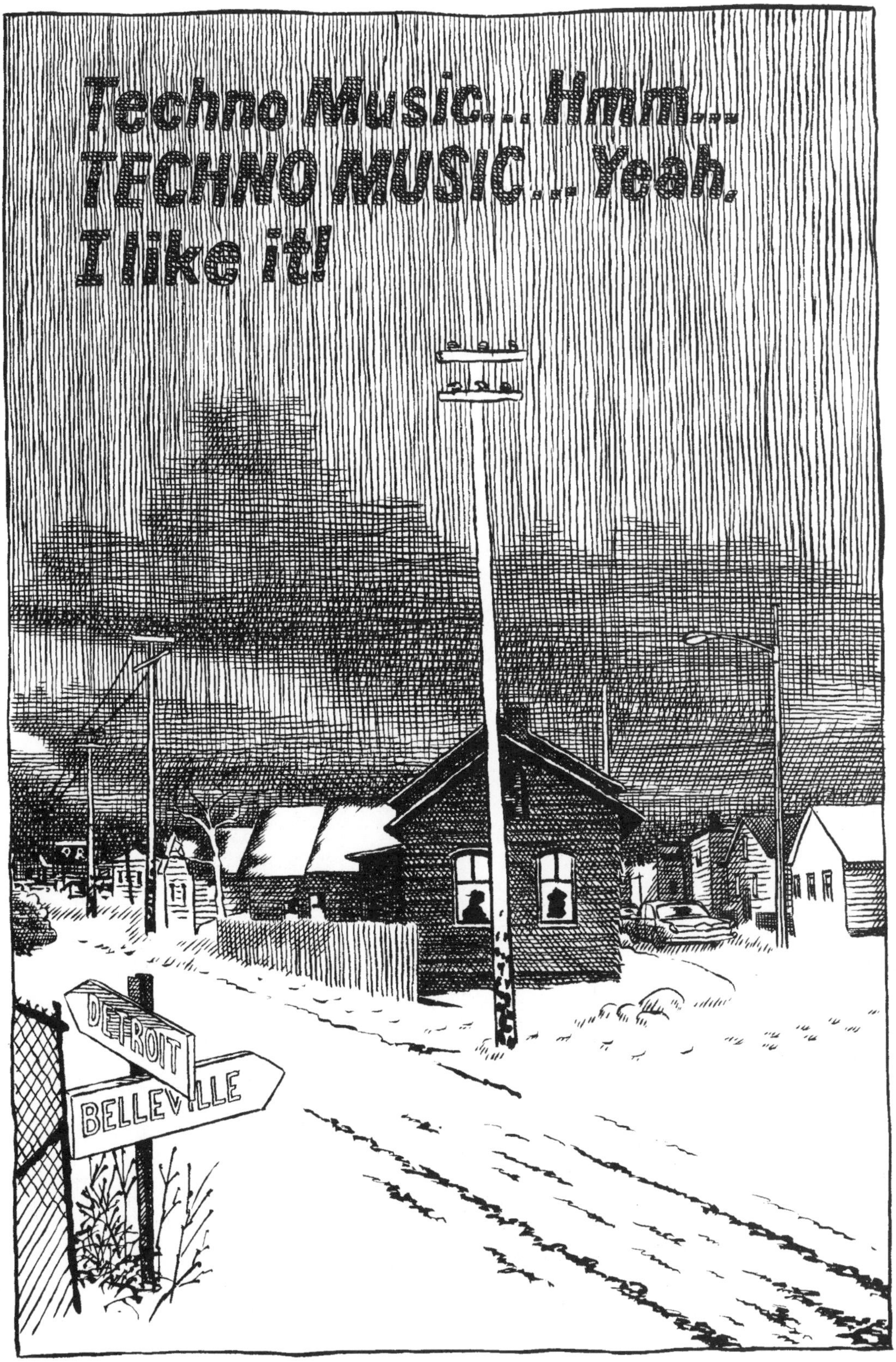
Techno Music... Hmm...
TECHNO MUSIC... Yeah.
I like it!
DETROIT
BELLEVILLE

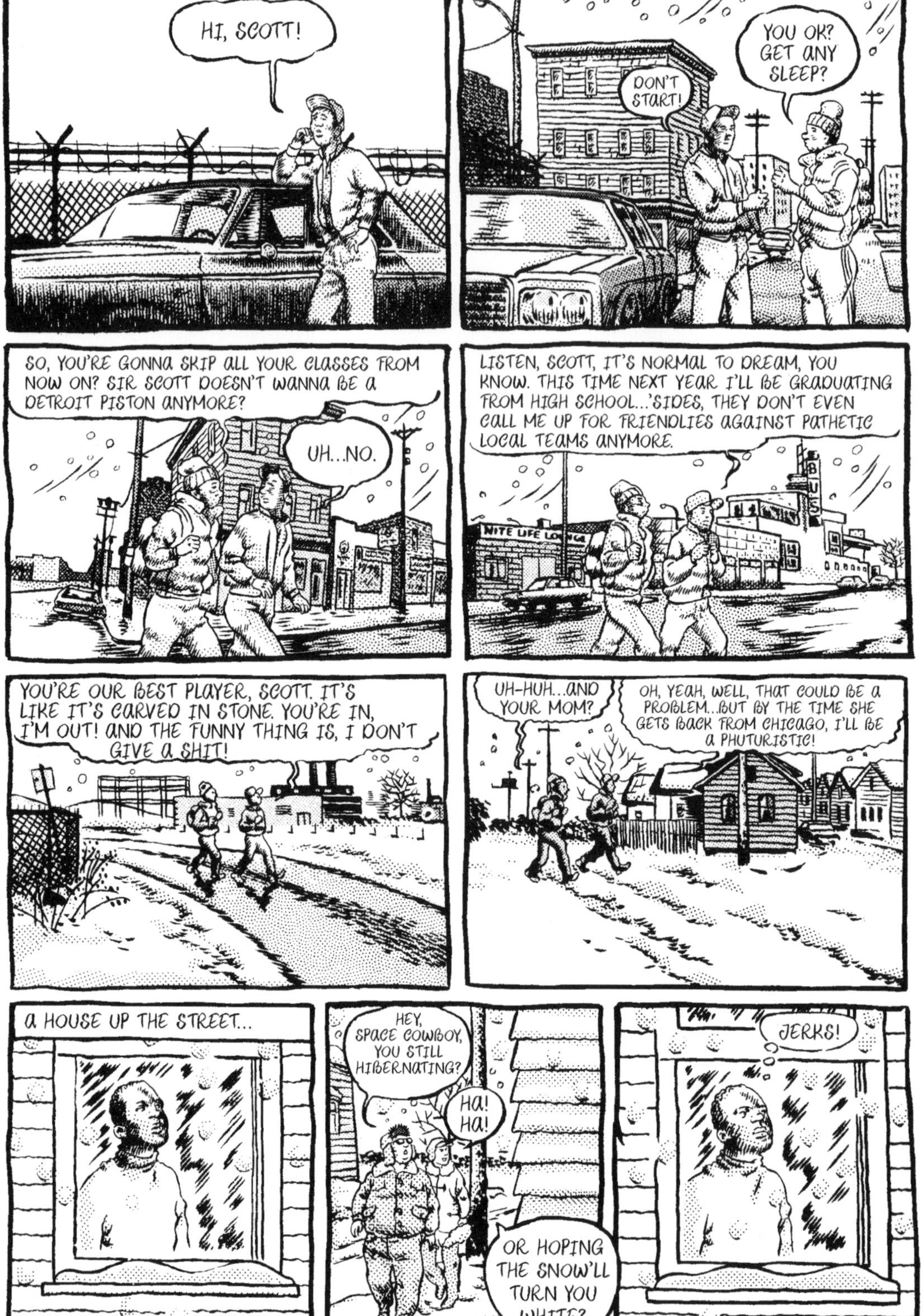
HI, SCOTT!
DON'T START!
YOU OK? GET ANY SLEEP?
SO, YOU'RE GONNA SKIP ALL YOUR CLASSES FROM NOW ON? SIR SCOTT DOESN'T WANNA BE A DETROIT PISTON ANYMORE?
UH...NO.
LISTEN, SCOTT, IT'S NORMAL TO DREAM, YOU KNOW. THIS TIME NEXT YEAR I'LL BE GRADUATING FROM HIGH SCHOOL...'SIDES, THEY DON'T EVEN CALL ME UP FOR FRIENDLIES AGAINST PATHETIC LOCAL TEAMS ANYMORE.
NITE LIFE LOUNGE
BUS
YOU'RE OUR BEST PLAYER, SCOTT. IT'S LIKE IT'S CARVED IN STONE. YOU'RE IN, I'M OUT! AND THE FUNNY THING IS, I DON'T GIVE A SHIT!
UH-HUH...AND YOUR MOM?
OH, YEAH, WELL, THAT COULD BE A PROBLEM...BUT BY THE TIME SHE GETS BACK FROM CHICAGO, I'LL BE A PHUTURISTIC!
A HOUSE UP THE STREET...
HEY, SPACE COWBOY, YOU STILL HIBERNATING?
HA! HA!
OR HOPING THE SNOW'LL TURN YOU WHITE?
JERKS!

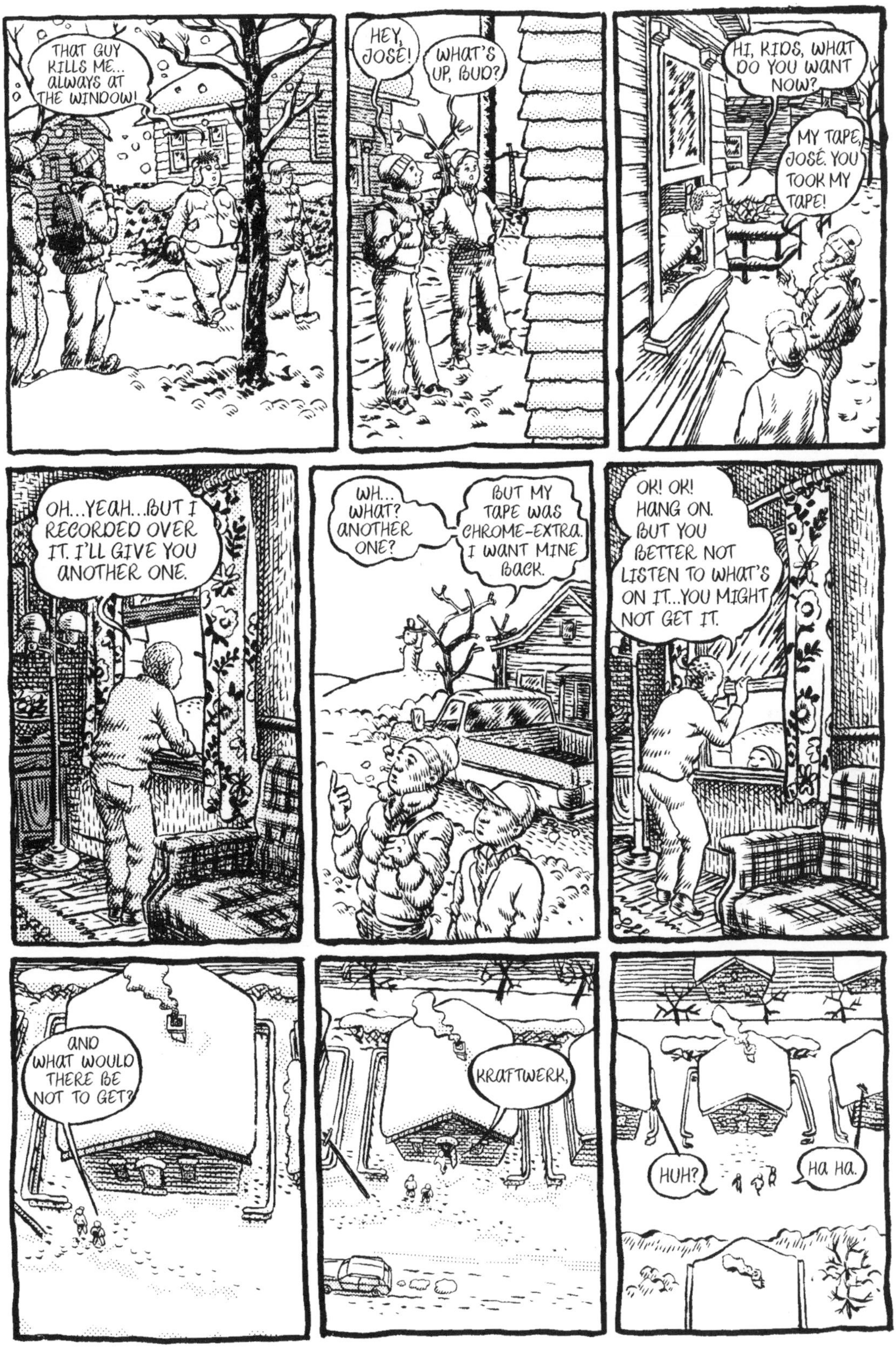

THAT GUY KILLS ME... ALWAYS AT THE WINDOW!
HEY, JOSÉ!
WHAT'S UP, BUD?
HI, KIDS, WHAT DO YOU WANT NOW?
MY TAPE, JOSÉ. YOU TOOK MY TAPE!
OH...YEAH...BUT I RECORDED OVER IT. I'LL GIVE YOU ANOTHER ONE.
WH... WHAT? ANOTHER ONE?
BUT MY TAPE WAS CHROME-EXTRA. I WANT MINE BACK.
OK! OK! HANG ON. BUT YOU BETTER NOT LISTEN TO WHAT'S ON IT...YOU MIGHT NOT GET IT.
AND WHAT WOULD THERE BE NOT TO GET?
KRAFTWERK,
HUH?
HA HA.

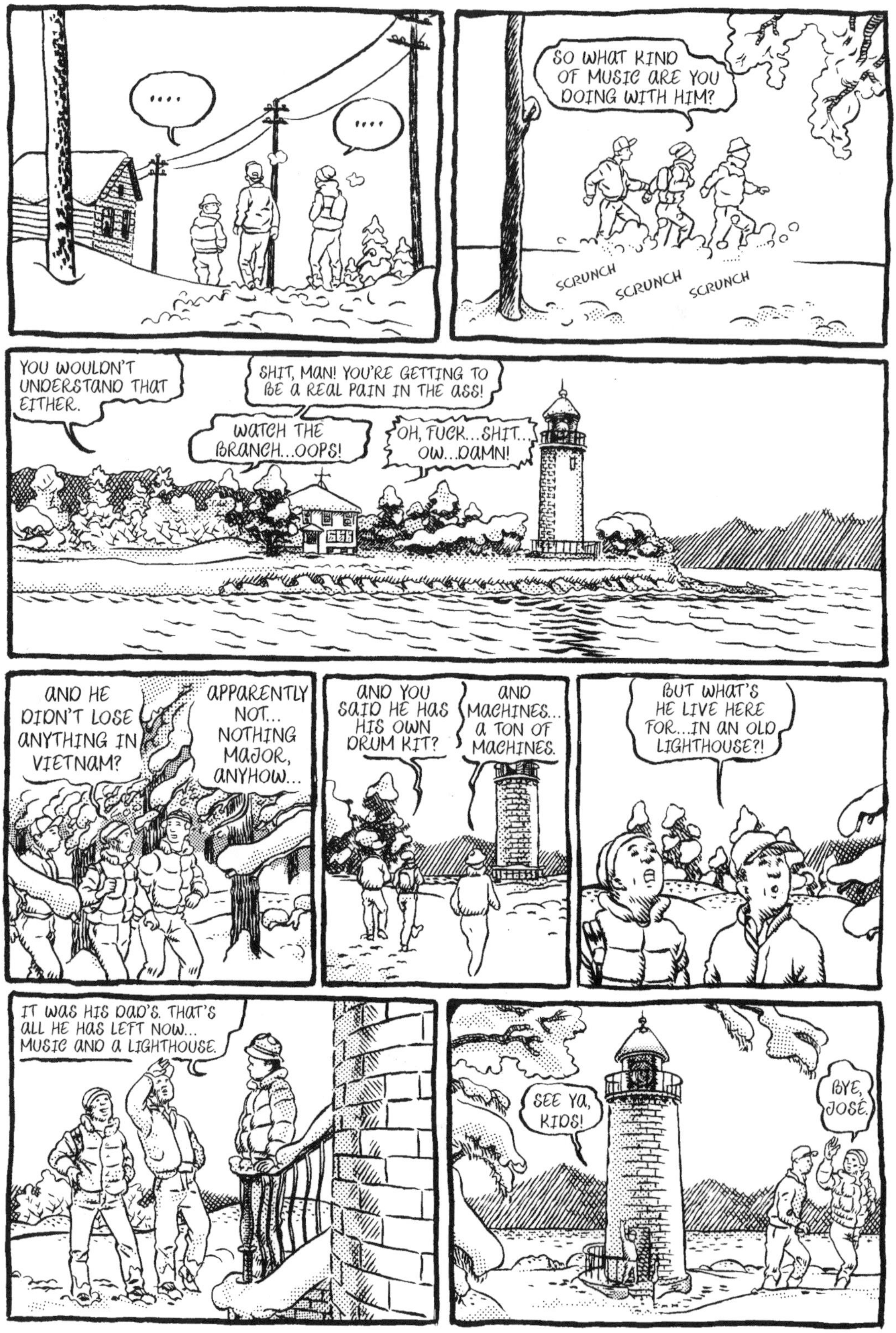
....
....
SO WHAT KIND OF MUSIC ARE YOU DOING WITH HIM?
SCRUNCH
SCRUNCH
SCRUNCH
YOU WOULDN'T UNDERSTAND THAT EITHER.
SHIT, MAN! YOU'RE GETTING TO BE A REAL PAIN IN THE ASS!
WATCH THE BRANCH...OOPS!
OH, FUCK...SHIT... OW...DAMN!
AND HE DIDN'T LOSE ANYTHING IN VIETNAM?
APPARENTLY NOT... NOTHING MAJOR, ANYHOW...
AND YOU SAID HE HAS HIS OWN DRUM KIT?
AND MACHINES... A TON OF MACHINES.
BUT WHAT'S HE LIVE HERE FOR...IN AN OLD LIGHTHOUSE?!
IT WAS HIS DAD'S. THAT'S ALL HE HAS LEFT NOW... MUSIC AND A LIGHTHOUSE.
SEE YA, KIDS!
BYE, JOSÉ.

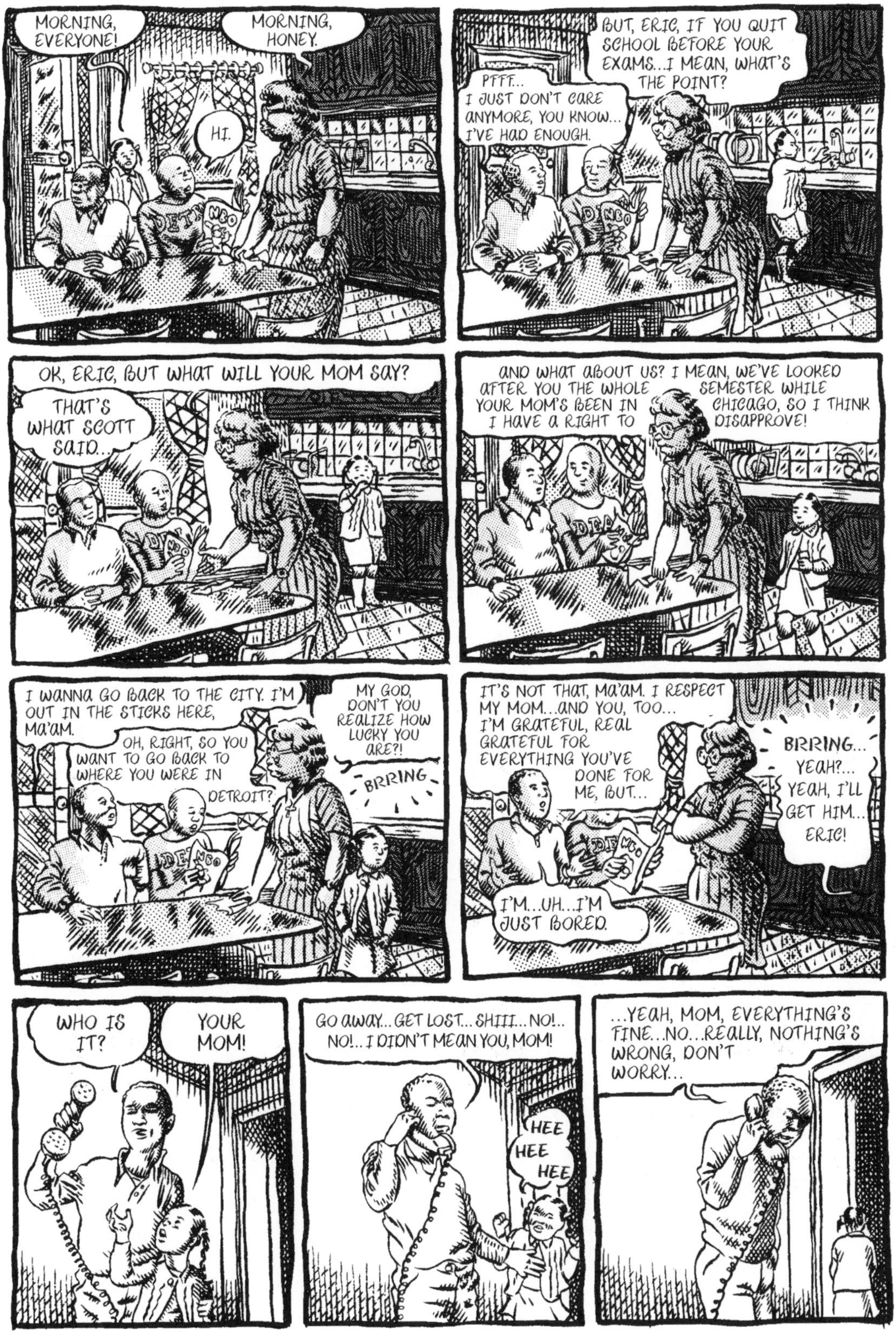
MORNING, EVERYONE!
MORNING, HONEY.
HI.
BUT, ERIC, IF YOU QUIT SCHOOL BEFORE YOUR EXAMS...I MEAN, WHAT'S THE POINT?
PFFF... I JUST DON'T CARE ANYMORE, YOU KNOW... I'VE HAD ENOUGH.
OK, ERIC, BUT WHAT WILL YOUR MOM SAY?
THAT'S WHAT SCOTT SAID...
AND WHAT ABOUT US? I MEAN, WE'VE LOOKED AFTER YOU THE WHOLE SEMESTER WHILE YOUR MOM'S BEEN IN CHICAGO, SO I THINK I HAVE A RIGHT TO DISAPPROVE!
I WANNA GO BACK TO THE CITY. I'M OUT IN THE STICKS HERE, MA'AM.
OH, RIGHT, SO YOU WANT TO GO BACK TO WHERE YOU WERE IN DETROIT?
MY GOD, DON'T YOU REALIZE HOW LUCKY YOU ARE?!
BRRING
IT'S NOT THAT, MA'AM. I RESPECT MY MOM...AND YOU, TOO... I'M GRATEFUL, REAL GRATEFUL FOR EVERYTHING YOU'VE DONE FOR ME, BUT...
I'M...UH...I'M JUST BORED.
BRRING...
YEAH?... YEAH, I'LL GET HIM... ERIC!
WHO IS IT?
YOUR MOM!
GO AWAY...GET LOST...SHIII...NO!.. NO!...I DIDN'T MEAN YOU, MOM!
HEE HEE HEE
...YEAH, MOM, EVERYTHING'S FINE...NO...REALLY, NOTHING'S WRONG, DON'T WORRY...

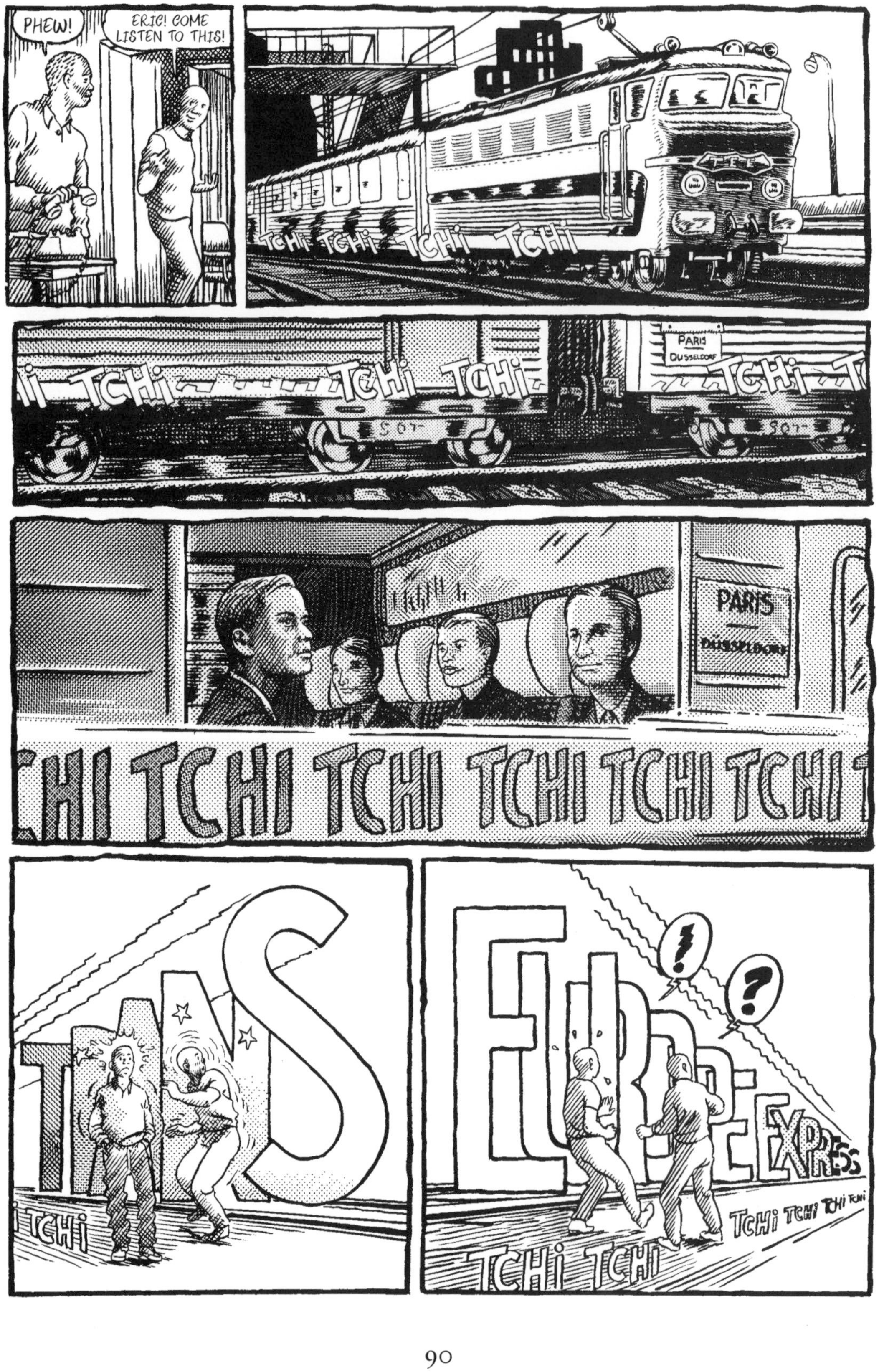
PHEW!
ERIC! COME LISTEN TO THIS!
TCHI TCHI TCHI TCHI
PARIS DUSSELDORF
TCHI TCHI TCHI TCHI
PARIS DÜSSELDORF
TCHI TCHI TCHI TCHI TCHI TCHI
TCHI
!
?
EXPRESS
TCHI TCHI TCHI TCHI
TCHI TCHI

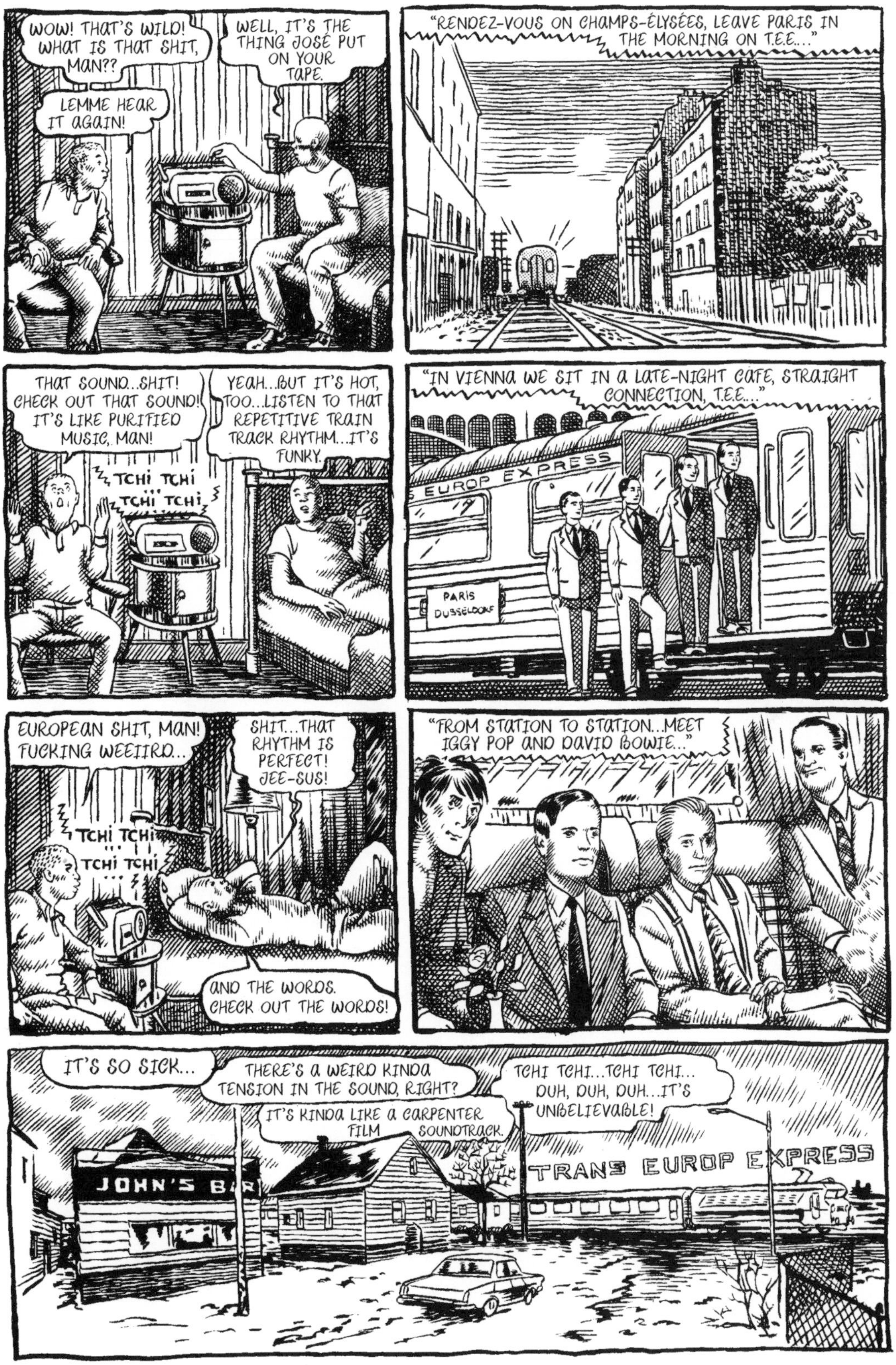
WOW! THAT'S WILD! WHAT IS THAT SHIT, MAN??
WELL, IT'S THE THING JOSÉ PUT ON YOUR TAPE.
LEMME HEAR IT AGAIN!
"RENDEZ-VOUS ON CHAMPS-ÉLYSÉES, LEAVE PARIS IN THE MORNING ON T.E.E..."
THAT SOUND...SHIT! CHECK OUT THAT SOUND! IT'S LIKE PURIFIED MUSIC, MAN!
YEAH...BUT IT'S HOT, TOO...LISTEN TO THAT REPETITIVE TRAIN TRACK RHYTHM...IT'S FUNKY.
TCHI TCHI ... TCHI TCHI
"IN VIENNA WE SIT IN A LATE-NIGHT CAFE, STRAIGHT CONNECTION, T.E.E..."
EUROP EXPRESS
PARIS DUSSELDORF
EUROPEAN SHIT, MAN! FUCKING WEEIIRD...
SHIT...THAT RHYTHM IS PERFECT! JEE-SUS!
TCHI TCHI ... TCHI TCHI ...
AND THE WORDS. CHECK OUT THE WORDS!
"FROM STATION TO STATION...MEET IGGY POP AND DAVID BOWIE..."
IT'S SO SICK...
THERE'S A WEIRD KINDA TENSION IN THE SOUND, RIGHT?
IT'S KINDA LIKE A CARPENTER FILM SOUNDTRACK.
TCHI TCHI...TCHI TCHI... DUH, DUH, DUH...IT'S UNBELIEVABLE!
JOHN'S BAR
TRANS EUROP EXPRESS

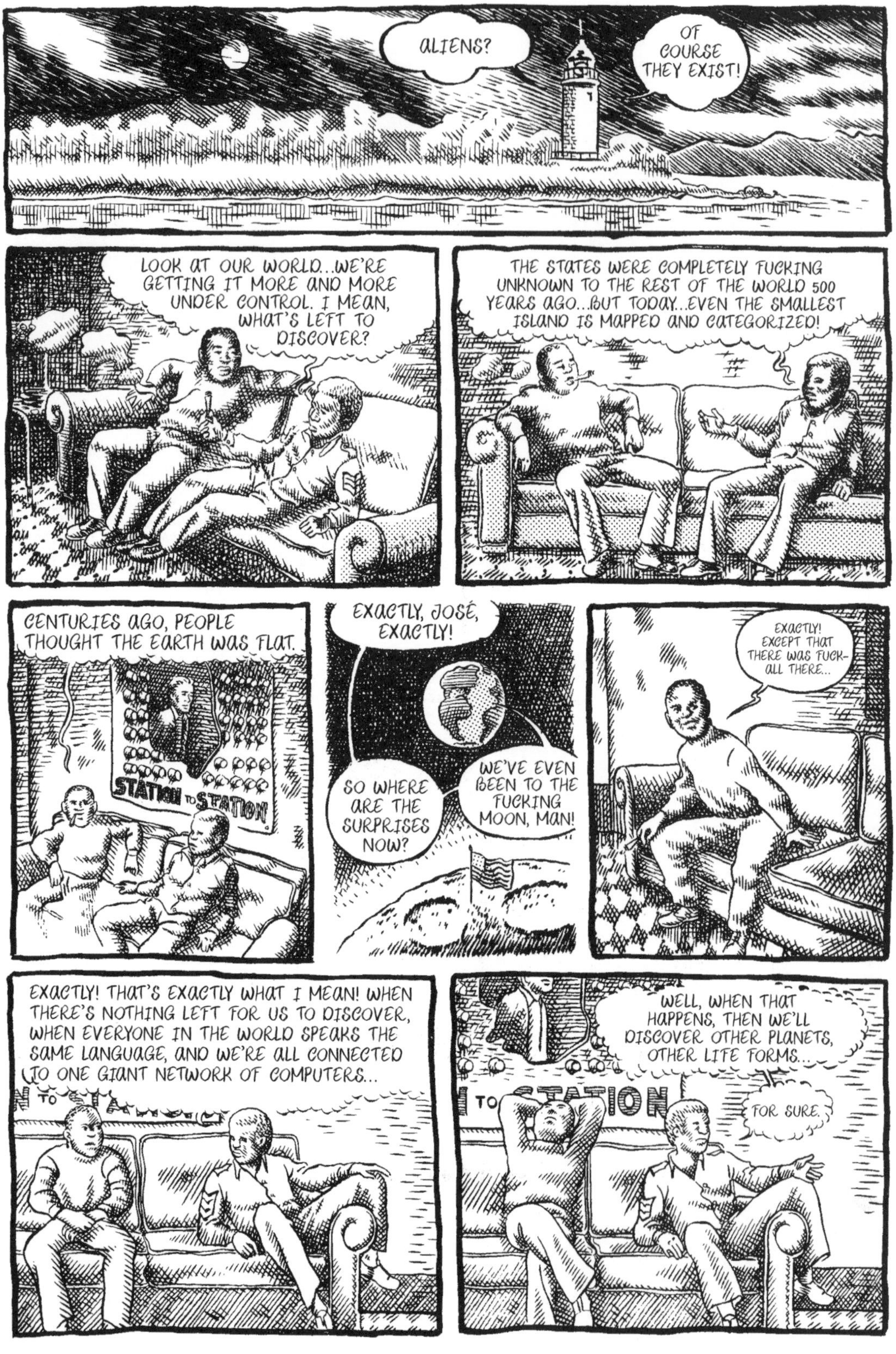
ALIENS?
OF COURSE THEY EXIST!
LOOK AT OUR WORLD...WE'RE GETTING IT MORE AND MORE UNDER CONTROL. I MEAN, WHAT'S LEFT TO DISCOVER?
THE STATES WERE COMPLETELY FUCKING UNKNOWN TO THE REST OF THE WORLD 500 YEARS AGO...BUT TODAY...EVEN THE SMALLEST ISLAND IS MAPPED AND CATEGORIZED!
CENTURIES AGO, PEOPLE THOUGHT THE EARTH WAS FLAT.
STATION TO STATION
EXACTLY, JOSÉ, EXACTLY!
SO WHERE ARE THE SURPRISES NOW?
WE'VE EVEN BEEN TO THE FUCKING MOON, MAN!
EXACTLY! EXCEPT THAT THERE WAS FUCK-ALL THERE...
EXACTLY! THAT'S EXACTLY WHAT I MEAN! WHEN THERE'S NOTHING LEFT FOR US TO DISCOVER, WHEN EVERYONE IN THE WORLD SPEAKS THE SAME LANGUAGE, AND WE'RE ALL CONNECTED TO ONE GIANT NETWORK OF COMPUTERS...
WELL, WHEN THAT HAPPENS, THEN WE'LL DISCOVER OTHER PLANETS, OTHER LIFE FORMS...
FOR SURE.

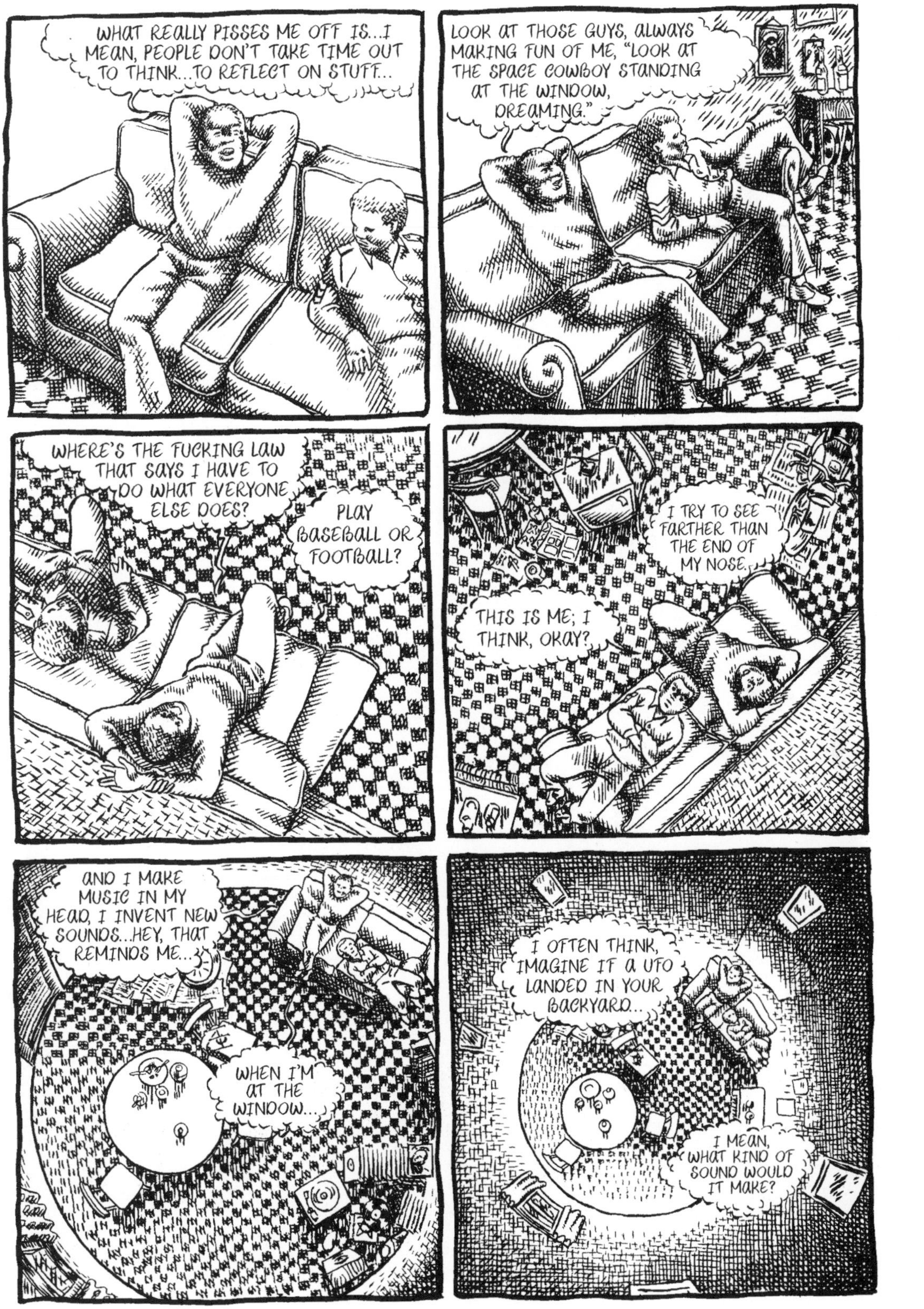
WHAT REALLY PISSES ME OFF IS...I MEAN, PEOPLE DON'T TAKE TIME OUT TO THINK...TO REFLECT ON STUFF...
LOOK AT THOSE GUYS, ALWAYS MAKING FUN OF ME, "LOOK AT THE SPACE COWBOY STANDING AT THE WINDOW, DREAMING."
WHERE'S THE FUCKING LAW THAT SAYS I HAVE TO DO WHAT EVERYONE ELSE DOES?
PLAY BASEBALL OR FOOTBALL?
I TRY TO SEE FARTHER THAN THE END OF MY NOSE.
THIS IS ME; I THINK, OKAY?
AND I MAKE MUSIC IN MY HEAD, I INVENT NEW SOUNDS...HEY, THAT REMINDS ME...
WHEN I'M AT THE WINDOW...
I OFTEN THINK, IMAGINE IF A UFO LANDED IN YOUR BACKYARD...
I MEAN, WHAT KIND OF SOUND WOULD IT MAKE?

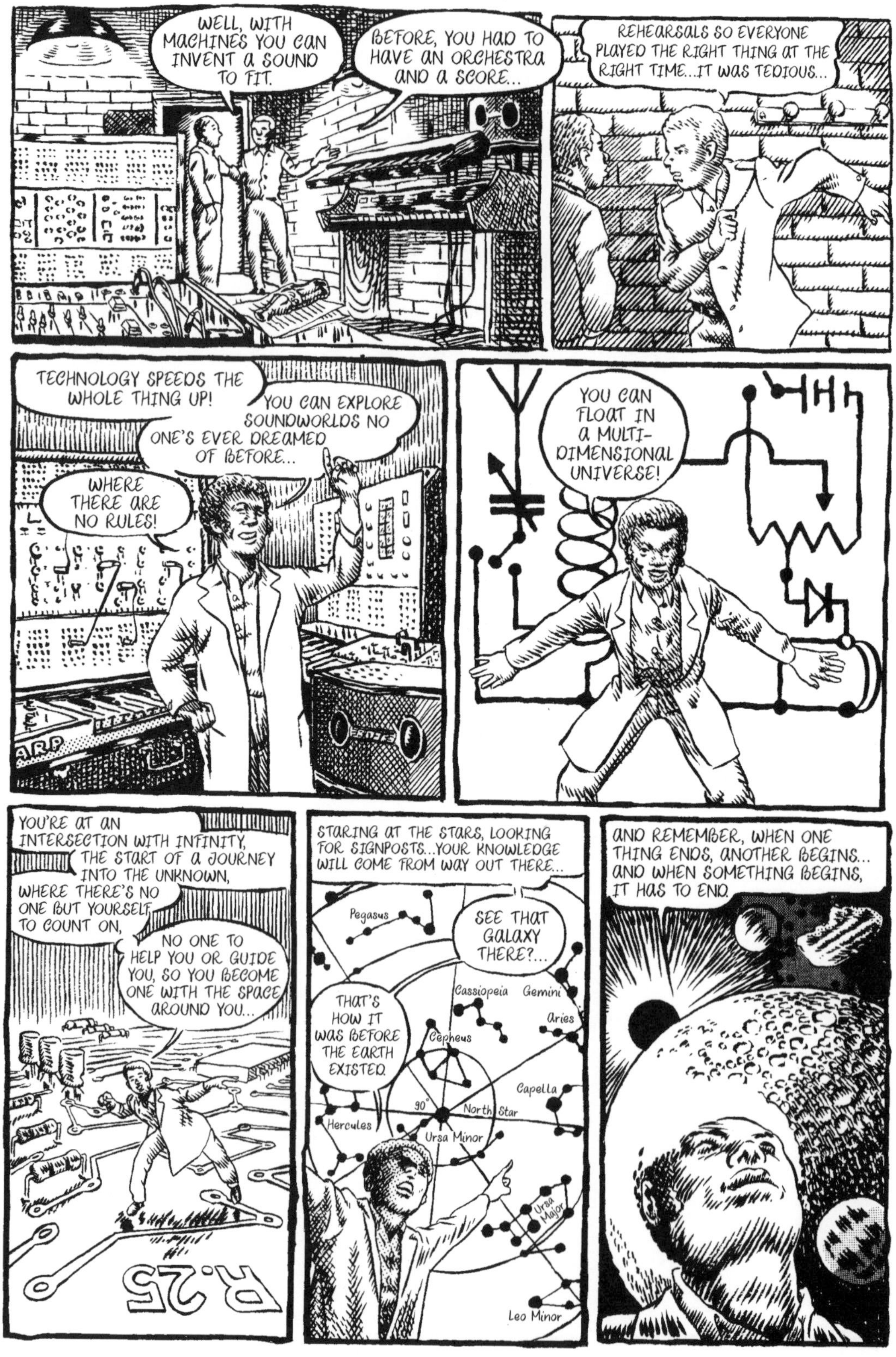
WELL, WITH MACHINES YOU CAN INVENT A SOUND TO FIT.
BEFORE, YOU HAD TO HAVE AN ORCHESTRA AND A SCORE...
REHEARSALS SO EVERYONE PLAYED THE RIGHT THING AT THE RIGHT TIME...IT WAS TEDIOUS...
TECHNOLOGY SPEEDS THE WHOLE THING UP!
YOU CAN EXPLORE SOUNDWORLDS NO ONE'S EVER DREAMED OF BEFORE...
WHERE THERE ARE NO RULES!
ARP
YOU CAN FLOAT IN A MULTI-DIMENSIONAL UNIVERSE!
YOU'RE AT AN INTERSECTION WITH INFINITY,
THE START OF A JOURNEY INTO THE UNKNOWN,
WHERE THERE'S NO ONE BUT YOURSELF TO COUNT ON,
NO ONE TO HELP YOU OR GUIDE YOU, SO YOU BECOME ONE WITH THE SPACE AROUND YOU...
R.25
STARING AT THE STARS, LOOKING FOR SIGNPOSTS...YOUR KNOWLEDGE WILL COME FROM WAY OUT THERE...
SEE THAT GALAXY THERE?...
THAT'S HOW IT WAS BEFORE THE EARTH EXISTED.
Pegasus
Cassiopeia
Gemini
Aries
Cepheus
Capella
90°
North Star
Hercules
Ursa Minor
Ursa Major
Leo Minor
AND REMEMBER, WHEN ONE THING ENDS, ANOTHER BEGINS... AND WHEN SOMETHING BEGINS, IT HAS TO END.

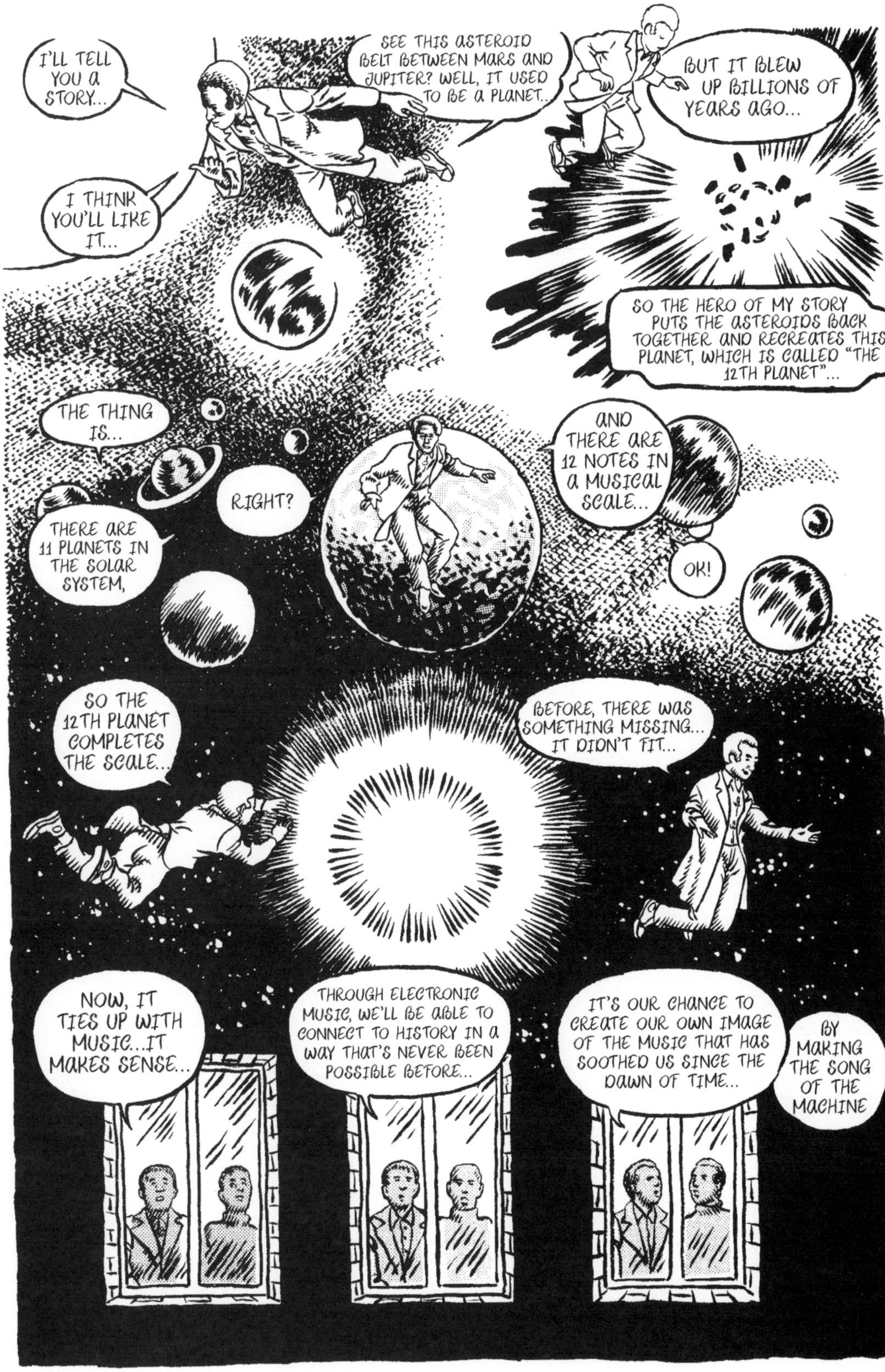
I'LL TELL YOU A STORY...
I THINK YOU'LL LIKE IT...
SEE THIS ASTEROID BELT BETWEEN MARS AND JUPITER? WELL, IT USED TO BE A PLANET...
BUT IT BLEW UP BILLIONS OF YEARS AGO...
SO THE HERO OF MY STORY PUTS THE ASTEROIDS BACK TOGETHER AND RECREATES THIS PLANET, WHICH IS CALLED "THE 12TH PLANET"...
THE THING IS...
THERE ARE 11 PLANETS IN THE SOLAR SYSTEM,
RIGHT?
AND THERE ARE 12 NOTES IN A MUSICAL SCALE...
OK!
SO THE 12TH PLANET COMPLETES THE SCALE...
BEFORE, THERE WAS SOMETHING MISSING... IT DIDN'T FIT...
NOW, IT TIES UP WITH MUSIC...IT MAKES SENSE...
THROUGH ELECTRONIC MUSIC, WE'LL BE ABLE TO CONNECT TO HISTORY IN A WAY THAT'S NEVER BEEN POSSIBLE BEFORE...
IT'S OUR CHANCE TO CREATE OUR OWN IMAGE OF THE MUSIC THAT HAS SOOTHED US SINCE THE DAWN OF TIME...
BY MAKING THE SONG OF THE MACHINE

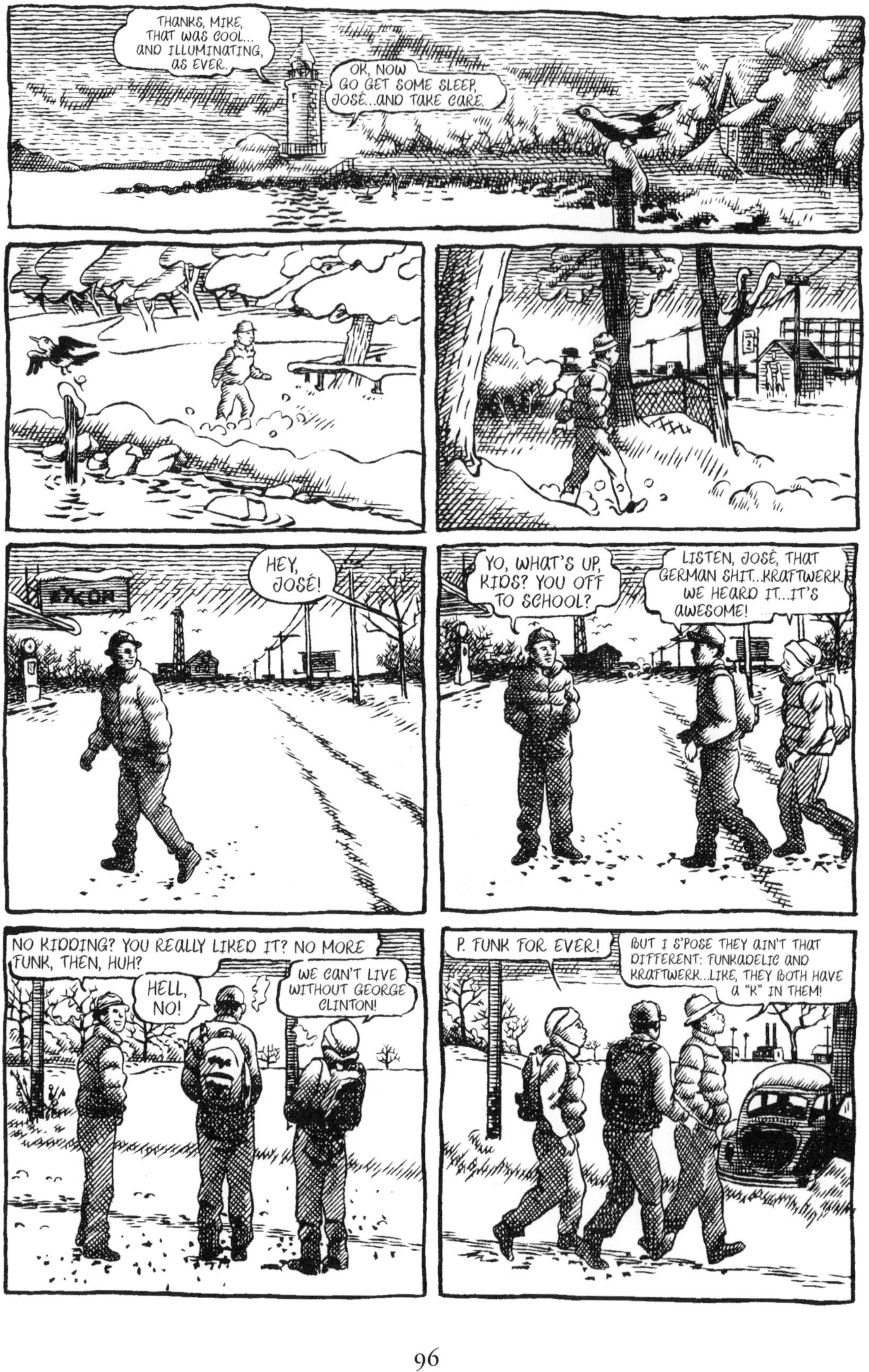
THANKS, MIKE, THAT WAS COOL... AND ILLUMINATING, AS EVER.
OK, NOW GO GET SOME SLEEP, JOSÉ...AND TAKE CARE.
HEY, JOSÉ!
YO, WHAT'S UP, KIDS? YOU OFF TO SCHOOL?
LISTEN, JOSÉ, THAT GERMAN SHIT...KRAFTWERK. WE HEARD IT...IT'S AWESOME!
NO KIDDING? YOU REALLY LIKED IT? NO MORE FUNK, THEN, HUH?
HELL, NO!
WE CAN'T LIVE WITHOUT GEORGE CLINTON!
P. FUNK FOR EVER!
BUT I S'POSE THEY AIN'T THAT DIFFERENT: FUNKADELIC AND KRAFTWERK...LIKE, THEY BOTH HAVE A "K" IN THEM!

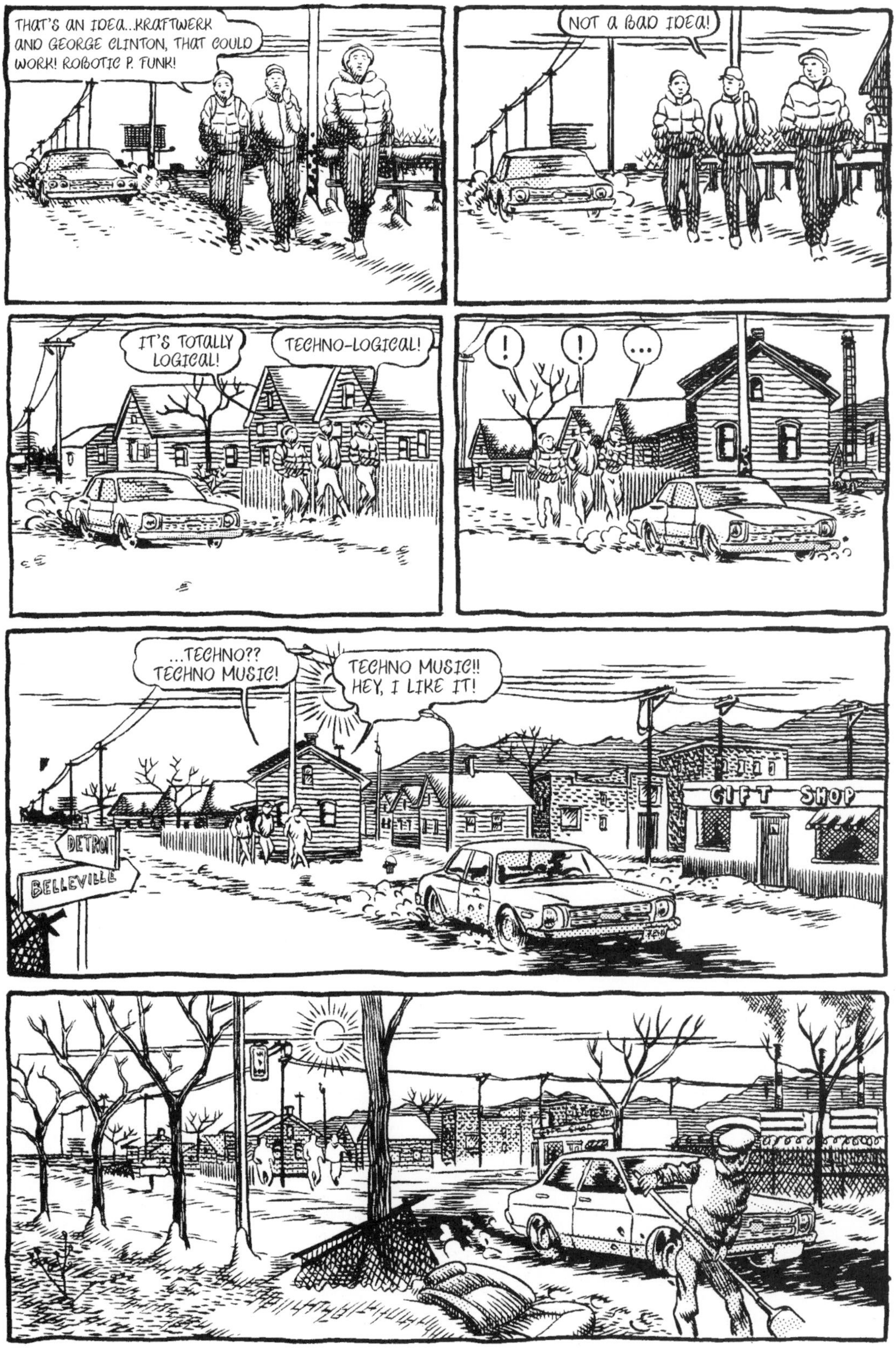
THAT'S AN IDEA...KRAFTWERK AND GEORGE CLINTON, THAT COULD WORK! ROBOTIC P. FUNK!
NOT A BAD IDEA!
IT'S TOTALLY LOGICAL!
TECHNO-LOGICAL!
!
!
...
...TECHNO?? TECHNO MUSIC!
TECHNO MUSIC!! HEY, I LIKE IT!
DETROIT
BELLEVILLE
GIFT SHOP

CHAPTER 6

MANCHESTER

SO MUCH TO ANSWER FOR

NEW ORDER CLUB CLASSICS

New Order
Everything's Gone Green—1981

New Order
Temptation—1982

52nd Street
Cool As Ice
(Bernard Sumner Production)—1983

New Order
Confusion (Arthur Baker Dub)—1983

New Order
Thieves Like Us—1984

New Order
Bizarre Love Triangle
(Shep Pettibone Mix)—1986

New Order
Fine Time (Steve Silk Hurley Mix)—1988

New Order
Mr. Disco—1989

New Order
Round and Round
(Kevin Saunderson Detroit Mix)—1989

Technotronic
Rockin' over the Beat
(Bernard Sumner Mix)—1990

Electronic
(Bernard Sumner and Johnny Marr)
Getting Away with It—1990

MANCHESTER

Herman's Hermits
No Milk Today—1966

Throbbing Gristle
United—1977

Buzzcocks
Sixteen Again—1978

A Certain Ratio
Shack Up—1979

The Durutti Column
Sketch for Summer—1979

Dislocation Dance
Show Me (12" Dennis Bovell Mix)—1983

The Smiths
This Charming Man—1983

The Fall
Mr. Pharmacist—1986

The Railway Children
Brighter—1987

Happy Mondays
Kuff Dam—1987

The Stone Roses
Fools Gold—1990

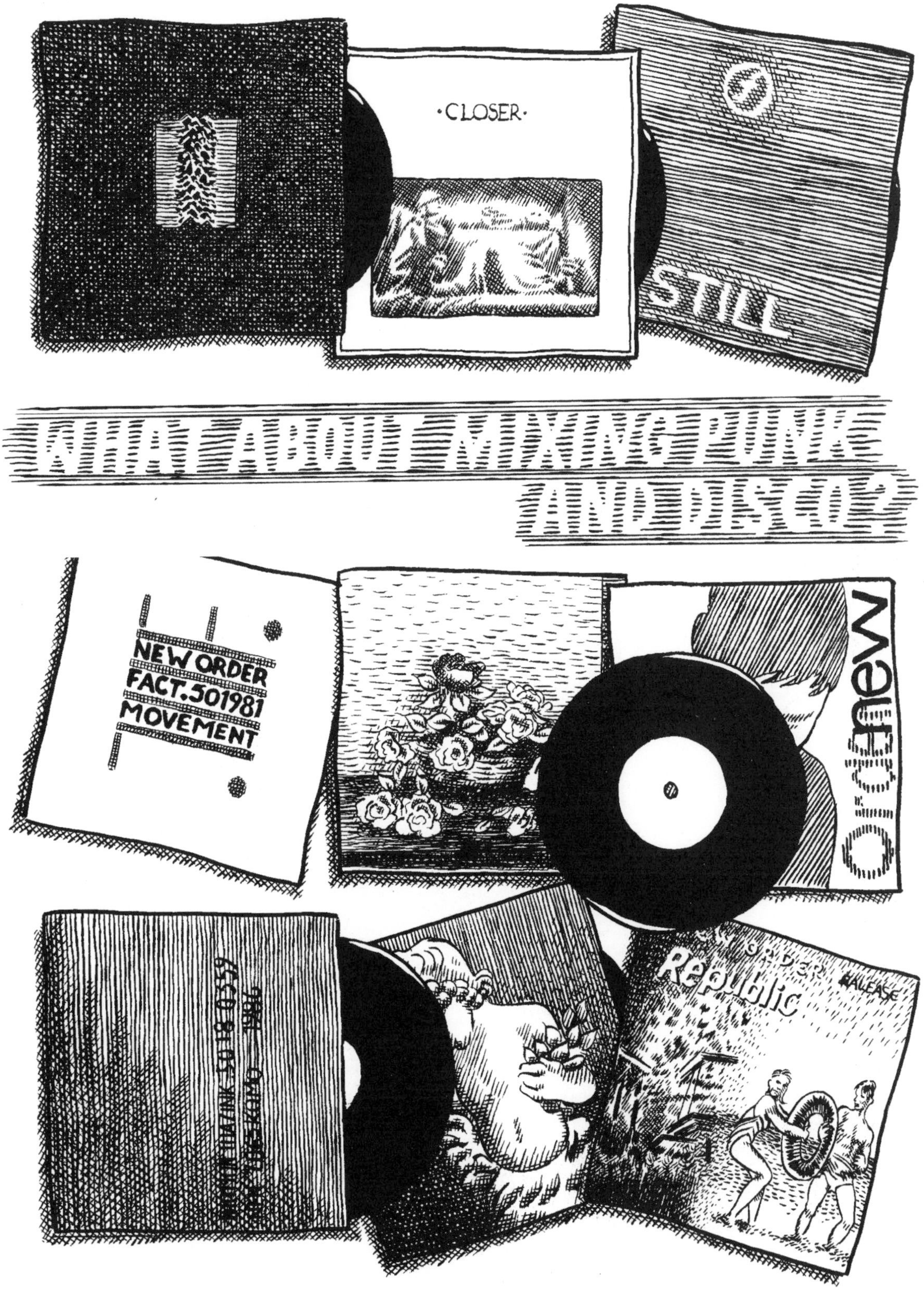
·CLOSER·
STILL
WHAT ABOUT MIXING PUNK AND DISCO?
NEW ORDER
FACT.50 1981
MOVEMENT
Republic

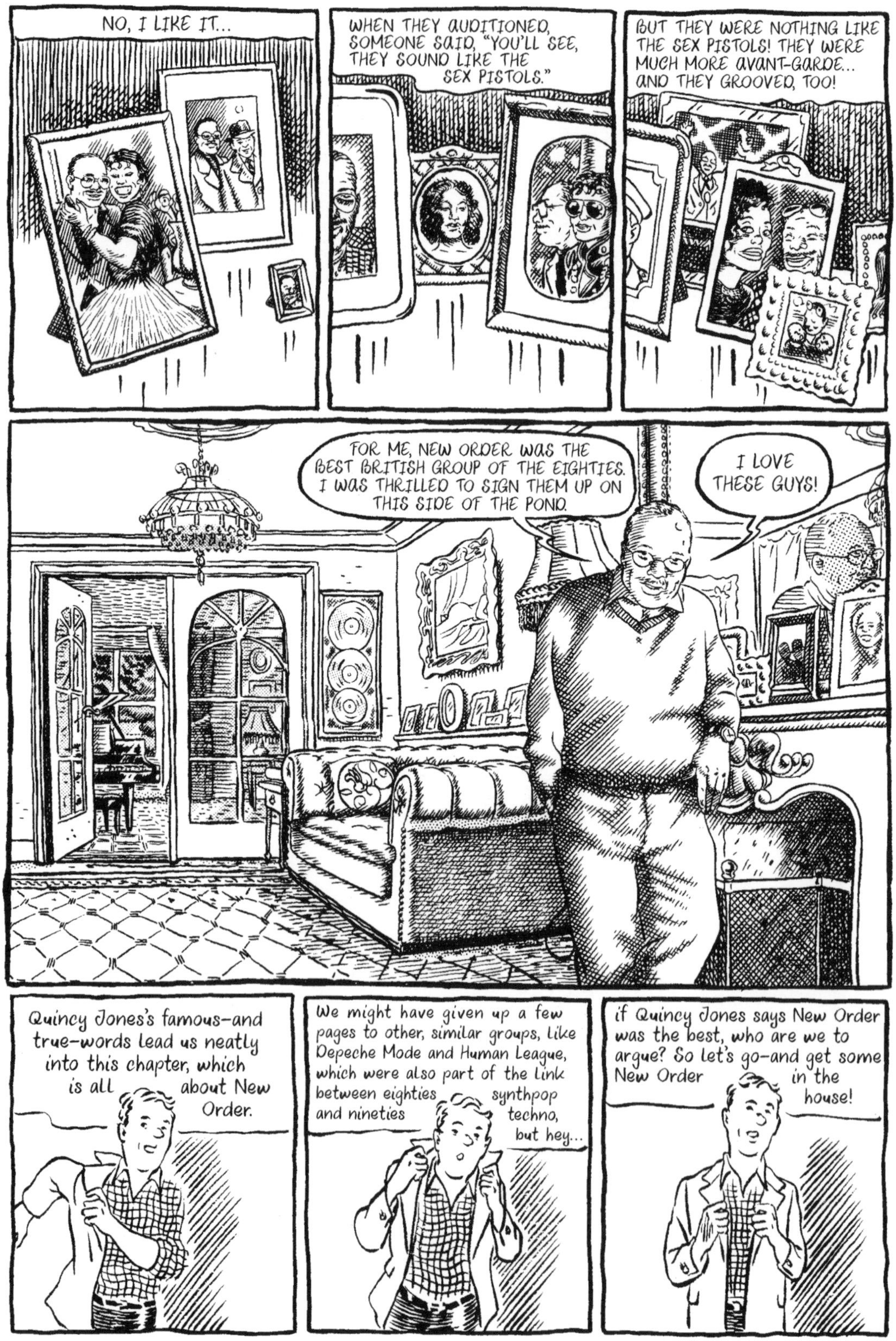

NO, I LIKE IT...
WHEN THEY AUDITIONED, SOMEONE SAID, "YOU'LL SEE, THEY SOUND LIKE THE SEX PISTOLS."
BUT THEY WERE NOTHING LIKE THE SEX PISTOLS! THEY WERE MUCH MORE AVANT-GARDE... AND THEY GROOVED, TOO!
FOR ME, NEW ORDER WAS THE BEST BRITISH GROUP OF THE EIGHTIES. I WAS THRILLED TO SIGN THEM UP ON THIS SIDE OF THE POND.
I LOVE THESE GUYS!
Quincy Jones's famous—and true—words lead us neatly into this chapter, which is all about New Order.
We might have given up a few pages to other, similar groups, like Depeche Mode and Human League, which were also part of the link between eighties synthpop and nineties techno, but hey...
if Quincy Jones says New Order was the best, who are we to argue? So let's go—and get some New Order in the house!

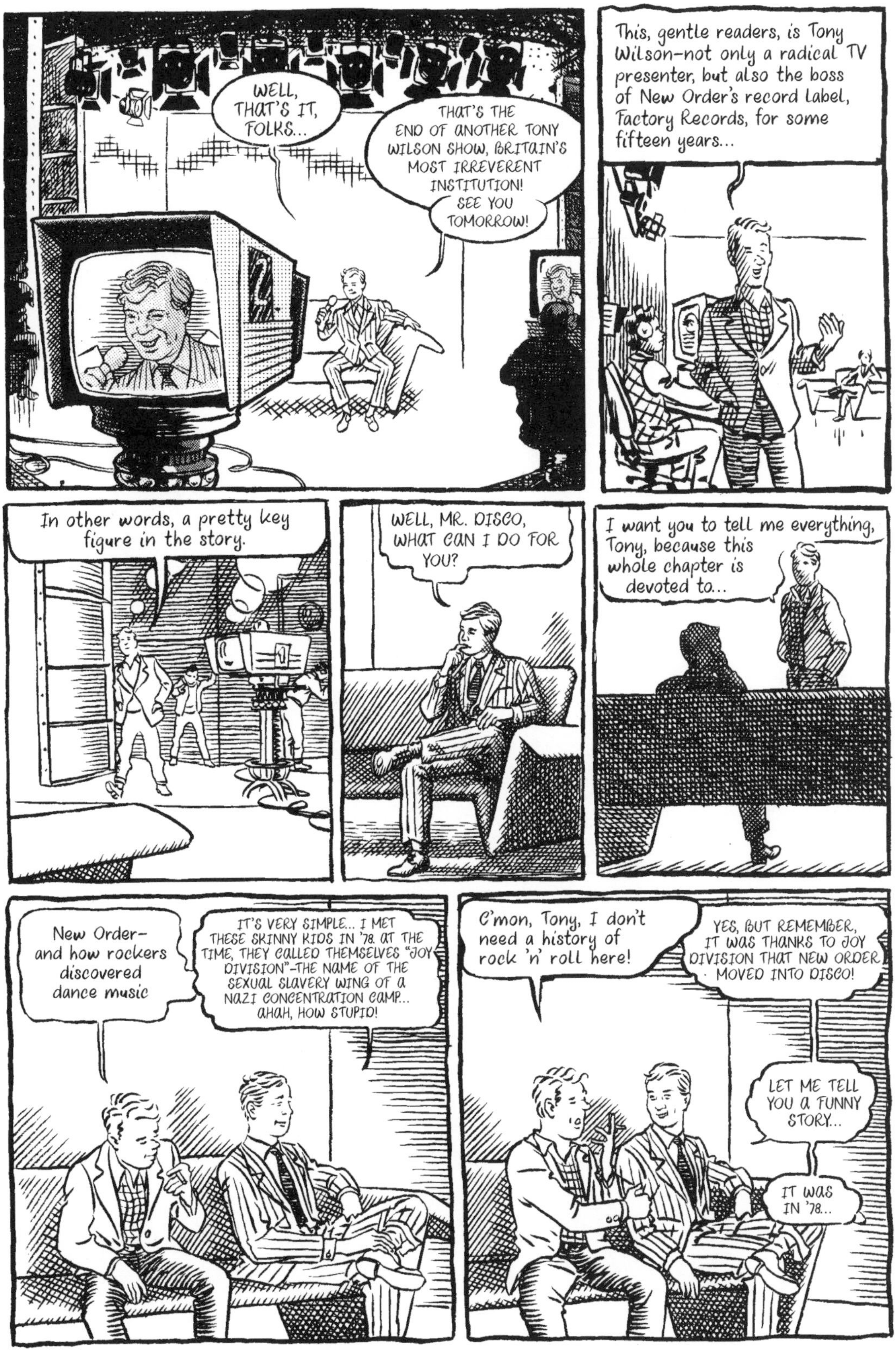
WELL, THAT'S IT, FOLKS...
THAT'S THE END OF ANOTHER TONY WILSON SHOW, BRITAIN'S MOST IRREVERENT INSTITUTION!
SEE YOU TOMORROW!
This, gentle readers, is Tony Wilson–not only a radical TV presenter, but also the boss of New Order's record label, Factory Records, for some fifteen years...
In other words, a pretty key figure in the story.
WELL, MR. DISCO, WHAT CAN I DO FOR YOU?
I want you to tell me everything, Tony, because this whole chapter is devoted to...
New Order–and how rockers discovered dance music
IT'S VERY SIMPLE... I MET THESE SKINNY KIDS IN '78. AT THE TIME, THEY CALLED THEMSELVES "JOY DIVISION"–THE NAME OF THE SEXUAL SLAVERY WING OF A NAZI CONCENTRATION CAMP... AHAH, HOW STUPID!
C'mon, Tony, I don't need a history of rock 'n' roll here!
YES, BUT REMEMBER, IT WAS THANKS TO JOY DIVISION THAT NEW ORDER MOVED INTO DISCO!
LET ME TELL YOU A FUNNY STORY...
IT WAS IN '78...

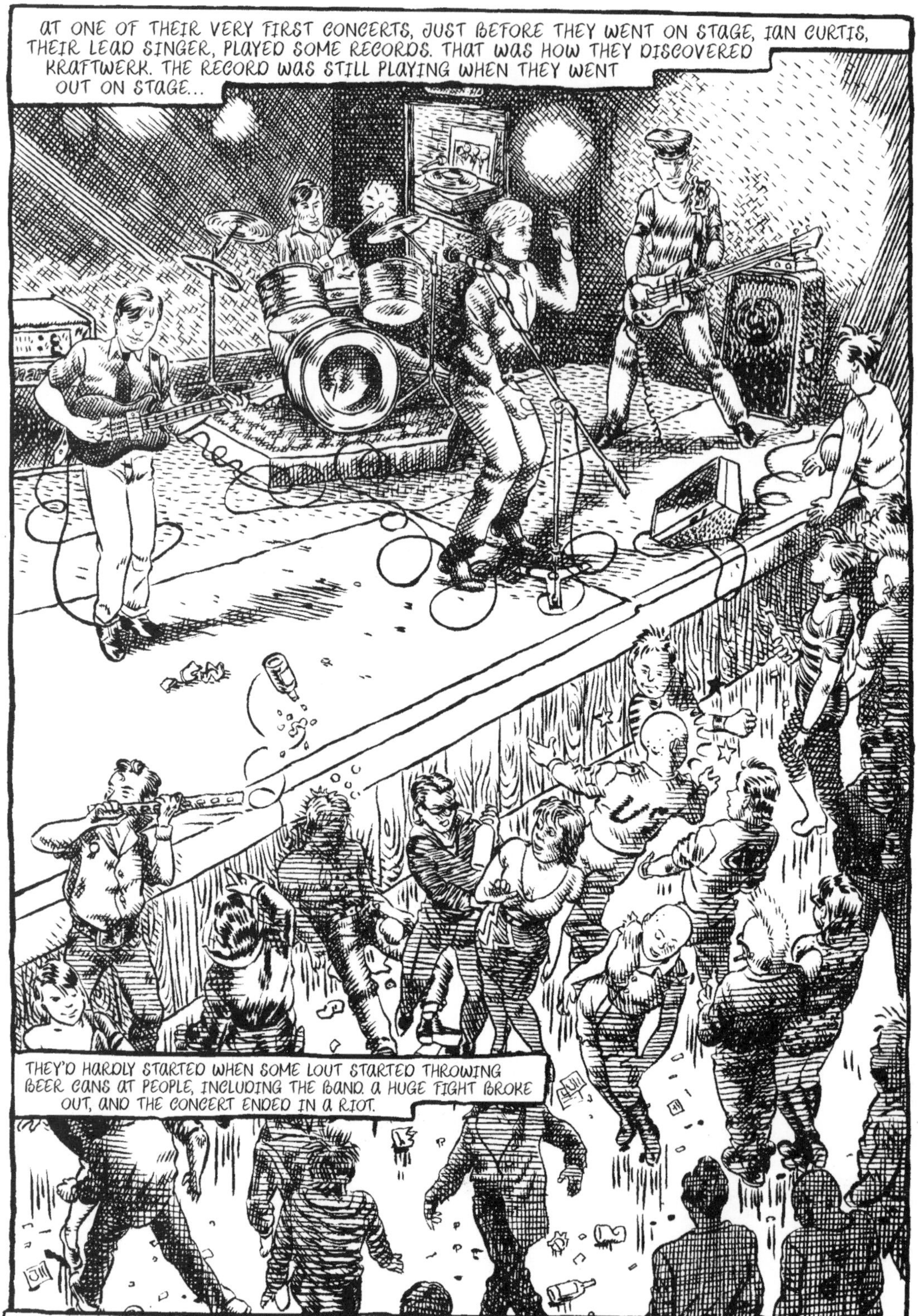

AT ONE OF THEIR VERY FIRST CONCERTS, JUST BEFORE THEY WENT ON STAGE, IAN CURTIS, THEIR LEAD SINGER, PLAYED SOME RECORDS. THAT WAS HOW THEY DISCOVERED KRAFTWERK. THE RECORD WAS STILL PLAYING WHEN THEY WENT OUT ON STAGE...
THEY'D HARDLY STARTED WHEN SOME LOUT STARTED THROWING BEER CANS AT PEOPLE, INCLUDING THE BAND. A HUGE FIGHT BROKE OUT, AND THE CONCERT ENDED IN A RIOT.
WHEN THEY GOT BACK TO THE DRESSING ROOM, THE KRAFTWERK RECORD WAS STILL PLAYING! FROM THEN ON, THEY BECAME OBSESSED WITH HYPNOTIC, MACHINE-MADE RHYTHMS.

THANKS TO KRAFTWERK, STEPHEN STARTED PLAYING AROUND WITH RHYTHM MACHINES AND BARNEY ABANDONED HIS GUITAR TO EXPERIMENT WITH SYNTHS. OF COURSE, AT THAT TIME, MACHINES LIKE THAT WERE ANTEDILUVIAN...

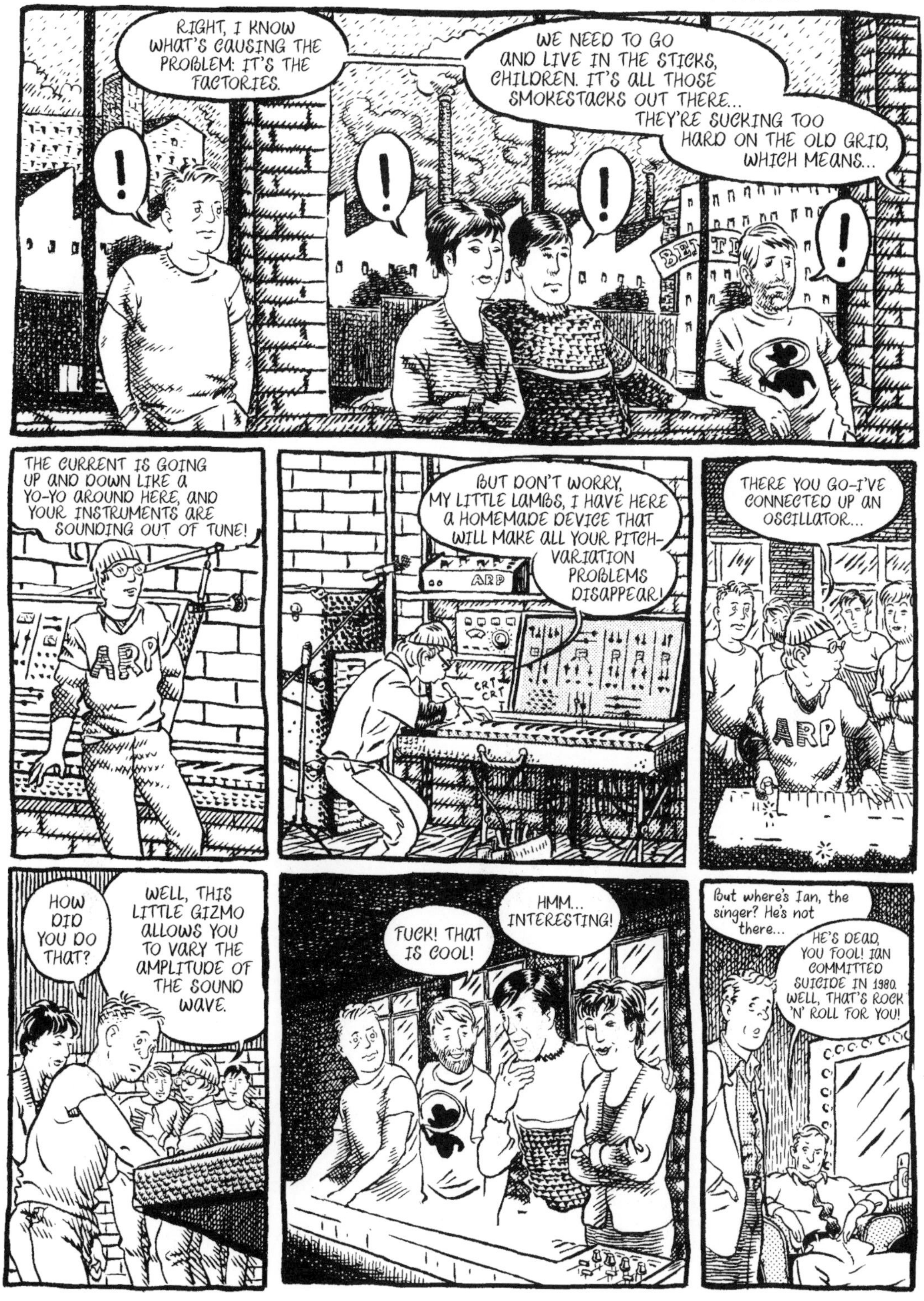
RIGHT, I KNOW WHAT'S CAUSING THE PROBLEM: IT'S THE FACTORIES.
WE NEED TO GO AND LIVE IN THE STICKS, CHILDREN. IT'S ALL THOSE SMOKESTACKS OUT THERE...
THEY'RE SUCKING TOO HARD ON THE OLD GRID, WHICH MEANS...
!
!
!
!
THE CURRENT IS GOING UP AND DOWN LIKE A YO-YO AROUND HERE, AND YOUR INSTRUMENTS ARE SOUNDING OUT OF TUNE!
BUT DON'T WORRY, MY LITTLE LAMBS, I HAVE HERE A HOMEMADE DEVICE THAT WILL MAKE ALL YOUR PITCH-
VARIATION PROBLEMS DISAPPEAR!
THERE YOU GO–I'VE CONNECTED UP AN OSCILLATOR...
HOW DID YOU DO THAT?
WELL, THIS LITTLE GIZMO ALLOWS YOU TO VARY THE AMPLITUDE OF THE SOUND WAVE.
FUCK! THAT IS COOL!
HMM... INTERESTING!
But where's Ian, the singer? He's not there...
HE'S DEAD, YOU FOOL! IAN COMMITTED SUICIDE IN 1980. WELL, THAT'S ROCK 'N' ROLL FOR YOU!

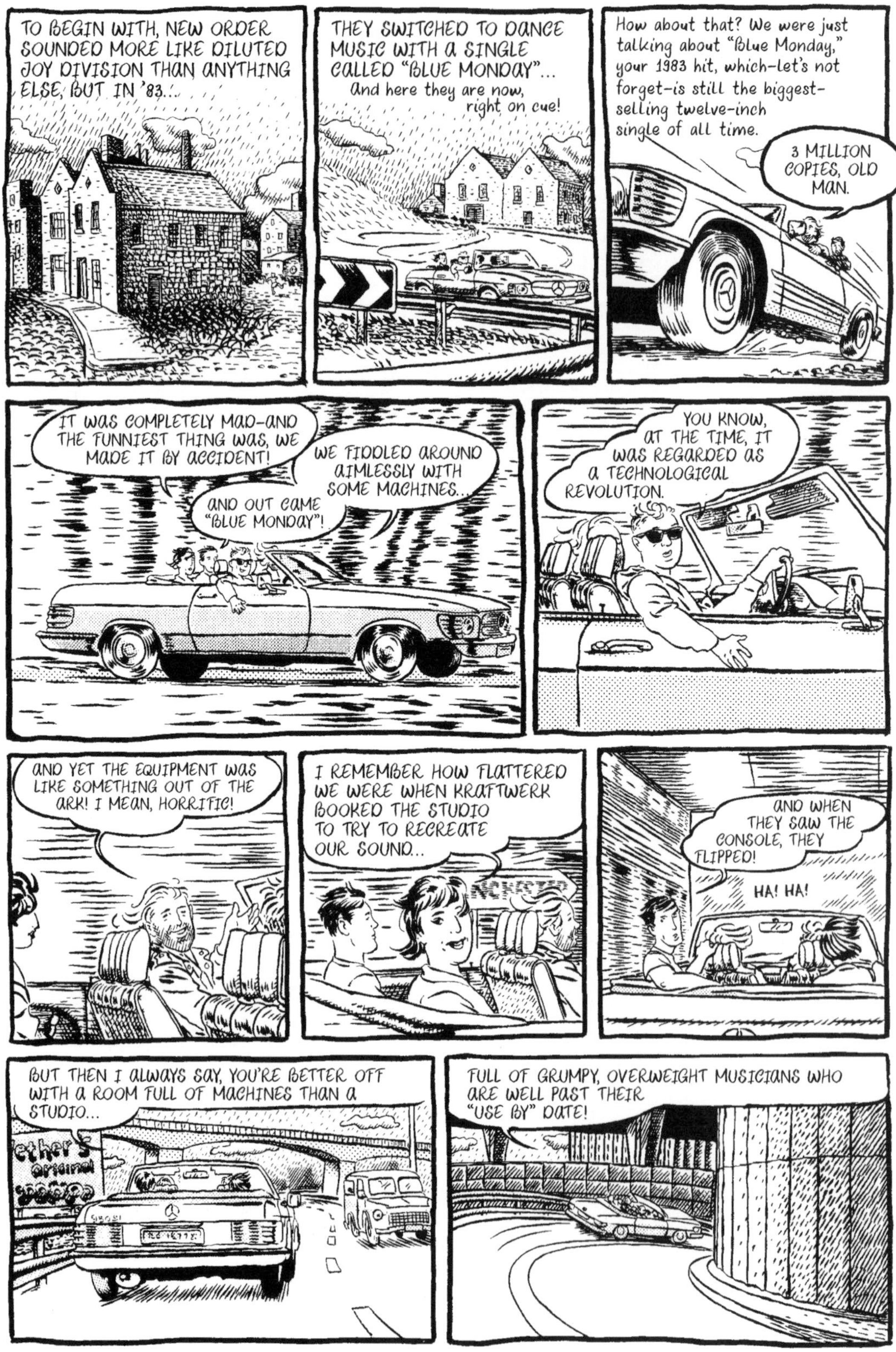
TO BEGIN WITH, NEW ORDER SOUNDED MORE LIKE DILUTED JOY DIVISION THAN ANYTHING ELSE, BUT IN '83...
THEY SWITCHED TO DANCE MUSIC WITH A SINGLE CALLED "BLUE MONDAY"...
And here they are now, right on cue!
How about that? We were just talking about "Blue Monday," your 1983 hit, which–let's not forget–is still the biggest-selling twelve-inch single of all time.
3 MILLION COPIES, OLD MAN.
IT WAS COMPLETELY MAD–AND THE FUNNIEST THING WAS, WE MADE IT BY ACCIDENT!
WE FIDDLED AROUND AIMLESSLY WITH SOME MACHINES...
AND OUT CAME "BLUE MONDAY"!
YOU KNOW, AT THE TIME, IT WAS REGARDED AS A TECHNOLOGICAL REVOLUTION.
AND YET THE EQUIPMENT WAS LIKE SOMETHING OUT OF THE ARK! I MEAN, HORRIFIC!
I REMEMBER HOW FLATTERED WE WERE WHEN KRAFTWERK BOOKED THE STUDIO TO TRY TO RECREATE OUR SOUND...
AND WHEN THEY SAW THE CONSOLE, THEY FLIPPED!
HA! HA!
BUT THEN I ALWAYS SAY, YOU'RE BETTER OFF WITH A ROOM FULL OF MACHINES THAN A STUDIO...
FULL OF GRUMPY, OVERWEIGHT MUSICIANS WHO ARE WELL PAST THEIR "USE BY" DATE!

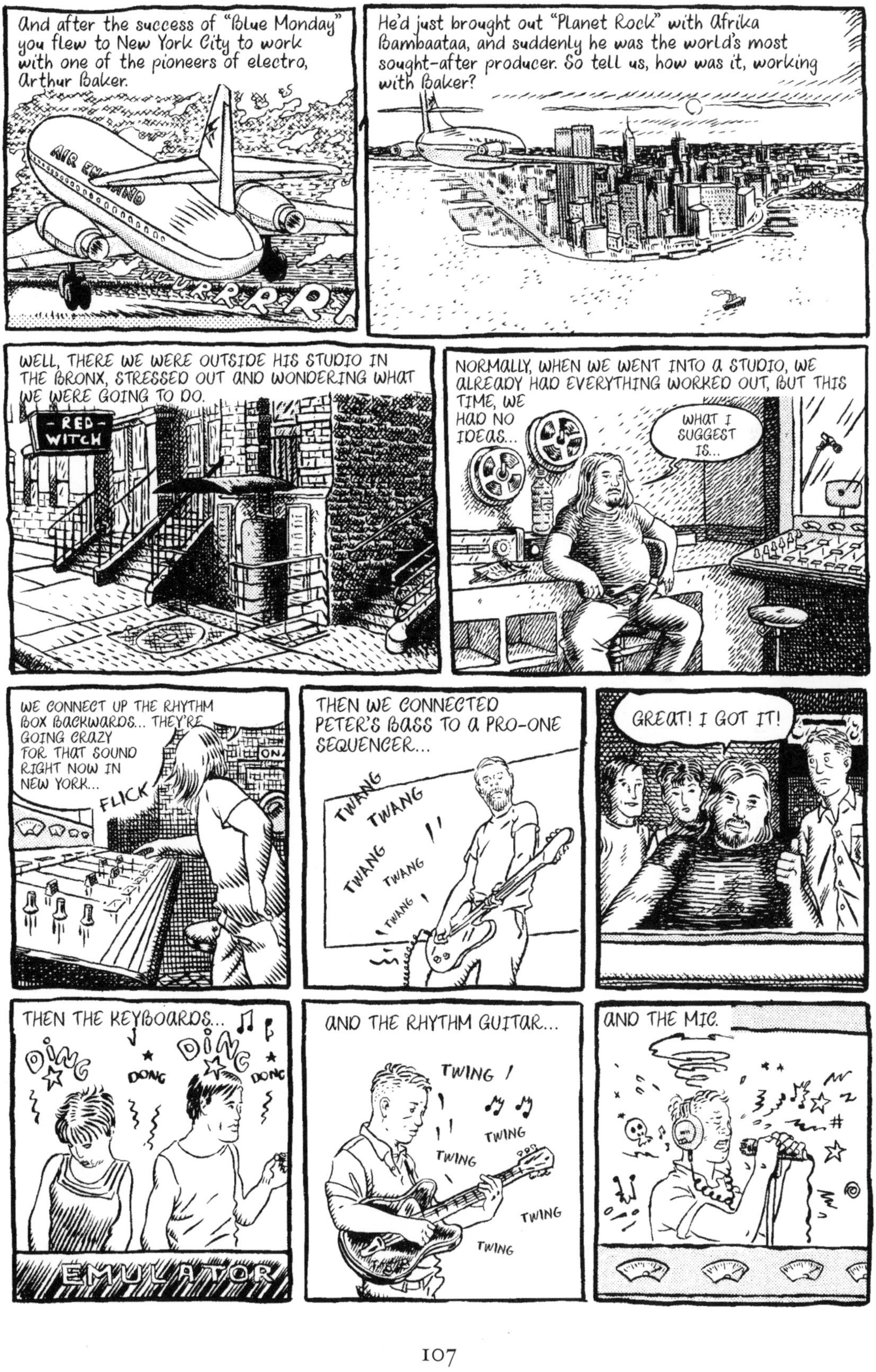
And after the success of "Blue Monday" you flew to New York City to work with one of the pioneers of electro, Arthur Baker.
AIR ENGLAND
VRRRRRR
He'd just brought out "Planet Rock" with Afrika Bambaataa, and suddenly he was the world's most sought-after producer. So tell us, how was it, working with Baker?
WELL, THERE WE WERE OUTSIDE HIS STUDIO IN THE BRONX, STRESSED OUT AND WONDERING WHAT WE WERE GOING TO DO.
- RED - WITCH
NORMALLY, WHEN WE WENT INTO A STUDIO, WE ALREADY HAD EVERYTHING WORKED OUT, BUT THIS TIME, WE HAD NO IDEAS...
WHAT I SUGGEST IS...
WE CONNECT UP THE RHYTHM BOX BACKWARDS... THEY'RE GOING CRAZY FOR THAT SOUND RIGHT NOW IN NEW YORK...
FLICK
ON
THEN WE CONNECTED PETER'S BASS TO A PRO-ONE SEQUENCER...
TWANG TWANG TWANG TWANG TWANG
GREAT! I GOT IT!
THEN THE KEYBOARDS...
DING DONG DING DONG
EMULATOR
AND THE RHYTHM GUITAR...
TWING ! TWING TWING TWING TWING
AND THE MIC.

BUT THE MOST AMAZING THING WAS, WHEN WE'D FINISHED RECORDING...

ARTHUR TOOK US ALL OUT...

AND WE WENT TO THIS INCREDIBLE CLUB CALLED THE FUN HOUSE...

WHERE HE PUT THE TAPE ON, JUST LIKE THAT.

LISTEN UP, BOYS AND GIRLS...IF YOU'RE JUMPING UP AND DOWN WONDERING WHO'S THE COOLEST CAT AROUND...

WELL, YOU'RE ABOUT TO HEAR THE COOLEST, GROOVIEST CAT THAT EVER WALKED THE PLANET OF SWING!

USUALLY, WHEN YOU FINISH A SESSION, YOU DON'T HEAR THE RECORDING AGAIN FOR MONTHS...

BUT HERE WAS THE MASTER TAPE, PLAYING IN A CLUB...

WE ACTUALLY SAW PEOPLE'S REACTION.

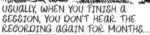 IT BLEW US AWAY.

THE ATMOSPHERE IN THOSE NEW YORK CLUBS MADE SUCH AN IMPRESSION ON US THAT, WHEN WE GOT BACK TO MANCHESTER, WE SAID:

FUCKING HELL! LET'S OPEN OUR OWN CLUB!

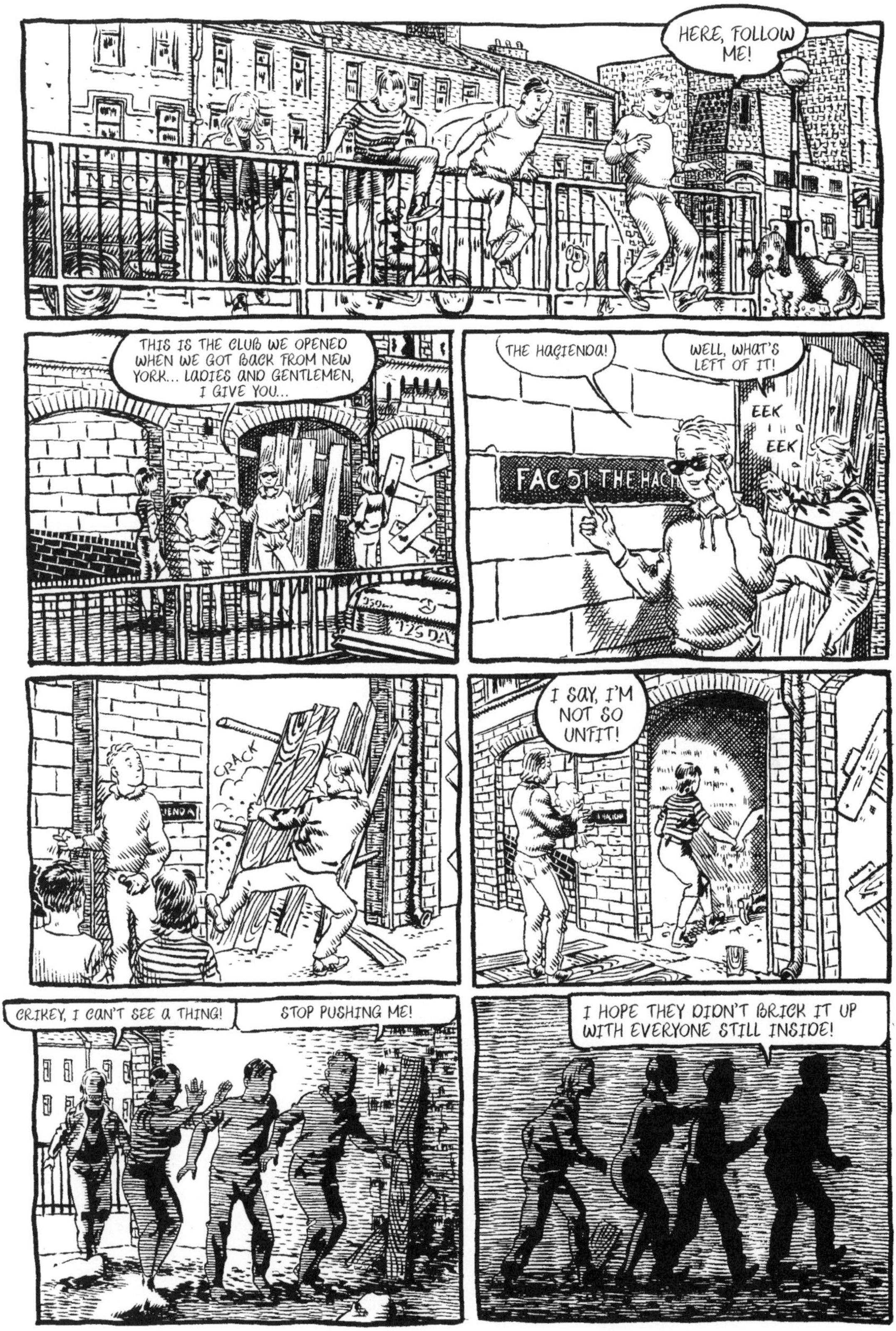
HERE, FOLLOW ME!
THIS IS THE CLUB WE OPENED WHEN WE GOT BACK FROM NEW YORK... LADIES AND GENTLEMEN, I GIVE YOU...
THE HAÇIENDA!
WELL, WHAT'S LEFT OF IT!
EEK
EEK
CRACK
I SAY, I'M NOT SO UNFIT!
CRIKEY, I CAN'T SEE A THING!
STOP PUSHING ME!
I HOPE THEY DIDN'T BRICK IT UP WITH EVERYONE STILL INSIDE!

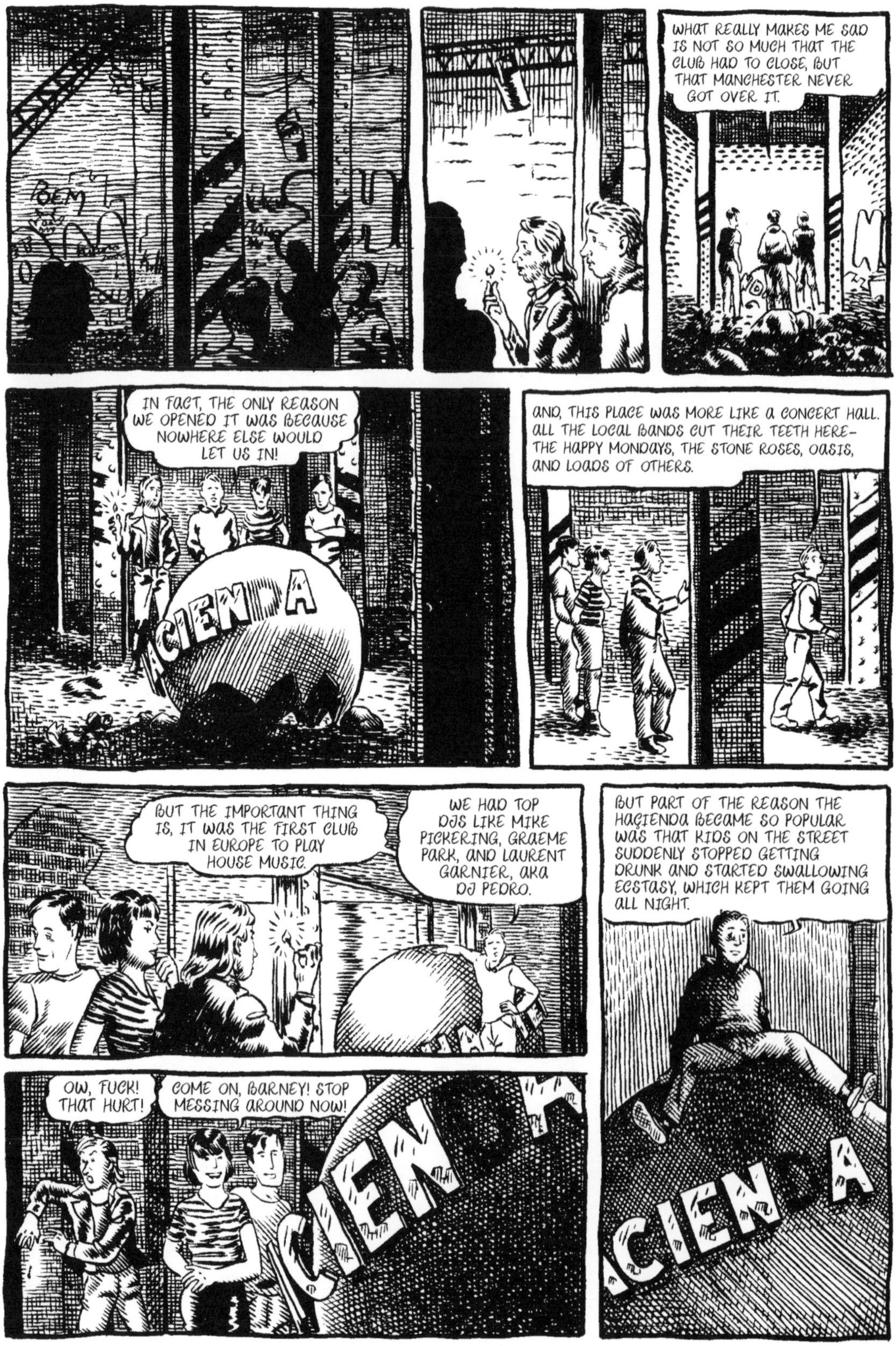
WHAT REALLY MAKES ME SAD IS NOT SO MUCH THAT THE CLUB HAD TO CLOSE, BUT THAT MANCHESTER NEVER GOT OVER IT.
IN FACT, THE ONLY REASON WE OPENED IT WAS BECAUSE NOWHERE ELSE WOULD LET US IN!
ACIENDA
AND, THIS PLACE WAS MORE LIKE A CONCERT HALL. ALL THE LOCAL BANDS CUT THEIR TEETH HERE– THE HAPPY MONDAYS, THE STONE ROSES, OASIS, AND LOADS OF OTHERS.
BUT THE IMPORTANT THING IS, IT WAS THE FIRST CLUB IN EUROPE TO PLAY HOUSE MUSIC.
WE HAD TOP DJS LIKE MIKE PICKERING, GRAEME PARK, AND LAURENT GARNIER, AKA DJ PEDRO.
OW, FUCK! THAT HURT!
COME ON, BARNEY! STOP MESSING AROUND NOW!
CIEND
BUT PART OF THE REASON THE HAÇIENDA BECAME SO POPULAR WAS THAT KIDS ON THE STREET SUDDENLY STOPPED GETTING DRUNK AND STARTED SWALLOWING ECSTASY, WHICH KEPT THEM GOING ALL NIGHT.
ACIENDA

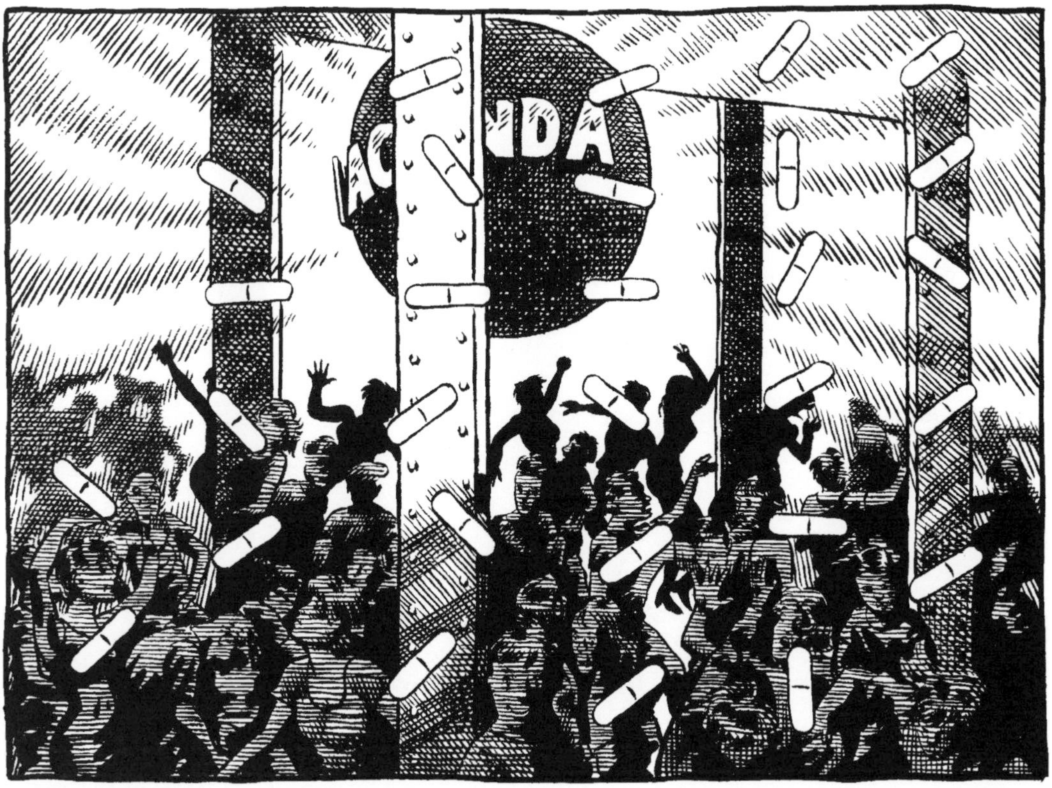

Sorry to interrupt you guys, but before we end this chapter I really wanted to ask you about your fifth album, *Technique*. You started recording it in Ibiza, surrounded by Brits on vacation, discovering sex and house at the same time. So, tell us...

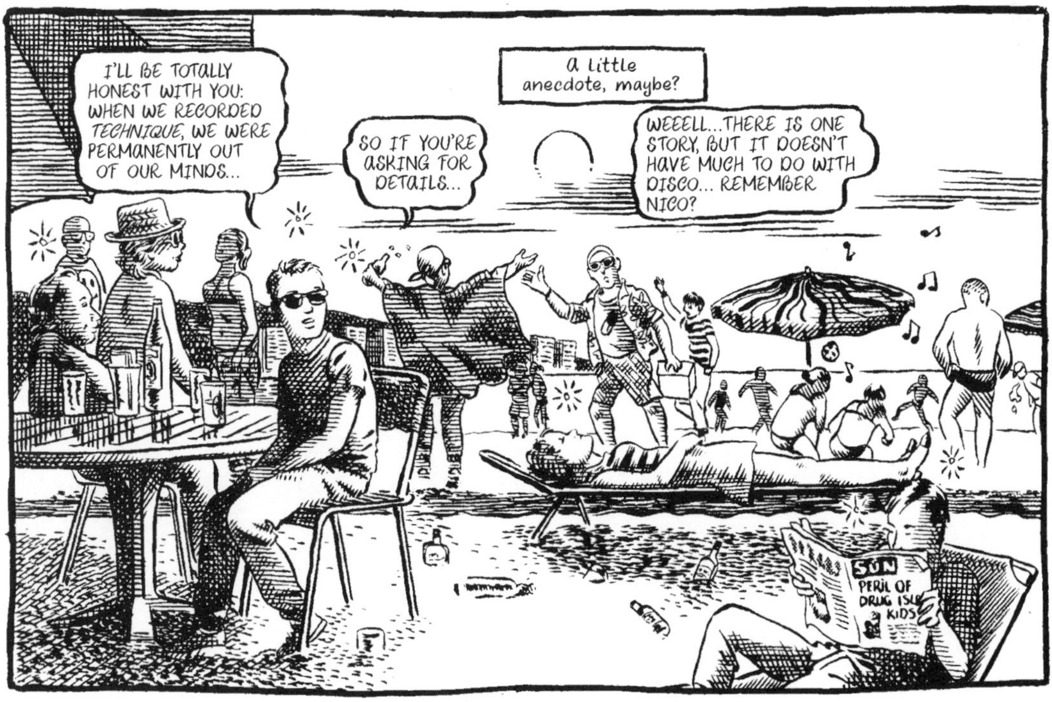

I'LL BE TOTALLY HONEST WITH YOU: WHEN WE RECORDED *TECHNIQUE*, WE WERE PERMANENTLY OUT OF OUR MINDS...
SO IF YOU'RE ASKING FOR DETAILS...
A little anecdote, maybe?
WEEELL...THERE IS ONE STORY, BUT IT DOESN'T HAVE MUCH TO DO WITH DISCO... REMEMBER NICO?
SUN
PERIL OF DRUG ISL KIDS

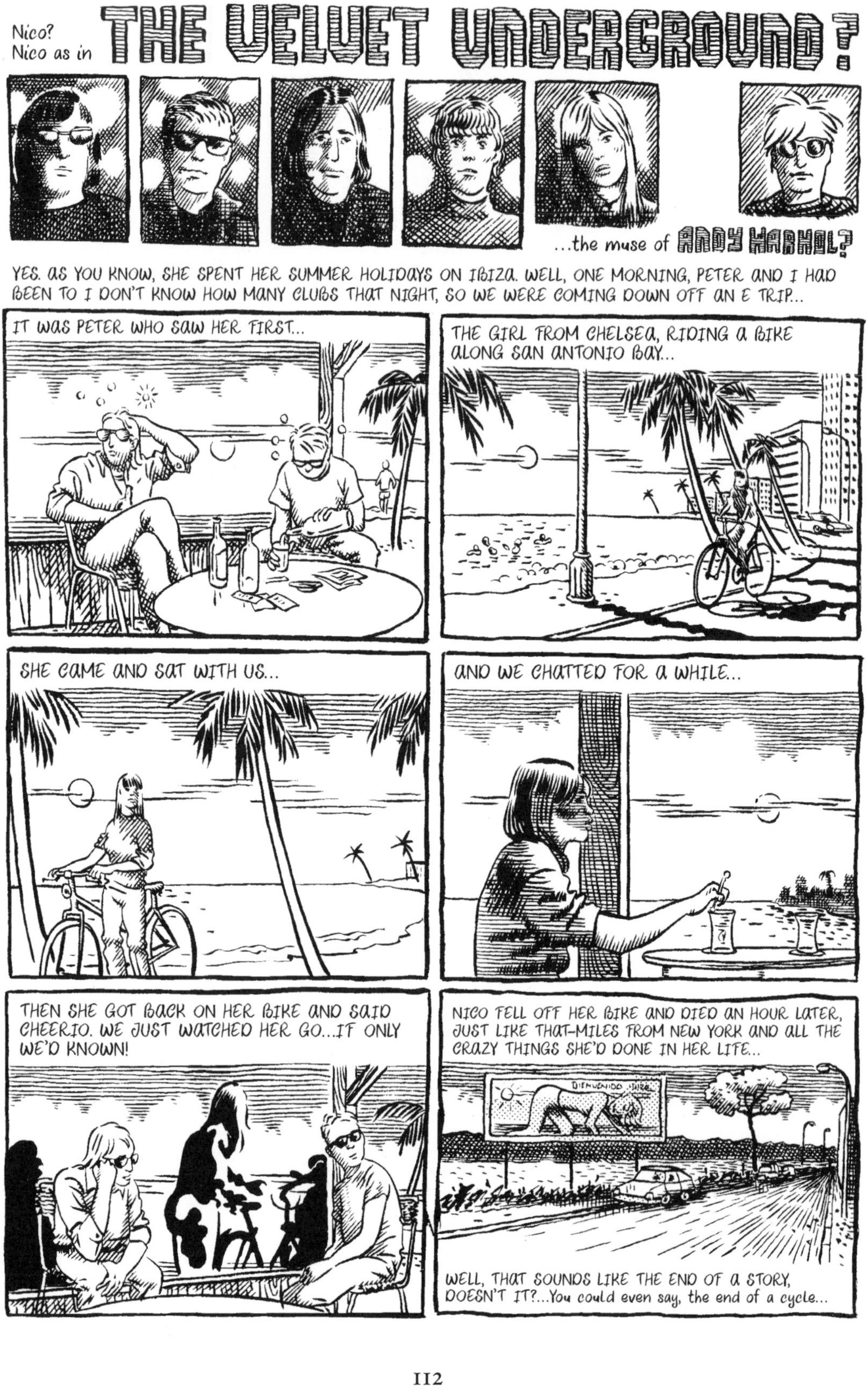
Nico?
Nico as in THE VELVET UNDERGROUND?
...the muse of ANDY WARHOL?
YES. AS YOU KNOW, SHE SPENT HER SUMMER HOLIDAYS ON IBIZA. WELL, ONE MORNING, PETER AND I HAD BEEN TO I DON'T KNOW HOW MANY CLUBS THAT NIGHT, SO WE WERE COMING DOWN OFF AN E TRIP...
IT WAS PETER WHO SAW HER FIRST...
THE GIRL FROM CHELSEA, RIDING A BIKE ALONG SAN ANTONIO BAY...
SHE CAME AND SAT WITH US...
AND WE CHATTED FOR A WHILE...
THEN SHE GOT BACK ON HER BIKE AND SAID CHEERIO. WE JUST WATCHED HER GO...IF ONLY WE'D KNOWN!
NICO FELL OFF HER BIKE AND DIED AN HOUR LATER, JUST LIKE THAT–MILES FROM NEW YORK AND ALL THE CRAZY THINGS SHE'D DONE IN HER LIFE...
WELL, THAT SOUNDS LIKE THE END OF A STORY, DOESN'T IT?...You could even say, the end of a cycle...

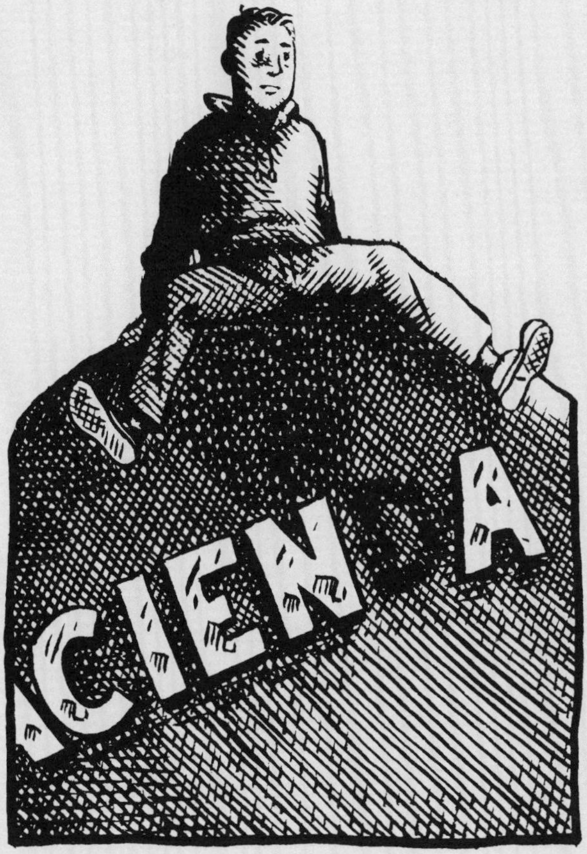
CIEN A

If music be the food of love...

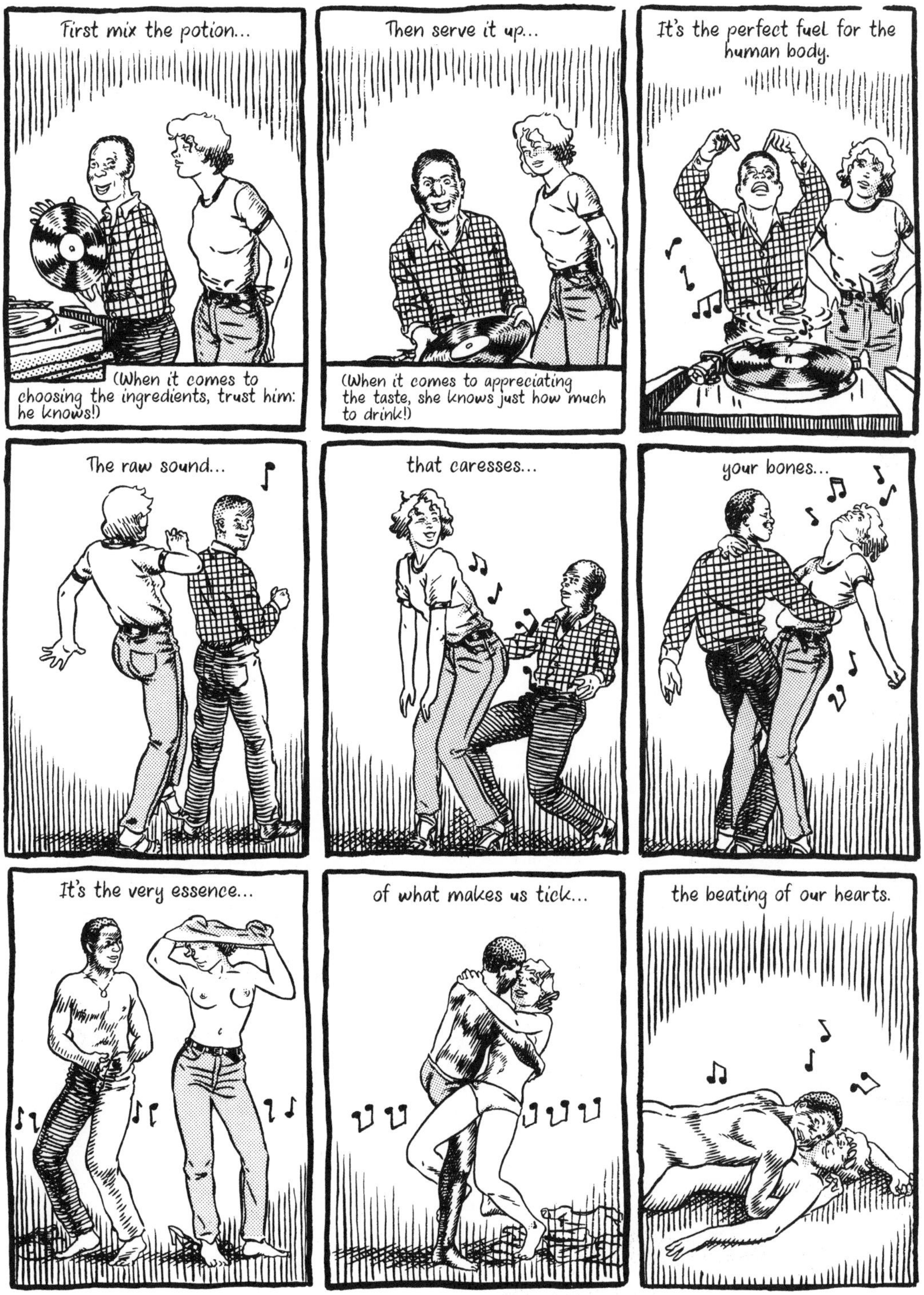

First mix the potion...
(When it comes to choosing the ingredients, trust him: he knows!)
Then serve it up...
(When it comes to appreciating the taste, she knows just how much to drink!)
It's the perfect fuel for the human body.
The raw sound...
that caresses...
your bones...
It's the very essence...
of what makes us tick...
the beating of our hearts.

CHAPTER 7

THE FOURTH DIMENSION

THE STORY OF MDMA

Thelonious Monk
Epistrophy ("Monk's Music" LP version) — 1957

Chico Hamilton Quintet with John Pisano
Blue Sands (Live at Newport) — 1958

John Cale
Eat/Kiss (LP) — 1963

Lee Hazlewood and Nancy Sinatra
Summer Wine — 1967

Velvet Underground
Pale Blue Eyes — 1968

Pentangle
Pentangling — 1968

The West Coast Pop Art Experimental Band
A Child's Guide to Good and Evil (LP) — 1968

Principal Edwards Magic Theatre
Enigmatic Insomniac Machine — 1969

Mayo Thompson
Fortune — 1970

Aquarius (Herman Chin Loy)
Rest Yourself — 1971

Herbie Hancock
Nobu — 1974

Devon Irons
*When Jah Come
(Lee Perry Extended Mix)* — 1975

Dillinger
Cocaine in My Brain — 1976

Cat Stevens
Was Dog a Doughnut? — 1976

David Bowie
Low (LP) — 1977

Public Image Ltd.
Fooderstompf — 1978

Riz Ortolani
Cannibal Holocaust (Main Theme) — 1979

Blackbear
Electrocharge — 1980

Kenneth Higney
Funky Kinky — 1980

Manuel Göttsching
E2-E4 — 1984

Arthur Russell
A Little Lost — 1986

Steve Reich
Electric Counterpoint — 1987

WELCOME TO THE '90S

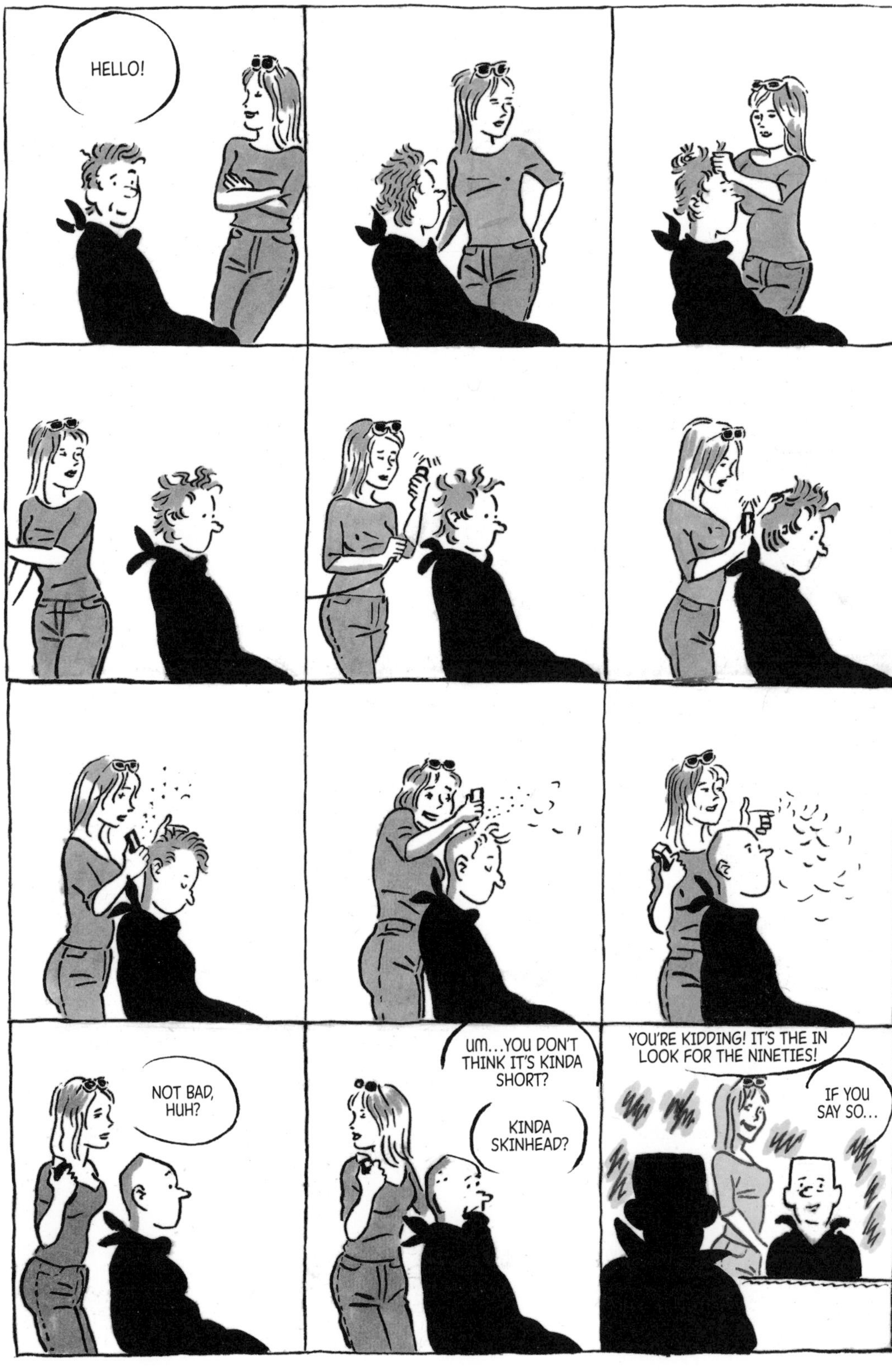
HELLO!
NOT BAD, HUH?
UM...YOU DON'T THINK IT'S KINDA SHORT?
KINDA SKINHEAD?
YOU'RE KIDDING! IT'S THE IN LOOK FOR THE NINETIES!
IF YOU SAY SO...

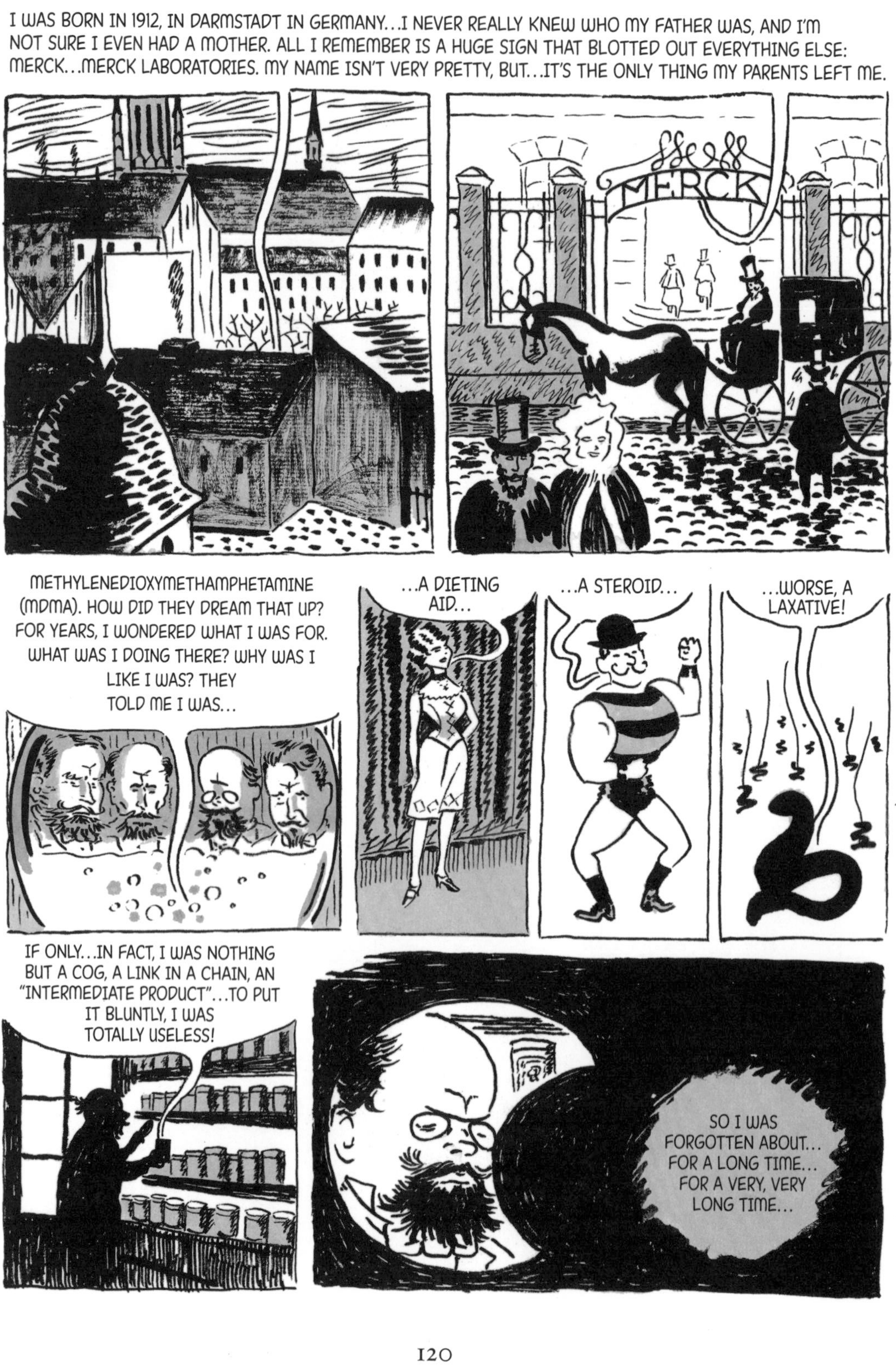
I WAS BORN IN 1912, IN DARMSTADT IN GERMANY...I NEVER REALLY KNEW WHO MY FATHER WAS, AND I'M NOT SURE I EVEN HAD A MOTHER. ALL I REMEMBER IS A HUGE SIGN THAT BLOTTED OUT EVERYTHING ELSE: MERCK...MERCK LABORATORIES. MY NAME ISN'T VERY PRETTY, BUT...IT'S THE ONLY THING MY PARENTS LEFT ME.
MERCK
METHYLENEDIOXYMETHAMPHETAMINE (MDMA). HOW DID THEY DREAM THAT UP? FOR YEARS, I WONDERED WHAT I WAS FOR. WHAT WAS I DOING THERE? WHY WAS I LIKE I WAS? THEY TOLD ME I WAS...
...A DIETING AID...
...A STEROID...
...WORSE, A LAXATIVE!
IF ONLY...IN FACT, I WAS NOTHING BUT A COG, A LINK IN A CHAIN, AN "INTERMEDIATE PRODUCT"...TO PUT IT BLUNTLY, I WAS TOTALLY USELESS!
SO I WAS FORGOTTEN ABOUT... FOR A LONG TIME... FOR A VERY, VERY LONG TIME...

SO LONG THAT I MISSED TWO WORLD WARS...AT THE END OF THE SECOND ONE, I WAS RESCUED BY AMERICANS, WHO BECAME MY NEW PARENTS...AND HANDED ME OVER TO A BUNCH OF FACELESS SCIENTISTS...

THEY TESTED ME ON JUST ABOUT EVERYTHING...

STUCK ME UP THE ASS-END OF A WHOLE ZOO...

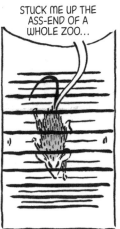

AND THEN TESTED ME ON A BUNCH OF POOR BROKE-DICKS.

THEY THOUGHT I COULD BE USED AS A TRUTH SERUM, BUT...

THERE WAS LITTLE POINT, SO I WAS PUT BACK...   IN A HOLE!

I DIDN'T FIND MY REAL FAMILY UNTIL THE SIXTIES. MY REAL FATHER, MY FAVORITE OF ALL, WAS ALEXANDER "SASHA" SHULGIN, A PROFESSOR AT BERKELEY WHO GOT SUPPORT FROM THE U.S. GOVERNMENT TO TEST WHATEVER CHEMICAL PRODUCTS HE WANTED TO...

THAT'S WHEN I REALLY STARTED TO HAVE FUN, LET ME TELL YOU! EVERY WEEKEND I WOUND UP AT HIS PLACE, IN LAFAYETTE, CALIFORNIA, WITH A WHOLE LOT OF PEOPLE WHO'D VOLUNTEERED TO TRY OUT ONE OF SASHA'S 159 CONCOCTIONS.

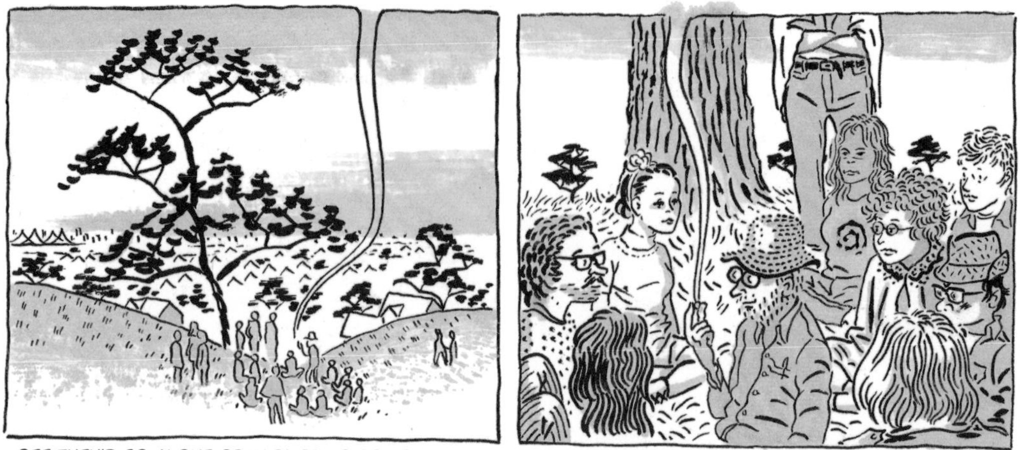

OFF THEY'D GO, ALONE OR IN PAIRS, TO DO SOME KIND OF "PRACTICAL TEST"!

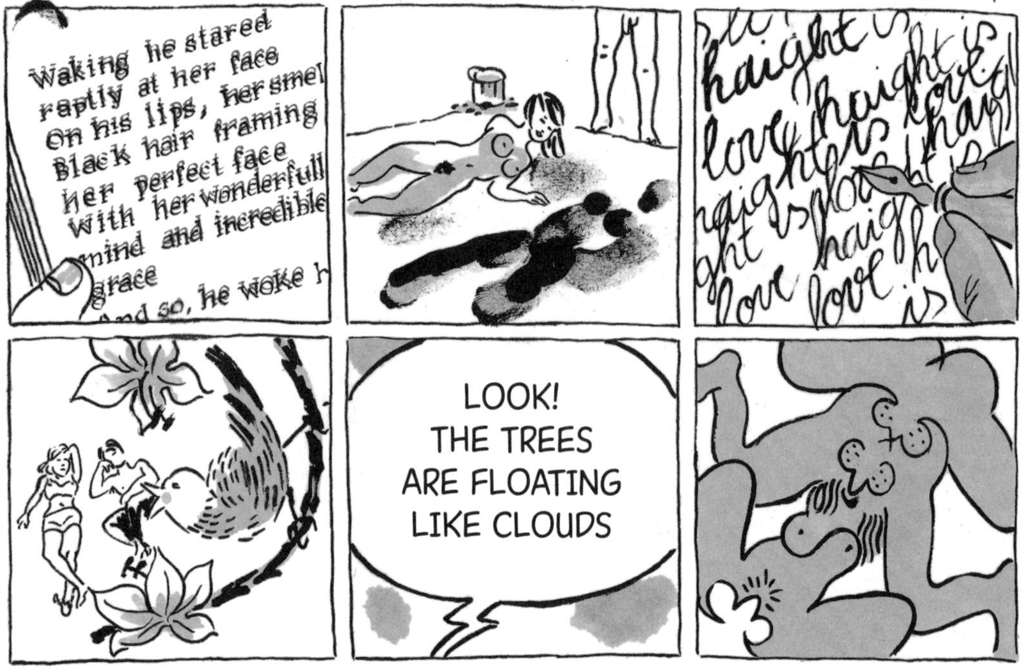
Waking he stared
raptly at her face
On his lips, her smel
Black hair framing
her perfect face
With her wonderfull
mind and incredible
grace
nd so, he woke h
haight is love
LOOK! THE TREES ARE FLOATING LIKE CLOUDS

BUT AFTER THAT, IT WAS BACK TO WORK...THEY ALL HAD TO WRITE A DETAILED ACCOUNT OF THEIR TRIP...AND OF ALL THE PILLS AND POTIONS, I WAS THE FAVORITE! "A MIRACLE DRUG...INCREASES EMPATHY...A HONEY." BUT THIS TIME, THEY WEREN'T GOING TO LET THE PUBLIC GET HOLD OF ME, LIKE THEY DID WITH LSD. OH, NO. THEY WERE KEEPING ME SECRET—THE SECRET OF HAPPINESS.

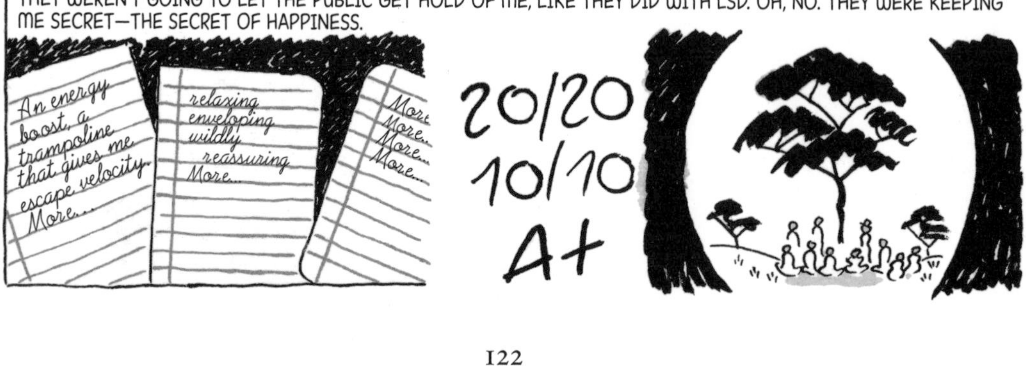
An energy boost, a trampoline that gives me escape velocity. More...
relaxing enveloping wildly reassuring More...
More... More... More... More...
20/20
10/10
A+

THE UPS AND DOWNS...

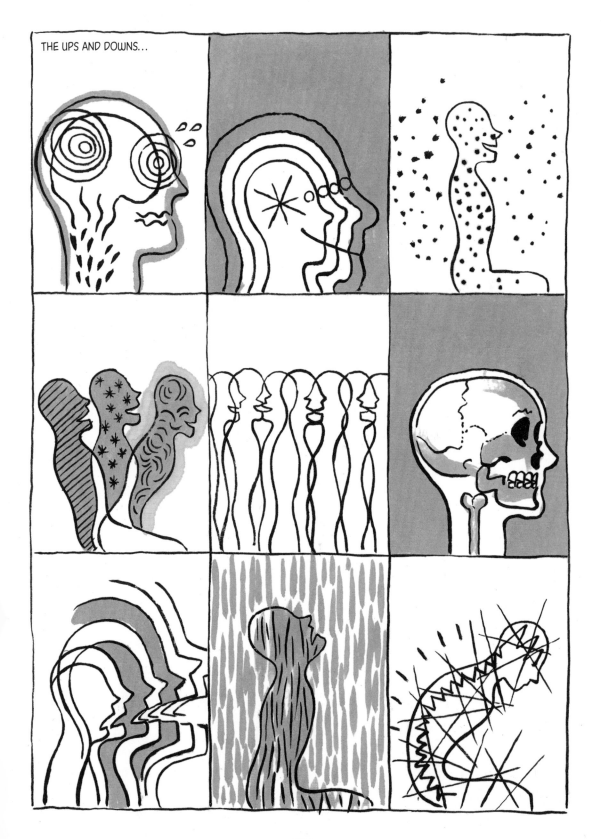

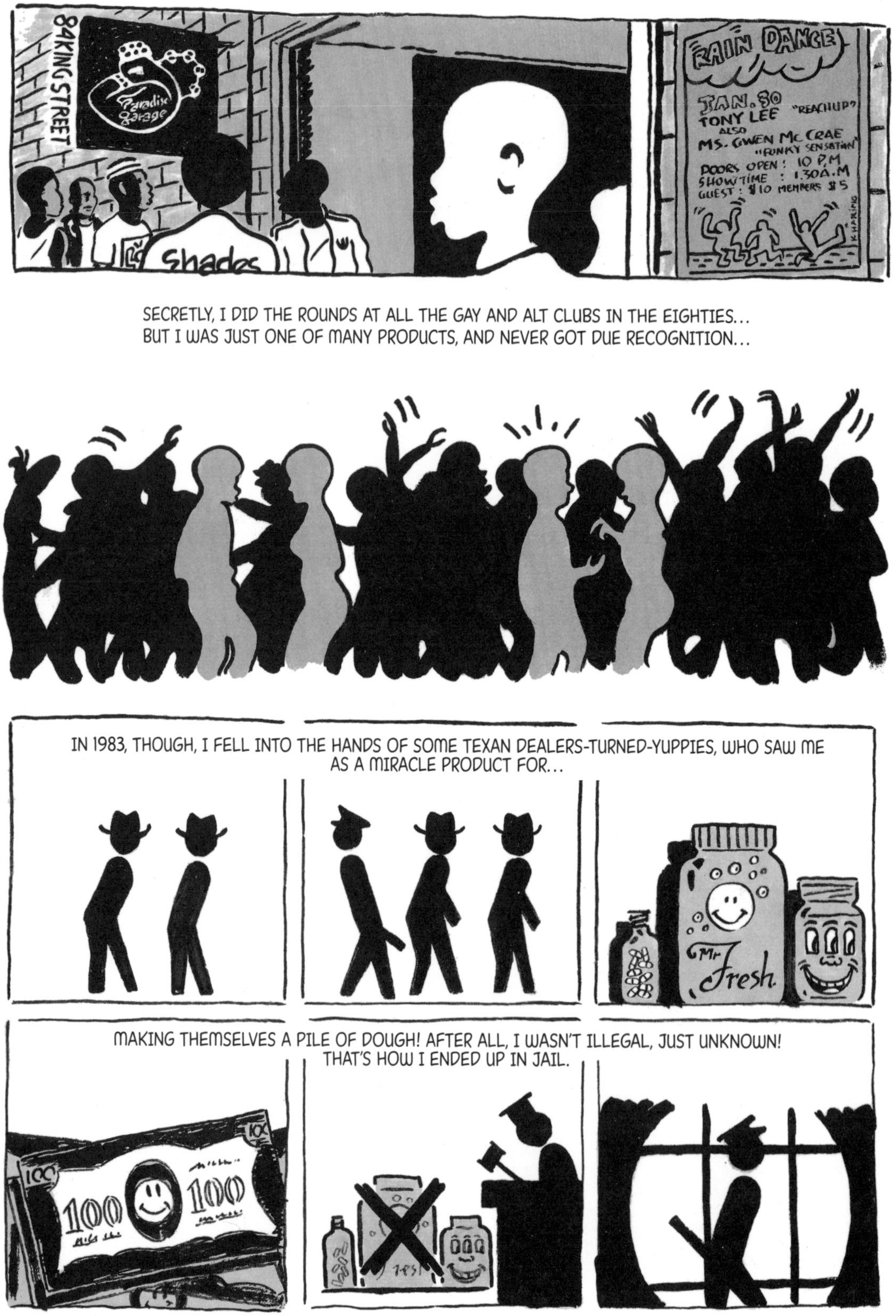
84 KING STREET
Paradise Garage
Shades
RAIN DANCE
JAN. 30
TONY LEE "REACH UP"
ALSO
MS. GWEN McCRAE "FUNKY SENSATION"
DOORS OPEN: 10 P.M
SHOWTIME: 1.30 A.M
GUEST: $10 MEMBERS $5
K. HARING
SECRETLY, I DID THE ROUNDS AT ALL THE GAY AND ALT CLUBS IN THE EIGHTIES...
BUT I WAS JUST ONE OF MANY PRODUCTS, AND NEVER GOT DUE RECOGNITION...
IN 1983, THOUGH, I FELL INTO THE HANDS OF SOME TEXAN DEALERS-TURNED-YUPPIES, WHO SAW ME AS A MIRACLE PRODUCT FOR...
Mr Fresh
MAKING THEMSELVES A PILE OF DOUGH! AFTER ALL, I WASN'T ILLEGAL, JUST UNKNOWN!
THAT'S HOW I ENDED UP IN JAIL.
100
100

JULY 1, 1985:
THE U.S. GOVERNMENT DECIDED IT WAS ILLEGAL TO SELL, POSSESS, OR USE ME...

SO SUDDENLY, AT THE AGE OF 73, I WAS AN OUTLAW AND EVERYONE WAS AFTER ME.

THE END OF THE LINE?

ARE YOU KIDDING?

IT WAS ALL I NEEDED TO MAKE ME FAMOUS!

SINCE THE NINETIES, MORE THAN HALF A MILLION PEOPLE USED ME EVERY WEEKEND IN THE U.K. THAT'S MORE THAN 50 MILLION PILLS PER YEAR.

IN THE U.S., I WASN'T THAT POPULAR UNTIL THE YEAR 2000.

I WAS EVEN PROMOTED BY RAP STARS LIKE EMINEM, JA RULE, AND MISSY ELLIOTT.

PROFESSOR SHULGIN NEVER GUESSED I'D BE SUCH A BIG STAR. BUT THEN, HE NEVER TOOK ECSTASY AND STAYED UP ALL NIGHT DANCING! FROM THE PERFECT FEEL-GOOD TREATMENT FOR A SMALL CIRCLE OF INITIATES, I'D BECOME THE DRUG OF CHOICE FOR MILLIONS OF HEDONISTS!

AND HEY ...

IT'S PARTY TIME!

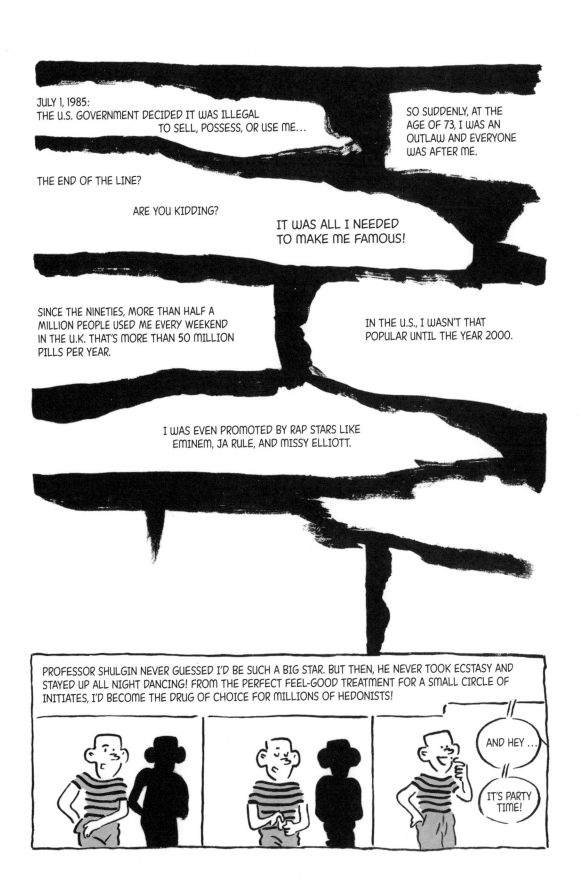

125

CHAPTER 8

RAVE ON

EVERYTHING STARTS WITH AN E

M|A|R|R|S
Pump Up The Volume — 1987

A Guy Called Gerald
Voodoo Ray — 1988

Bomb the Bass
Beat Dis — 1988

The Beloved
The Sun Rising — 1989

808 State
Ninety (LP) — 1989

Technotronic
Get Up! (Before the Night Is Over) — 1989

The KLF
Chill Out (LP) — 1990

N-Joi
Anthem — 1990

Xpansions
Move Your Body — 1990

Primal Scream
Come Together (Andrew Weatherall Mix) — 1990

Cartouche
Feel The Groove — 1990

Adamski
N-R-G — 1990

D-Shake
Techno Trance — 1990

LFO
LFO — 1991

Orbital
Halcyon (Life at Glastonbury) — 1992

B.M. EX
Appolonia (Sasha Mix) (EP) — 1992

The Age of Love
The Age of Love (The Jam & Spoon Mix) — 1992

Dave Clarke
Wisdom to the Wise — 1994

UK Apachi and Shy FX
Original Nuttah — 1994

The Prodigy
No Good (Start the Dance) — 1994

Nookie
The Sound of Music — 1995

LTJ Bukem
Horizons — 1996

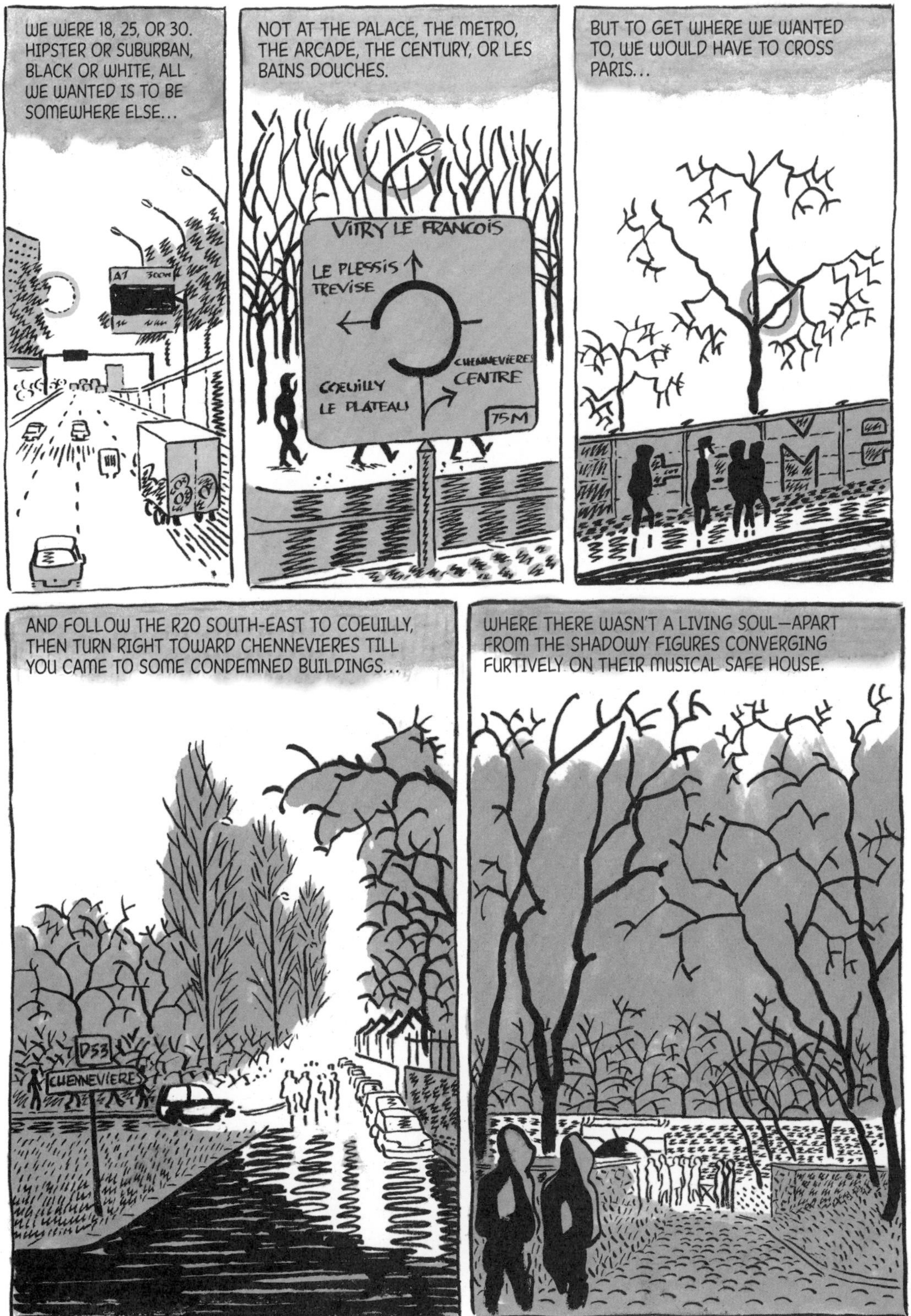
WE WERE 18, 25, OR 30. HIPSTER OR SUBURBAN, BLACK OR WHITE, ALL WE WANTED IS TO BE SOMEWHERE ELSE...
A1
NOT AT THE PALACE, THE METRO, THE ARCADE, THE CENTURY, OR LES BAINS DOUCHES.
VITRY LE FRANCOIS
LE PLESSIS TREVISE
CHENNEVIERES CENTRE
COEUILLY LE PLATEAU
75M
BUT TO GET WHERE WE WANTED TO, WE WOULD HAVE TO CROSS PARIS...
AND FOLLOW THE R20 SOUTH-EAST TO COEUILLY, THEN TURN RIGHT TOWARD CHENNEVIERES TILL YOU CAME TO SOME CONDEMNED BUILDINGS...
D33
CHENNEVIERE
WHERE THERE WASN'T A LIVING SOUL—APART FROM THE SHADOWY FIGURES CONVERGING FURTIVELY ON THEIR MUSICAL SAFE HOUSE.

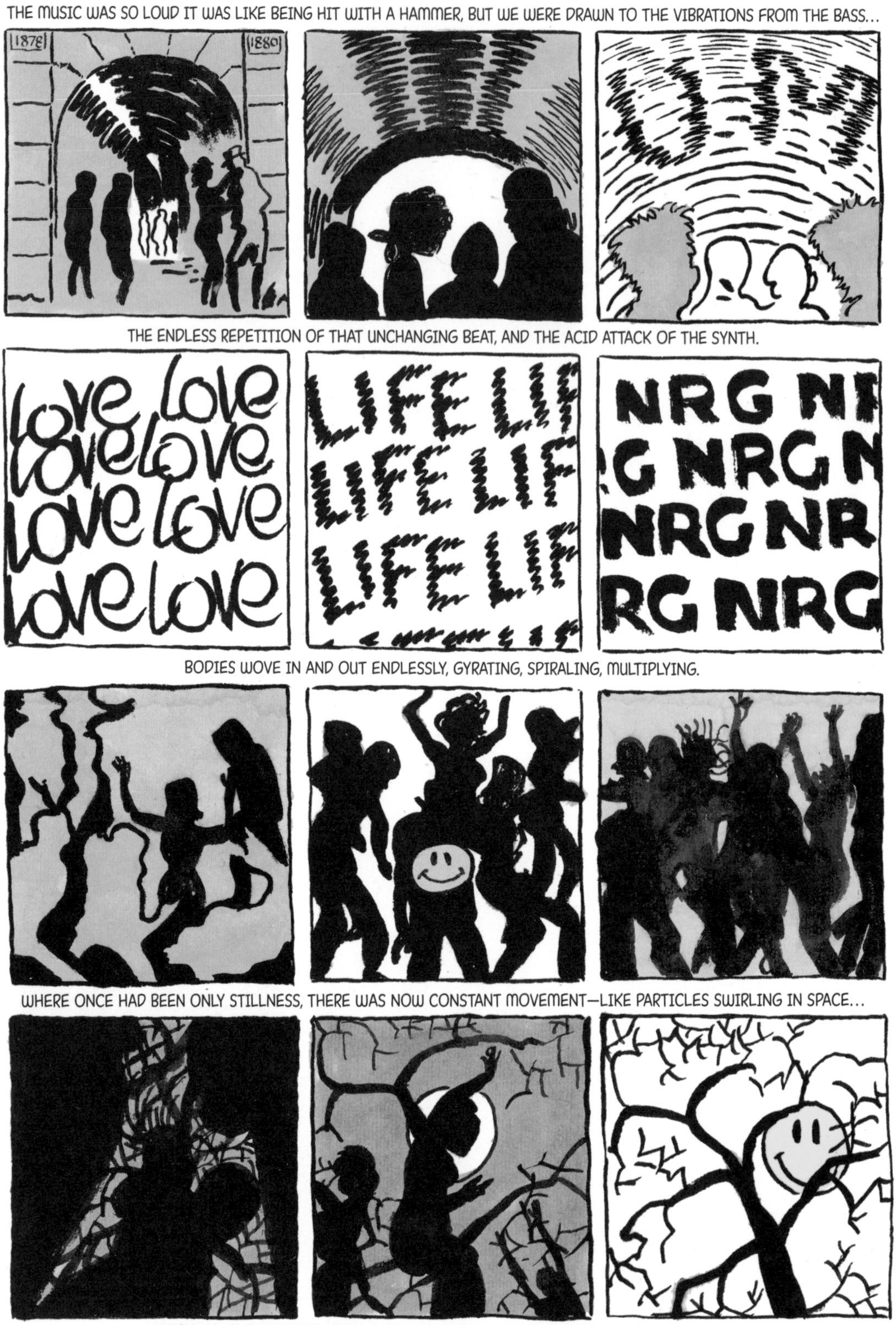
THE MUSIC WAS SO LOUD IT WAS LIKE BEING HIT WITH A HAMMER, BUT WE WERE DRAWN TO THE VIBRATIONS FROM THE BASS...
1878
1880
THE ENDLESS REPETITION OF THAT UNCHANGING BEAT, AND THE ACID ATTACK OF THE SYNTH.
love love love love love love love love
LIFE LIFE LIFE
NRG NRG NRG NRG
BODIES WOVE IN AND OUT ENDLESSLY, GYRATING, SPIRALING, MULTIPLYING.
WHERE ONCE HAD BEEN ONLY STILLNESS, THERE WAS NOW CONSTANT MOVEMENT—LIKE PARTICLES SWIRLING IN SPACE...
WHICH NEVER REST UNTIL THEY SUDDENLY MELT AWAY AT THE FIRST LIGHT OF DAWN.

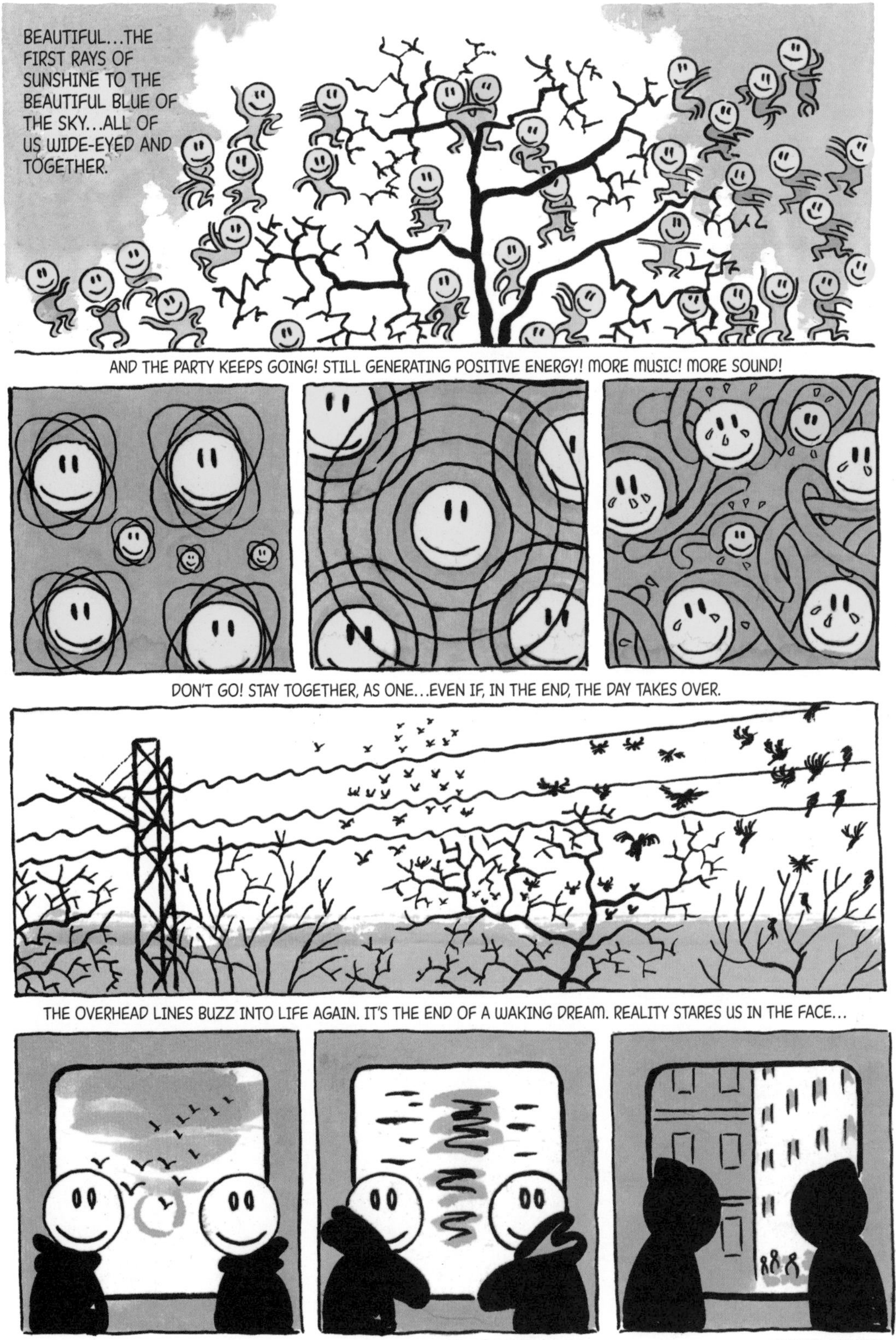
BEAUTIFUL...THE FIRST RAYS OF SUNSHINE TO THE BEAUTIFUL BLUE OF THE SKY...ALL OF US WIDE-EYED AND TOGETHER.
AND THE PARTY KEEPS GOING! STILL GENERATING POSITIVE ENERGY! MORE MUSIC! MORE SOUND!
DON'T GO! STAY TOGETHER, AS ONE...EVEN IF, IN THE END, THE DAY TAKES OVER.
THE OVERHEAD LINES BUZZ INTO LIFE AGAIN. IT'S THE END OF A WAKING DREAM. REALITY STARES US IN THE FACE...
THERE'S NO MORE MUSIC.
AND I'M SCARED.

NOVEMBER 3, 1994: BUCKINGHAM PALACE

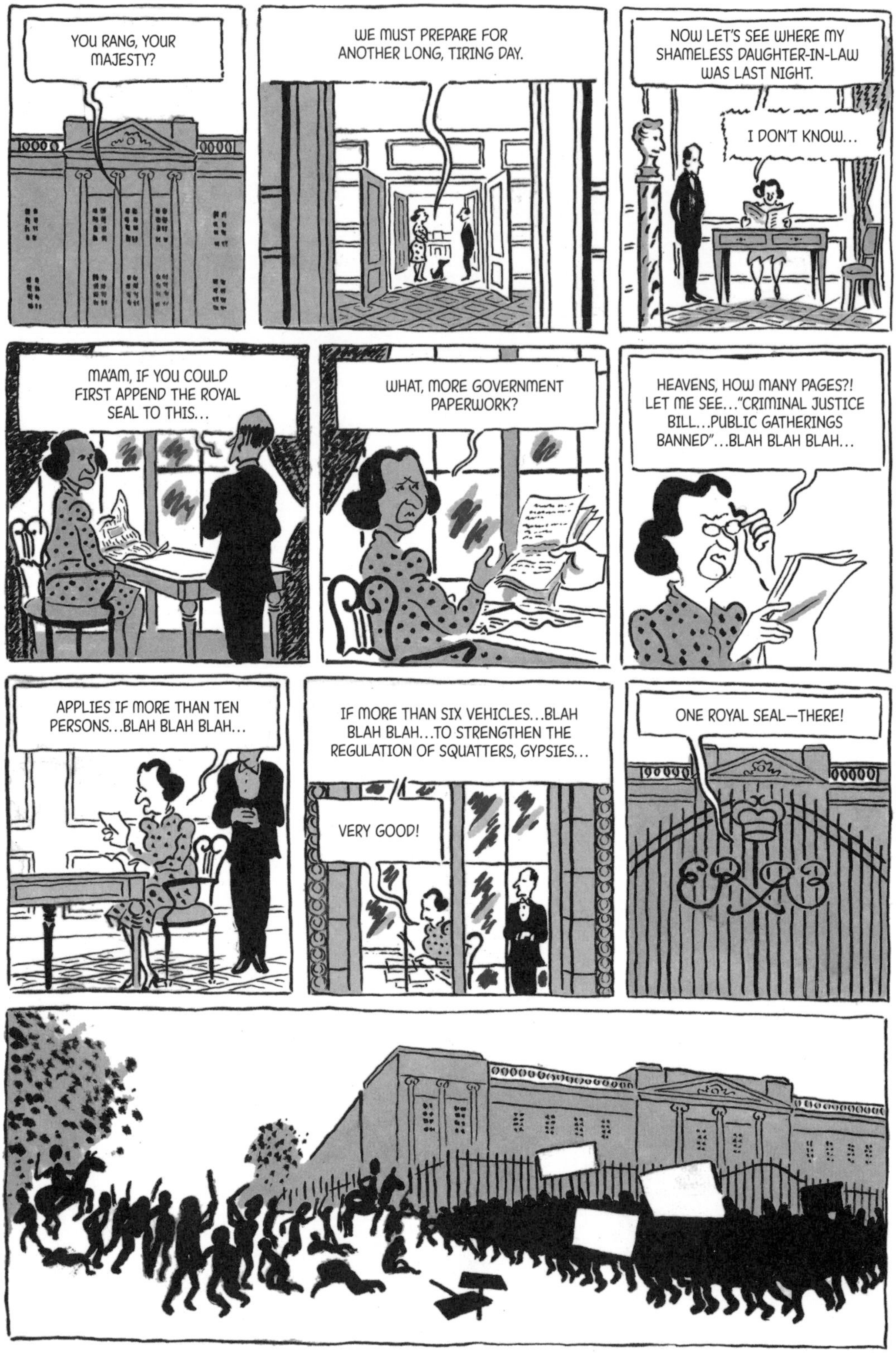
YOU RANG, YOUR MAJESTY?
WE MUST PREPARE FOR ANOTHER LONG, TIRING DAY.
NOW LET'S SEE WHERE MY SHAMELESS DAUGHTER-IN-LAW WAS LAST NIGHT.
I DON'T KNOW...
MA'AM, IF YOU COULD FIRST APPEND THE ROYAL SEAL TO THIS...
WHAT, MORE GOVERNMENT PAPERWORK?
HEAVENS, HOW MANY PAGES?! LET ME SEE..."CRIMINAL JUSTICE BILL...PUBLIC GATHERINGS BANNED"...BLAH BLAH BLAH...
APPLIES IF MORE THAN TEN PERSONS...BLAH BLAH BLAH...
IF MORE THAN SIX VEHICLES...BLAH BLAH BLAH...TO STRENGTHEN THE REGULATION OF SQUATTERS, GYPSIES...
VERY GOOD!
ONE ROYAL SEAL—THERE!

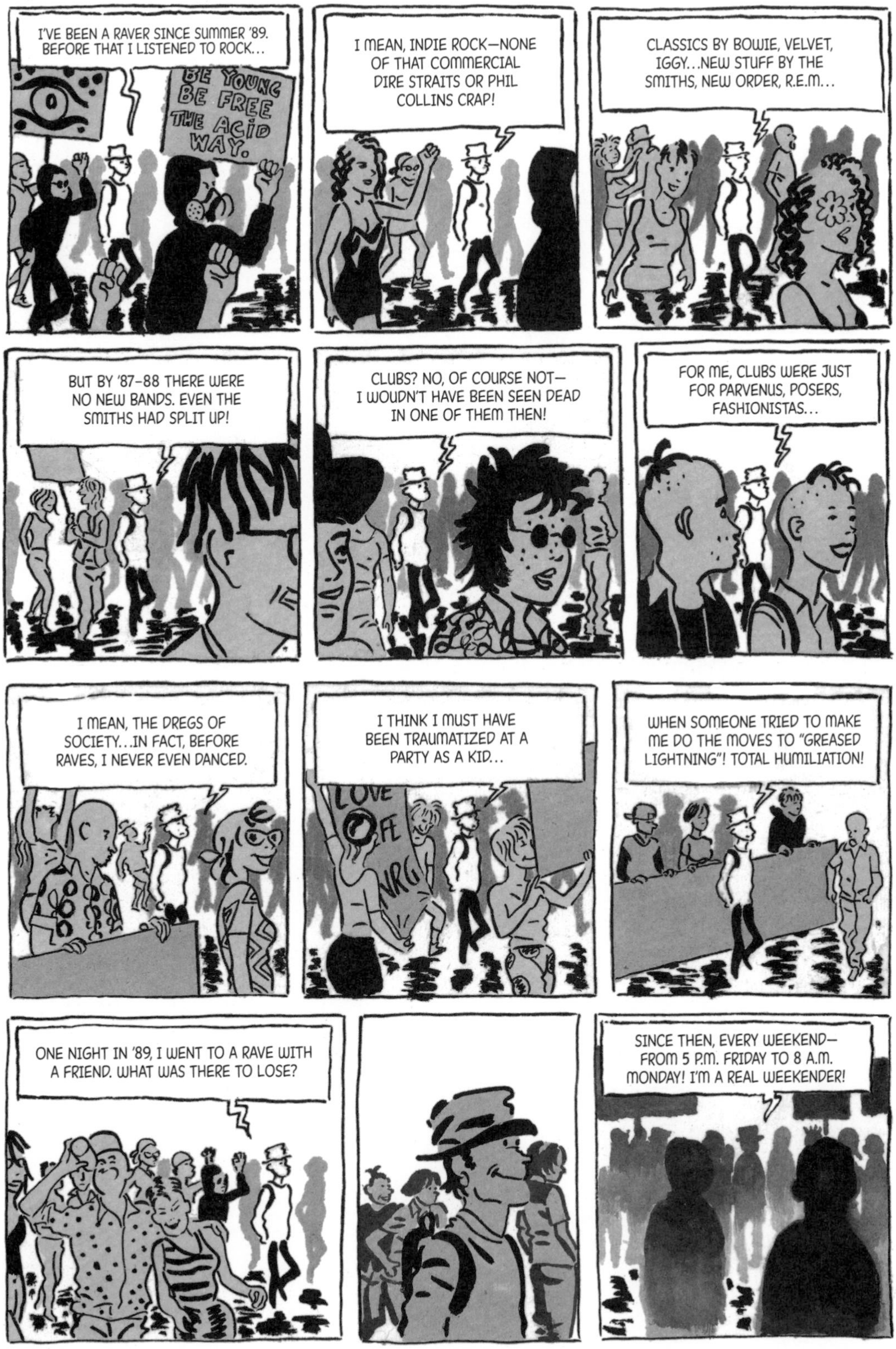
I'VE BEEN A RAVER SINCE SUMMER '89. BEFORE THAT I LISTENED TO ROCK...
BE YOUNG BE FREE THE ACID WAY.
I MEAN, INDIE ROCK—NONE OF THAT COMMERCIAL DIRE STRAITS OR PHIL COLLINS CRAP!
CLASSICS BY BOWIE, VELVET, IGGY...NEW STUFF BY THE SMITHS, NEW ORDER, R.E.M...
BUT BY '87–88 THERE WERE NO NEW BANDS. EVEN THE SMITHS HAD SPLIT UP!
CLUBS? NO, OF COURSE NOT—I WOUDN'T HAVE BEEN SEEN DEAD IN ONE OF THEM THEN!
FOR ME, CLUBS WERE JUST FOR PARVENUS, POSERS, FASHIONISTAS...
I MEAN, THE DREGS OF SOCIETY...IN FACT, BEFORE RAVES, I NEVER EVEN DANCED.
I THINK I MUST HAVE BEEN TRAUMATIZED AT A PARTY AS A KID...
LOVE
WHEN SOMEONE TRIED TO MAKE ME DO THE MOVES TO "GREASED LIGHTNING"! TOTAL HUMILIATION!
ONE NIGHT IN '89, I WENT TO A RAVE WITH A FRIEND. WHAT WAS THERE TO LOSE?
SINCE THEN, EVERY WEEKEND—FROM 5 P.M. FRIDAY TO 8 A.M. MONDAY! I'M A REAL WEEKENDER!

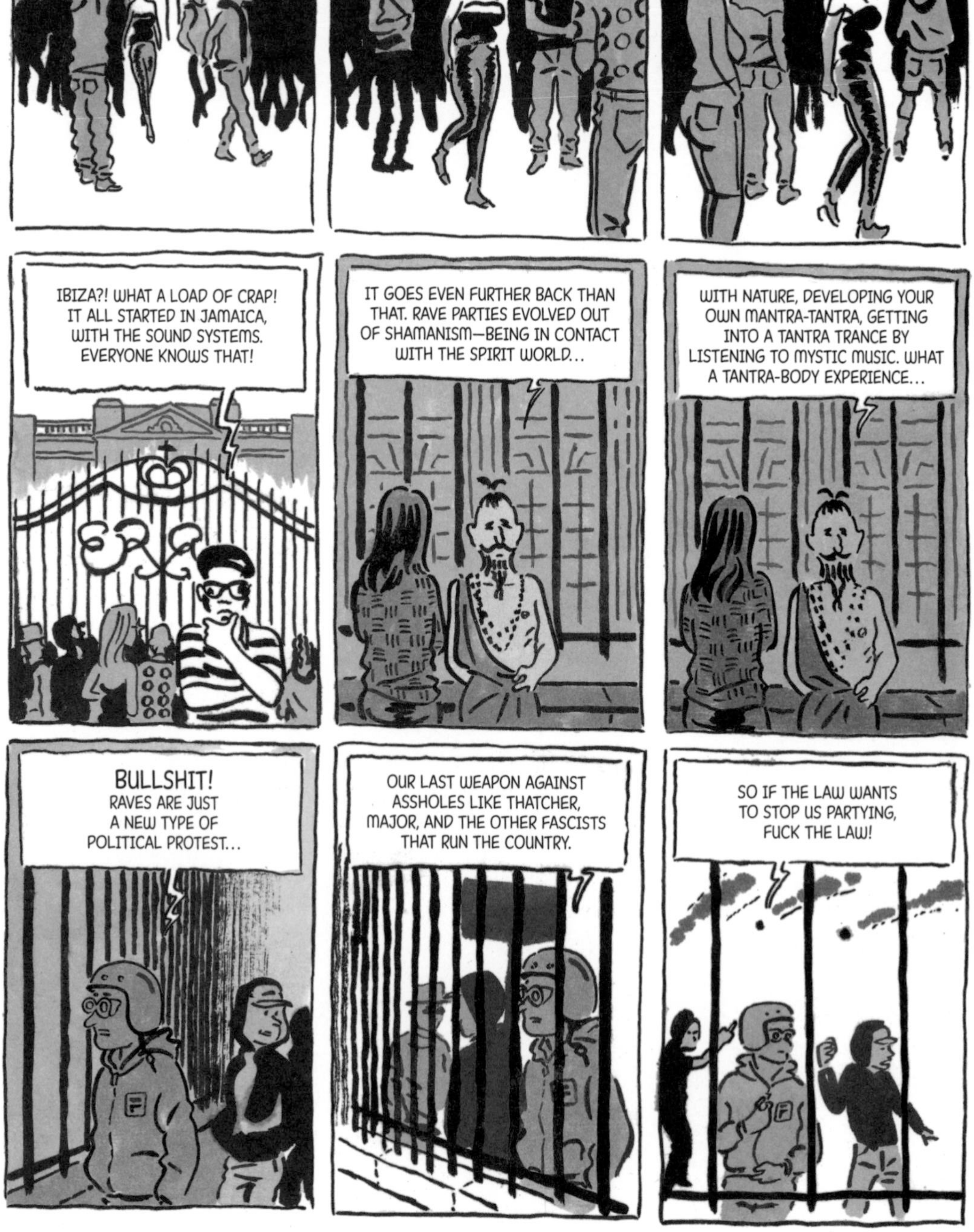
FOR ME, RAVES CAME OUT OF THE IBIZA CRAZE—WHERE WE ALL WENT ON VACATION.
ONCE YOU START PARTYING OUTDOORS, YOU NEVER WANT TO BE SHUT INSIDE A CLUB AGAIN…
SO WHEN WE GOT HOME, WE DECIDED TO DO THE SAME THING OUT IN THE FIELDS!
IBIZA?! WHAT A LOAD OF CRAP! IT ALL STARTED IN JAMAICA, WITH THE SOUND SYSTEMS. EVERYONE KNOWS THAT!
IT GOES EVEN FURTHER BACK THAN THAT. RAVE PARTIES EVOLVED OUT OF SHAMANISM—BEING IN CONTACT WITH THE SPIRIT WORLD…
WITH NATURE, DEVELOPING YOUR OWN MANTRA-TANTRA, GETTING INTO A TANTRA TRANCE BY LISTENING TO MYSTIC MUSIC. WHAT A TANTRA-BODY EXPERIENCE…
BULLSHIT! RAVES ARE JUST A NEW TYPE OF POLITICAL PROTEST…
OUR LAST WEAPON AGAINST ASSHOLES LIKE THATCHER, MAJOR, AND THE OTHER FASCISTS THAT RUN THE COUNTRY.
SO IF THE LAW WANTS TO STOP US PARTYING, FUCK THE LAW!

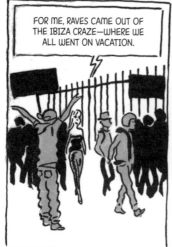

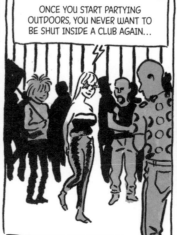

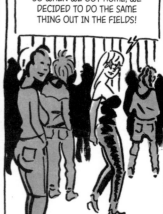

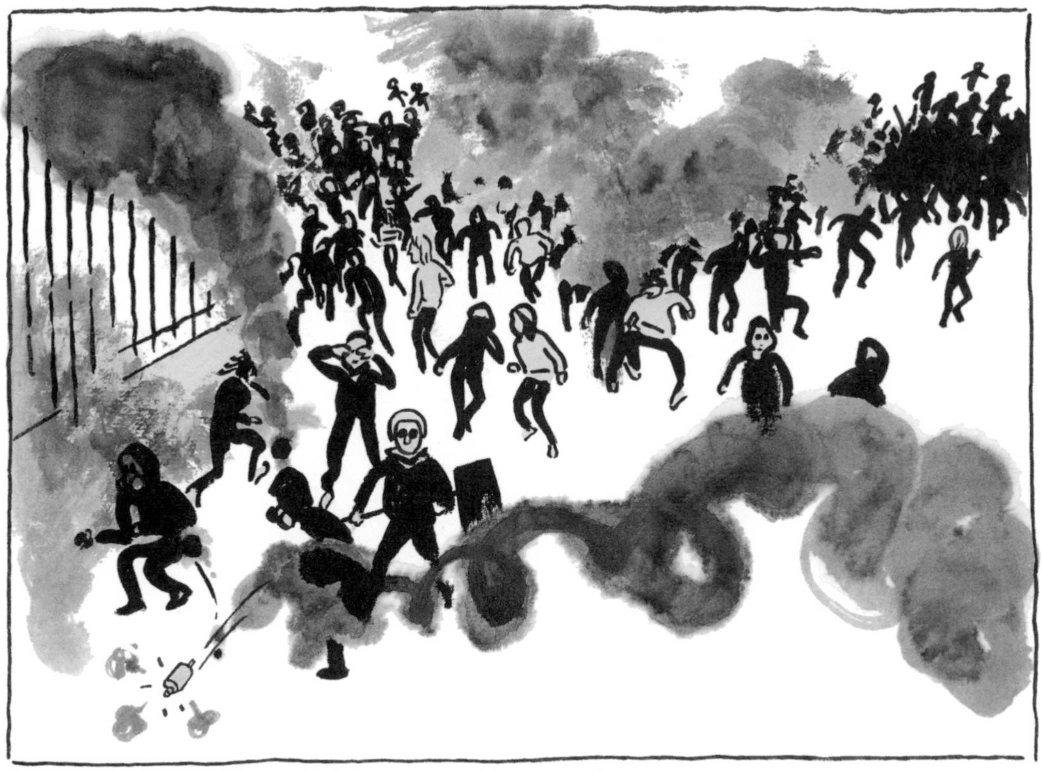

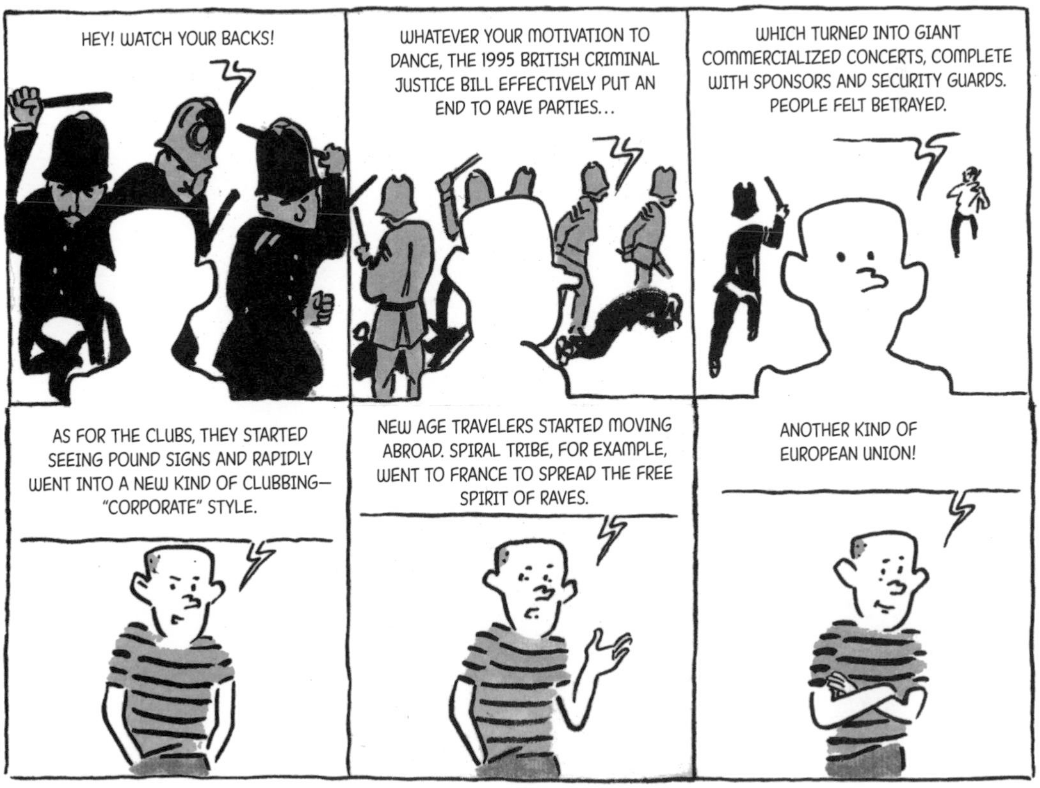
HEY! WATCH YOUR BACKS!
WHATEVER YOUR MOTIVATION TO DANCE, THE 1995 BRITISH CRIMINAL JUSTICE BILL EFFECTIVELY PUT AN END TO RAVE PARTIES...
WHICH TURNED INTO GIANT COMMERCIALIZED CONCERTS, COMPLETE WITH SPONSORS AND SECURITY GUARDS. PEOPLE FELT BETRAYED.
AS FOR THE CLUBS, THEY STARTED SEEING POUND SIGNS AND RAPIDLY WENT INTO A NEW KIND OF CLUBBING—"CORPORATE" STYLE.
NEW AGE TRAVELERS STARTED MOVING ABROAD. SPIRAL TRIBE, FOR EXAMPLE, WENT TO FRANCE TO SPREAD THE FREE SPIRIT OF RAVES.
ANOTHER KIND OF EUROPEAN UNION!

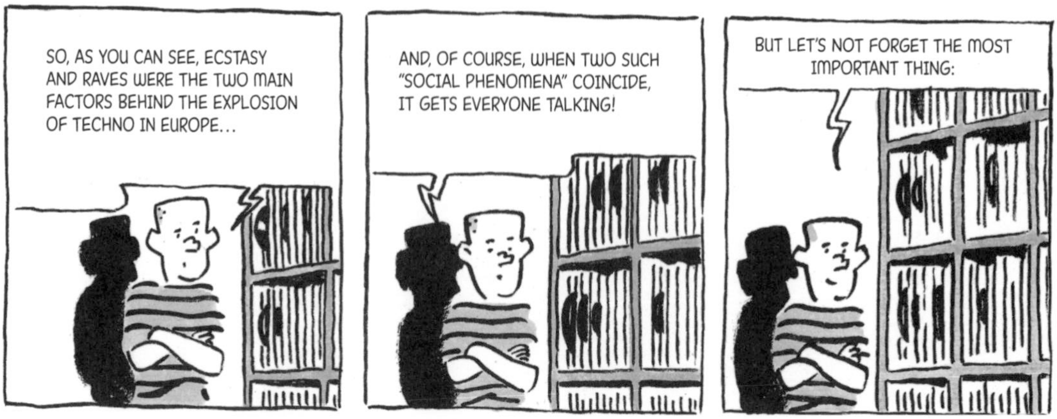
SO, AS YOU CAN SEE, ECSTASY AND RAVES WERE THE TWO MAIN FACTORS BEHIND THE EXPLOSION OF TECHNO IN EUROPE...
AND, OF COURSE, WHEN TWO SUCH "SOCIAL PHENOMENA" COINCIDE, IT GETS EVERYONE TALKING!
BUT LET'S NOT FORGET THE MOST IMPORTANT THING:

IN THE U.K., HOUSE WASN'T SOMETHING THAT HAD BEEN CREATED AND LIVED THROUGH; IT HAD BEEN IMPORTED FROM THE STATES, LIKE HIP-HOP, DISCO, ROCK, FUNK, AND JAZZ BEFORE IT. ALL THE EARLY U.K. HITS WERE AMERICAN, INITIALLY FROM CHICAGO—LARRY HEARD AND HIS DEEP HOUSE, DJ PIERRE AND ACID HOUSE, NOT FORGETTING LIL LOUIS BLOWING EVERYONE AWAY WITH HIS MULTI-MILLION-SELLING "FRENCH KISS."

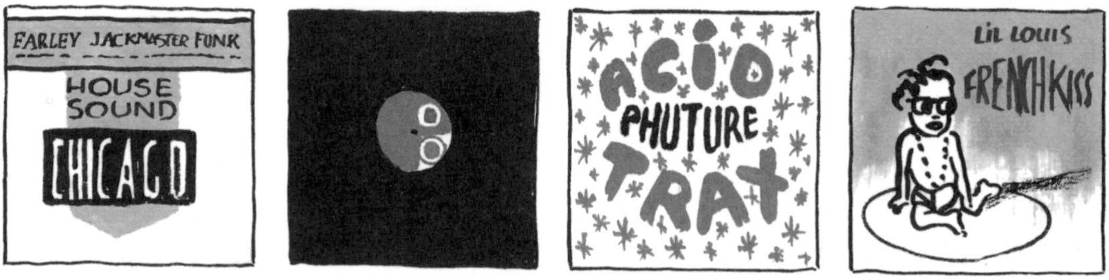
EARLEY JACKMASTER FUNK
HOUSE SOUND
CHICAGO
ACID
PHUTURE
TRAX
LIL LOUIS
FRENCH KISS

IN DETROIT, TECHNO WAS ENNOBLED BY "STRINGS OF LIFE," DERRICK MAY'S CLASSIC RAVE SONG—AKA FUTURISTIC INNER-CITY SOUL. IN NEW JERSEY, TONY HUMPHRIES ESTABLISHED HIMSELF AT CLUB ZANZIBAR, AND BLAZE WAS FORMED. AND FINALLY, IN NEW YORK, TODD TERRY OBLITERATED THE ENTIRE ELECTRO LEGACY SOMEWHERE BETWEEN HIP-HOP AND HOUSE. ALL OF THESE WENT TO THE TOP OF THE U.K. CHARTS...

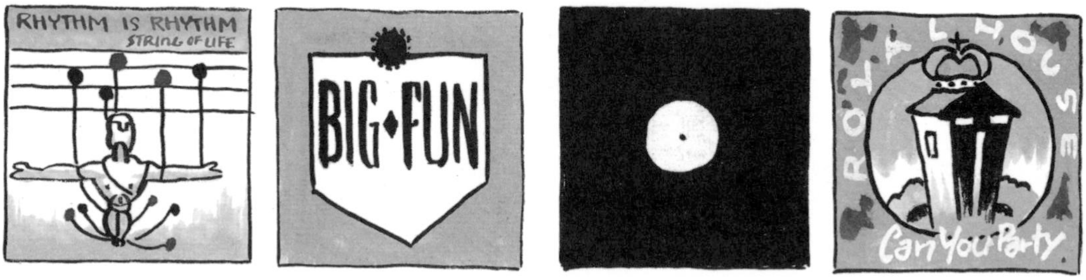
RHYTHM IS RHYTHM
STRING OF LIFE
BIG FUN
ROYAL HOUSE
Can You Party.

FROM LONDON, THE VISIONARY "PUMP UP THE VOLUME" BY M|A|R|R|S LED TO HOUSE BECOMING 100% SAMPLED, ALLOWING KNOB-TWIDDLERS LIKE COLDCUT AND THE WHOLE RHYTHM KING RECORDS STABLE TO MAKE BIG HITS.

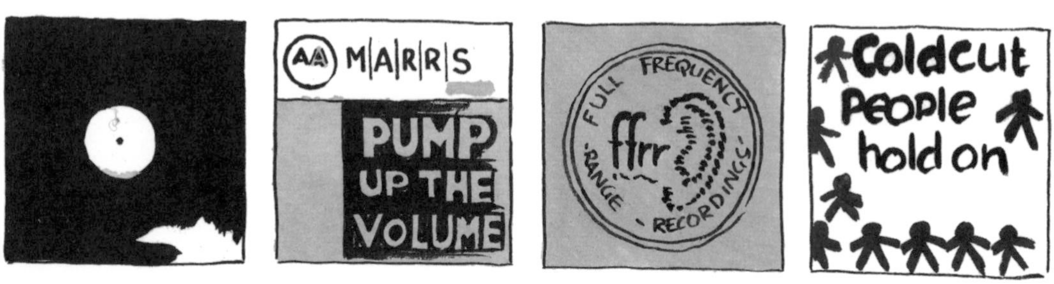
AA M|A|R|R|S
PUMP UP THE VOLUME
FULL FREQUENCY RANGE RECORDINGS
ffrr
Coldcut
People hold on

S'EXPRESS AND BOMB THE BASS PRODUCED THEIR EARLY HITS, WHEN SAMPLING WAS IN ITS INFANCY AND COULD BE FORGIVEN FOR ANYTHING, AND THE GOOD OLD '70S SMILEY, REINVENTED BY MOORE AND GIBBONS IN THE *WATCHMEN* COMIC BOOKS, BECAME THE SYMBOL OF ACID HOUSE—A NEW LONDON CULTURE DRIVEN BY THE TRENDY MEDIA…CAUGHT BETWEEN THE HYPE AND THE POLITIC, THE YOUTH OF THE U.K. DIDN'T (YET) KNOW WHICH WAY TO DANCE.

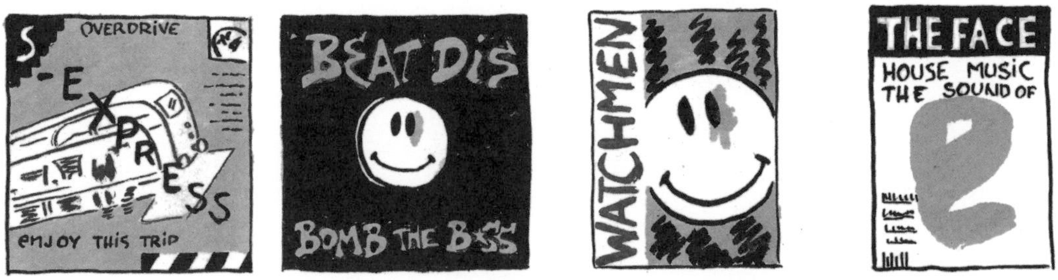
OVERDRIVE
S-EXPRESS
ENJOY THIS TRIP
BEAT DIS
WATCHMEN
THE FACE
HOUSE MUSIC
THE SOUND OF
e

BUT IF HOUSE WAS TO CONVERT A WHOLE GENERATION OF PARTY PEOPLE RAISED ON GUITAR-LED INDIE ROCK, IT NEEDED A WORLDWIDE POPULAR IMPULSE, A THIRD "SOCIAL PHENOMENON": ENTER, MANCHESTER! HOME OF THE SMITHS, THE NORTHERN INDUSTRIAL CITY BECAME THE EPICENTER OF RAVE CULTURE—MINUS THE SOUTHERN SNOBBERY OF THE CAPITAL. HOUSE HAD FOUND A HOME.

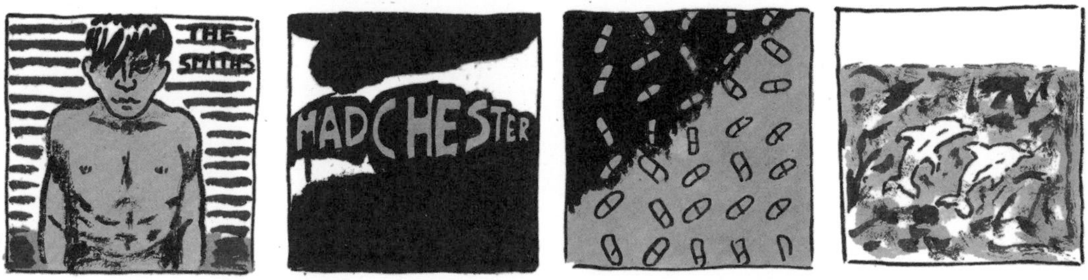
THE SMITHS
MADCHESTER

ALL OF ENGLAND WENT "MADCHESTER." EVEN ROCKERS LIKE THE STONE ROSES AND PRIMAL SCREAM JOINED THE PARTY. THE CROSSOVER WAS COMPLETE. HOUSE HAD WRAPPED ITSELF AROUND ROCK, AND ITS TENTACLES NOW SPREAD FAR AND WIDE. 808 STATE AND ORBITAL WERE AMONG THE LEADING HOUSE BANDS.

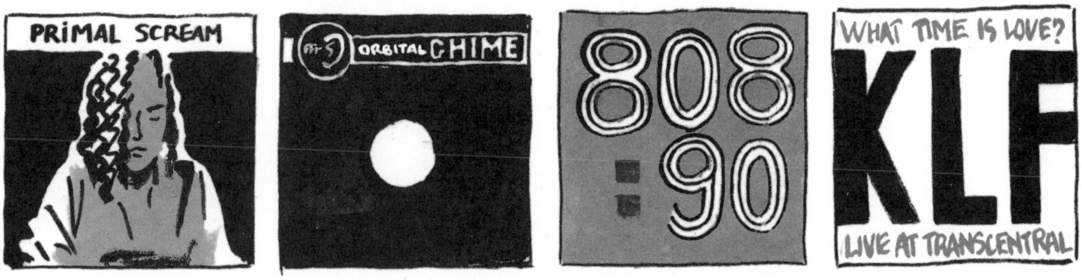
PRIMAL SCREAM
ORBITAL CHIME
808
90
WHAT TIME IS LOVE?
KLF
LIVE AT TRANSCENTRAL

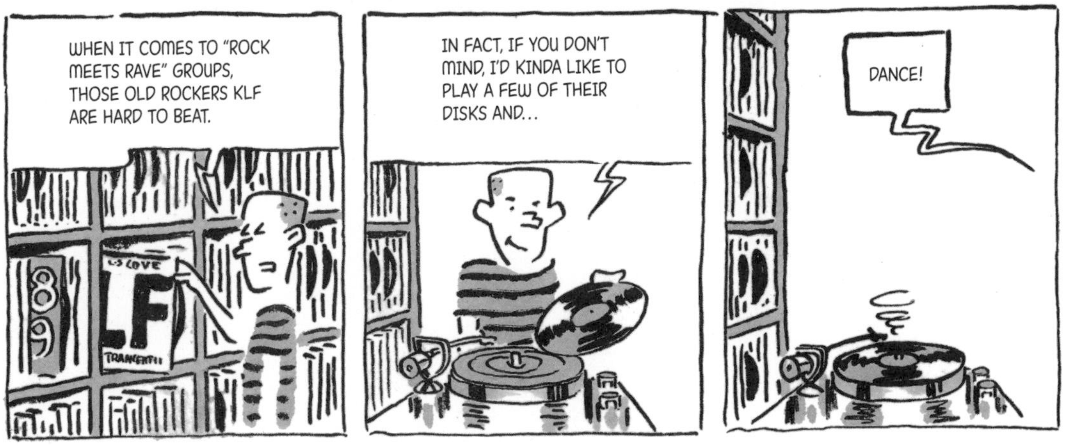
WHEN IT COMES TO "ROCK MEETS RAVE" GROUPS, THOSE OLD ROCKERS KLF ARE HARD TO BEAT.
KLF
IN FACT, IF YOU DON'T MIND, I'D KINDA LIKE TO PLAY A FEW OF THEIR DISKS AND…
DANCE!

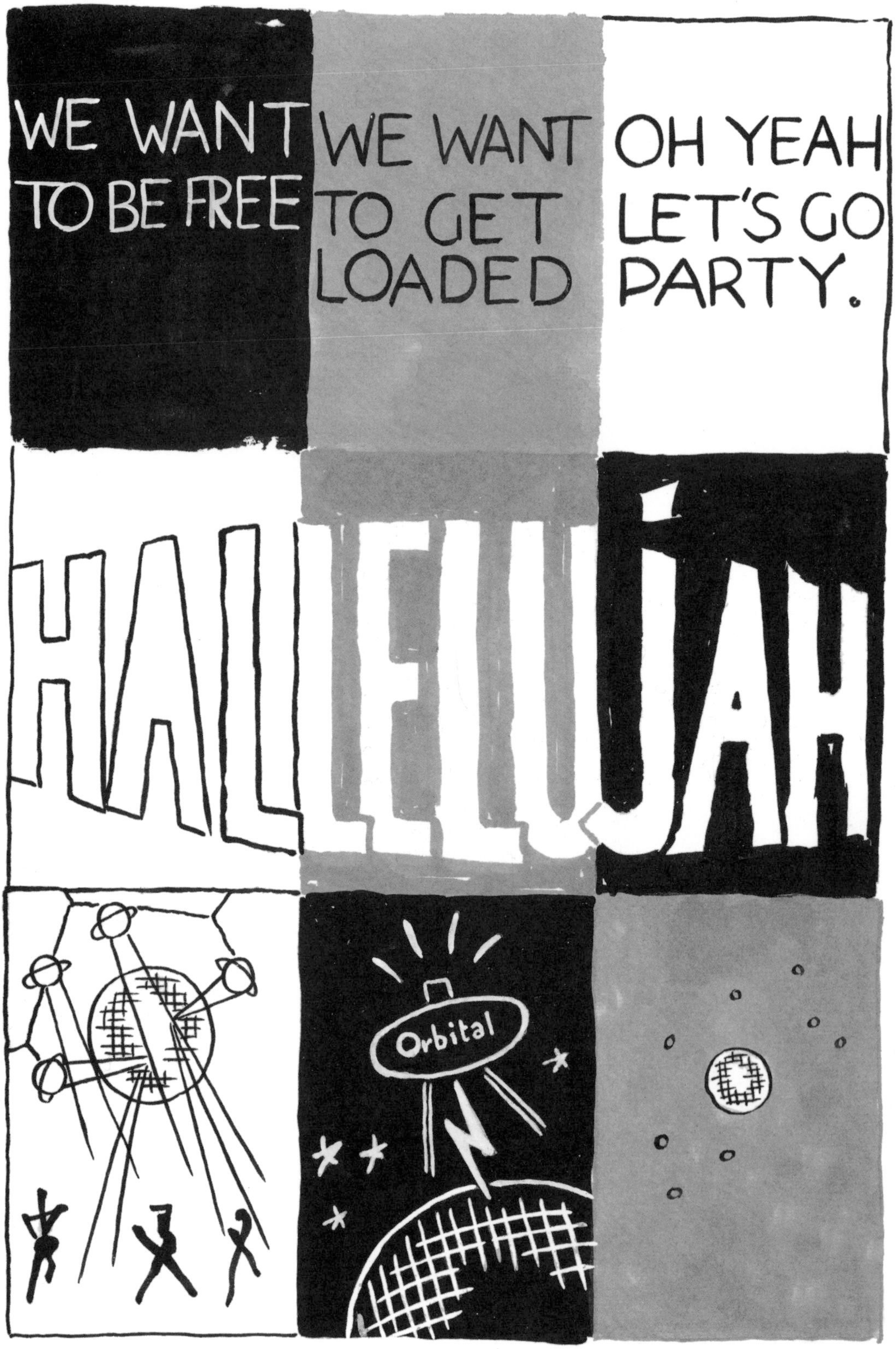
WE WANT TO BE FREE
WE WANT TO GET LOADED
OH YEAH LET'S GO PARTY.
HALLELUJAH
Orbital

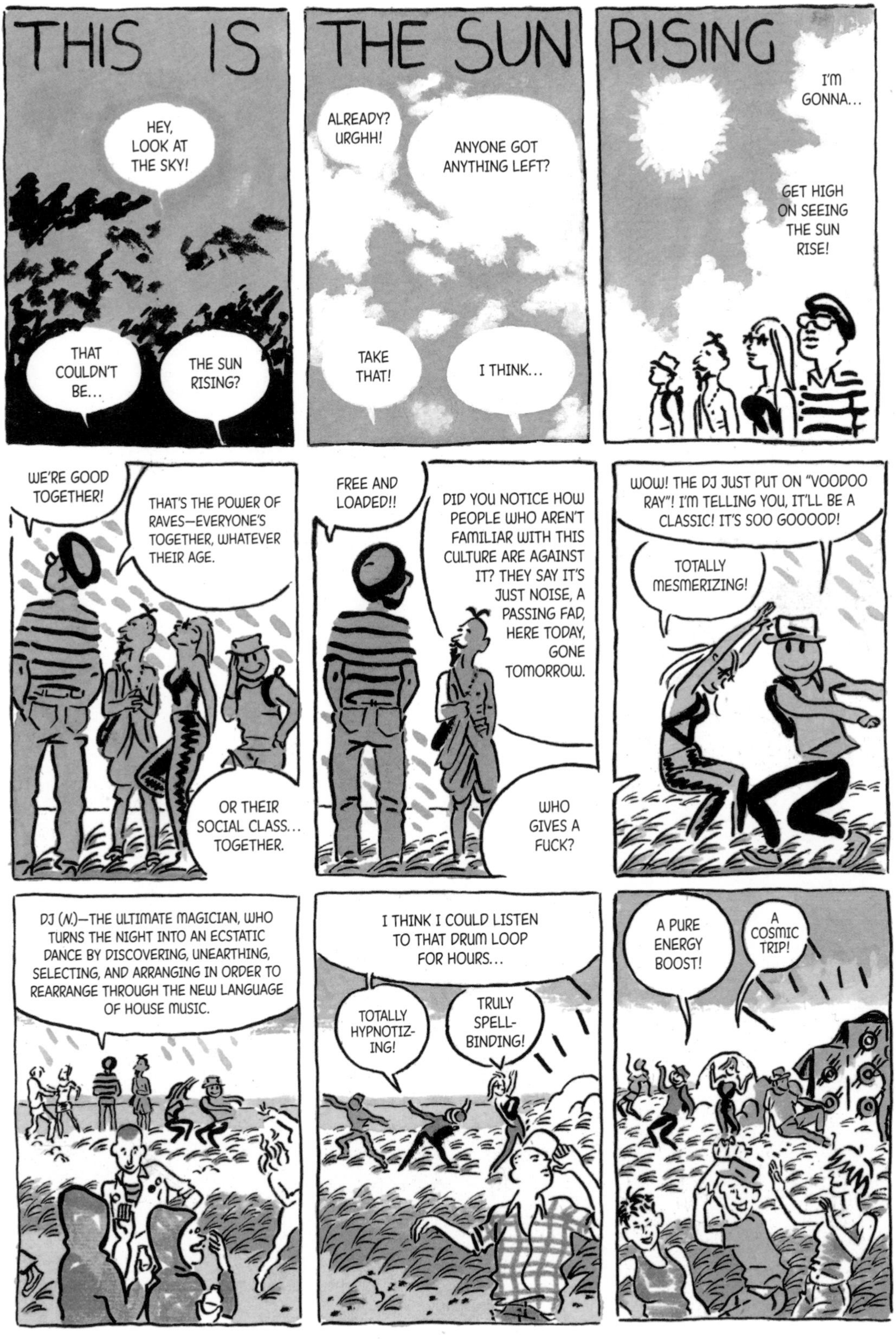
THIS IS
HEY, LOOK AT THE SKY!
THAT COULDN'T BE...
THE SUN RISING?
THE SUN
ALREADY? URGHH!
ANYONE GOT ANYTHING LEFT?
TAKE THAT!
I THINK...
RISING
I'M GONNA...
GET HIGH ON SEEING THE SUN RISE!
WE'RE GOOD TOGETHER!
THAT'S THE POWER OF RAVES—EVERYONE'S TOGETHER, WHATEVER THEIR AGE.
OR THEIR SOCIAL CLASS... TOGETHER.
FREE AND LOADED!!
DID YOU NOTICE HOW PEOPLE WHO AREN'T FAMILIAR WITH THIS CULTURE ARE AGAINST IT? THEY SAY IT'S JUST NOISE, A PASSING FAD, HERE TODAY, GONE TOMORROW.
WHO GIVES A FUCK?
WOW! THE DJ JUST PUT ON "VOODOO RAY"! I'M TELLING YOU, IT'LL BE A CLASSIC! IT'S SOO GOOOOD!
TOTALLY MESMERIZING!
DJ (N.)—THE ULTIMATE MAGICIAN, WHO TURNS THE NIGHT INTO AN ECSTATIC DANCE BY DISCOVERING, UNEARTHING, SELECTING, AND ARRANGING IN ORDER TO REARRANGE THROUGH THE NEW LANGUAGE OF HOUSE MUSIC.
I THINK I COULD LISTEN TO THAT DRUM LOOP FOR HOURS...
TOTALLY HYPNOTIZ-ING!
TRULY SPELL-BINDING!
A PURE ENERGY BOOST!
A COSMIC TRIP!

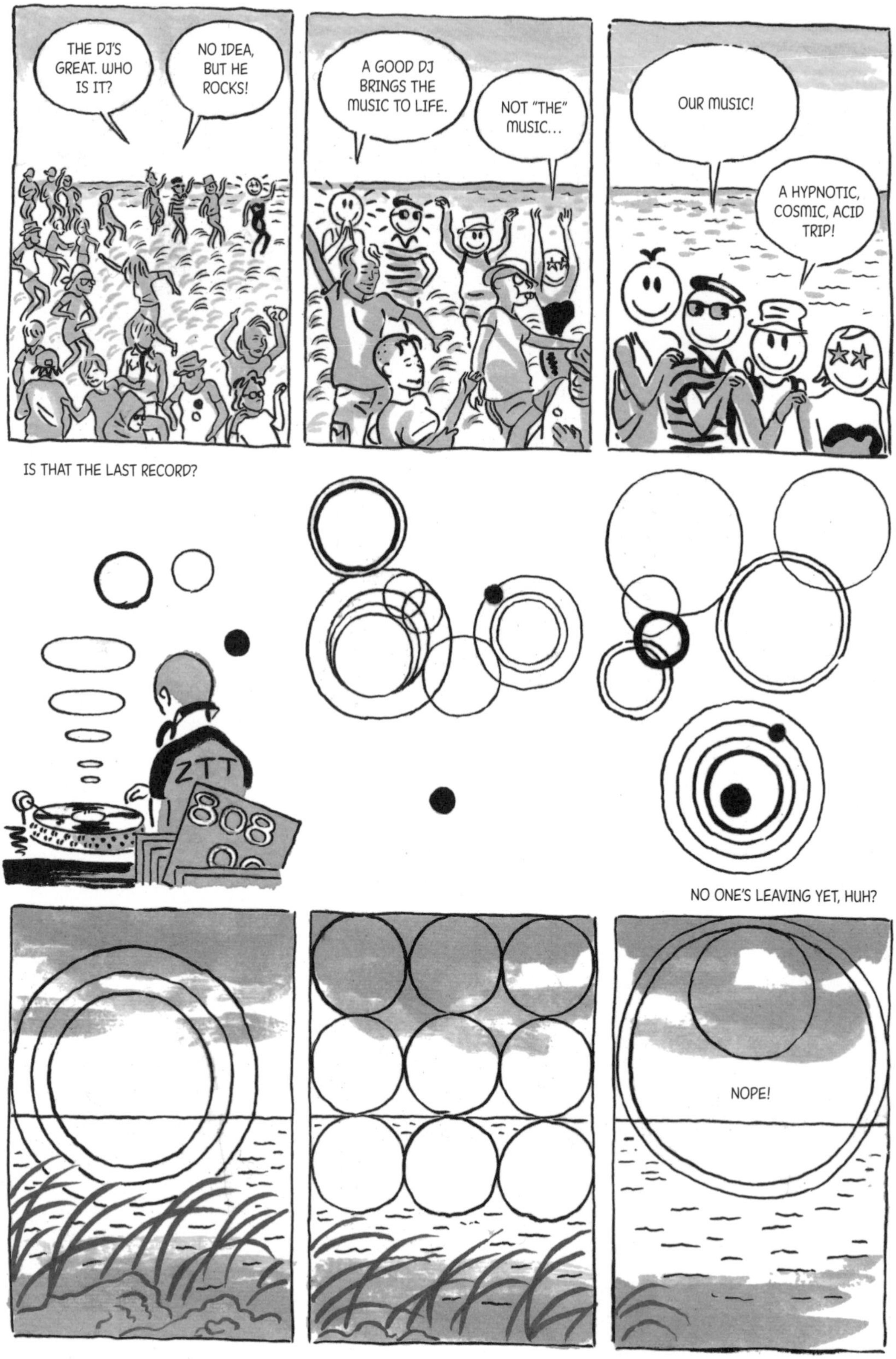
THE DJ'S GREAT. WHO IS IT?
NO IDEA, BUT HE ROCKS!
A GOOD DJ BRINGS THE MUSIC TO LIFE.
NOT "THE" MUSIC...
OUR MUSIC!
A HYPNOTIC, COSMIC, ACID TRIP!
IS THAT THE LAST RECORD?
ZTT
808
NO ONE'S LEAVING YET, HUH?
NOPE!

CHAPTER 9

REMEMBERING STANLEY ROSE

GARAGE, DEEP, AND HOUSE SELECTION

Arnold Jarvis and Tommy Musto
Take Some Time Out — 1987

Phase II (Blaze)
Reachin' — 1988

The Todd Terry Project
To the Batmobile Let's Go (LP) — 1988

Ten City and Marshall Jefferson
Foundation (LP) — 1989

Teulé
Drink on Me (Kerri Chandler Club Mix) — 1990

Robert Owens
I'll Be Your Friend (Glamorous Mix) — 1992

Lil Louis and The World
Journey with the Lonely (LP) — 1992

Jaydee
Plastic Dreams — 1992

Nuyorican Soul (Masters at Work)
The Nervous Track — 1993

4th Measure Men
4 You (Mark Kinchen Remix) — 1993

Hardive (Masters at Work)
Deep Inside (dub) — 1993

Erick Morillo
Dancing (A Little More Dub) — 1994

Chanté Moore
This Time (Frankie Knuckles Bomb Mix) — 1995

KenLou (Masters at Work)
What a Sensation — 1995

Funky People (Blaze)
The Blaze Tracks (EP) — 1995

Moodymann
The Day We Lost Soul
(original Marvin Gaye Intro Version) — 1995

Romanthony
Romanworld (LP) — 1996

Mood II Swing
All Night Long — 1996

Kerri Chandler
Rain (Mood EP Version) — 1998

Kimara Lovelace
When Can Our Love Begin (Timmy Regisford Shelter Anthem) — 1998

Kings of Tomorrow feat. Julie McKnight
Finally — 2000

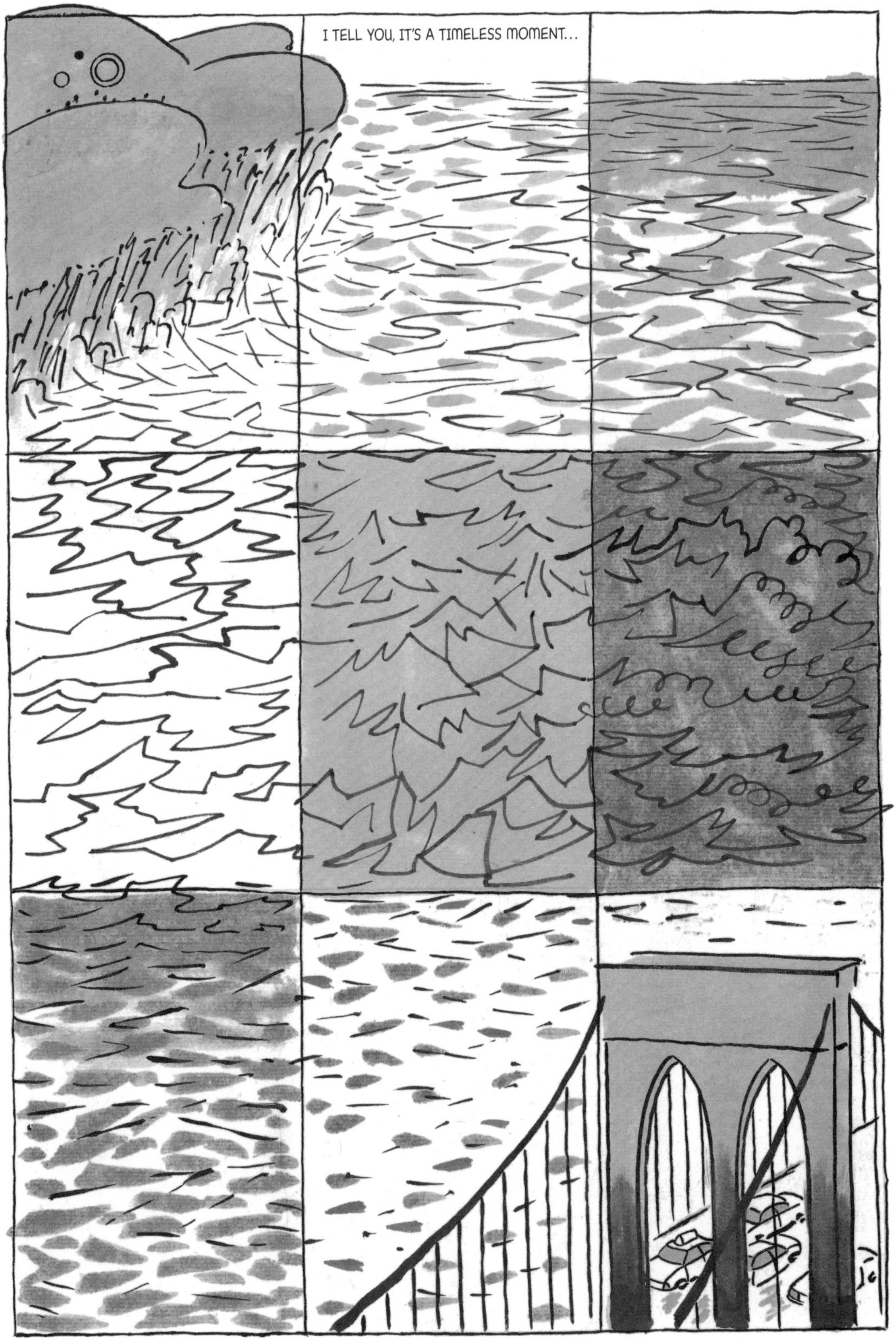
I TELL YOU, IT'S A TIMELESS MOMENT...

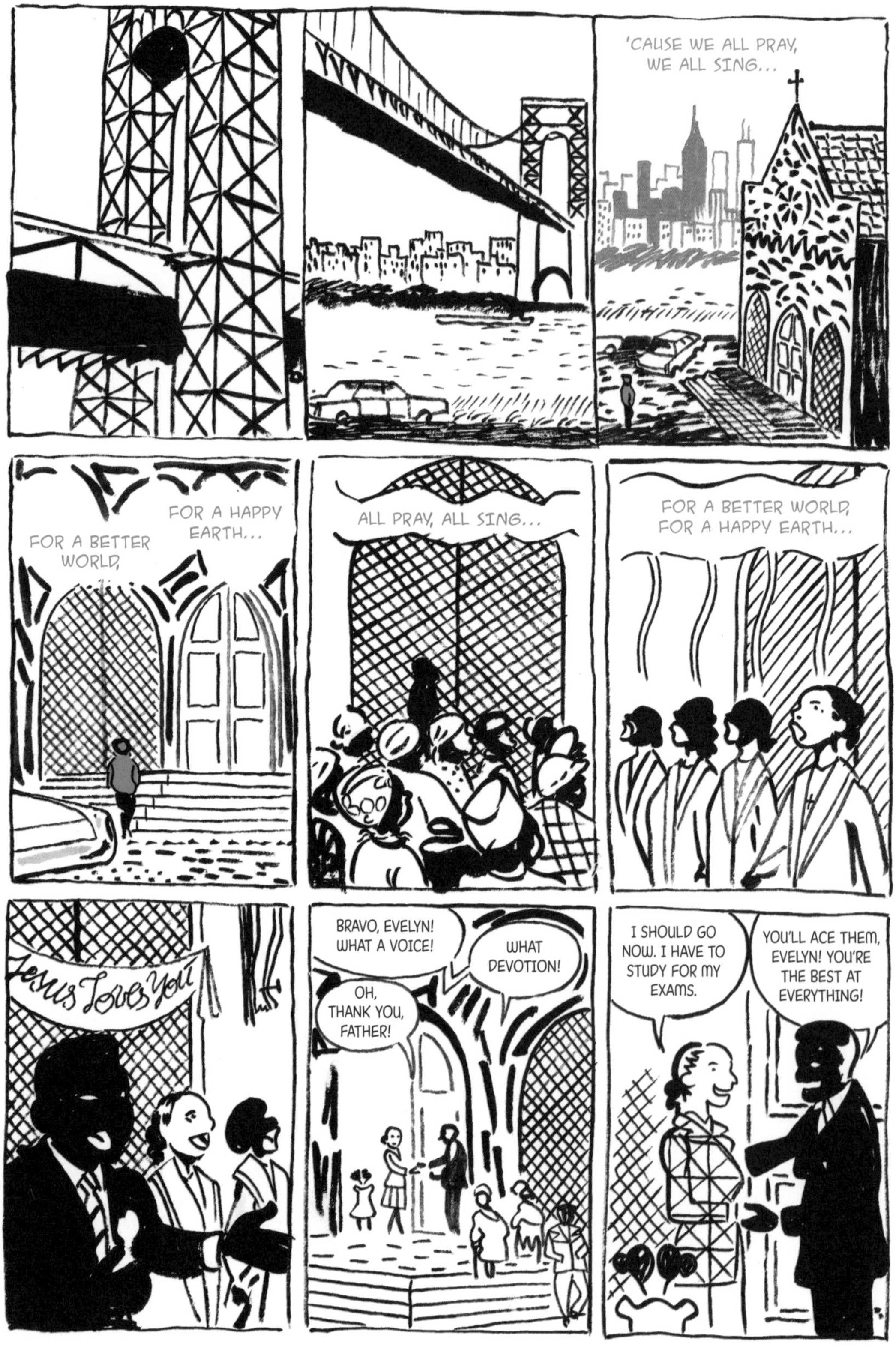
'CAUSE WE ALL PRAY, WE ALL SING...
FOR A BETTER WORLD,
FOR A HAPPY EARTH...
ALL PRAY, ALL SING...
FOR A BETTER WORLD, FOR A HAPPY EARTH...
Jesus Loves You
BRAVO, EVELYN! WHAT A VOICE!
WHAT DEVOTION!
OH, THANK YOU, FATHER!
I SHOULD GO NOW. I HAVE TO STUDY FOR MY EXAMS.
YOU'LL ACE THEM, EVELYN! YOU'RE THE BEST AT EVERYTHING!

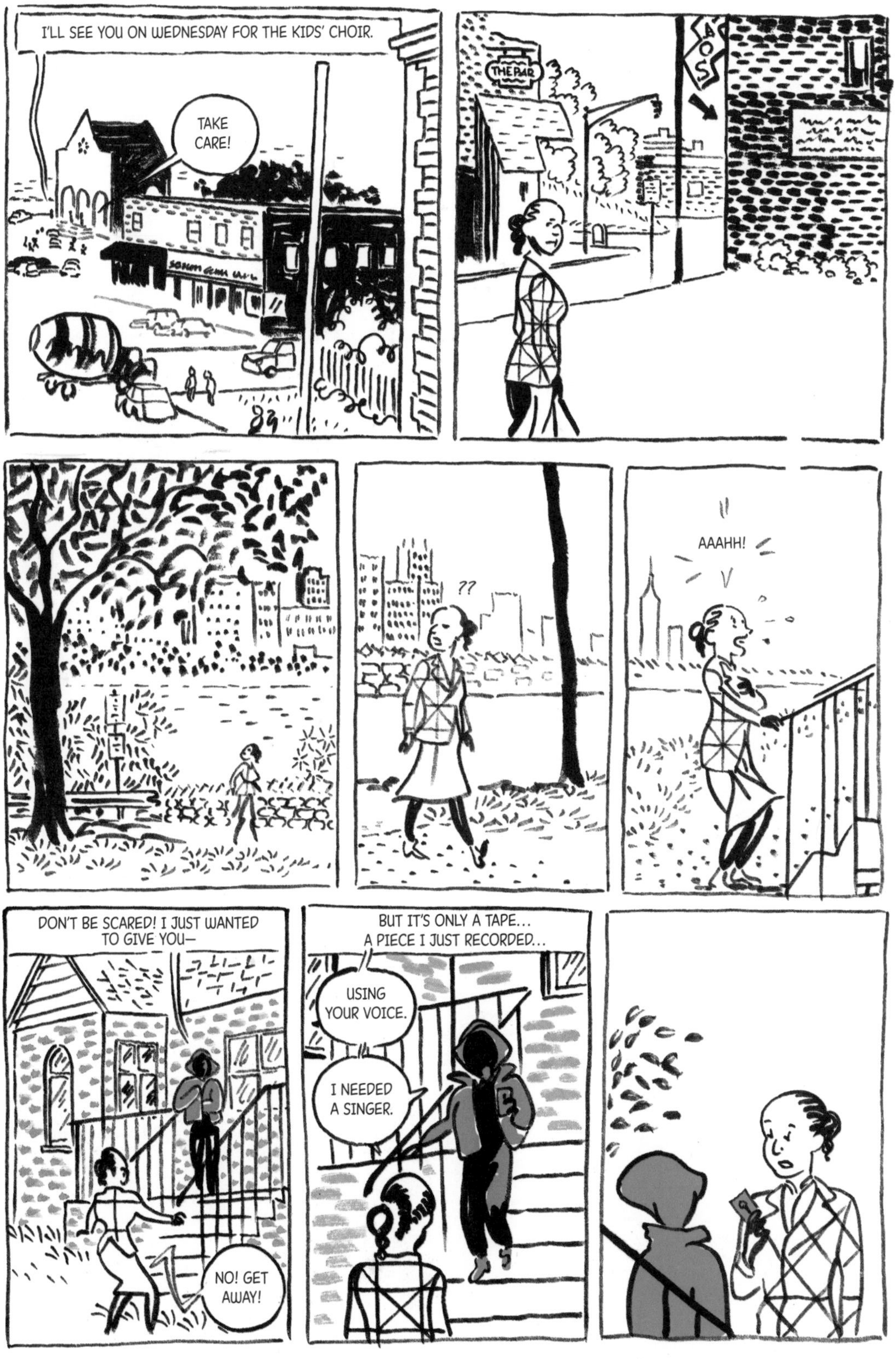
I'LL SEE YOU ON WEDNESDAY FOR THE KIDS' CHOIR.
TAKE CARE!
THE PAR
??
AAAHH!
DON'T BE SCARED! I JUST WANTED TO GIVE YOU—
NO! GET AWAY!
BUT IT'S ONLY A TAPE... A PIECE I JUST RECORDED...
USING YOUR VOICE.
I NEEDED A SINGER.

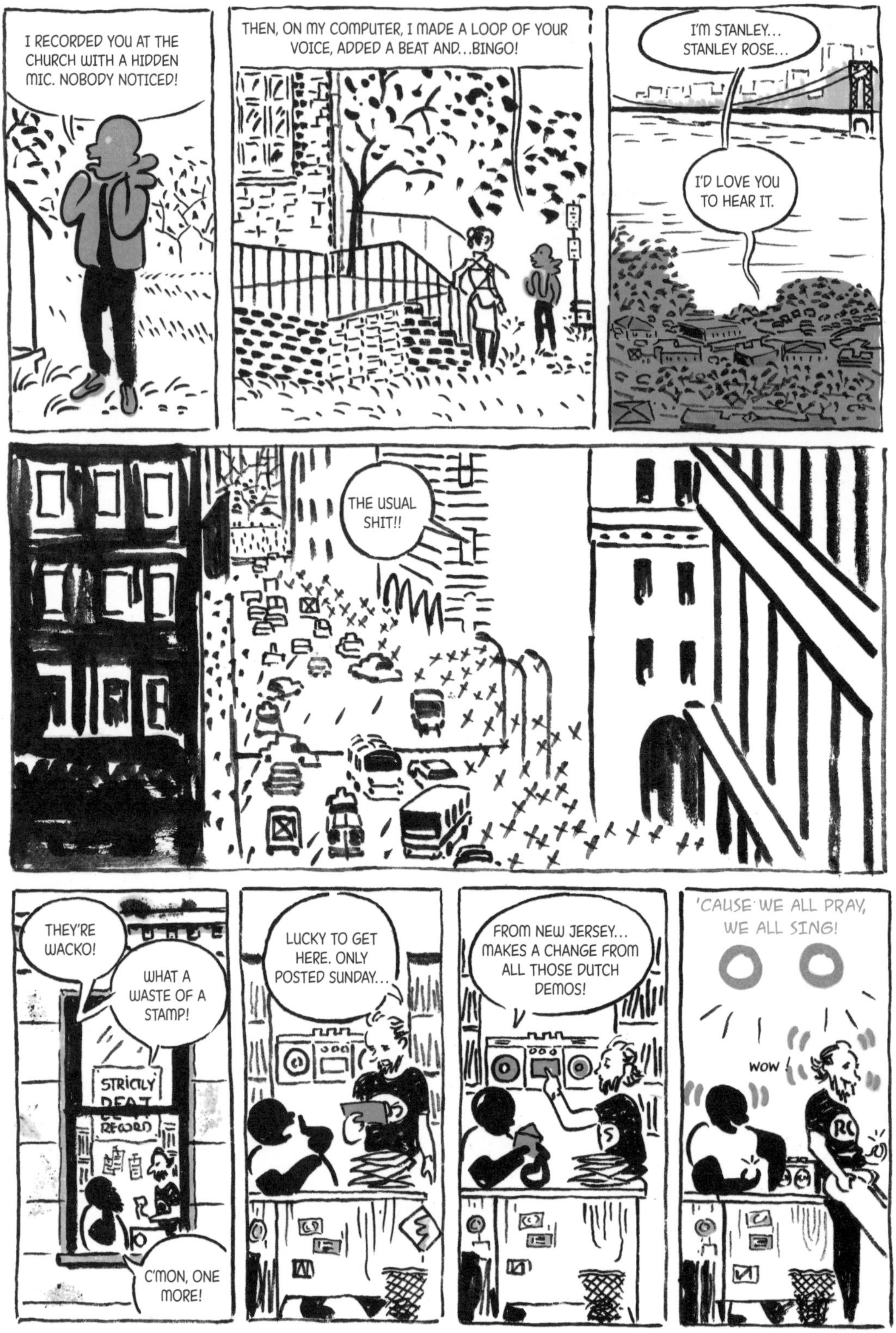
I RECORDED YOU AT THE CHURCH WITH A HIDDEN MIC. NOBODY NOTICED!
THEN, ON MY COMPUTER, I MADE A LOOP OF YOUR VOICE, ADDED A BEAT AND...BINGO!
I'M STANLEY... STANLEY ROSE...
I'D LOVE YOU TO HEAR IT.
THE USUAL SHIT!!
THEY'RE WACKO!
WHAT A WASTE OF A STAMP!
STRICTLY
C'MON, ONE MORE!
LUCKY TO GET HERE. ONLY POSTED SUNDAY...
FROM NEW JERSEY... MAKES A CHANGE FROM ALL THOSE DUTCH DEMOS!
'CAUSE WE ALL PRAY, WE ALL SING!
WOW!

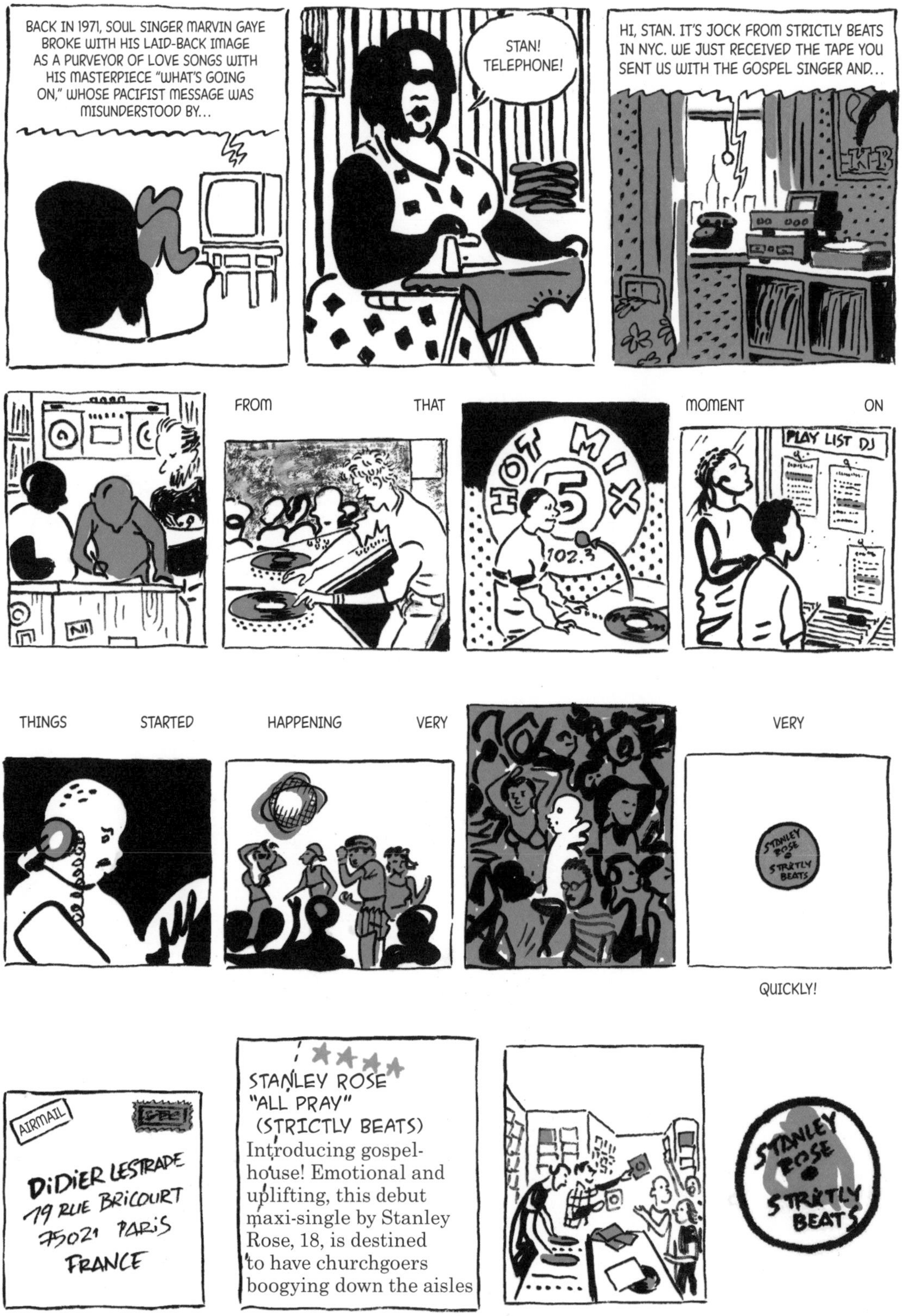
BACK IN 1971, SOUL SINGER MARVIN GAYE BROKE WITH HIS LAID-BACK IMAGE AS A PURVEYOR OF LOVE SONGS WITH HIS MASTERPIECE "WHAT'S GOING ON," WHOSE PACIFIST MESSAGE WAS MISUNDERSTOOD BY...
STAN! TELEPHONE!
HI, STAN. IT'S JOCK FROM STRICTLY BEATS IN NYC. WE JUST RECEIVED THE TAPE YOU SENT US WITH THE GOSPEL SINGER AND...
KB
FROM
THAT
HOT MIX 5
102.3
MOMENT
ON
PLAY LIST DJ
THINGS
STARTED
HAPPENING
VERY
VERY
STANLEY ROSE STRICTLY BEATS
QUICKLY!
AIRMAIL
DIDIER LESTRADE
79 RUE BRICOURT
75021 PARIS
FRANCE
STANLEY ROSE
"ALL PRAY"
(STRICTLY BEATS)
Introducing gospel-house! Emotional and uplifting, this debut maxi-single by Stanley Rose, 18, is destined to have churchgoers boogying down the aisles
STANLEY ROSE STRICTLY BEATS

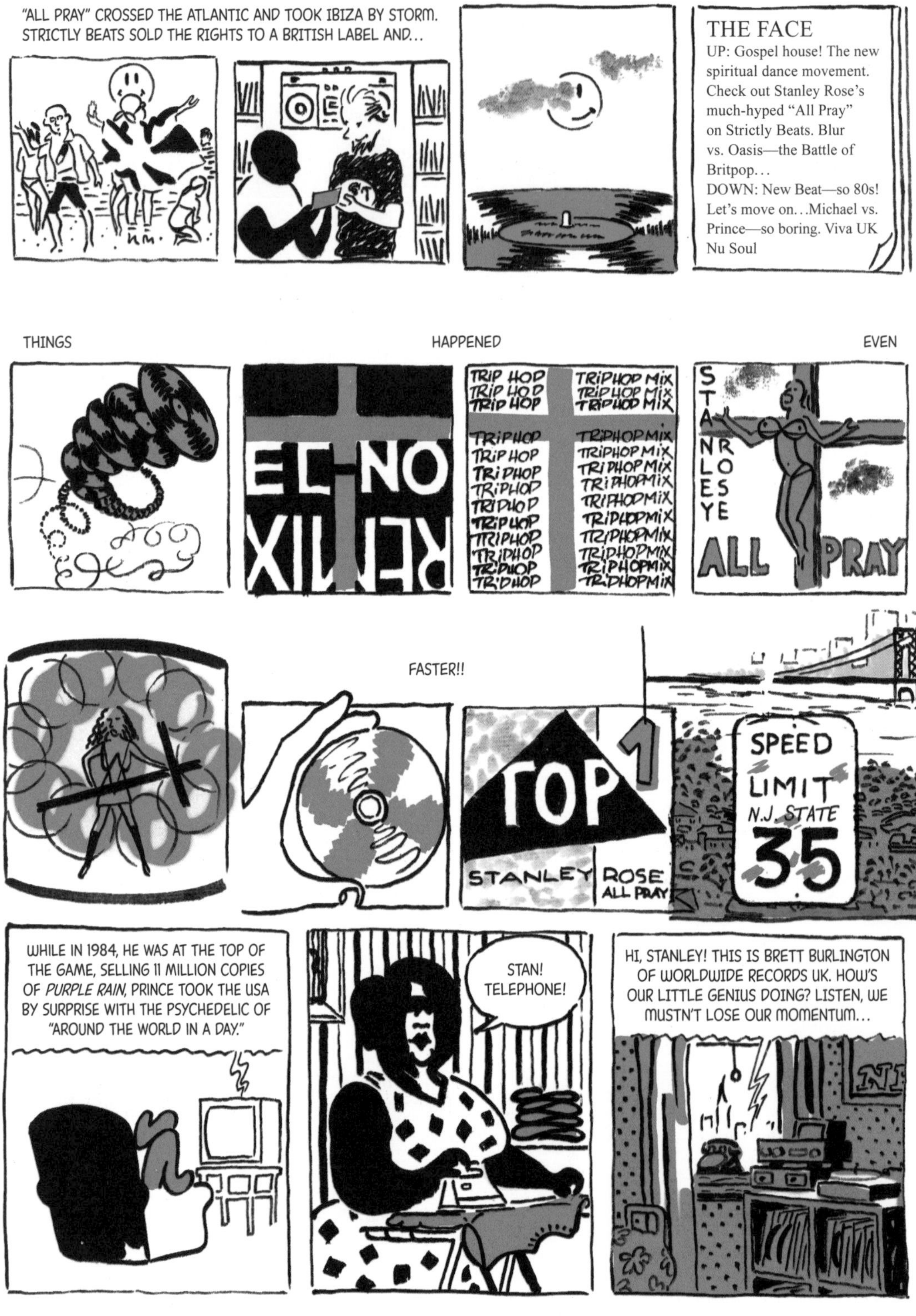
"ALL PRAY" CROSSED THE ATLANTIC AND TOOK IBIZA BY STORM. STRICTLY BEATS SOLD THE RIGHTS TO A BRITISH LABEL AND...
THE FACE
UP: Gospel house! The new spiritual dance movement. Check out Stanley Rose's much-hyped "All Pray" on Strictly Beats. Blur vs. Oasis—the Battle of Britpop...
DOWN: New Beat—so 80s! Let's move on...Michael vs. Prince—so boring. Viva UK Nu Soul
THINGS
HAPPENED
EVEN
EC NO REMIX
TRIP HOP
TRIPHOP MIX
STANLEY ROSE
ALL PRAY
FASTER!!
TOP 1
STANLEY ROSE
ALL PRAY
SPEED LIMIT
N.J. STATE
35
WHILE IN 1984, HE WAS AT THE TOP OF THE GAME, SELLING 11 MILLION COPIES OF *PURPLE RAIN*, PRINCE TOOK THE USA BY SURPRISE WITH THE PSYCHEDELIC OF "AROUND THE WORLD IN A DAY."
STAN! TELEPHONE!
HI, STANLEY! THIS IS BRETT BURLINGTON OF WORLDWIDE RECORDS UK. HOW'S OUR LITTLE GENIUS DOING? LISTEN, WE MUSTN'T LOSE OUR MOMENTUM...

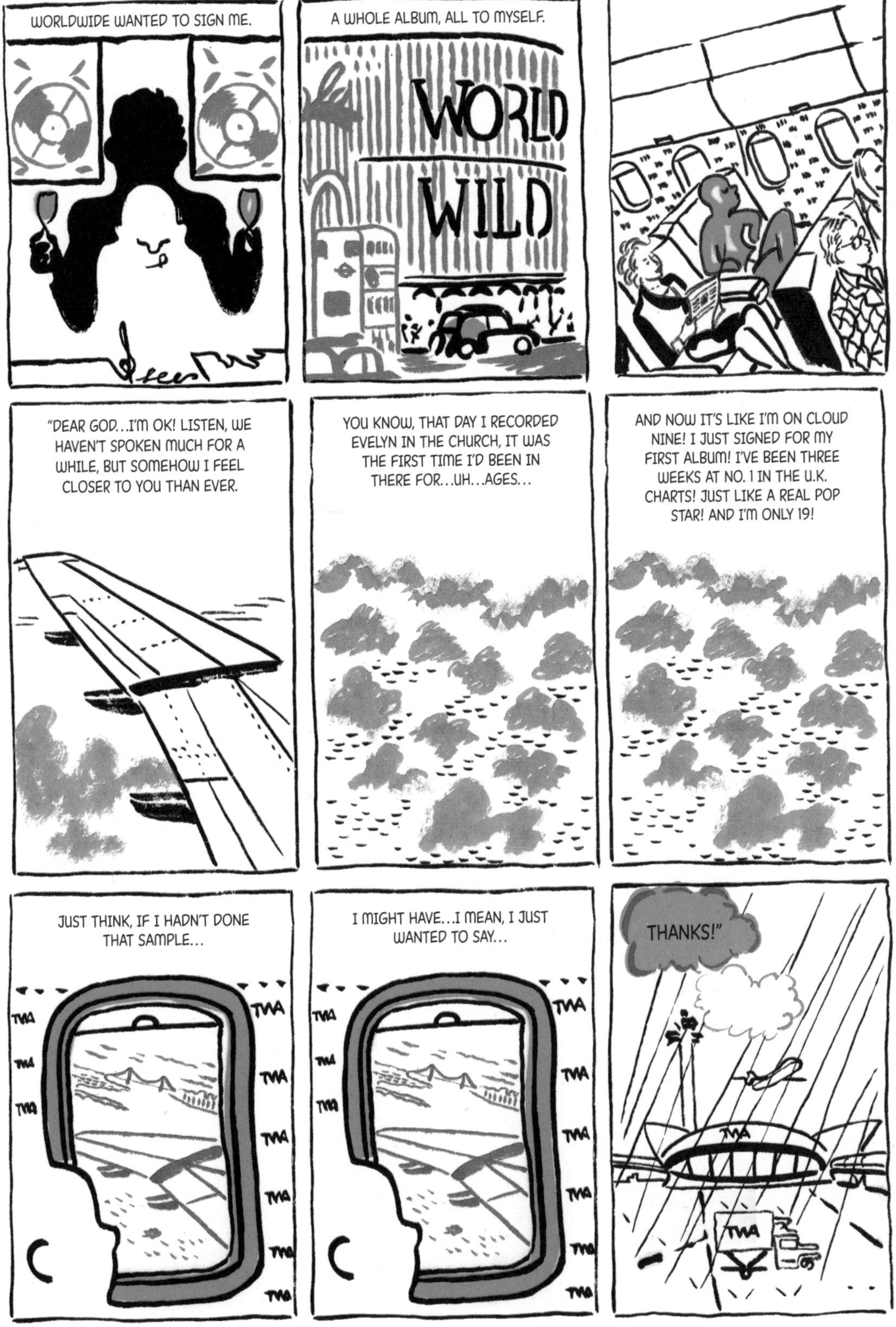
WORLDWIDE WANTED TO SIGN ME.
A WHOLE ALBUM, ALL TO MYSELF.
WORLD WILD
"DEAR GOD...I'M OK! LISTEN, WE HAVEN'T SPOKEN MUCH FOR A WHILE, BUT SOMEHOW I FEEL CLOSER TO YOU THAN EVER.
YOU KNOW, THAT DAY I RECORDED EVELYN IN THE CHURCH, IT WAS THE FIRST TIME I'D BEEN IN THERE FOR...UH...AGES...
AND NOW IT'S LIKE I'M ON CLOUD NINE! I JUST SIGNED FOR MY FIRST ALBUM! I'VE BEEN THREE WEEKS AT NO. 1 IN THE U.K. CHARTS! JUST LIKE A REAL POP STAR! AND I'M ONLY 19!
JUST THINK, IF I HADN'T DONE THAT SAMPLE...
TWA
I MIGHT HAVE...I MEAN, I JUST WANTED TO SAY...
TWA
THANKS!"
TWA

I GOT BACK TO WORK RIGHT AWAY. I SPENT MY WHOLE ADVANCE FROM WORLDWIDE RECORDS ON MACHINES. THERE WERE SO MANY NEW SOUNDS TO DISCOVER...

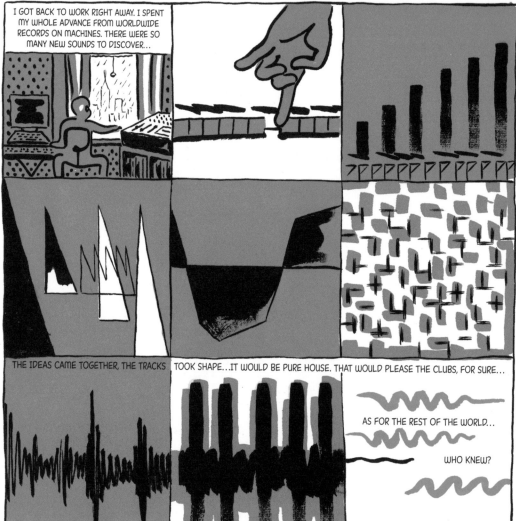

THE IDEAS CAME TOGETHER, THE TRACKS TOOK SHAPE...IT WOULD BE PURE HOUSE. THAT WOULD PLEASE THE CLUBS, FOR SURE...

AS FOR THE REST OF THE WORLD...

WHO KNEW?

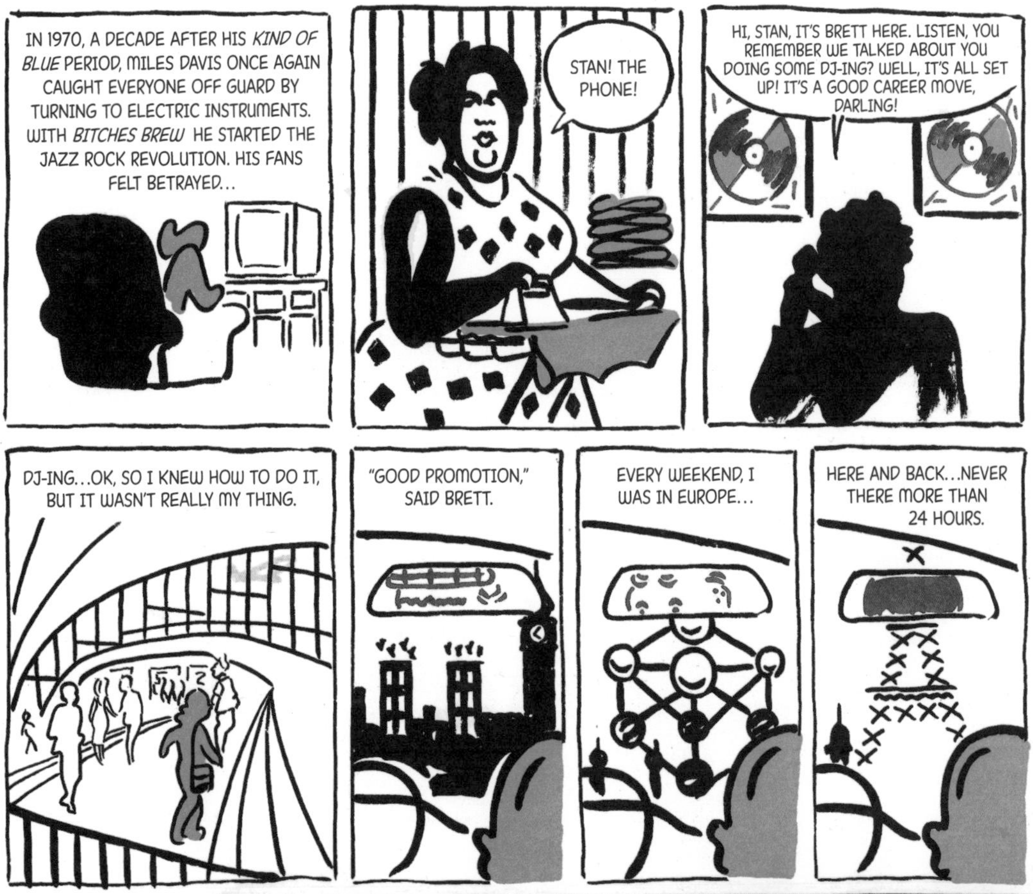
IN 1970, A DECADE AFTER HIS *KIND OF BLUE* PERIOD, MILES DAVIS ONCE AGAIN CAUGHT EVERYONE OFF GUARD BY TURNING TO ELECTRIC INSTRUMENTS. WITH *BITCHES BREW* HE STARTED THE JAZZ ROCK REVOLUTION. HIS FANS FELT BETRAYED...
STAN! THE PHONE!
HI, STAN, IT'S BRETT HERE. LISTEN, YOU REMEMBER WE TALKED ABOUT YOU DOING SOME DJ-ING? WELL, IT'S ALL SET UP! IT'S A GOOD CAREER MOVE, DARLING!
DJ-ING...OK, SO I KNEW HOW TO DO IT, BUT IT WASN'T REALLY MY THING.
"GOOD PROMOTION," SAID BRETT.
EVERY WEEKEND, I WAS IN EUROPE...
HERE AND BACK...NEVER THERE MORE THAN 24 HOURS.

Of course, at first it was fun. Everywhere I went, the disk was in the top 10. The single had sold 1.5 million copies in Europe. In the U.S., nada. But here: number 1 in the U.K., Germany, and Sweden. I spent my whole time promoting it, doing interviews left, right, and center, and DJ-ing in out-of-the-way clubs. Europe's weird. It's like here... only different. When you order a cola, for example, you don't get ice. I think I just got homesick...

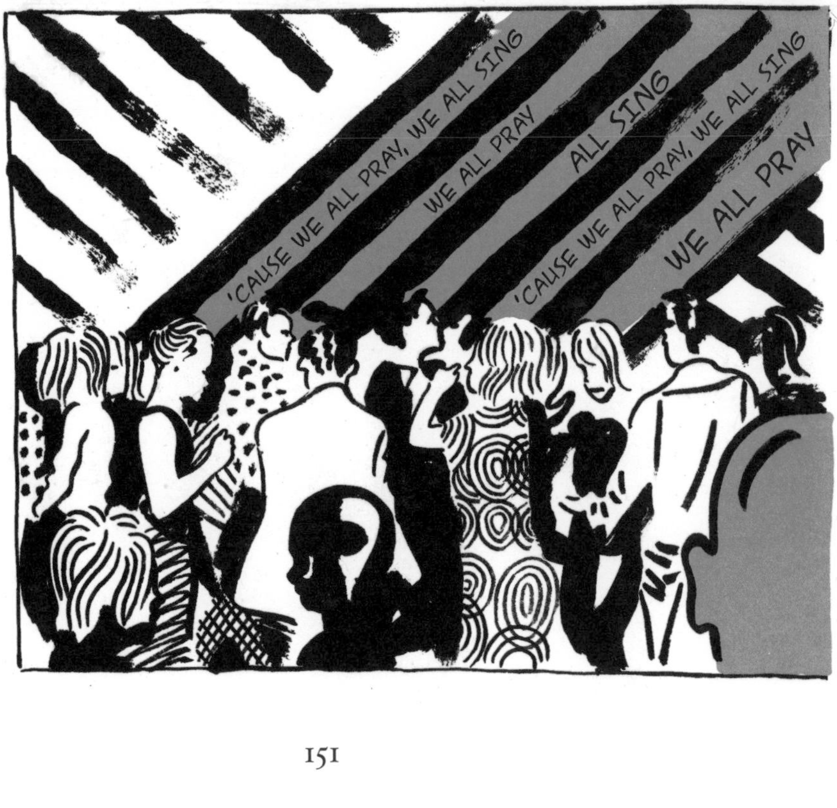
'CAUSE WE ALL PRAY, WE ALL SING
WE ALL PRAY
ALL SING
'CAUSE WE ALL PRAY, WE ALL SING
WE ALL PRAY

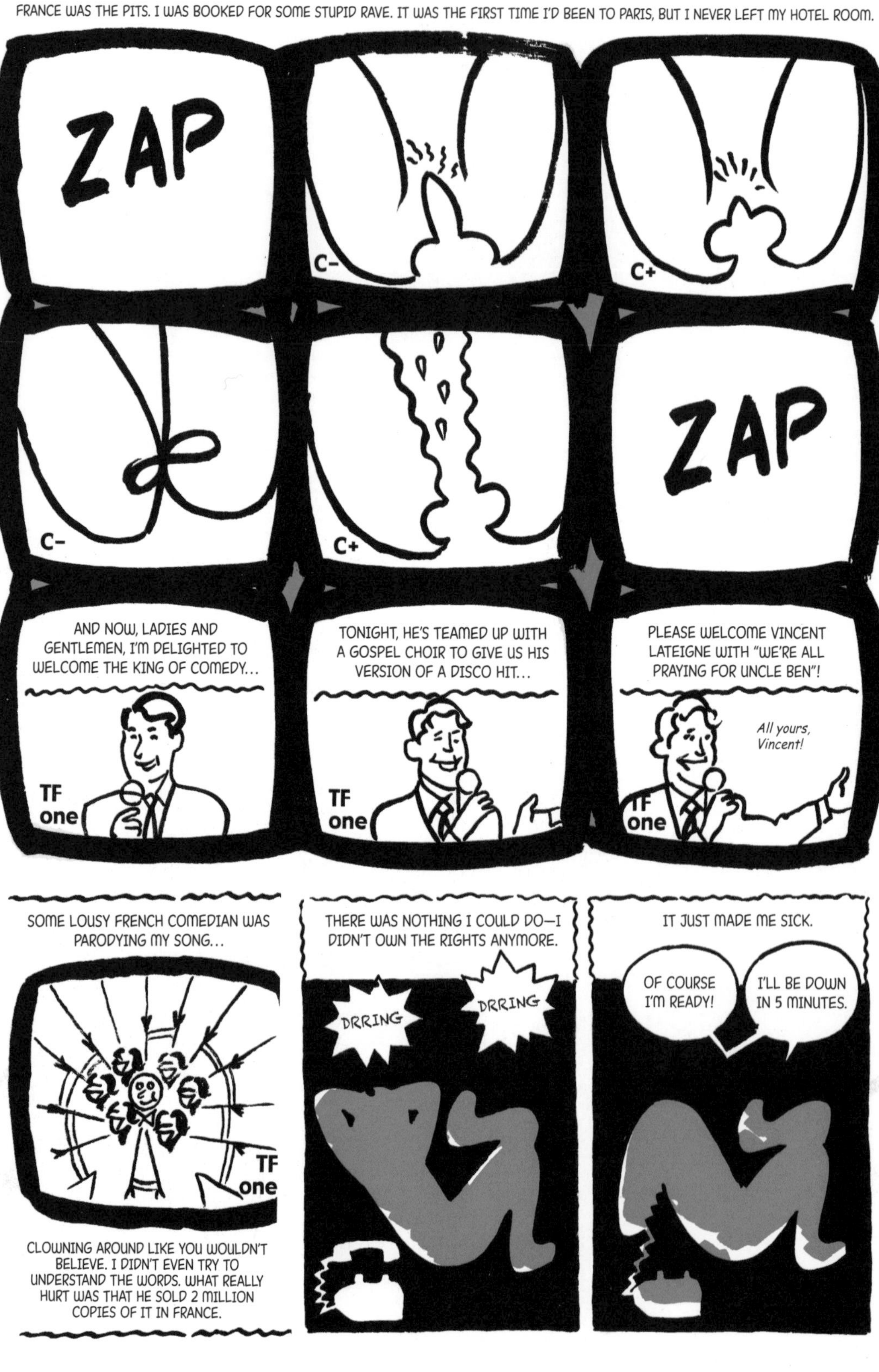
FRANCE WAS THE PITS. I WAS BOOKED FOR SOME STUPID RAVE. IT WAS THE FIRST TIME I'D BEEN TO PARIS, BUT I NEVER LEFT MY HOTEL ROOM.
ZAP
C–
C+
C–
C+
ZAP
AND NOW, LADIES AND GENTLEMEN, I'M DELIGHTED TO WELCOME THE KING OF COMEDY...
TF one
TONIGHT, HE'S TEAMED UP WITH A GOSPEL CHOIR TO GIVE US HIS VERSION OF A DISCO HIT...
TF one
PLEASE WELCOME VINCENT LATEIGNE WITH "WE'RE ALL PRAYING FOR UNCLE BEN"!
All yours, Vincent!
TF one
SOME LOUSY FRENCH COMEDIAN WAS PARODYING MY SONG...
TF one
CLOWNING AROUND LIKE YOU WOULDN'T BELIEVE. I DIDN'T EVEN TRY TO UNDERSTAND THE WORDS. WHAT REALLY HURT WAS THAT HE SOLD 2 MILLION COPIES OF IT IN FRANCE.
THERE WAS NOTHING I COULD DO—I DIDN'T OWN THE RIGHTS ANYMORE.
DRRING
DRRING
IT JUST MADE ME SICK.
OF COURSE I'M READY!
I'LL BE DOWN IN 5 MINUTES.

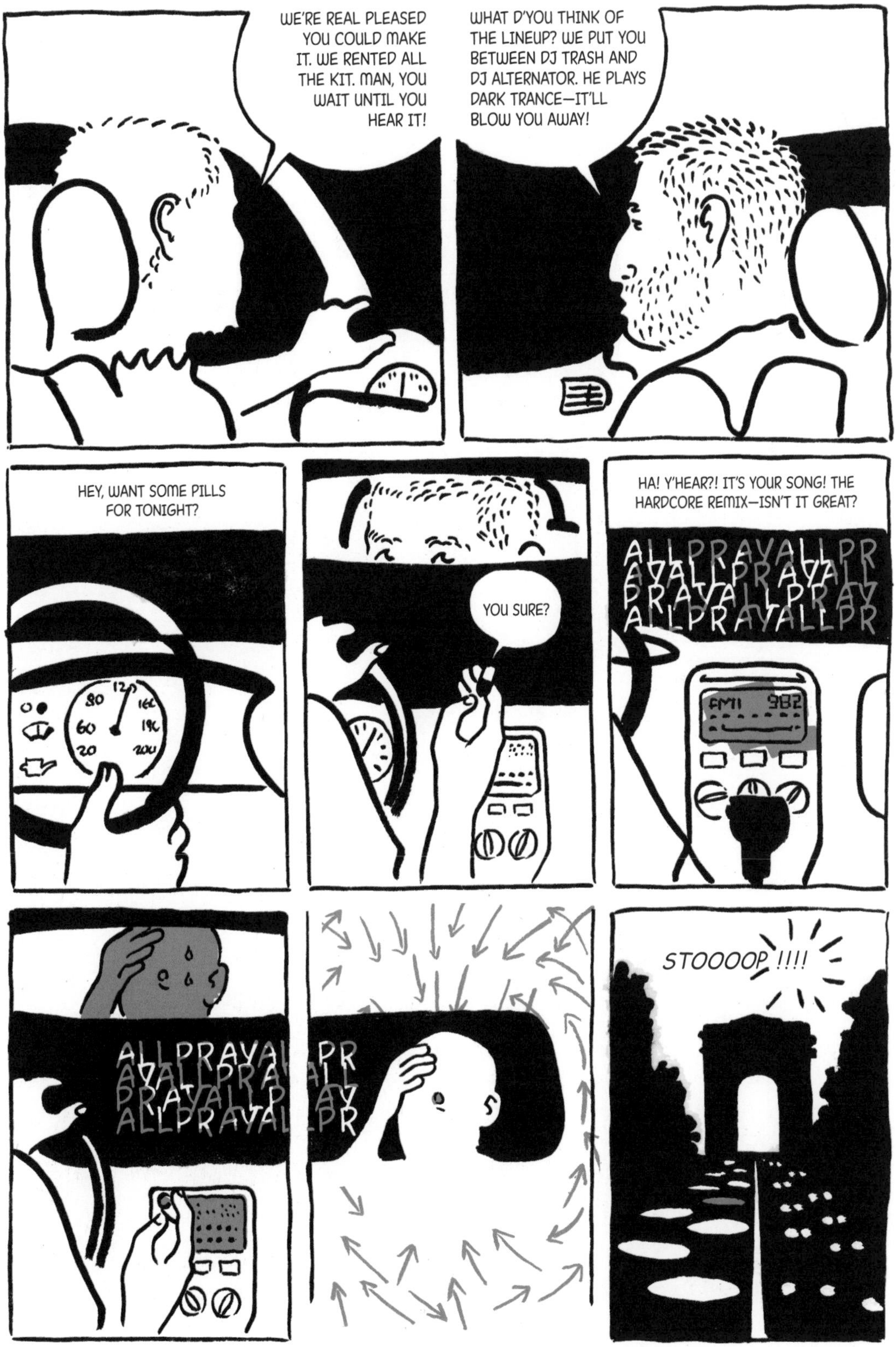
WE'RE REAL PLEASED YOU COULD MAKE IT. WE RENTED ALL THE KIT. MAN, YOU WAIT UNTIL YOU HEAR IT!
WHAT D'YOU THINK OF THE LINEUP? WE PUT YOU BETWEEN DJ TRASH AND DJ ALTERNATOR. HE PLAYS DARK TRANCE—IT'LL BLOW YOU AWAY!
HEY, WANT SOME PILLS FOR TONIGHT?
YOU SURE?
HA! Y'HEAR?! IT'S YOUR SONG! THE HARDCORE REMIX—ISN'T IT GREAT?
ALLPRAYALLPR
AYALLPRAYALL
PRAYALLPRAY
ALLPRAYALLPR
STOOOOP !!!!

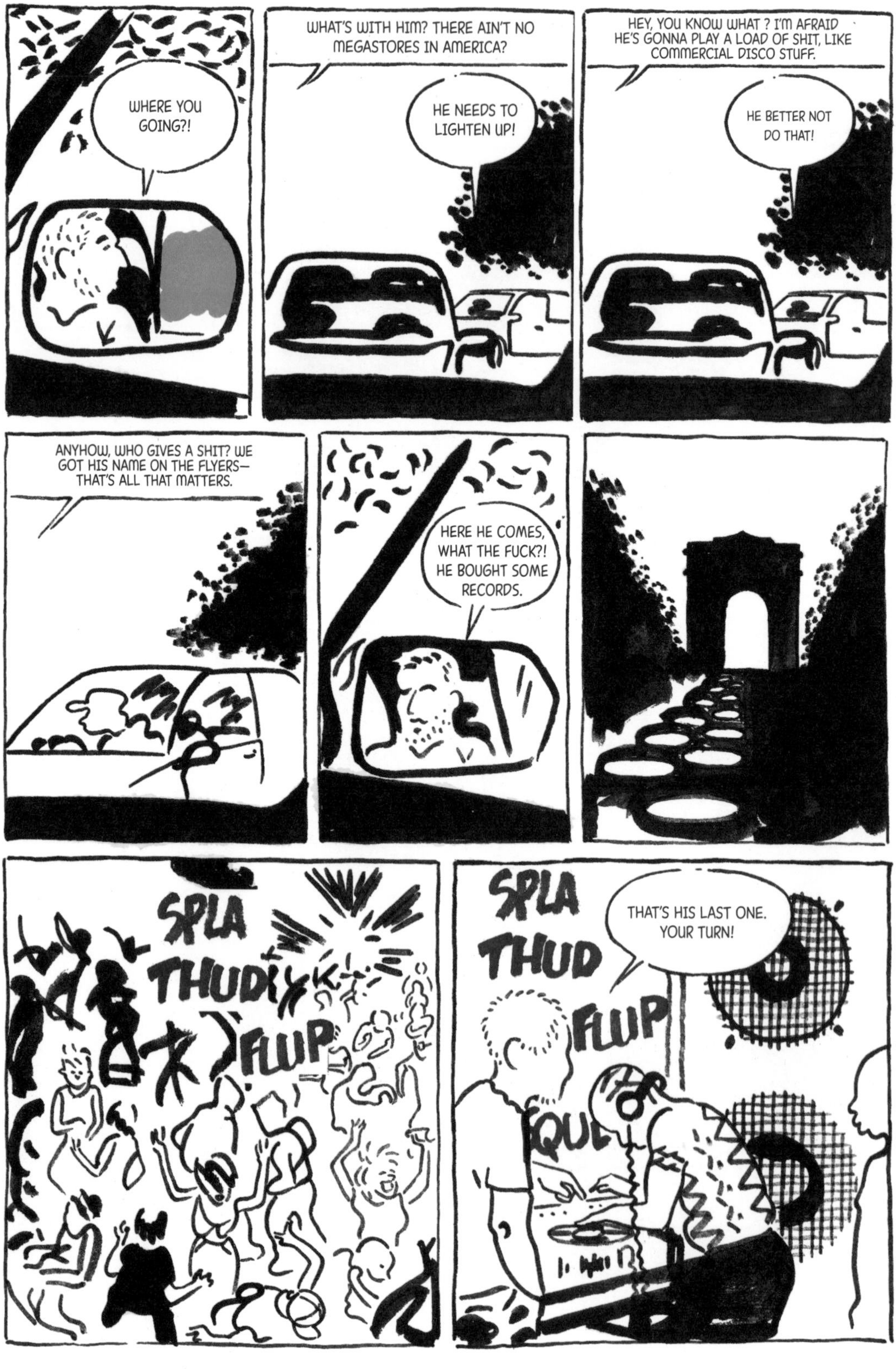
WHERE YOU GOING?!
WHAT'S WITH HIM? THERE AIN'T NO MEGASTORES IN AMERICA?
HE NEEDS TO LIGHTEN UP!
HEY, YOU KNOW WHAT ? I'M AFRAID HE'S GONNA PLAY A LOAD OF SHIT, LIKE COMMERCIAL DISCO STUFF.
HE BETTER NOT DO THAT!
ANYHOW, WHO GIVES A SHIT? WE GOT HIS NAME ON THE FLYERS— THAT'S ALL THAT MATTERS.
HERE HE COMES, WHAT THE FUCK?! HE BOUGHT SOME RECORDS.
SPLA
THUD
FLUP
SPLA
THUD
FLUP
THAT'S HIS LAST ONE. YOUR TURN!

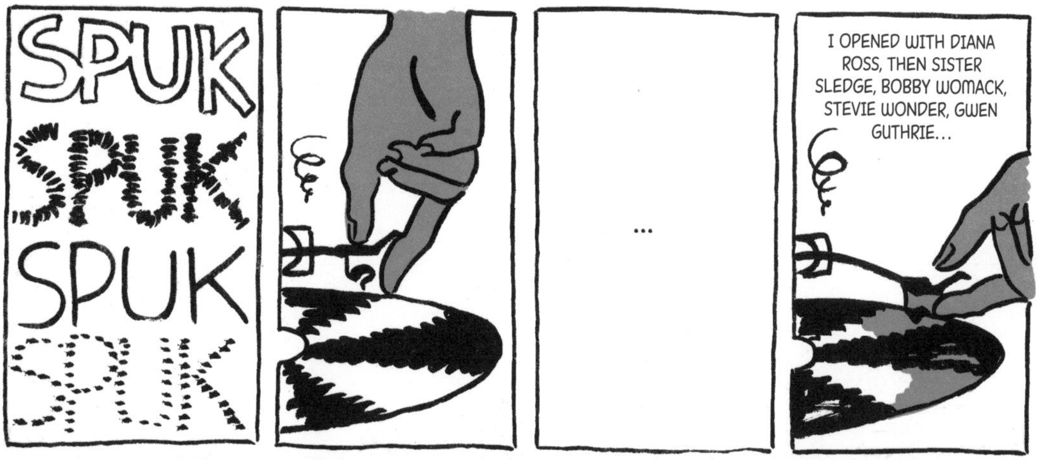
SPUK
SPUK
SPUK
SPUK
...
I OPENED WITH DIANA ROSS, THEN SISTER SLEDGE, BOBBY WOMACK, STEVIE WONDER, GWEN GUTHRIE...

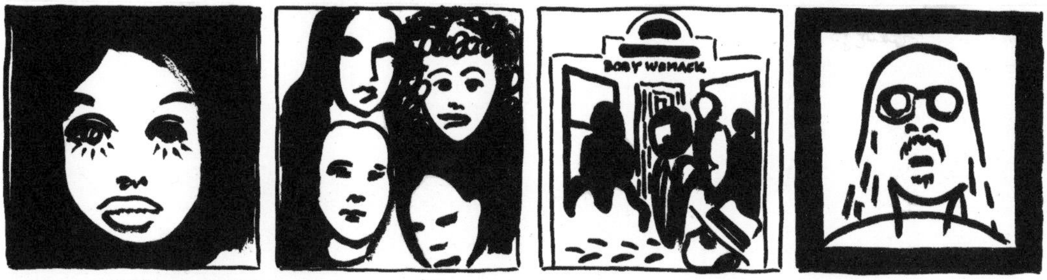
BOBY WOMACK

EVERYONE WAS BOOING, CATCALLING...AFTER THE PRINCE "CONTROVERSY" I LEFT ANOTHER GAP, THEN CONTINUED WITH JAMES BROWN'S 1971 "SEX MACHINE"...NO ONE WAS DANCING. PEOPLE EVEN SPAT AT ME.

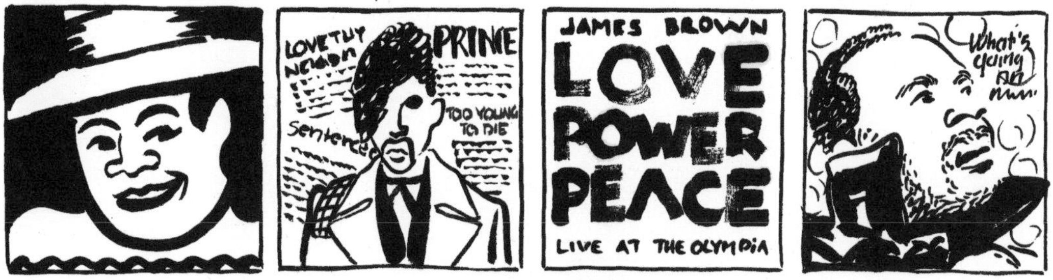
PRINCE
TOO YOUNG TO DIE
JAMES BROWN
LOVE
POWER
PEACE
LIVE AT THE OLYMPIA
What's going on

I LET THEM YELL A BIT AND THEN I PUT ON MARVIN GAYE'S "WHAT'S GOING ON." I THINK THAT WAS WHEN I GOT SOCKED IN THE MOUTH.

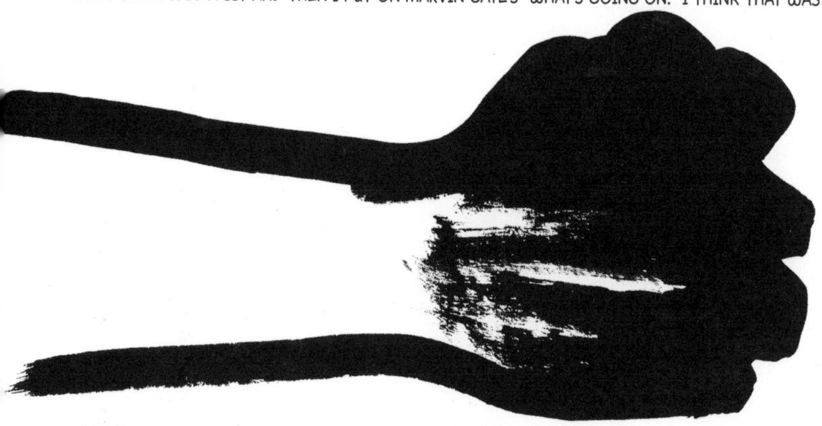

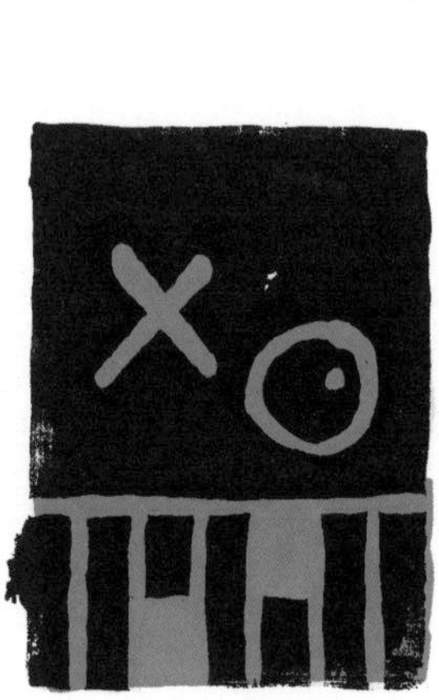

AFTER THAT, ALL I COULD HEAR WAS BOOM, BOOM—NOT JUST THE MUSIC, BUT THE FISTS AS WELL...

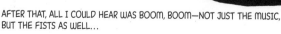

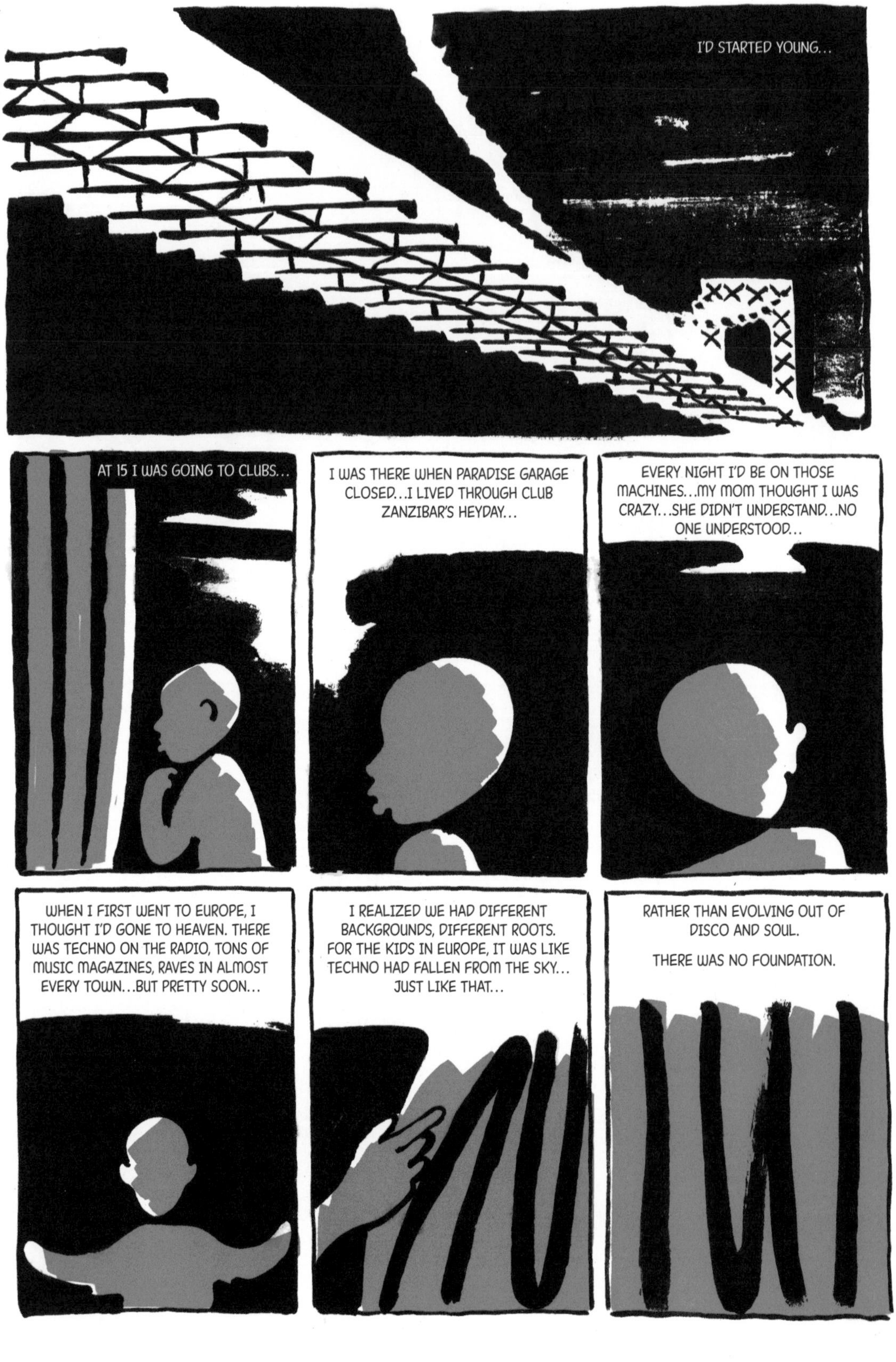
I'D STARTED YOUNG...
AT 15 I WAS GOING TO CLUBS...
I WAS THERE WHEN PARADISE GARAGE CLOSED...I LIVED THROUGH CLUB ZANZIBAR'S HEYDAY...
EVERY NIGHT I'D BE ON THOSE MACHINES...MY MOM THOUGHT I WAS CRAZY...SHE DIDN'T UNDERSTAND...NO ONE UNDERSTOOD...
WHEN I FIRST WENT TO EUROPE, I THOUGHT I'D GONE TO HEAVEN. THERE WAS TECHNO ON THE RADIO, TONS OF MUSIC MAGAZINES, RAVES IN ALMOST EVERY TOWN...BUT PRETTY SOON...
I REALIZED WE HAD DIFFERENT BACKGROUNDS, DIFFERENT ROOTS. FOR THE KIDS IN EUROPE, IT WAS LIKE TECHNO HAD FALLEN FROM THE SKY... JUST LIKE THAT...
RATHER THAN EVOLVING OUT OF DISCO AND SOUL.
THERE WAS NO FOUNDATION.

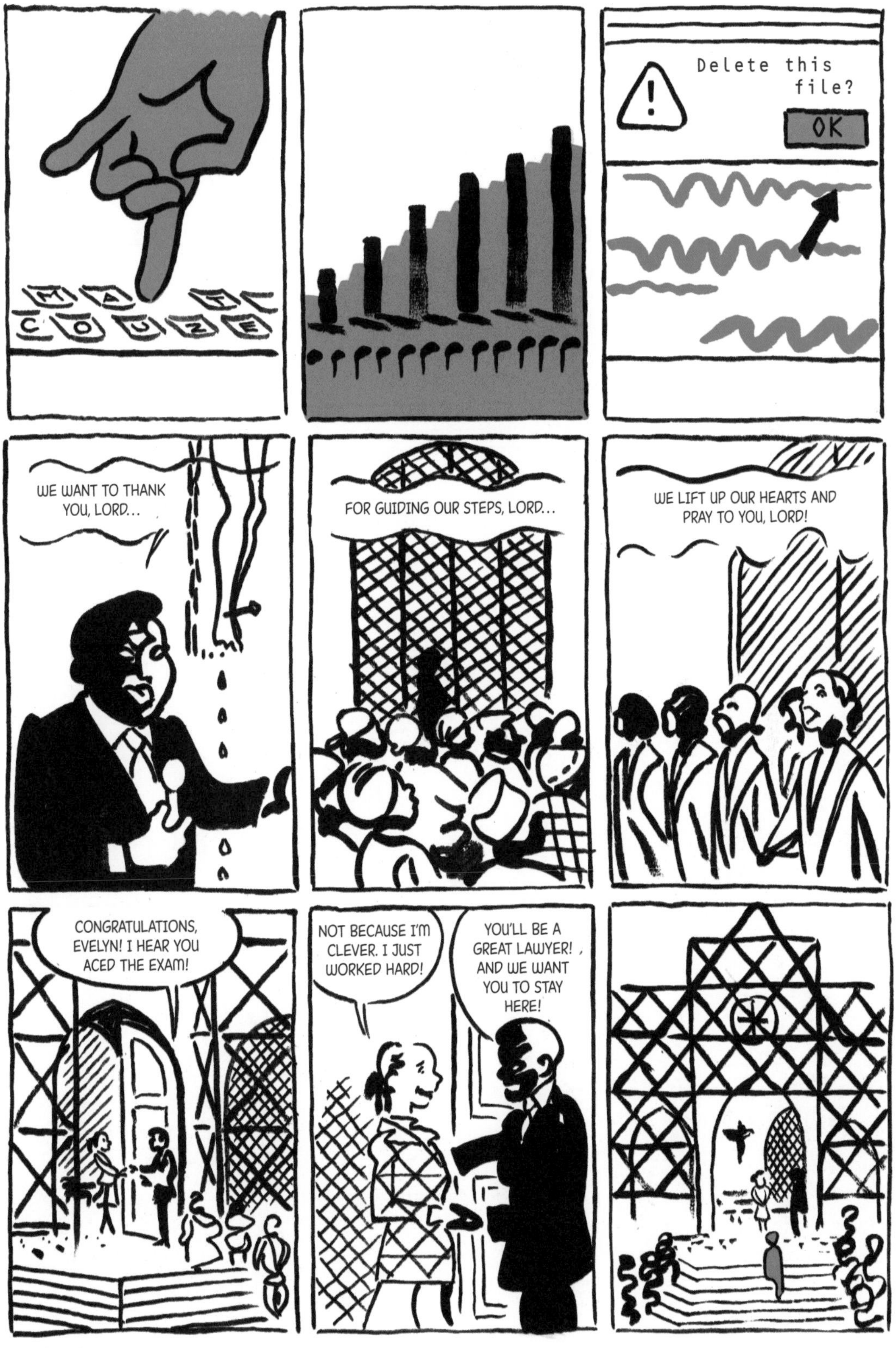
Delete this file?
OK
WE WANT TO THANK YOU, LORD...
FOR GUIDING OUR STEPS, LORD...
WE LIFT UP OUR HEARTS AND PRAY TO YOU, LORD!
CONGRATULATIONS, EVELYN! I HEAR YOU ACED THE EXAM!
NOT BECAUSE I'M CLEVER. I JUST WORKED HARD!
YOU'LL BE A GREAT LAWYER! AND WE WANT YOU TO STAY HERE!

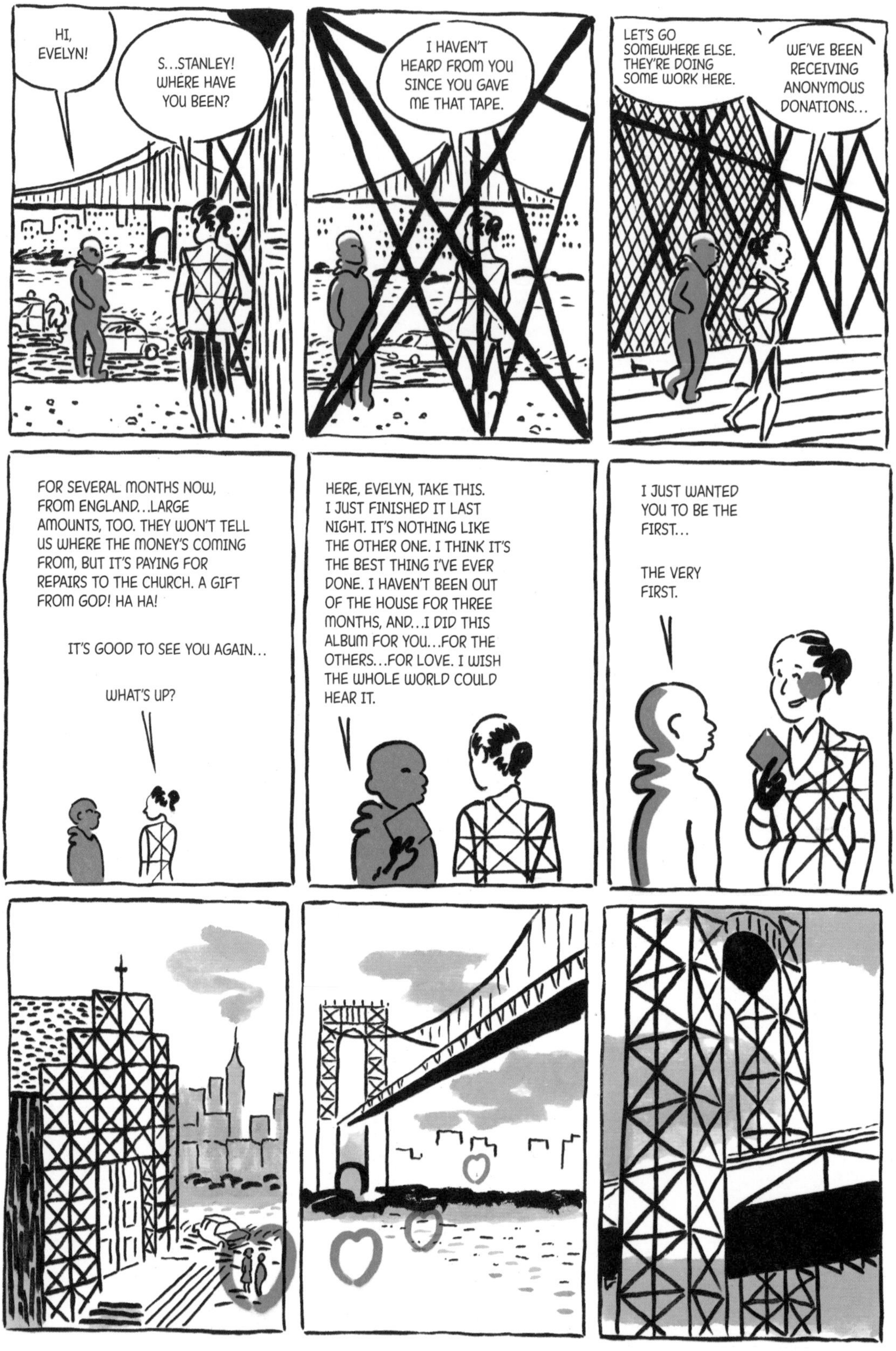
HI, EVELYN!
S...STANLEY! WHERE HAVE YOU BEEN?
I HAVEN'T HEARD FROM YOU SINCE YOU GAVE ME THAT TAPE.
LET'S GO SOMEWHERE ELSE. THEY'RE DOING SOME WORK HERE.
WE'VE BEEN RECEIVING ANONYMOUS DONATIONS...
FOR SEVERAL MONTHS NOW, FROM ENGLAND...LARGE AMOUNTS, TOO. THEY WON'T TELL US WHERE THE MONEY'S COMING FROM, BUT IT'S PAYING FOR REPAIRS TO THE CHURCH. A GIFT FROM GOD! HA HA!
IT'S GOOD TO SEE YOU AGAIN...
WHAT'S UP?
HERE, EVELYN, TAKE THIS. I JUST FINISHED IT LAST NIGHT. IT'S NOTHING LIKE THE OTHER ONE. I THINK IT'S THE BEST THING I'VE EVER DONE. I HAVEN'T BEEN OUT OF THE HOUSE FOR THREE MONTHS, AND...I DID THIS ALBUM FOR YOU...FOR THE OTHERS...FOR LOVE. I WISH THE WHOLE WORLD COULD HEAR IT.
I JUST WANTED YOU TO BE THE FIRST...
THE VERY FIRST.

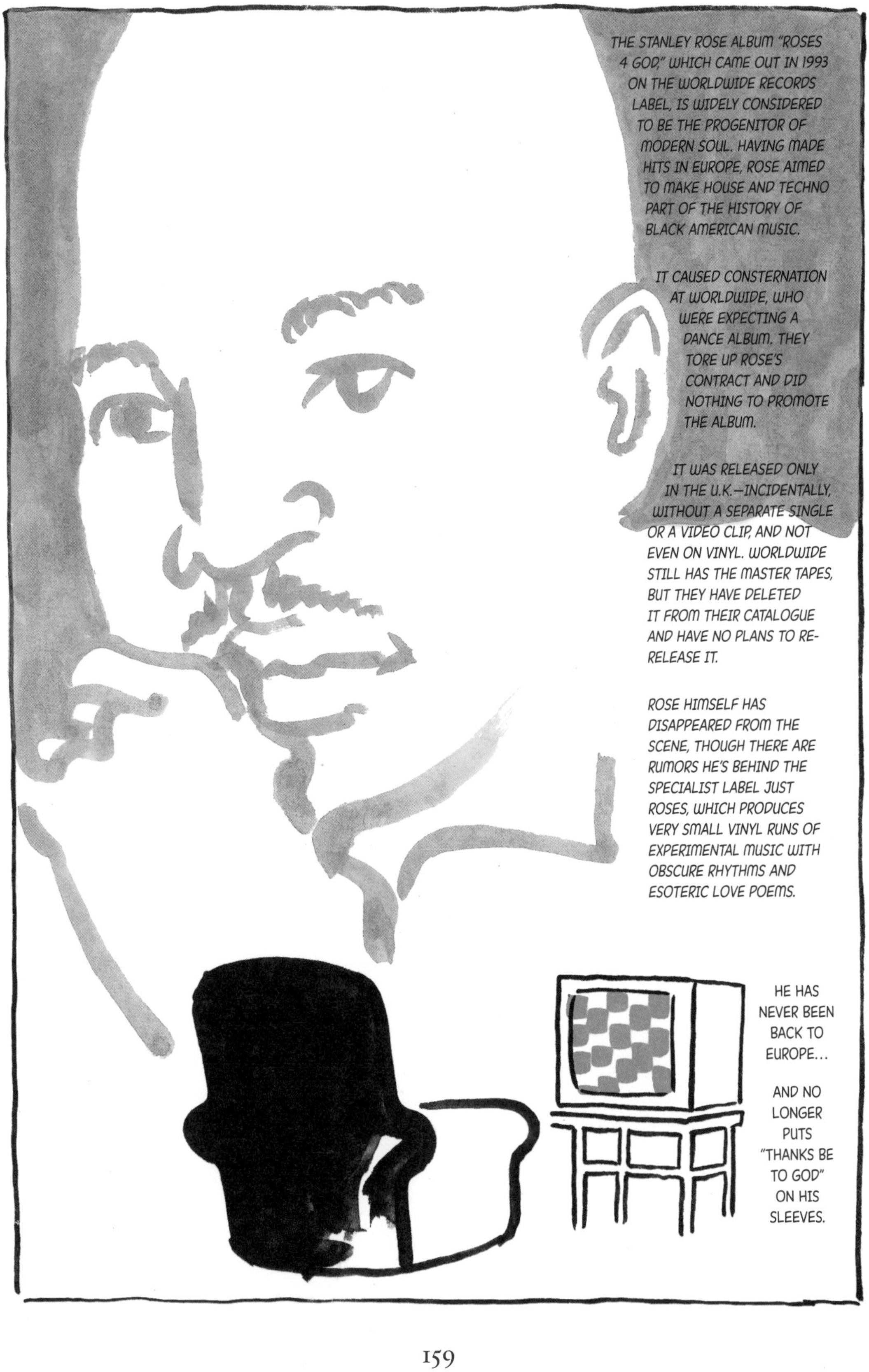
THE STANLEY ROSE ALBUM "ROSES 4 GOD," WHICH CAME OUT IN 1993 ON THE WORLDWIDE RECORDS LABEL, IS WIDELY CONSIDERED TO BE THE PROGENITOR OF MODERN SOUL. HAVING MADE HITS IN EUROPE, ROSE AIMED TO MAKE HOUSE AND TECHNO PART OF THE HISTORY OF BLACK AMERICAN MUSIC.
IT CAUSED CONSTERNATION AT WORLDWIDE, WHO WERE EXPECTING A DANCE ALBUM. THEY TORE UP ROSE'S CONTRACT AND DID NOTHING TO PROMOTE THE ALBUM.
IT WAS RELEASED ONLY IN THE U.K.—INCIDENTALLY, WITHOUT A SEPARATE SINGLE OR A VIDEO CLIP, AND NOT EVEN ON VINYL. WORLDWIDE STILL HAS THE MASTER TAPES, BUT THEY HAVE DELETED IT FROM THEIR CATALOGUE AND HAVE NO PLANS TO RE-RELEASE IT.
ROSE HIMSELF HAS DISAPPEARED FROM THE SCENE, THOUGH THERE ARE RUMORS HE'S BEHIND THE SPECIALIST LABEL JUST ROSES, WHICH PRODUCES VERY SMALL VINYL RUNS OF EXPERIMENTAL MUSIC WITH OBSCURE RHYTHMS AND ESOTERIC LOVE POEMS.
HE HAS NEVER BEEN BACK TO EUROPE…
AND NO LONGER PUTS "THANKS BE TO GOD" ON HIS SLEEVES.

CHAPTER 10

PARADISE LOST

A NINETIES SOUNDTRACK

Dr. Dre feat. Snoop Dogg
Nuthin' But a 'G' Thang — 1992

Wu-Tang Clan
Enter the Wu-Tang (LP) — 1993

Robin S.
Show Me Love — 1993

Nightcrawlers
Push the Feeling On (Mark Kinchen Dub) — 1994

The Notorious B.I.G.
Everything — 1994

Kenny Dope Presents The Bucketheads
The Bomb! — 1994

Jay-Z
Everything! — 1996

Suprême NTM
Paris sous les bombes (LP) — 1996

Motorbass
Pansoul (LP) — 1996

Cheek (DJ Gilb'R)
Venus (Sunshine People)
(DJ Gregory Remix) — 1996

Daft Punk
Homework (LP) — 1997

Air
Le Soleil Est Près de Moi — 1997

Lil' Kim
Hard Cord (LP) — 1996

Mary J. Blige
Share My World (LP) — 1997

Brandy feat. Ma$e
Top of the World — 1998

Stardust
Music Sounds Better With You — 1998

Alice Deejay
Better Off Alone — 1998

R. Kelly
R. — 1998

TLC
No Scrubs — 1999

Destiny's Child
Say My Name — 1999

Phoenix
If I Ever Feel Better — 2000

Aaliyah and Timbaland
Try Again — 2000

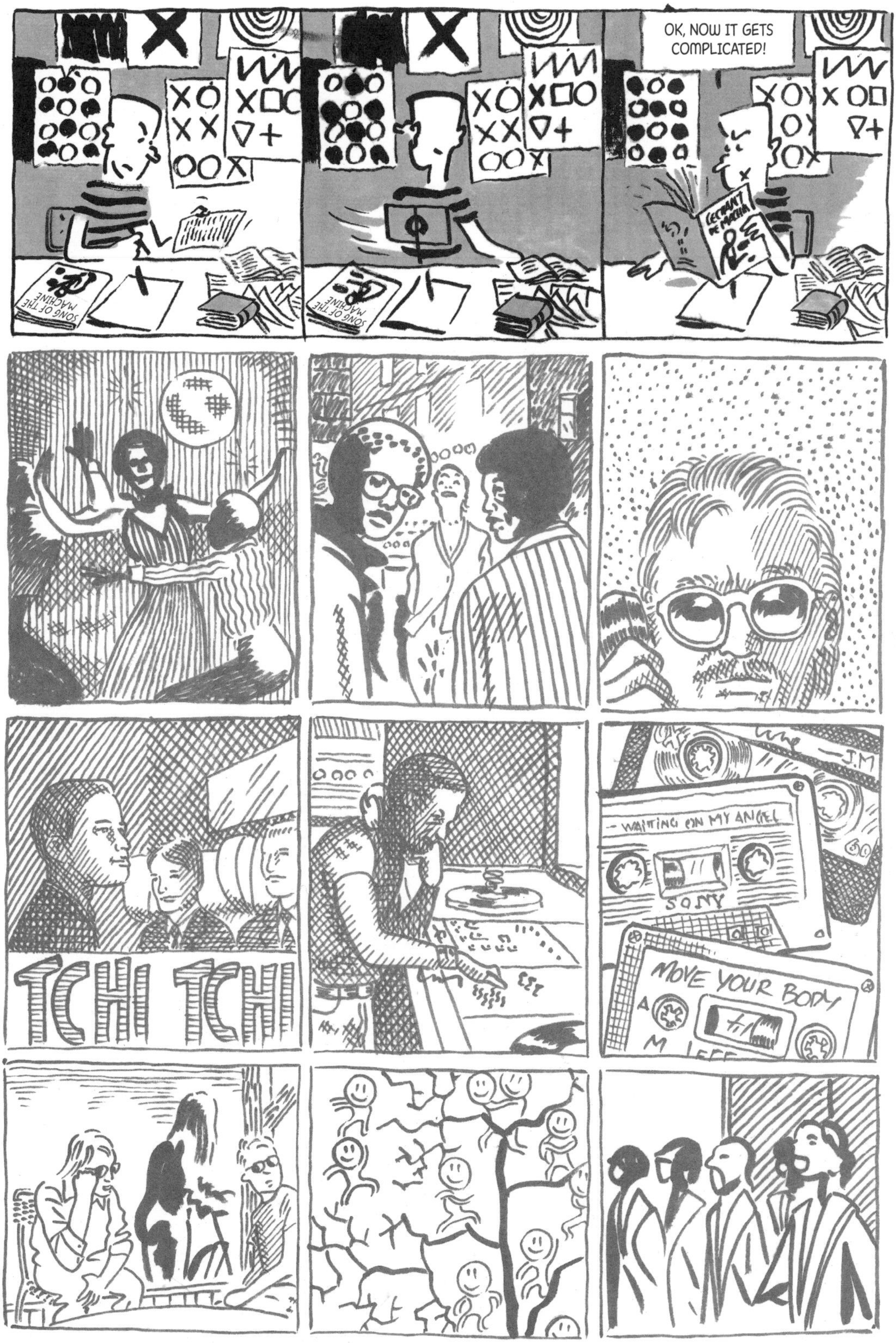
SONG OF THE MACHINE
SONG OF THE MACHINE
OK, NOW IT GETS COMPLICATED!
LE CHANT DE MACHIN
TCHI TCHI
J.M
WAITING ON MY ANGEL
SONY
MOVE YOUR BODY

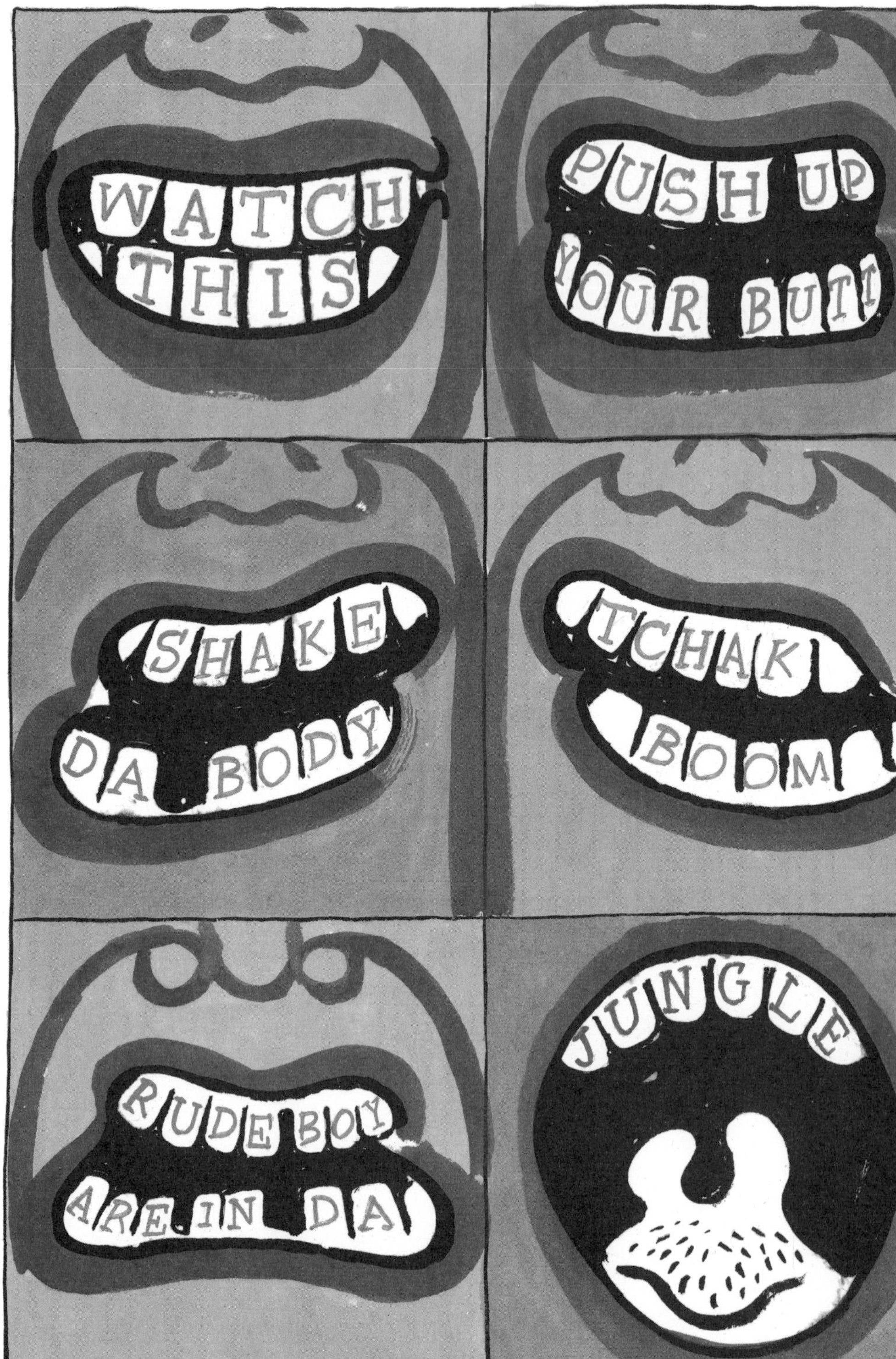
WATCH THIS
PUSH UP YOUR BUTT
SHAKE DA BODY
TCHAK BOOM
RUDE BOY ARE IN DA
JUNGLE

DRUM 'N' BASS: THE U.K. RAVE OFFSHOOT. CRUSADERS OF THE DUB EXPERIENCE.

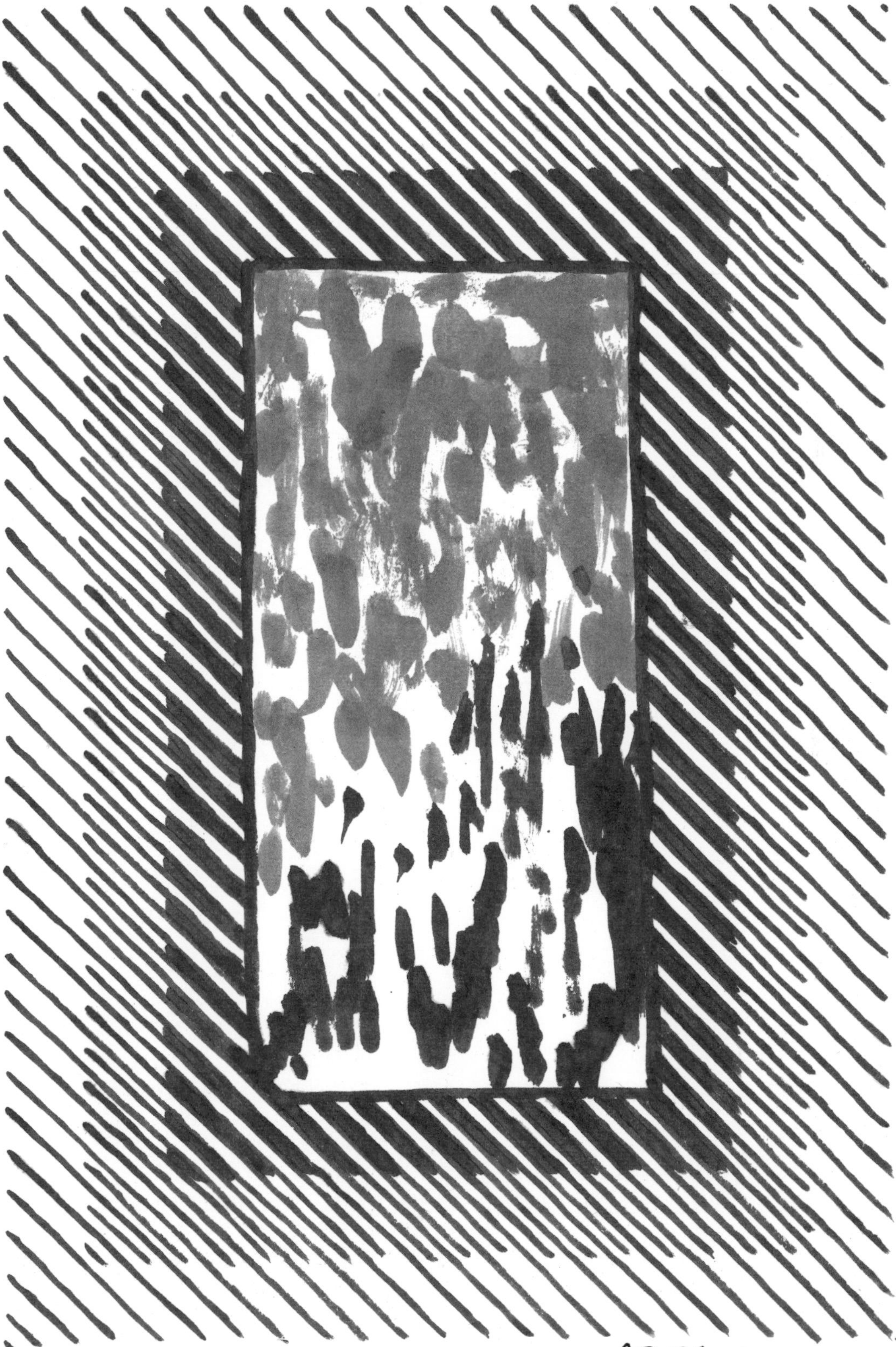

APHEX TWIN (NO TITLE)

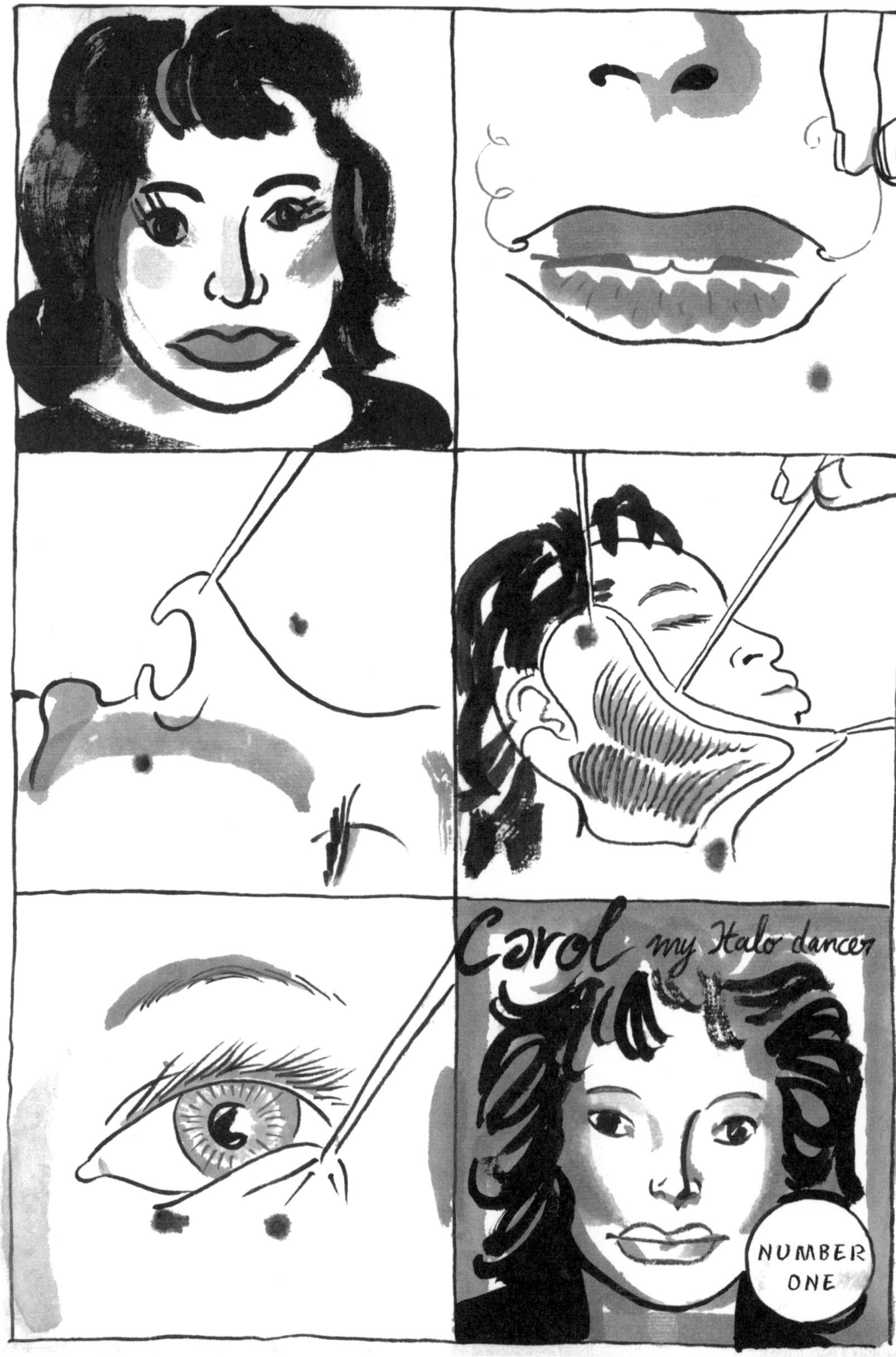
Carol my Italo dancer
NUMBER ONE

MANUFACTURED IN MILAN, STOCKHOLM, OR BRUSSELS, EURODANCE MUSIC TAKES OVER AND SPREADS FROM RIMINI TO BANGKOK.

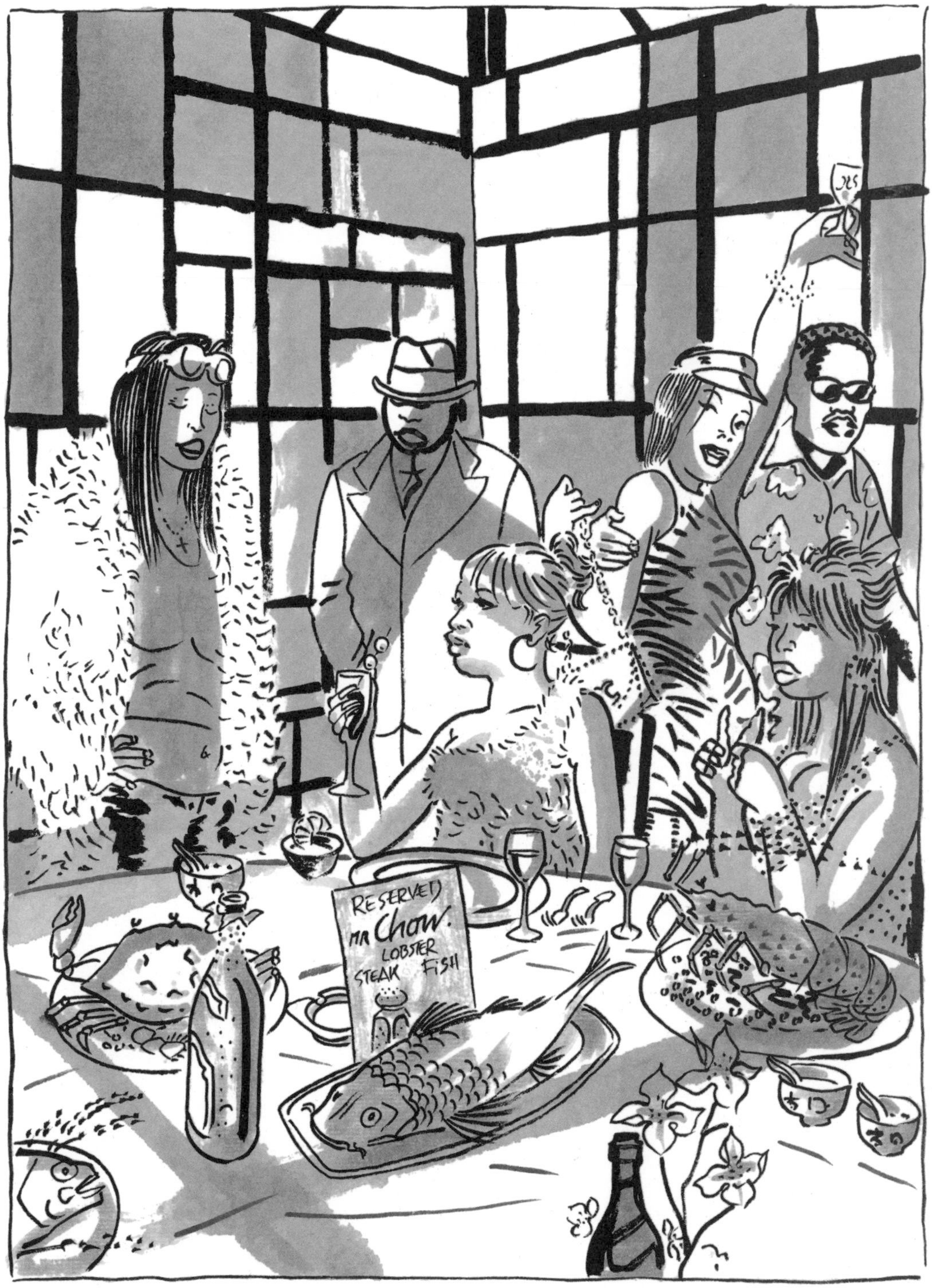
RESERVED
MR Chow.
LOBSTER
STEAK
FISH

AALIYAH, BIGGIE, MARY J., LIL' KIM, P. DIDDY, AND MISSY DINING AT MR. CHOW'S BEFORE CLUBBING AT THE TUNNEL.

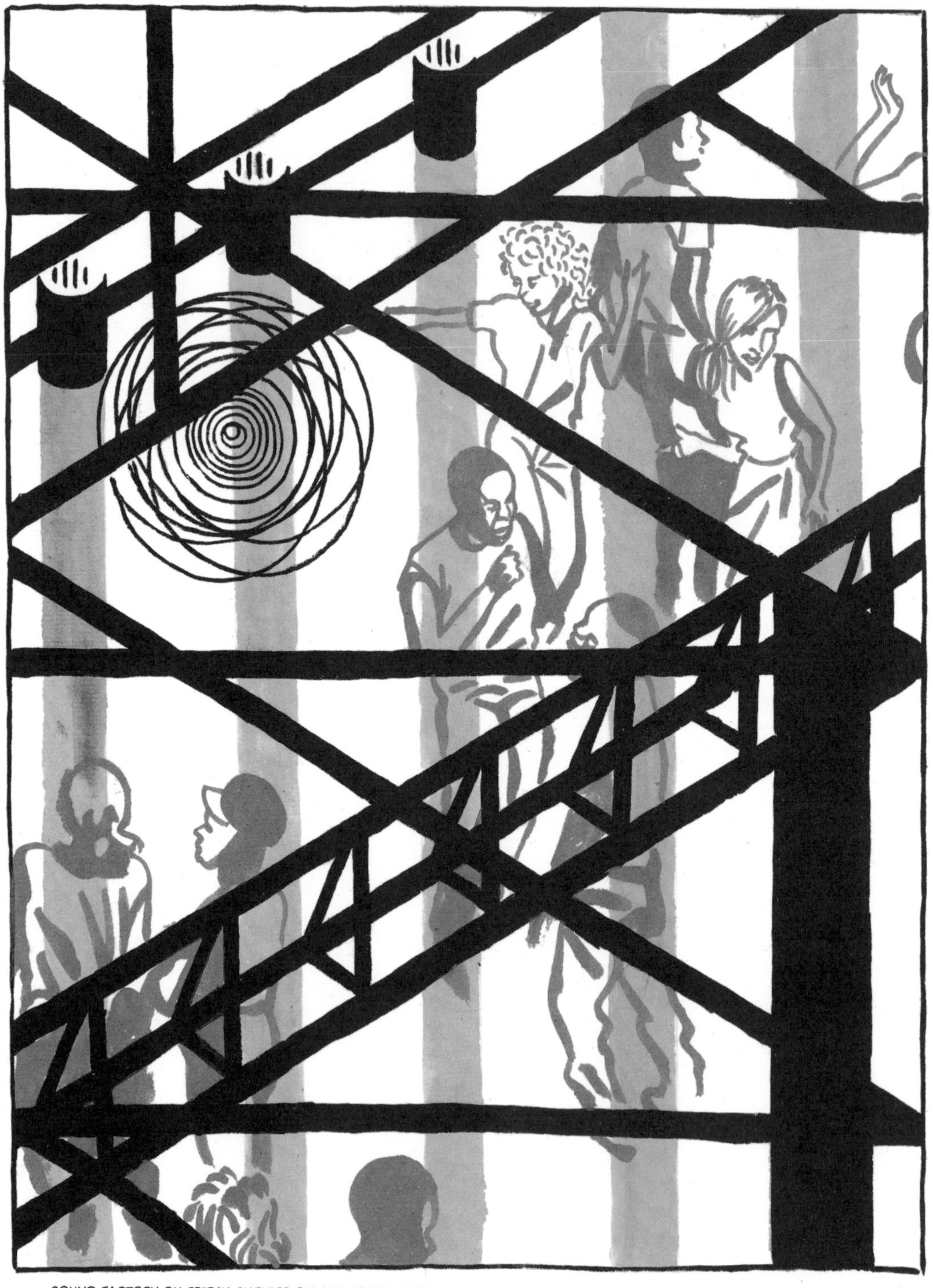

SOUND FACTORY ON FRIDAY, SHELTER ON SATURDAY, AND BODY AND SOUL ON SUNDAY AFTERNOON—WEEKEND CLUBBING IN NYC.

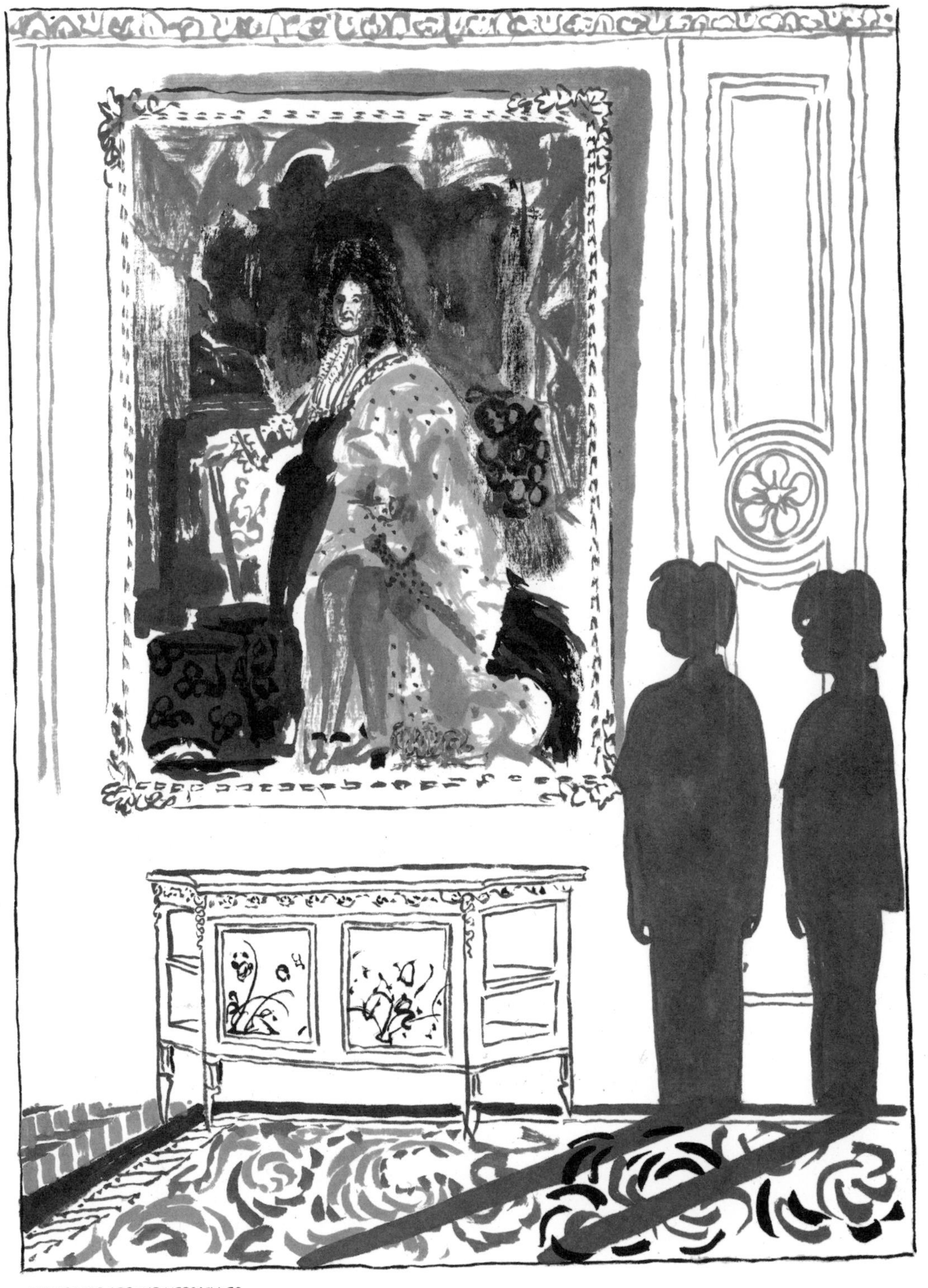

AIR NOSING AROUND VERSAILLES.

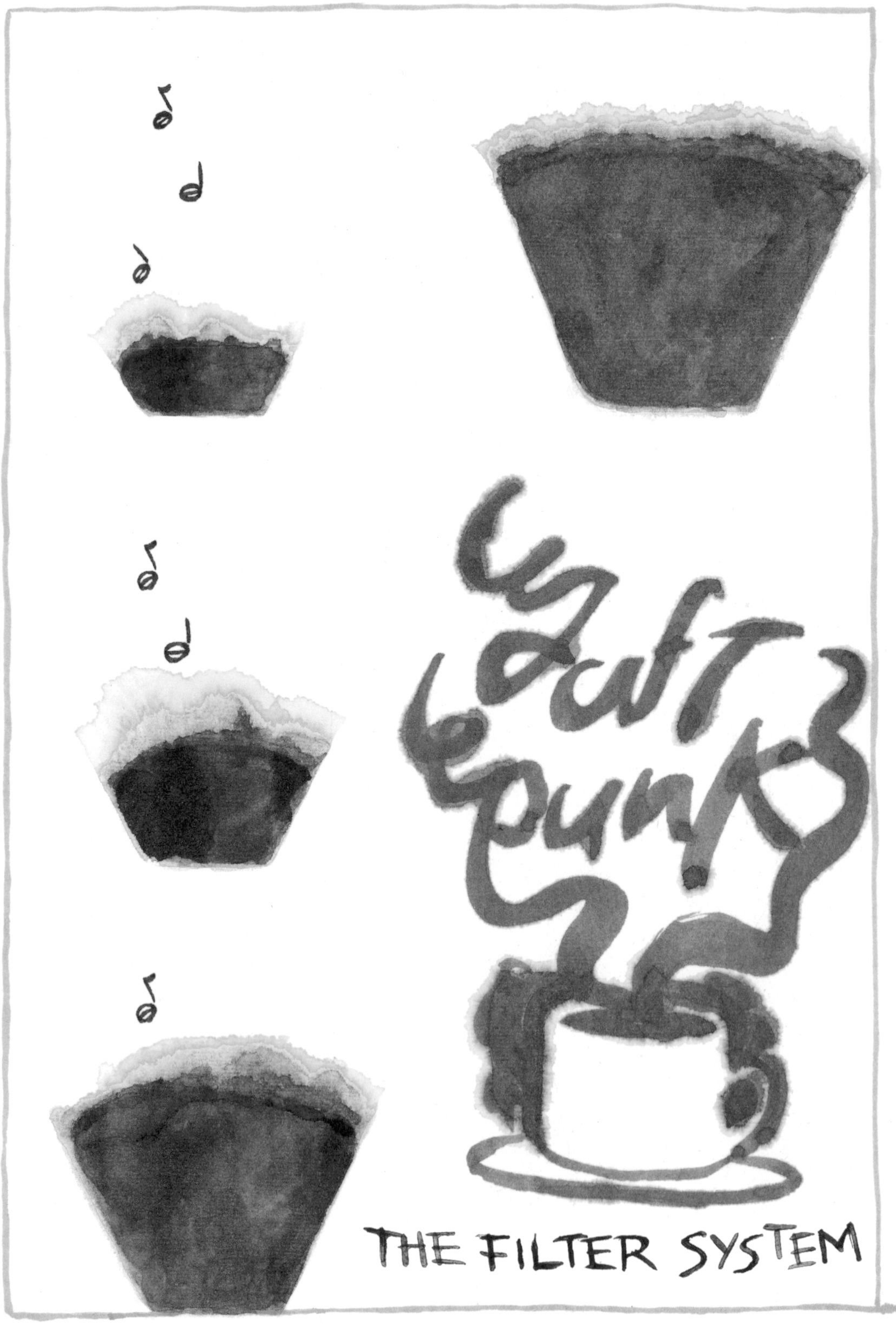
THE FILTER SYSTEM

OF COURSE...

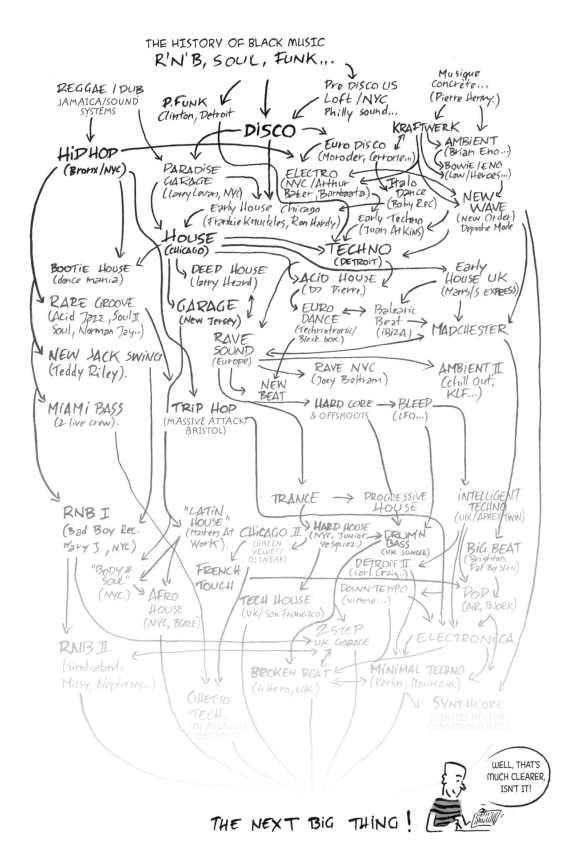

THE HISTORY OF BLACK MUSIC
R'N'B, SOUL, FUNK...

Musique concrete... (Pierre Henry.)

REGGAE / DUB
JAMAICA/SOUND SYSTEMS

P. FUNK
Clinton, Detroit

Pre DISCO US
Loft /NYC
Philly sound...

KRAFTWERK

DISCO

AMBIENT
(Brian Eno..)

HIP HOP
(Bronx /NYC)

Euro Disco
(Moroder, Cerrone...)

Bowie / ENO
(Low /Heroes...)

PARADISE GARAGE
(Larry Levan, NYC)

ELECTRO
(NYC /Arthur Baker, Bambaata)

Italo Dance
(Baby Rec.)

NEW WAVE
(New Order)
Depeche Mode

Early House Chicago
(Frankie Knuckles, Ron Hardy)

Early Techno
(Juan Atkins)

HOUSE
(CHICAGO)

TECHNO
(DETROIT)

Early House UK
(Marrs /S Express)

BOOTIE HOUSE
(dance mania)

DEEP HOUSE
(Larry Heard)

ACID HOUSE
(DJ Pierre.)

RARE GROOVE
(Acid Jazz, Soul II Soul, Norman Jay...)

GARAGE
(New Jersey)

EURO DANCE
(Technotronic/ Black box)

Balearic Beat
(Ibiza)

MADCHESTER

RAVE SOUND
(Europe)

NEW JACK SWING
(Teddy Riley).

RAVE NYC
(Joey Beltram)

AMBIENT II
(chill out, KLF...)

NEW BEAT

MIAMI BASS
(2 live crew).

TRIP HOP
(MASSIVE ATTACK, BRISTOL)

HARD CORE
& OFFSHOOTS

BLEEP
(LFO...)

TRANCE

PROGRESSIVE HOUSE

INTELLIGENT TECHNO
(UIX / APHEX TWIN)

RNB I
(Bad Boy Rec. Mary J, NYC)

"LATIN HOUSE"
(Masters At Work).

CHICAGO II
(GREEN VELVET/ DJ SNEAK)

HARD HOUSE
(NYC, Junior Vesquez)

DRUM'N BASS
(UK JUNGLE)

BIG BEAT
(Brighton, Fat Boy Slim)

"BODY & SOUL"
(NYC.)

AFRO HOUSE
(NYC, BLAZE)

FRENCH TOUCH

TECH HOUSE
(UK / San Francisco)

DETROIT II
(Carl Craig...)

DOWN TEMPO
(Vienne...)

POP
(AIR, BJORK)

RNB II
(Timbaland, Missy, Neptunes...)

2 STEP
UK GARAGE

ELECTRONICA

GHETTO TECH.
(DJ ASSAULT/ DETROIT)

BROKEN BEAT
(4 Hero, UK)

MINIMAL TECHNO
(Berlin, Maurizio.)

SYNTHCORE
EIGHTIES REVIVAL
(DFA/GIGOLO REC.)

WELL, THAT'S MUCH CLEARER, ISN'T IT!

THE NEXT BIG THING!

SOMEWHERE IN THE WORLD, 2001

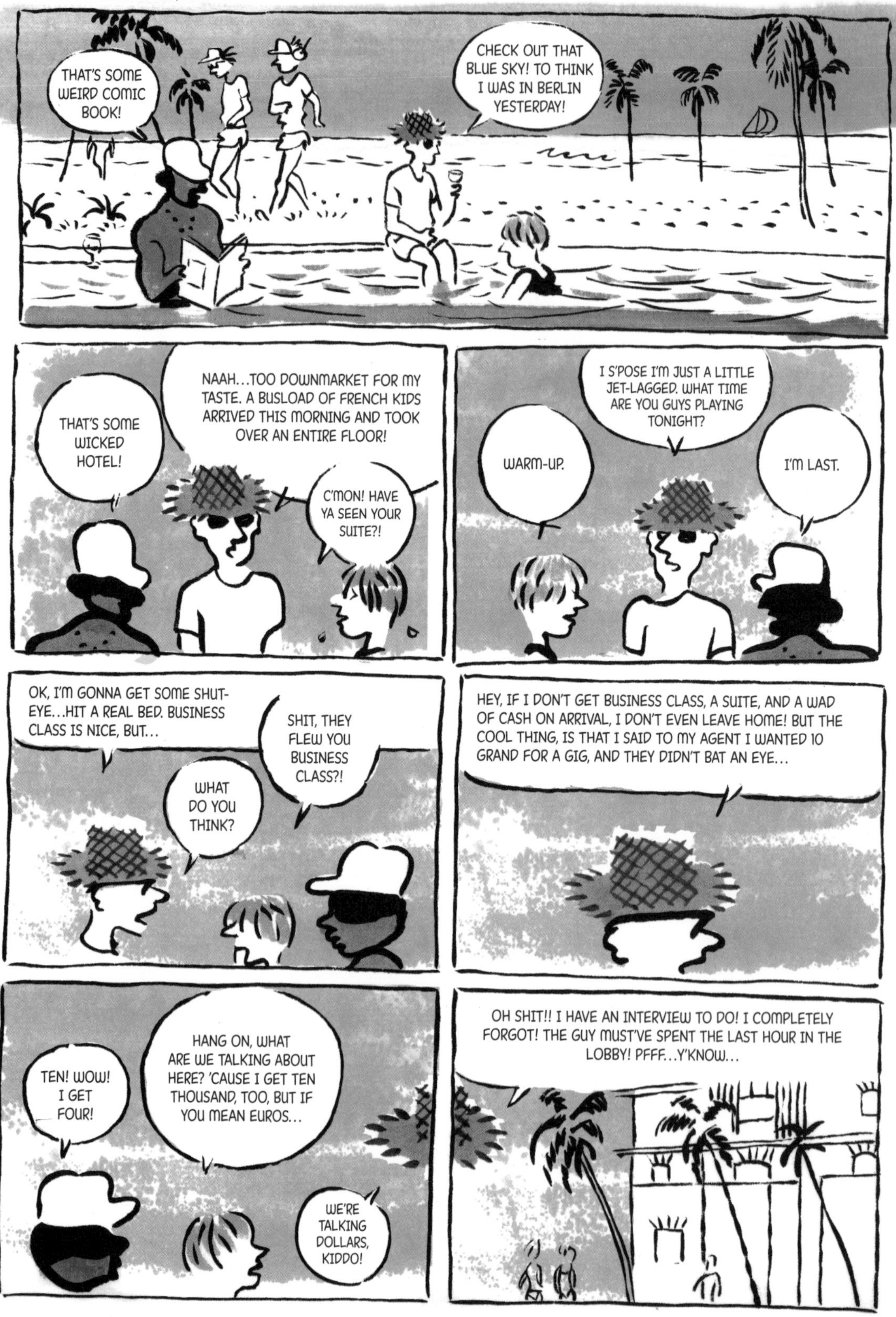

THAT'S SOME WEIRD COMIC BOOK!
CHECK OUT THAT BLUE SKY! TO THINK I WAS IN BERLIN YESTERDAY!
THAT'S SOME WICKED HOTEL!
NAAH...TOO DOWNMARKET FOR MY TASTE. A BUSLOAD OF FRENCH KIDS ARRIVED THIS MORNING AND TOOK OVER AN ENTIRE FLOOR!
C'MON! HAVE YA SEEN YOUR SUITE?!
I S'POSE I'M JUST A LITTLE JET-LAGGED. WHAT TIME ARE YOU GUYS PLAYING TONIGHT?
WARM-UP.
I'M LAST.
OK, I'M GONNA GET SOME SHUT-EYE...HIT A REAL BED. BUSINESS CLASS IS NICE, BUT...
SHIT, THEY FLEW YOU BUSINESS CLASS?!
WHAT DO YOU THINK?
HEY, IF I DON'T GET BUSINESS CLASS, A SUITE, AND A WAD OF CASH ON ARRIVAL, I DON'T EVEN LEAVE HOME! BUT THE COOL THING, IS THAT I SAID TO MY AGENT I WANTED 10 GRAND FOR A GIG, AND THEY DIDN'T BAT AN EYE...
TEN! WOW! I GET FOUR!
HANG ON, WHAT ARE WE TALKING ABOUT HERE? 'CAUSE I GET TEN THOUSAND, TOO, BUT IF YOU MEAN EUROS...
WE'RE TALKING DOLLARS, KIDDO!
OH SHIT!! I HAVE AN INTERVIEW TO DO! I COMPLETELY FORGOT! THE GUY MUST'VE SPENT THE LAST HOUR IN THE LOBBY! PFFF...Y'KNOW...

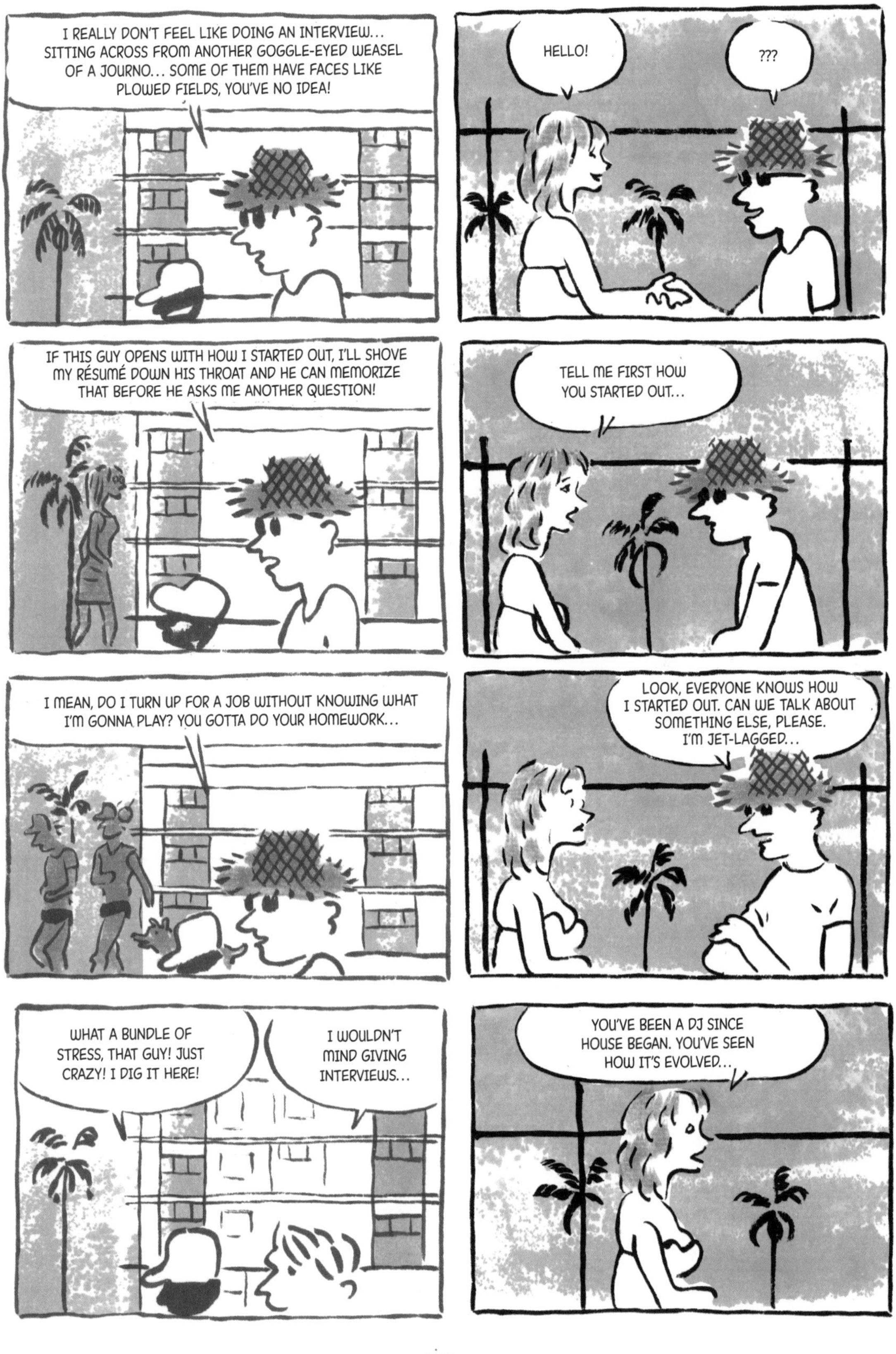
I REALLY DON'T FEEL LIKE DOING AN INTERVIEW... SITTING ACROSS FROM ANOTHER GOGGLE-EYED WEASEL OF A JOURNO... SOME OF THEM HAVE FACES LIKE PLOWED FIELDS, YOU'VE NO IDEA!
HELLO!
???
IF THIS GUY OPENS WITH HOW I STARTED OUT, I'LL SHOVE MY RÉSUMÉ DOWN HIS THROAT AND HE CAN MEMORIZE THAT BEFORE HE ASKS ME ANOTHER QUESTION!
TELL ME FIRST HOW YOU STARTED OUT...
I MEAN, DO I TURN UP FOR A JOB WITHOUT KNOWING WHAT I'M GONNA PLAY? YOU GOTTA DO YOUR HOMEWORK...
LOOK, EVERYONE KNOWS HOW I STARTED OUT. CAN WE TALK ABOUT SOMETHING ELSE, PLEASE. I'M JET-LAGGED...
WHAT A BUNDLE OF STRESS, THAT GUY! JUST CRAZY! I DIG IT HERE!
I WOULDN'T MIND GIVING INTERVIEWS...
YOU'VE BEEN A DJ SINCE HOUSE BEGAN. YOU'VE SEEN HOW IT'S EVOLVED...

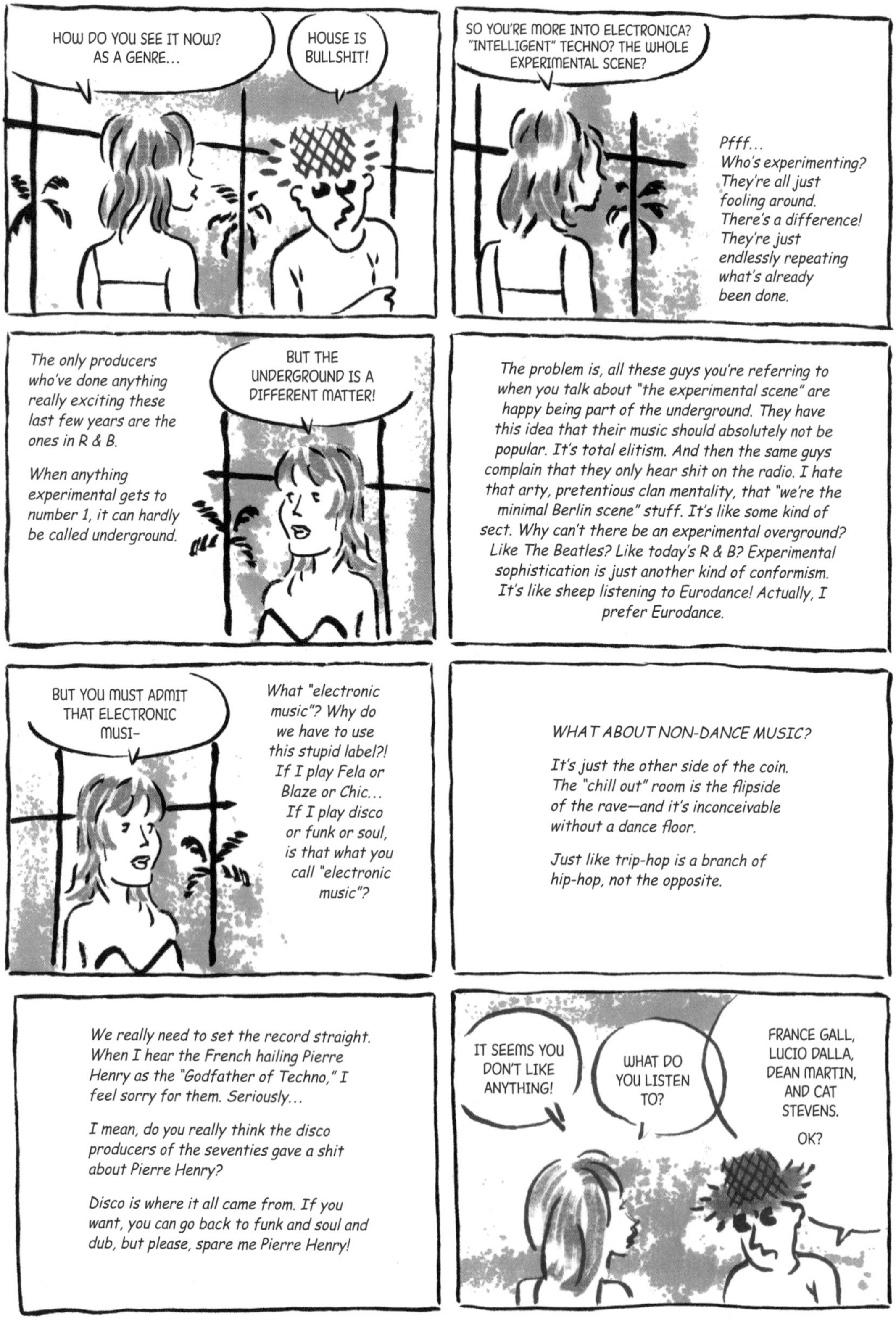
HOW DO YOU SEE IT NOW? AS A GENRE...
HOUSE IS BULLSHIT!
SO YOU'RE MORE INTO ELECTRONICA? "INTELLIGENT" TECHNO? THE WHOLE EXPERIMENTAL SCENE?
Pfff... Who's experimenting? They're all just fooling around. There's a difference! They're just endlessly repeating what's already been done.
The only producers who've done anything really exciting these last few years are the ones in R & B.
When anything experimental gets to number 1, it can hardly be called underground.
BUT THE UNDERGROUND IS A DIFFERENT MATTER!
The problem is, all these guys you're referring to when you talk about "the experimental scene" are happy being part of the underground. They have this idea that their music should absolutely not be popular. It's total elitism. And then the same guys complain that they only hear shit on the radio. I hate that arty, pretentious clan mentality, that "we're the minimal Berlin scene" stuff. It's like some kind of sect. Why can't there be an experimental overground? Like The Beatles? Like today's R & B? Experimental sophistication is just another kind of conformism. It's like sheep listening to Eurodance! Actually, I prefer Eurodance.
BUT YOU MUST ADMIT THAT ELECTRONIC MUSI–
What "electronic music"? Why do we have to use this stupid label?! If I play Fela or Blaze or Chic... If I play disco or funk or soul, is that what you call "electronic music"?
WHAT ABOUT NON-DANCE MUSIC?
It's just the other side of the coin. The "chill out" room is the flipside of the rave—and it's inconceivable without a dance floor.
Just like trip-hop is a branch of hip-hop, not the opposite.
We really need to set the record straight. When I hear the French hailing Pierre Henry as the "Godfather of Techno," I feel sorry for them. Seriously...
I mean, do you really think the disco producers of the seventies gave a shit about Pierre Henry?
Disco is where it all came from. If you want, you can go back to funk and soul and dub, but please, spare me Pierre Henry!
IT SEEMS YOU DON'T LIKE ANYTHING!
WHAT DO YOU LISTEN TO?
FRANCE GALL, LUCIO DALLA, DEAN MARTIN, AND CAT STEVENS.
OK?

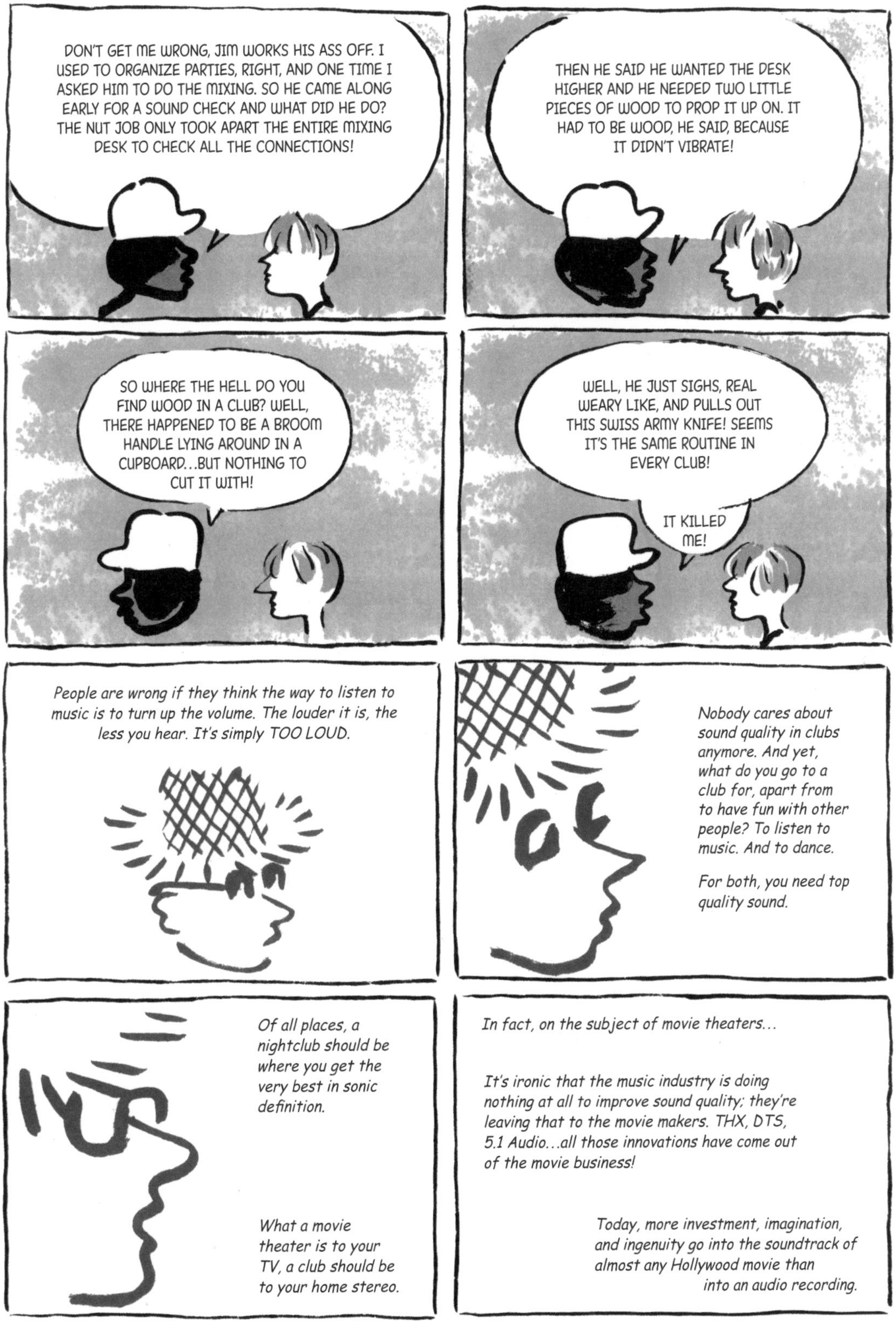
DON'T GET ME WRONG, JIM WORKS HIS ASS OFF. I USED TO ORGANIZE PARTIES, RIGHT, AND ONE TIME I ASKED HIM TO DO THE MIXING. SO HE CAME ALONG EARLY FOR A SOUND CHECK AND WHAT DID HE DO? THE NUT JOB ONLY TOOK APART THE ENTIRE MIXING DESK TO CHECK ALL THE CONNECTIONS!
THEN HE SAID HE WANTED THE DESK HIGHER AND HE NEEDED TWO LITTLE PIECES OF WOOD TO PROP IT UP ON. IT HAD TO BE WOOD, HE SAID, BECAUSE IT DIDN'T VIBRATE!
SO WHERE THE HELL DO YOU FIND WOOD IN A CLUB? WELL, THERE HAPPENED TO BE A BROOM HANDLE LYING AROUND IN A CUPBOARD...BUT NOTHING TO CUT IT WITH!
WELL, HE JUST SIGHS, REAL WEARY LIKE, AND PULLS OUT THIS SWISS ARMY KNIFE! SEEMS IT'S THE SAME ROUTINE IN EVERY CLUB!
IT KILLED ME!
People are wrong if they think the way to listen to music is to turn up the volume. The louder it is, the less you hear. It's simply TOO LOUD.
Nobody cares about sound quality in clubs anymore. And yet, what do you go to a club for, apart from to have fun with other people? To listen to music. And to dance.
For both, you need top quality sound.
Of all places, a nightclub should be where you get the very best in sonic definition.
What a movie theater is to your TV, a club should be to your home stereo.
In fact, on the subject of movie theaters...
It's ironic that the music industry is doing nothing at all to improve sound quality; they're leaving that to the movie makers. THX, DTS, 5.1 Audio...all those innovations have come out of the movie business!
Today, more investment, imagination, and ingenuity go into the soundtrack of almost any Hollywood movie than into an audio recording.

Which is why we need discotheques in the original sense of the term—"disk emporia." They should be listening centers...auditoria, in fact—that's just the word! And listening doesn't preclude dancing...or hooking up!

IS THAT YOUR IDEAL CLUB, THE CLUB OF THE FUTURE?

I'm too old for ideals, but OK... yes! I imagine a club where everything is perfect: the reception, the cocktails, the seats, the dancers, the decor, the lighting, the dance floor, even the bathrooms... the whole damn thing!

DO YOU HAVE OTHER VISIONS OF THE FUTURE LIKE THAT?

I don't really have visions of the future...and I don't think I'm the only one, either.

And that's worrying. We don't see the future as a real thing anymore.

We're in the twenty-first century now, but who cares? I remember when I was little, the year 2000 was like a giant full stop...Going beyond it was like leaping into the unknown.

Twentieth-century literature, movies, comic books, music...they all looked forward—to 1984, SPACE: 1999, 2001: A SPACE ODYSSEY

Everything was dated; everything was a vision of the future.

In the fifties, people imagined the future to be a nice straight line—a little totalitarian, maybe, but more laid-back, if you know what I mean. Everyone would dress the same, eat the same food, and live in places that were the ultimate in design, and there'd be universal peace because everything bad would have been wiped out.

People of the future were pictured as supercool and free of material need, because they had everything—wealth, freedom to travel, unlimited information...Progress with a capital P.

But, at the end of the sixties and the start of the seventies, when those illusions had evaporated, there was a crisis, and popular science-fiction presented an apocalyptic vision of the future—PLANET OF THE APES, SOYLENT GREEN, etc.—in fact, so apocalyptic that all anyone in the eighties could see was everyone turning back into savages. It was nothing but MAD MAX and zombies, all that kind of thing— the aftermath of nuclear war. Man fighting for survival...

And since then? Nothing. Nothing at all.

Ever since STAR WARS, we've been running away from the future: "A long time ago, in a galaxy far, far away...." In other words, look somewhere else; the future isn't tomorrow—it's inside your head.

As it turned out, the year 2000 was nothing special. Neither was 2001...And we can no longer invent the future.

The biggest thing at the turn of the millennium—the biggest thing in sci-fi, that is—was THE MATRIX. And what was its vision of the future?

Virtual reality.

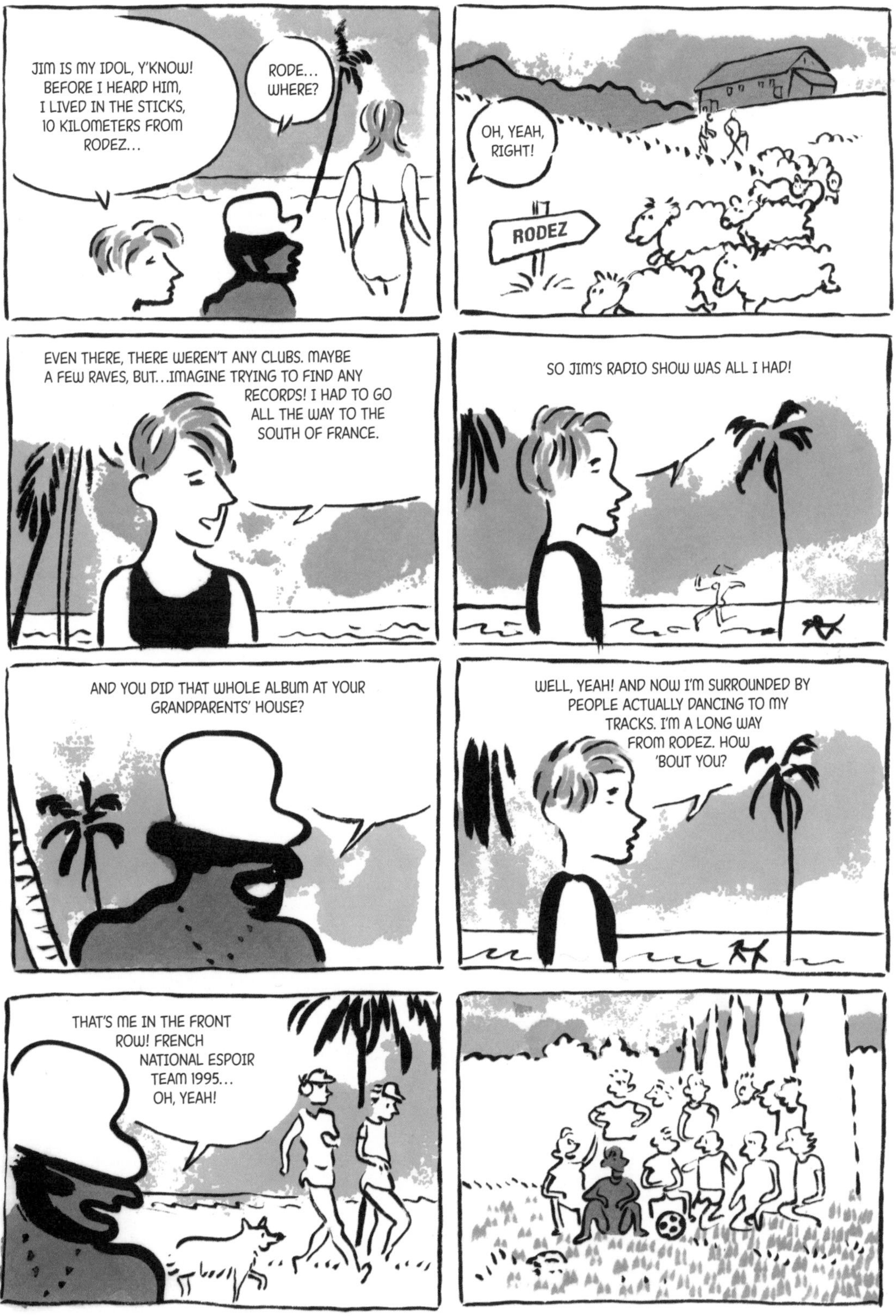
JIM IS MY IDOL, Y'KNOW! BEFORE I HEARD HIM, I LIVED IN THE STICKS, 10 KILOMETERS FROM RODEZ...
RODE... WHERE?
OH, YEAH, RIGHT!
RODEZ
EVEN THERE, THERE WEREN'T ANY CLUBS. MAYBE A FEW RAVES, BUT...IMAGINE TRYING TO FIND ANY RECORDS! I HAD TO GO ALL THE WAY TO THE SOUTH OF FRANCE.
SO JIM'S RADIO SHOW WAS ALL I HAD!
AND YOU DID THAT WHOLE ALBUM AT YOUR GRANDPARENTS' HOUSE?
WELL, YEAH! AND NOW I'M SURROUNDED BY PEOPLE ACTUALLY DANCING TO MY TRACKS. I'M A LONG WAY FROM RODEZ. HOW 'BOUT YOU?
THAT'S ME IN THE FRONT ROW! FRENCH NATIONAL ESPOIR TEAM 1995... OH, YEAH!

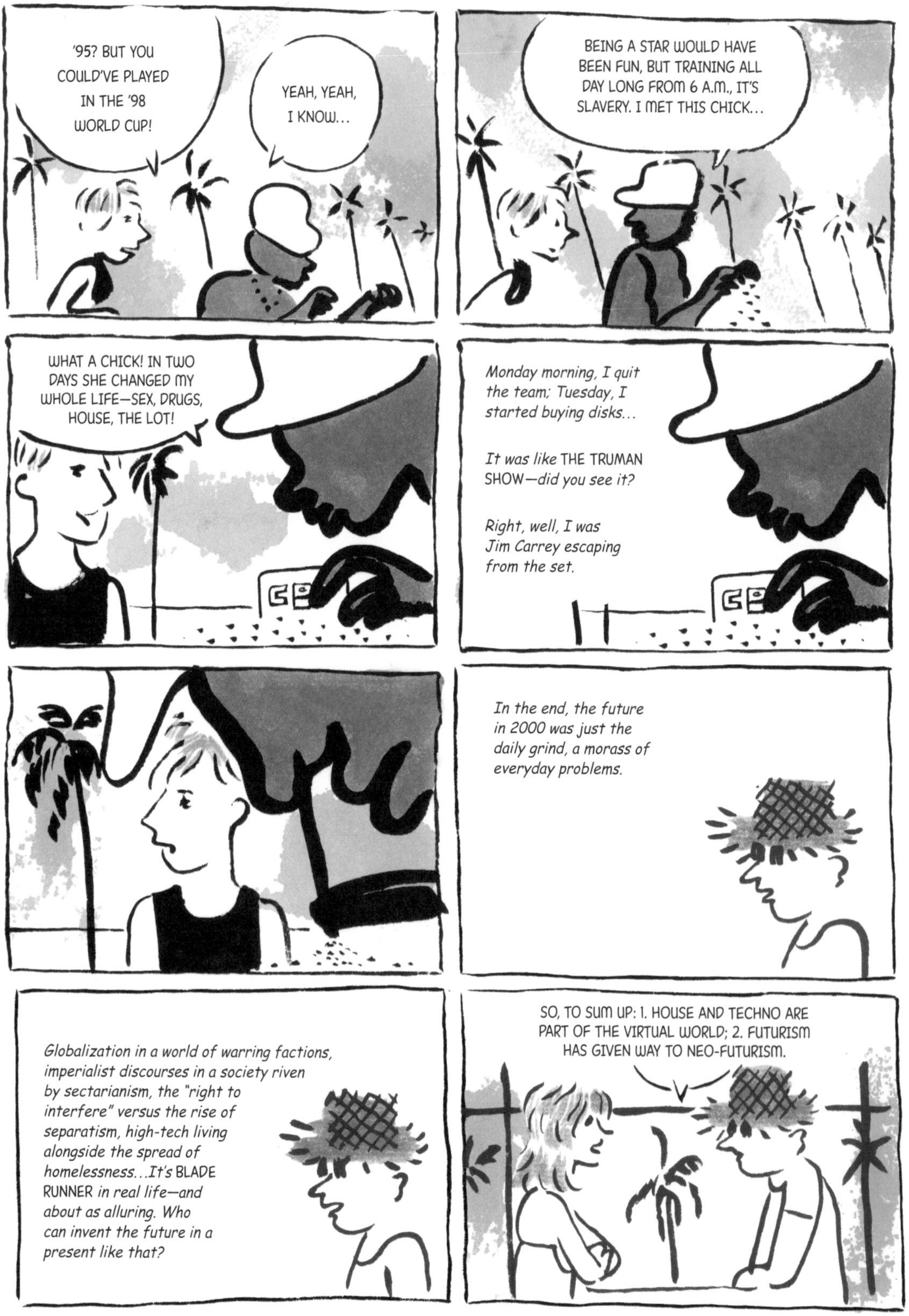
'95? BUT YOU COULD'VE PLAYED IN THE '98 WORLD CUP!
YEAH, YEAH, I KNOW...
BEING A STAR WOULD HAVE BEEN FUN, BUT TRAINING ALL DAY LONG FROM 6 A.M., IT'S SLAVERY. I MET THIS CHICK...
WHAT A CHICK! IN TWO DAYS SHE CHANGED MY WHOLE LIFE—SEX, DRUGS, HOUSE, THE LOT!
Monday morning, I quit the team; Tuesday, I started buying disks...
It was like THE TRUMAN SHOW—did you see it?
Right, well, I was Jim Carrey escaping from the set.
In the end, the future in 2000 was just the daily grind, a morass of everyday problems.
Globalization in a world of warring factions, imperialist discourses in a society riven by sectarianism, the "right to interfere" versus the rise of separatism, high-tech living alongside the spread of homelessness...It's BLADE RUNNER in real life—and about as alluring. Who can invent the future in a present like that?
SO, TO SUM UP: 1. HOUSE AND TECHNO ARE PART OF THE VIRTUAL WORLD; 2. FUTURISM HAS GIVEN WAY TO NEO-FUTURISM.

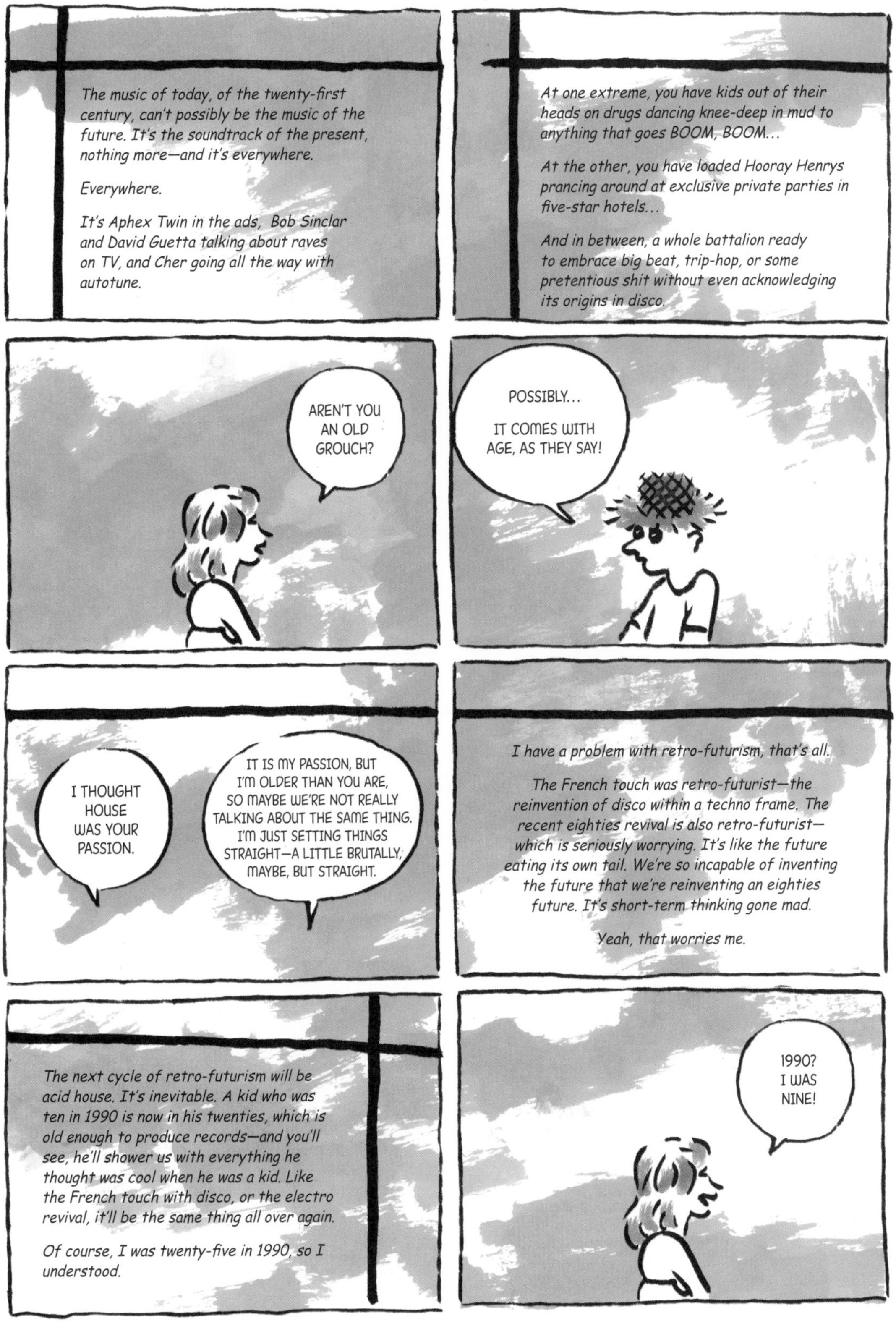
The music of today, of the twenty-first century, can't possibly be the music of the future. It's the soundtrack of the present, nothing more—and it's everywhere.
Everywhere.
It's Aphex Twin in the ads, Bob Sinclar and David Guetta talking about raves on TV, and Cher going all the way with autotune.
At one extreme, you have kids out of their heads on drugs dancing knee-deep in mud to anything that goes BOOM, BOOM...
At the other, you have loaded Hooray Henrys prancing around at exclusive private parties in five-star hotels...
And in between, a whole battalion ready to embrace big beat, trip-hop, or some pretentious shit without even acknowledging its origins in disco.
AREN'T YOU AN OLD GROUCH?
POSSIBLY... IT COMES WITH AGE, AS THEY SAY!
I THOUGHT HOUSE WAS YOUR PASSION.
IT IS MY PASSION, BUT I'M OLDER THAN YOU ARE, SO MAYBE WE'RE NOT REALLY TALKING ABOUT THE SAME THING. I'M JUST SETTING THINGS STRAIGHT—A LITTLE BRUTALLY, MAYBE, BUT STRAIGHT.
I have a problem with retro-futurism, that's all.
The French touch was retro-futurist—the reinvention of disco within a techno frame. The recent eighties revival is also retro-futurist—which is seriously worrying. It's like the future eating its own tail. We're so incapable of inventing the future that we're reinventing an eighties future. It's short-term thinking gone mad.
Yeah, that worries me.
The next cycle of retro-futurism will be acid house. It's inevitable. A kid who was ten in 1990 is now in his twenties, which is old enough to produce records—and you'll see, he'll shower us with everything he thought was cool when he was a kid. Like the French touch with disco, or the electro revival, it'll be the same thing all over again.
Of course, I was twenty-five in 1990, so I understood.
1990? I WAS NINE!

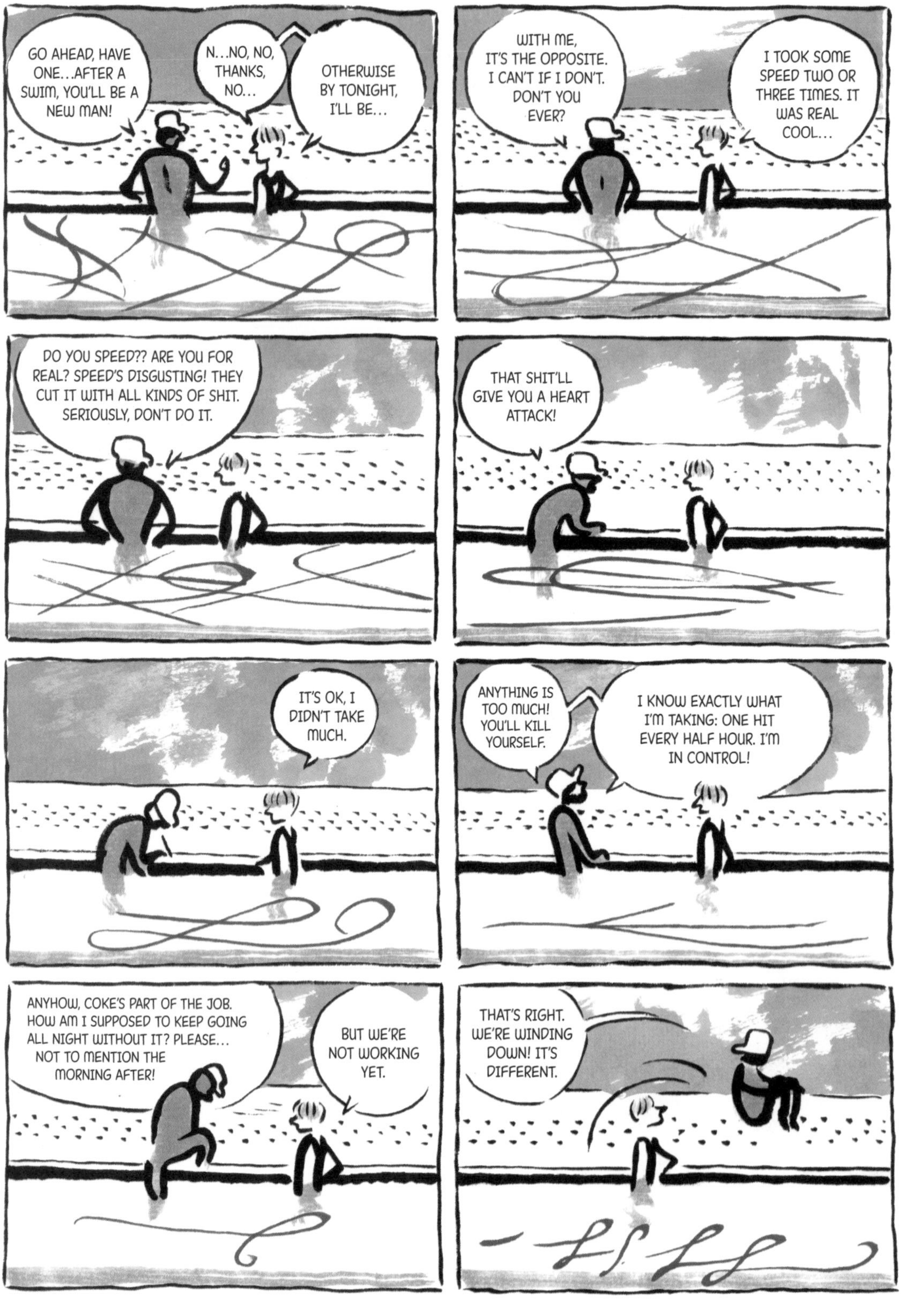
GO AHEAD, HAVE ONE...AFTER A SWIM, YOU'LL BE A NEW MAN!
N...NO, NO, THANKS, NO...
OTHERWISE BY TONIGHT, I'LL BE...
WITH ME, IT'S THE OPPOSITE. I CAN'T IF I DON'T. DON'T YOU EVER?
I TOOK SOME SPEED TWO OR THREE TIMES. IT WAS REAL COOL...
DO YOU SPEED?? ARE YOU FOR REAL? SPEED'S DISGUSTING! THEY CUT IT WITH ALL KINDS OF SHIT. SERIOUSLY, DON'T DO IT.
THAT SHIT'LL GIVE YOU A HEART ATTACK!
IT'S OK, I DIDN'T TAKE MUCH.
ANYTHING IS TOO MUCH! YOU'LL KILL YOURSELF.
I KNOW EXACTLY WHAT I'M TAKING: ONE HIT EVERY HALF HOUR. I'M IN CONTROL!
ANYHOW, COKE'S PART OF THE JOB. HOW AM I SUPPOSED TO KEEP GOING ALL NIGHT WITHOUT IT? PLEASE... NOT TO MENTION THE MORNING AFTER!
BUT WE'RE NOT WORKING YET.
THAT'S RIGHT. WE'RE WINDING DOWN! IT'S DIFFERENT.

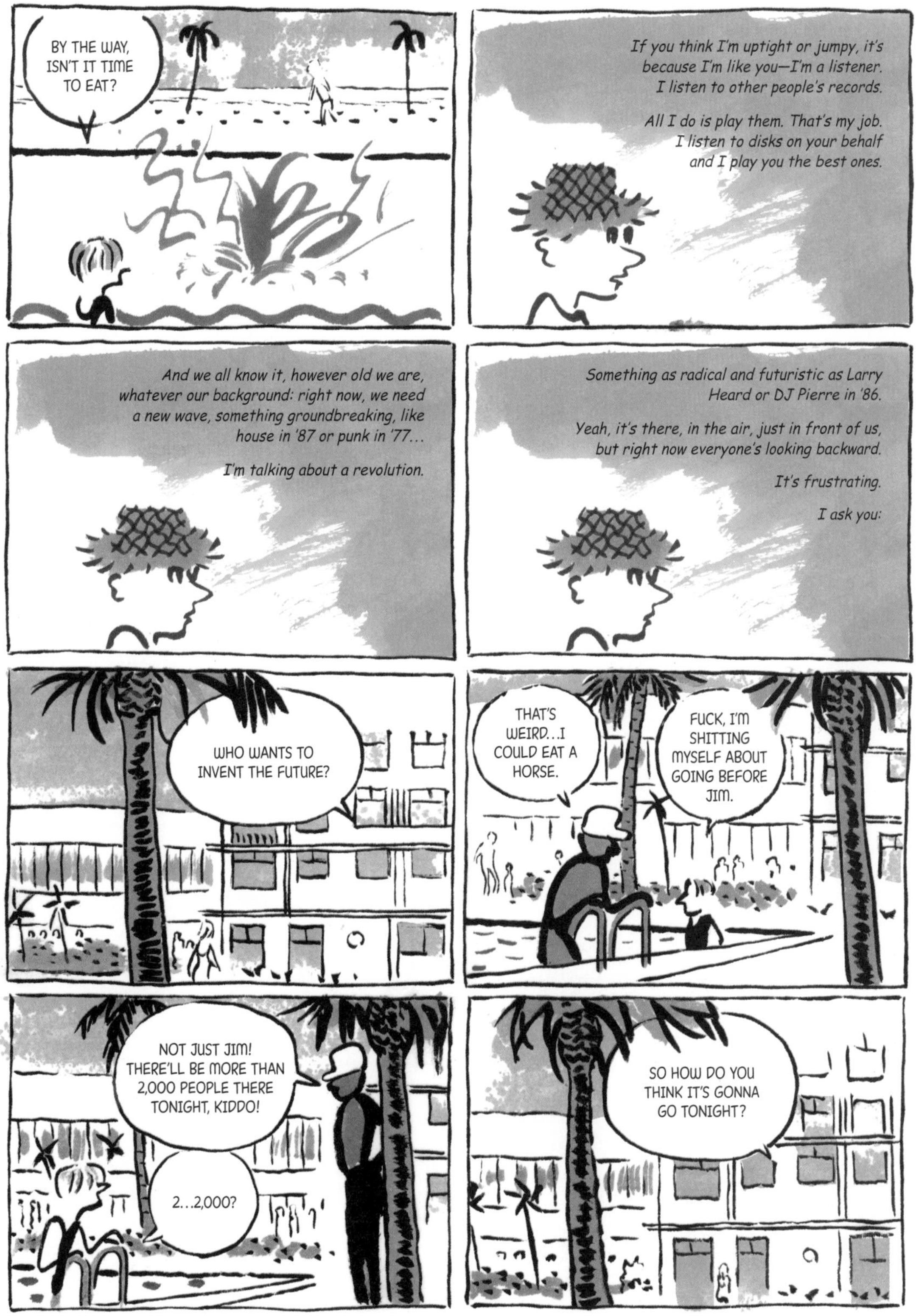
BY THE WAY, ISN'T IT TIME TO EAT?
If you think I'm uptight or jumpy, it's because I'm like you—I'm a listener. I listen to other people's records.
All I do is play them. That's my job. I listen to disks on your behalf and I play you the best ones.
And we all know it, however old we are, whatever our background: right now, we need a new wave, something groundbreaking, like house in '87 or punk in '77...
I'm talking about a revolution.
Something as radical and futuristic as Larry Heard or DJ Pierre in '86.
Yeah, it's there, in the air, just in front of us, but right now everyone's looking backward.
It's frustrating.
I ask you:
WHO WANTS TO INVENT THE FUTURE?
THAT'S WEIRD...I COULD EAT A HORSE.
FUCK, I'M SHITTING MYSELF ABOUT GOING BEFORE JIM.
NOT JUST JIM! THERE'LL BE MORE THAN 2,000 PEOPLE THERE TONIGHT, KIDDO!
2...2,000?
SO HOW DO YOU THINK IT'S GONNA GO TONIGHT?

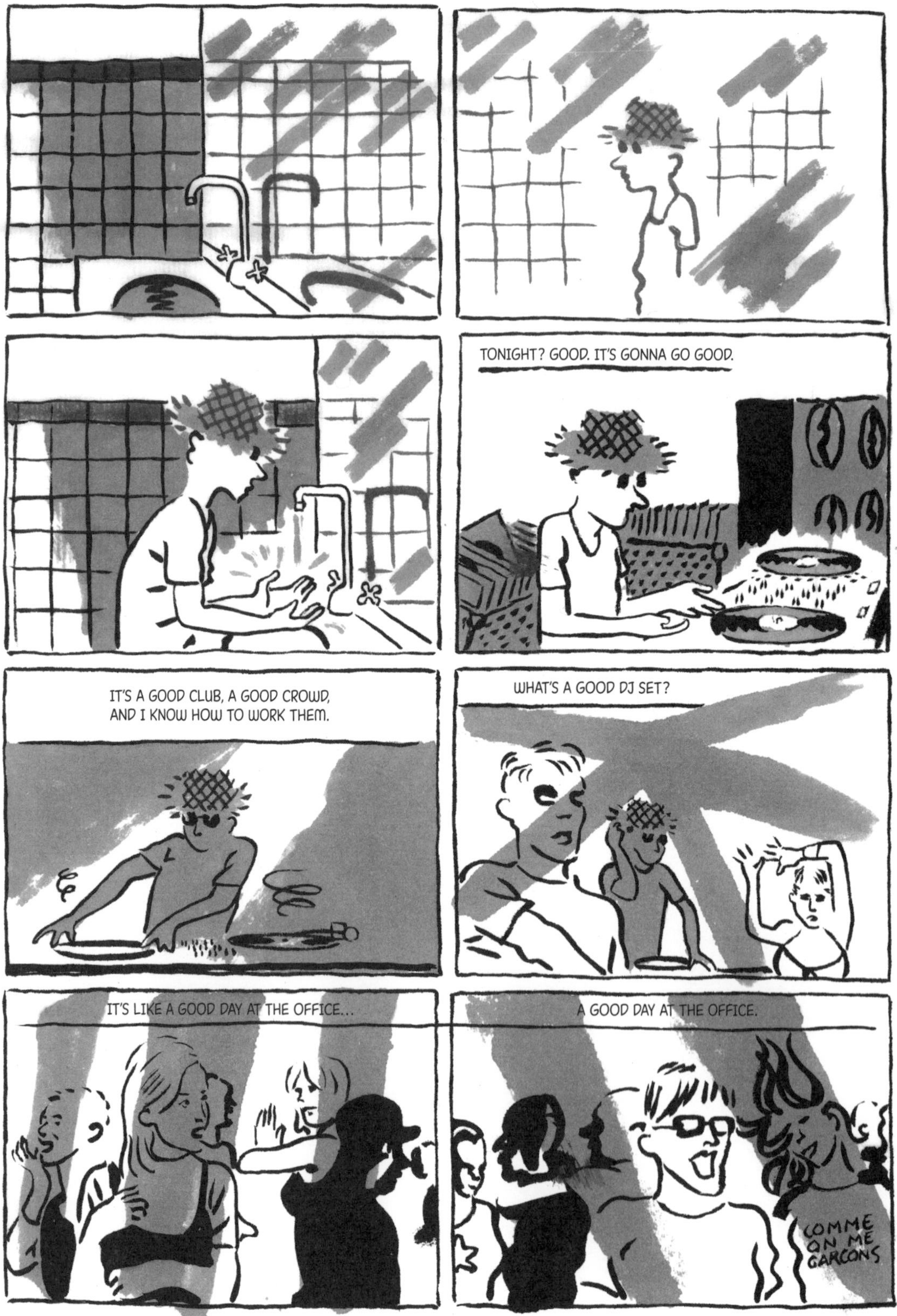
TONIGHT? GOOD. IT'S GONNA GO GOOD.
IT'S A GOOD CLUB, A GOOD CROWD, AND I KNOW HOW TO WORK THEM.
WHAT'S A GOOD DJ SET?
IT'S LIKE A GOOD DAY AT THE OFFICE...
A GOOD DAY AT THE OFFICE.
COMME ON ME GARCONS

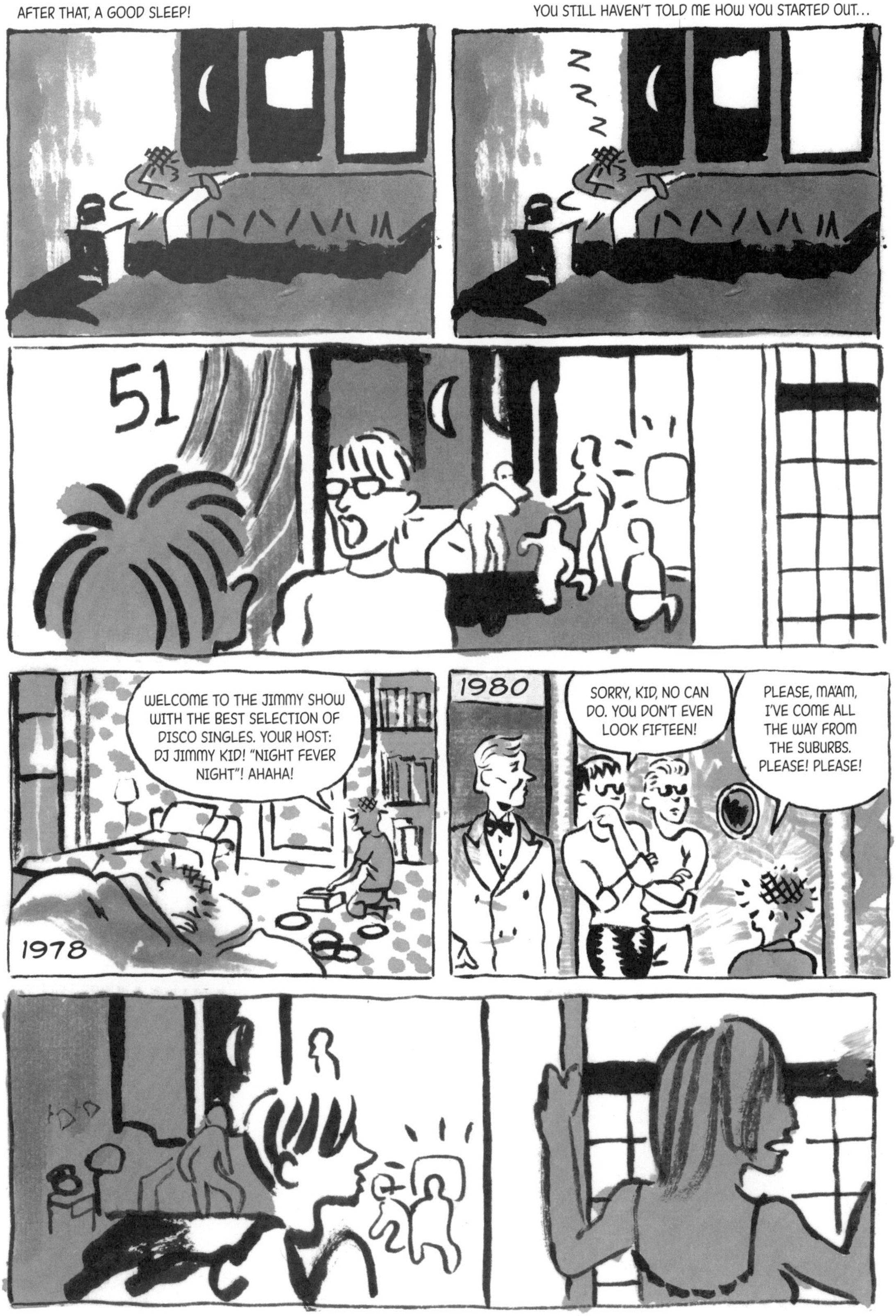
AFTER THAT, A GOOD SLEEP!
YOU STILL HAVEN'T TOLD ME HOW YOU STARTED OUT...
Z Z Z
51
WELCOME TO THE JIMMY SHOW WITH THE BEST SELECTION OF DISCO SINGLES. YOUR HOST: DJ JIMMY KID! "NIGHT FEVER NIGHT"! AHAHA!
1978
1980
SORRY, KID, NO CAN DO. YOU DON'T EVEN LOOK FIFTEEN!
PLEASE, MA'AM, I'VE COME ALL THE WAY FROM THE SUBURBS. PLEASE! PLEASE!

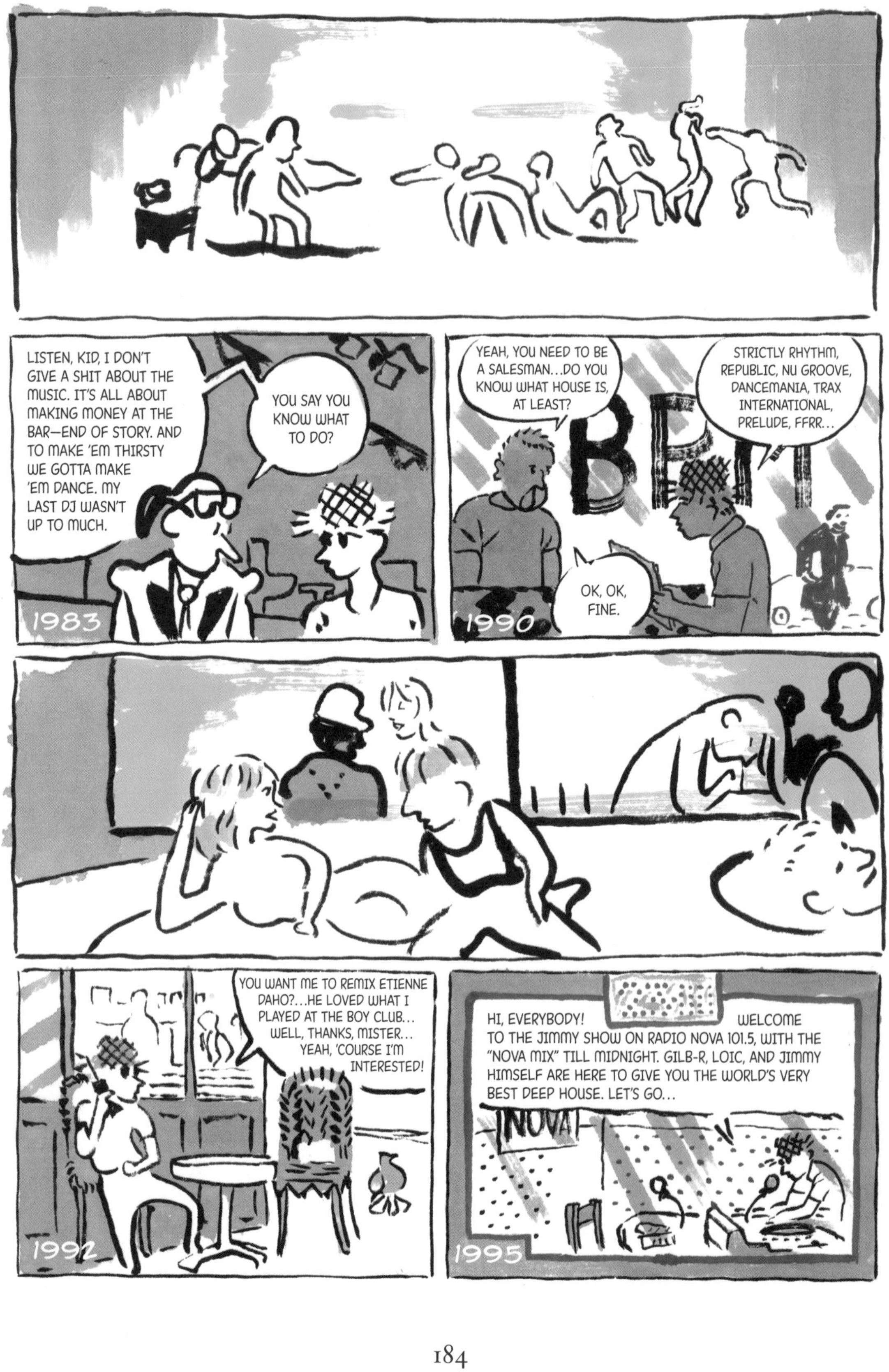
LISTEN, KID, I DON'T GIVE A SHIT ABOUT THE MUSIC. IT'S ALL ABOUT MAKING MONEY AT THE BAR—END OF STORY. AND TO MAKE 'EM THIRSTY WE GOTTA MAKE 'EM DANCE. MY LAST DJ WASN'T UP TO MUCH.
YOU SAY YOU KNOW WHAT TO DO?
1983
YEAH, YOU NEED TO BE A SALESMAN...DO YOU KNOW WHAT HOUSE IS, AT LEAST?
STRICTLY RHYTHM, REPUBLIC, NU GROOVE, DANCEMANIA, TRAX INTERNATIONAL, PRELUDE, FFRR...
OK, OK, FINE.
1990
YOU WANT ME TO REMIX ETIENNE DAHO?...HE LOVED WHAT I PLAYED AT THE BOY CLUB... WELL, THANKS, MISTER... YEAH, 'COURSE I'M INTERESTED!
1992
HI, EVERYBODY! WELCOME TO THE JIMMY SHOW ON RADIO NOVA 101.5, WITH THE "NOVA MIX" TILL MIDNIGHT. GILB-R, LOIC, AND JIMMY HIMSELF ARE HERE TO GIVE YOU THE WORLD'S VERY BEST DEEP HOUSE. LET'S GO...
NOVA
1995

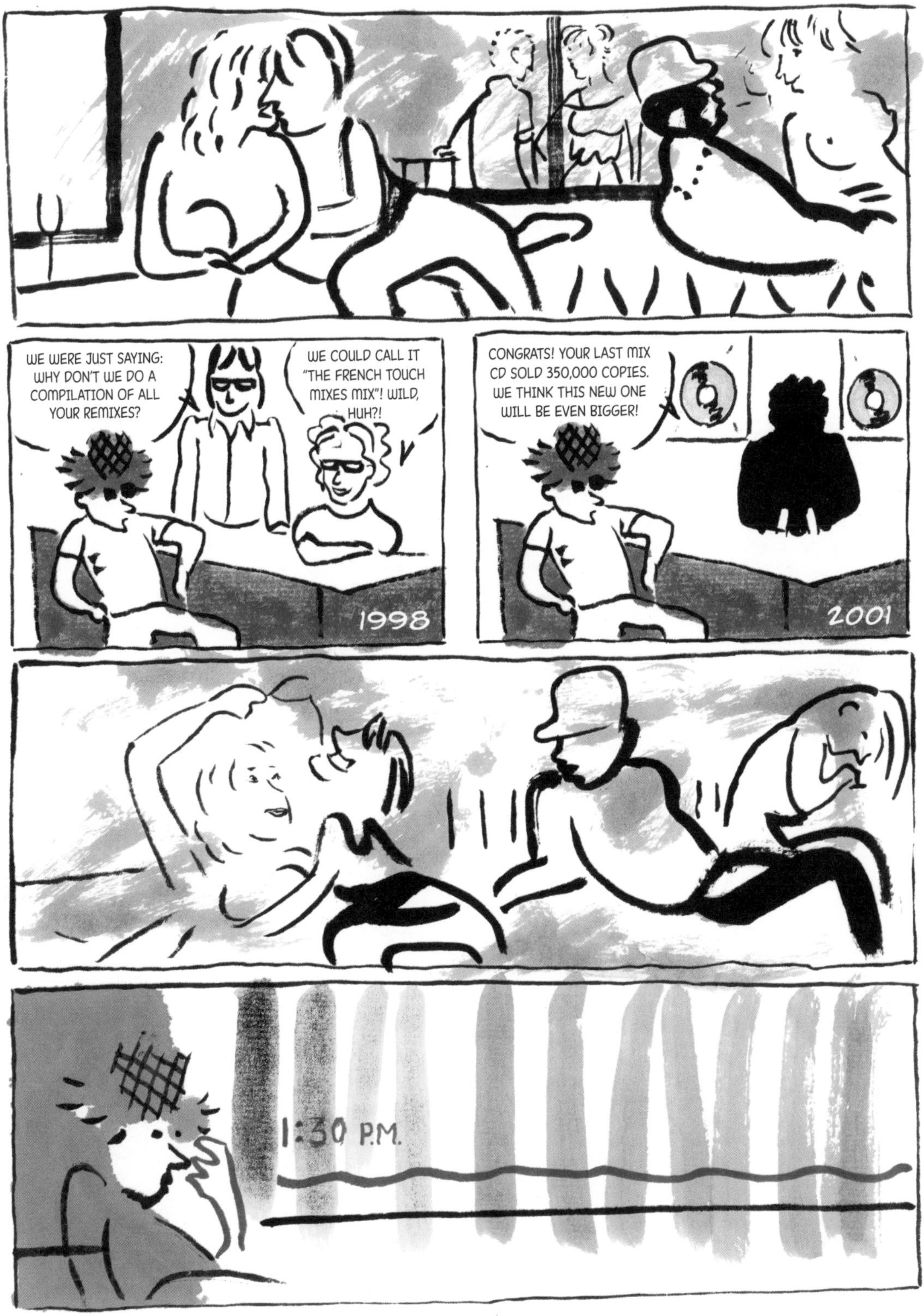
WE WERE JUST SAYING: WHY DON'T WE DO A COMPILATION OF ALL YOUR REMIXES?
WE COULD CALL IT "THE FRENCH TOUCH MIXES MIX"! WILD, HUH?!
1998
CONGRATS! YOUR LAST MIX CD SOLD 350,000 COPIES. WE THINK THIS NEW ONE WILL BE EVEN BIGGER!
2001
1:30 P.M.

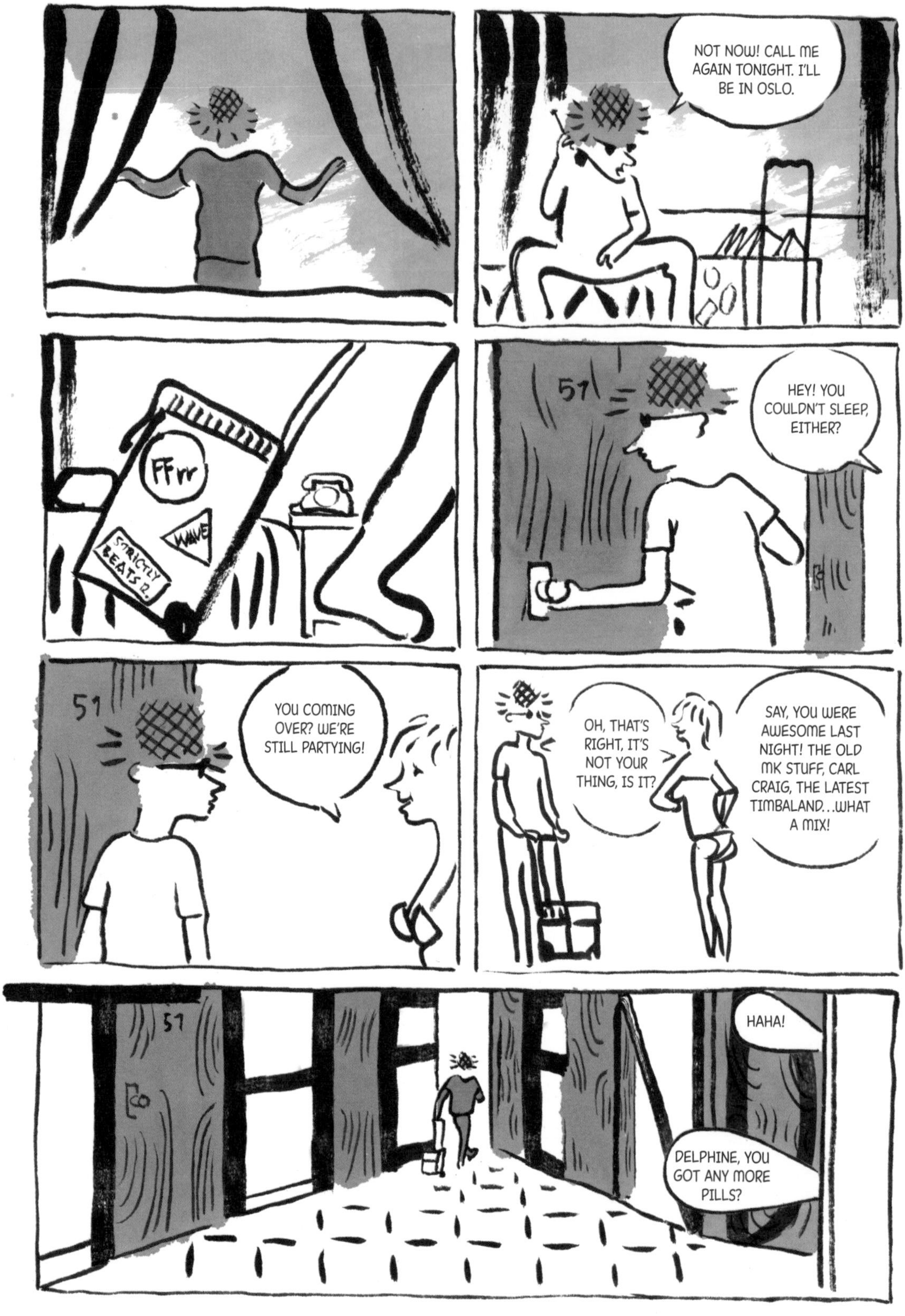
NOT NOW! CALL ME AGAIN TONIGHT. I'LL BE IN OSLO.
FFrr
WAVE
STRICTLY BEATS 12.
51
HEY! YOU COULDN'T SLEEP, EITHER?
51
YOU COMING OVER? WE'RE STILL PARTYING!
OH, THAT'S RIGHT, IT'S NOT YOUR THING, IS IT?
SAY, YOU WERE AWESOME LAST NIGHT! THE OLD MK STUFF, CARL CRAIG, THE LATEST TIMBALAND...WHAT A MIX!
51
HAHA!
DELPHINE, YOU GOT ANY MORE PILLS?

BONUS BEATS

189–209

In 2001, Mathias and David went to Liverpool to meet New Order, who were about to release *Get Ready*. These pages, which were not part of the original book, were first published in the independent music magazine *Magic* and then made available as an insert with the Warner France pressing of the album.

211–215

A tribute to Mathias Cousin by David Blot (2016).

216–217

Previously unpublished drawings by Mathias Cousin that were part of an alternative version of Volume 2 of *Le Chant de la Machine*.

218–219

Illustration for the inside of the vinyl compilation album *Le Chant de la Machine*, released by Source in 2000.

220–221

Illustration for *La Danse dans le monde*.

223

Tribute to Mathias Cousin by Pierre Le-Tan.

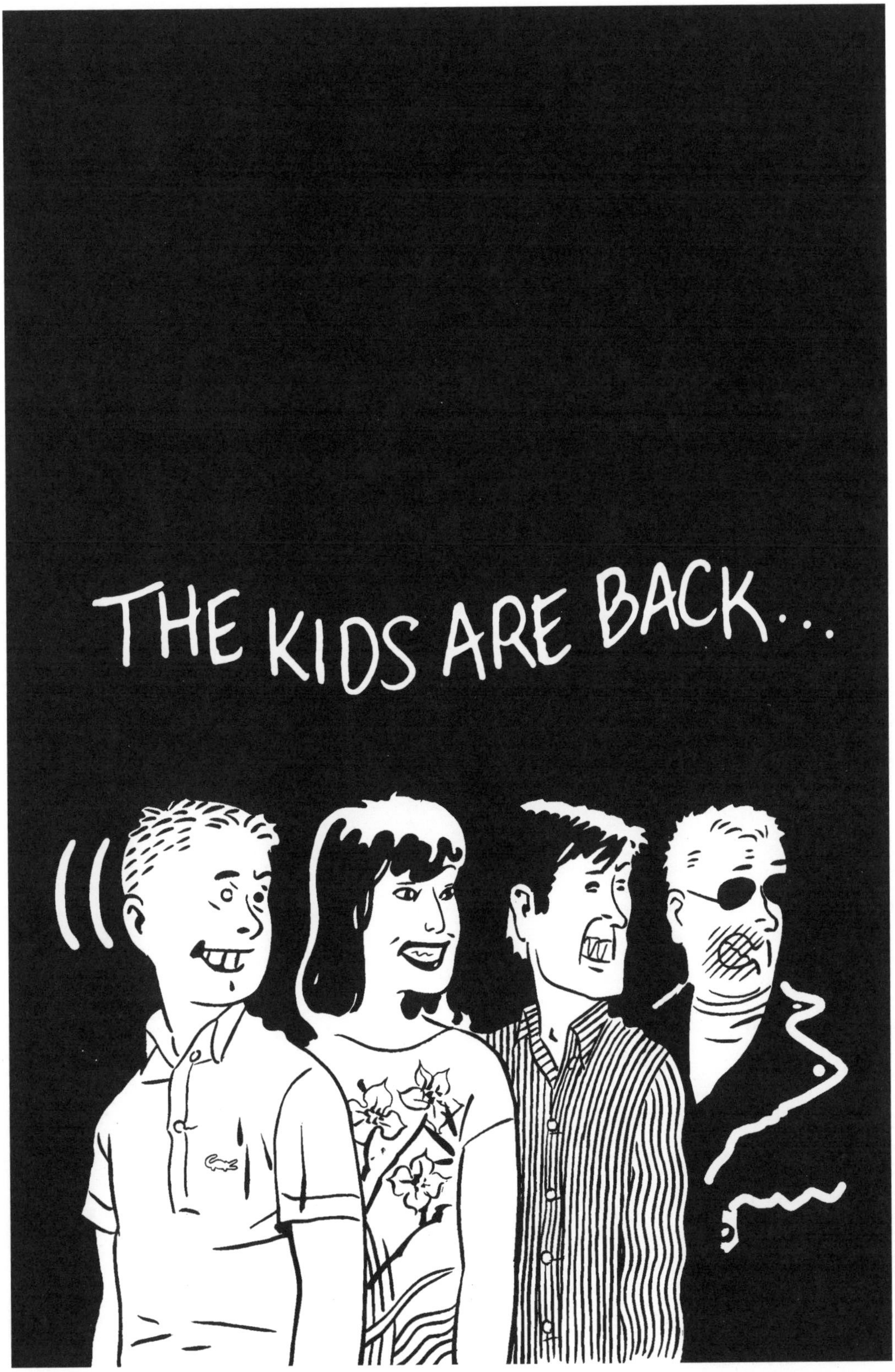
THE KIDS ARE BACK...

DAVID'S STORY

IN 1982, I WAS 12 YEARS OLD, AND THERE WAS NO OFFICIAL FRENCH HIT PARADE. EACH RADIO STATION HAD ITS OWN, AND IF THEY WERE REALLY SWITCHED ON, THEY HAD A "TOP CLUB HIT."

Just an illusion

EVERY WEEK, I'D LIST EACH STATION'S TOP HITS AND DO SOME KIND OF CALCULATION TO WORK OUT WHICH WERE THE BIGGEST SONGS OF THE WEEK.

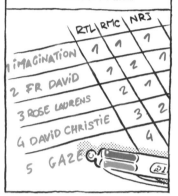

	RTL	RMC	NRJ
1 IMAGINATION	1	1	1
2 FR DAVID	1	2	1
3 ROSE LAURENS		2	
4 DAVID CHRISTIE		3	2
5 GAZE			4

THE HARDEST PART WAS CATCHING FRANCE-INTER'S CLUB HIT, WHICH WAS ON AT 3 A.M. ONE NIGHT IN JULY '83, AFTER ANNOUNCING THE CHARTS THE DJ PLAYED A "TEASER"

—A RECORD THAT WASN'T YET ON THE HIT PARADE BUT THAT EVERYONE WAS TALKING ABOUT...

NOO ORDER?

NEW ORDER'S "BLUE MONDAY." IT WAS LIKE NOTHING I'D EVER HEARD.

THE FOLLOWING SUNDAY, RTL PLAYED A NEW TRACK NOT ON THE CHARTS YET...I STARTED TO REALIZE THAT THE BEST DISKS NEVER MADE IT INTO THE HIT PARADE.

SO THAT MONDAY, I WENT TO LOOK FOR IT...

THIS IS IT!

IT WAS A TWELVE-INCH SINGLE!

I WAS EVEN COMPLIMENTED ON MY TASTE BY MY OLDER BROTHER!

AH! NOW THIS AIN'T ONE OF YOUR SHITTY HITS!

THE SOUND OF THE FUTURE!

I TELL YOU, KID: THIS IS...

THE INTRO IS JUST A BEAT—CLIPPED, LIKE A MACHINE GUN: TCHAK, TCHAK, TCHAK...THEN IT STARTS TO TAKE OFF... THE MACHINES KICK IN: SEQUENCER, BASS BOX...A DISTANT, DRAWLING VOICE... LYRICS, BUT NO REFRAIN... THE BREAK LITERALLY BREAKS UP THE BEAT...

I FEEL LIKE MY TURNTABLE IS A FLIGHT DECK AND I'M FLYING OVER IT, LOOKING FOR THE NEXT "BLUE MONDAY"...

THE CLIMAX IS CRAZY—RED ARMY CHOIR + COMPUTERS + KRAFTWERK + BASS SOUNDS FROM BEYOND THE GRAVE—ALL AT 130 BPM.

MONDAY BLUES OR A TRIP TO ANOTHER PLANET?

WHEN I GOT TO 14, I CHANGED DIRECTION. NO MORE HIT PARADE; IT WAS U.S. ROCK FOR ME...

IT WAS THE FLESHTONES AND BRUCE SPRINGSTEEN.

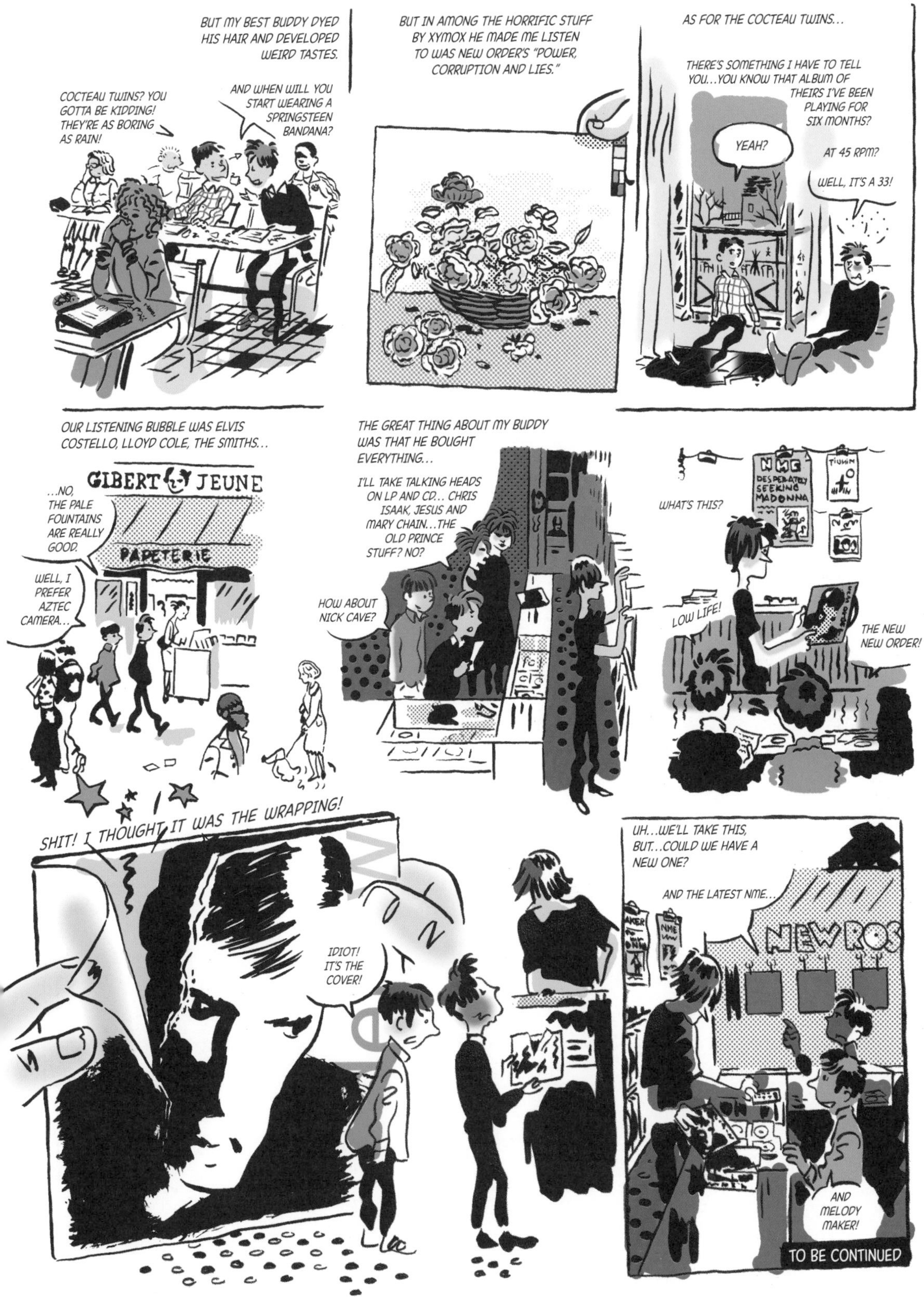

BUT MY BEST BUDDY DYED HIS HAIR AND DEVELOPED WEIRD TASTES.
COCTEAU TWINS? YOU GOTTA BE KIDDING! THEY'RE AS BORING AS RAIN!
AND WHEN WILL YOU START WEARING A SPRINGSTEEN BANDANA?
BUT IN AMONG THE HORRIFIC STUFF BY XYMOX HE MADE ME LISTEN TO WAS NEW ORDER'S "POWER, CORRUPTION AND LIES."
AS FOR THE COCTEAU TWINS...
THERE'S SOMETHING I HAVE TO TELL YOU...YOU KNOW THAT ALBUM OF THEIRS I'VE BEEN PLAYING FOR SIX MONTHS?
YEAH?
AT 45 RPM?
WELL, IT'S A 33!
OUR LISTENING BUBBLE WAS ELVIS COSTELLO, LLOYD COLE, THE SMITHS...
GIBERT JEUNE
PAPETERIE
...NO, THE PALE FOUNTAINS ARE REALLY GOOD.
WELL, I PREFER AZTEC CAMERA...
THE GREAT THING ABOUT MY BUDDY WAS THAT HE BOUGHT EVERYTHING...
I'LL TAKE TALKING HEADS ON LP AND CD... CHRIS ISAAK, JESUS AND MARY CHAIN...THE OLD PRINCE STUFF? NO?
HOW ABOUT NICK CAVE?
NME
WHAT'S THIS?
LOW LIFE!
THE NEW NEW ORDER!
SHIT! I THOUGHT IT WAS THE WRAPPING!
IDIOT! IT'S THE COVER!
UH...WE'LL TAKE THIS, BUT...COULD WE HAVE A NEW ONE?
AND THE LATEST NME...
AND MELODY MAKER!
TO BE CONTINUED

ON DECEMBER 12, 1985, NEW ORDER PLAYED LIVE IN FRANCE FOR THE FIRST TIME IN THREE YEARS.
NEW ORDER
& QUANDO QUANGO
CONCERT A 19H30
PLACEMENT LIBRE
L'ELDORADO
MY BIG BROTHER, WHO WOULD NEVER LISTEN TO ANYTHING BUT AFRO MUSIC, TOOK ME ALONG AS A TREAT.
AND I REMEMBER WE ARRIVED LATE—AT 9:30, TWO HOURS AFTER THE CONCERT STARTED.
NEW ORDER
DORAD
DON'T WORRY. THEY WON'T BE ON FOR HOURS...
BUT LOOK, ON THE TICKET IT SAYS 7:30!
SHIT! I CAN HEAR THEM. THEY'RE ON!
LDORADO
SORTIE
I TOLD YOU! WE'RE GONNA MISS THEM!
AAOHHRR
YOU DUMBASS! THERE'S PLENTY OF TIME. IT'S STILL THE OPENING ACT!
IDIOT!
TWO BEERS AND TWO SODAS LATER...
ALWAYS THE SAME WITH THESE NEW WAVE BANDS... THEY ALWAYS GOTTA MAKE YOU HANG AROUND!
JUST THINK... KING SUNNY ADE USED TO PLAY FOR TEN HOURS—JUST FOR THE HELL OF IT!
WAIT A MINUTE...IS THAT HIP-HOP?
HAHAHA! IT'S RAP! THAT'LL SHAKE UP THE OLD GOTHS!
DON'T PUSH ME HA HAN, COS I'M CLOSE TO THE EDGE...
LEMME TELL YOU, BRO, THAT'S THE SOUND OF THE FUTURE!
NOT LIKE THAT SHITTY...
COLD WAVE! OOOOOPS...
NEW ORDER
NEW ORDER
NEW ORDER

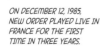

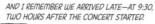

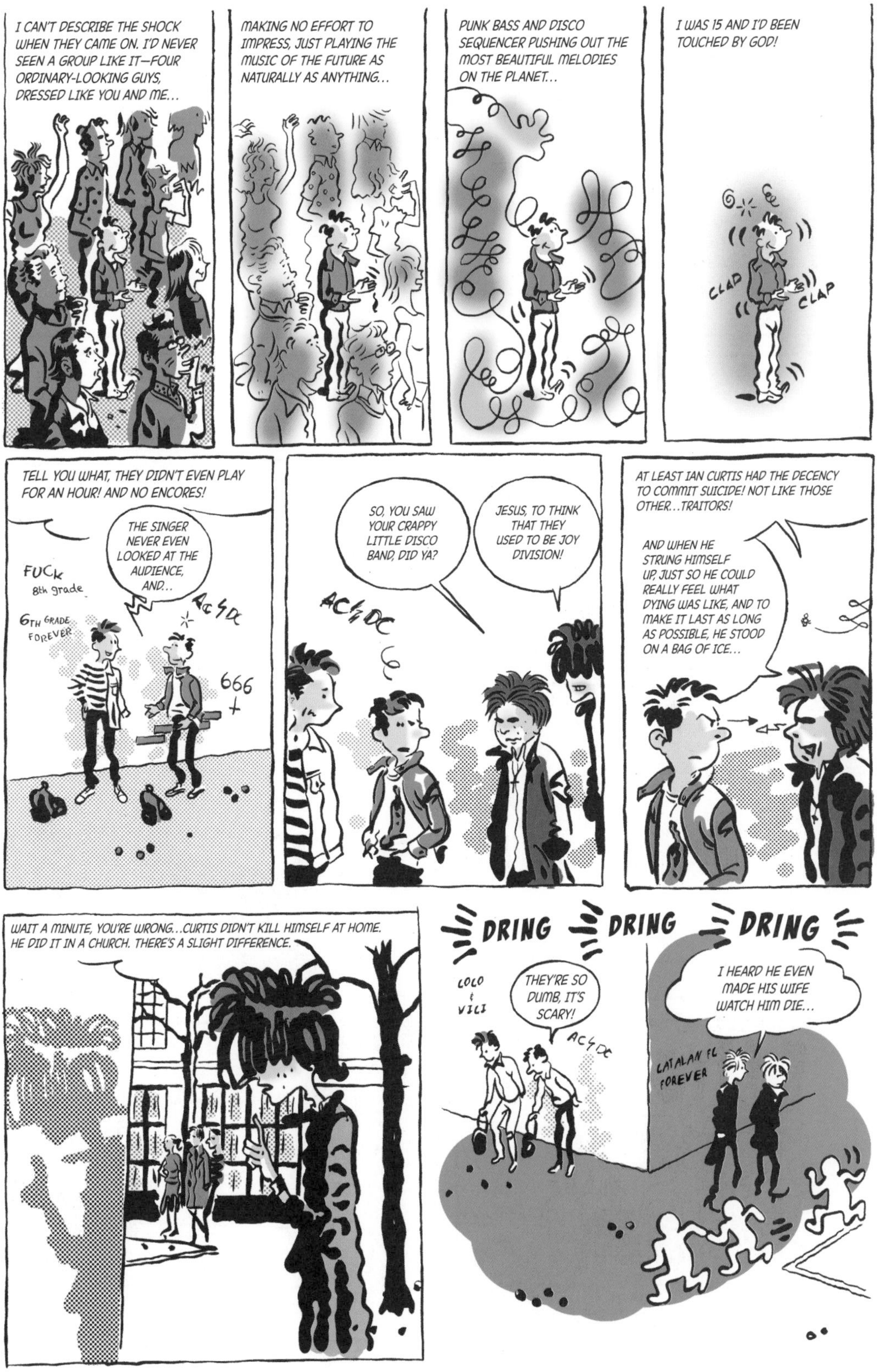
I CAN'T DESCRIBE THE SHOCK WHEN THEY CAME ON. I'D NEVER SEEN A GROUP LIKE IT—FOUR ORDINARY-LOOKING GUYS, DRESSED LIKE YOU AND ME...
MAKING NO EFFORT TO IMPRESS, JUST PLAYING THE MUSIC OF THE FUTURE AS NATURALLY AS ANYTHING...
PUNK BASS AND DISCO SEQUENCER PUSHING OUT THE MOST BEAUTIFUL MELODIES ON THE PLANET...
I WAS 15 AND I'D BEEN TOUCHED BY GOD!
CLAP
CLAP
TELL YOU WHAT, THEY DIDN'T EVEN PLAY FOR AN HOUR! AND NO ENCORES!
THE SINGER NEVER EVEN LOOKED AT THE AUDIENCE, AND...
FUCk 8th grade
6TH GRADE FOREVER
666
SO, YOU SAW YOUR CRAPPY LITTLE DISCO BAND, DID YA?
JESUS, TO THINK THAT THEY USED TO BE JOY DIVISION!
AT LEAST IAN CURTIS HAD THE DECENCY TO COMMIT SUICIDE! NOT LIKE THOSE OTHER...TRAITORS!
AND WHEN HE STRUNG HIMSELF UP, JUST SO HE COULD REALLY FEEL WHAT DYING WAS LIKE, AND TO MAKE IT LAST AS LONG AS POSSIBLE, HE STOOD ON A BAG OF ICE...
WAIT A MINUTE, YOU'RE WRONG...CURTIS DIDN'T KILL HIMSELF AT HOME. HE DID IT IN A CHURCH. THERE'S A SLIGHT DIFFERENCE.
DRING DRING DRING
LOLO & VILI
THEY'RE SO DUMB, IT'S SCARY!
I HEARD HE EVEN MADE HIS WIFE WATCH HIM DIE...
CATALAN FC FOREVER

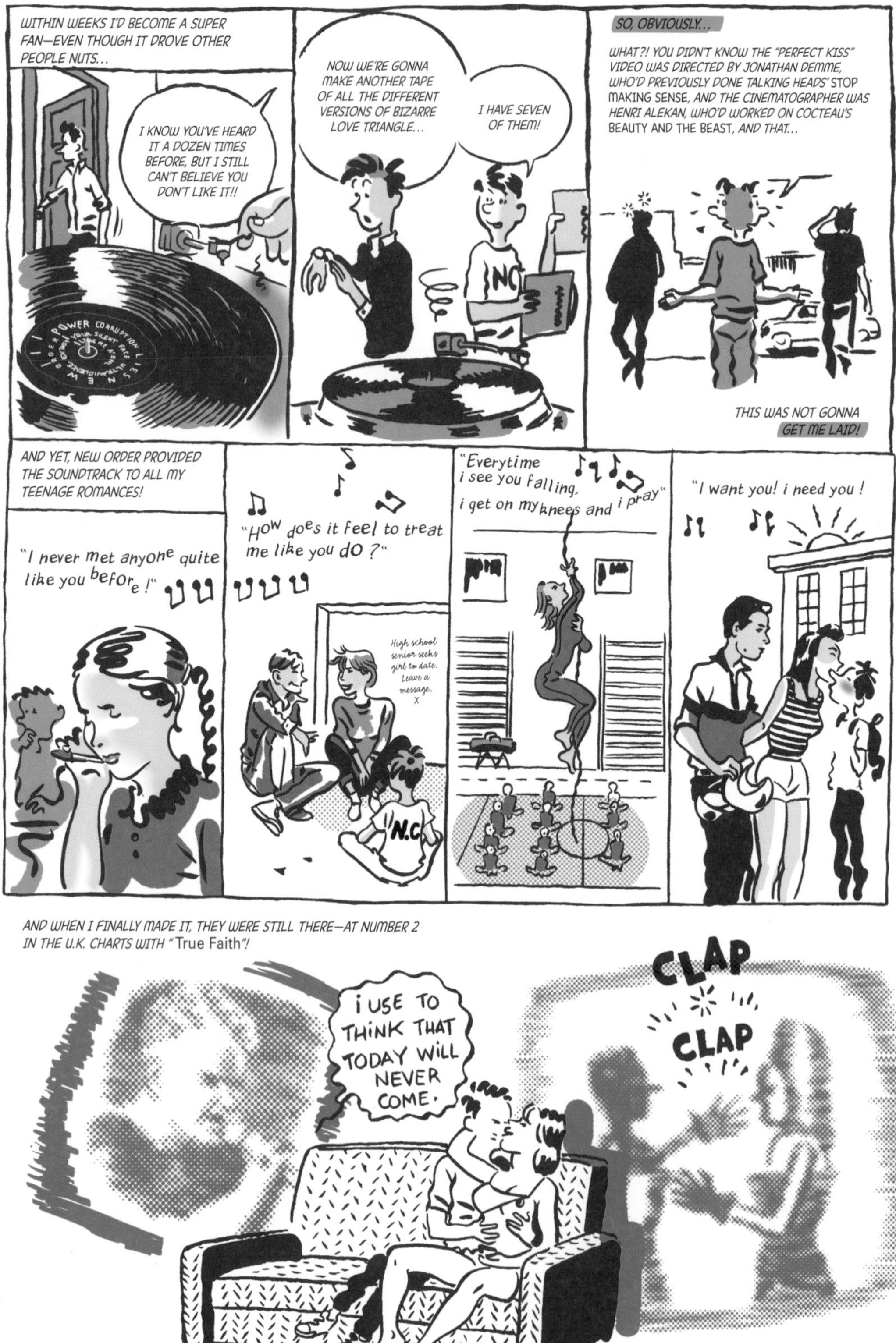
WITHIN WEEKS I'D BECOME A SUPER FAN—EVEN THOUGH IT DROVE OTHER PEOPLE NUTS...
I KNOW YOU'VE HEARD IT A DOZEN TIMES BEFORE, BUT I STILL CAN'T BELIEVE YOU DON'T LIKE IT!!
NOW WE'RE GONNA MAKE ANOTHER TAPE OF ALL THE DIFFERENT VERSIONS OF BIZARRE LOVE TRIANGLE...
I HAVE SEVEN OF THEM!
SO, OBVIOUSLY...
WHAT?! YOU DIDN'T KNOW THE "PERFECT KISS" VIDEO WAS DIRECTED BY JONATHAN DEMME, WHO'D PREVIOUSLY DONE TALKING HEADS' STOP MAKING SENSE, AND THE CINEMATOGRAPHER WAS HENRI ALEKAN, WHO'D WORKED ON COCTEAU'S BEAUTY AND THE BEAST, AND THAT...
THIS WAS NOT GONNA GET ME LAID!
AND YET, NEW ORDER PROVIDED THE SOUNDTRACK TO ALL MY TEENAGE ROMANCES!
"I never met anyone quite like you before!"
"How does it feel to treat me like you do?"
High school senior seeks girl to date. Leave a message. X
N.C
"Everytime i see you falling, i get on my knees and i pray"
"I want you! i need you!"
AND WHEN I FINALLY MADE IT, THEY WERE STILL THERE—AT NUMBER 2 IN THE U.K. CHARTS WITH "True Faith"!
i USE TO THINK THAT TODAY WILL NEVER COME.
CLAP
CLAP

AND I WASN'T THE ONLY ONE COMING OF AGE THAT SUMMER: IN DECEMBER '88, NEW ORDER MADE A COMEBACK WITH TECHNIQUE, WHICH WAS RECORDED IN IBIZA, AND APPEARED LIVE ON TOP OF THE POPS WITH BARNEY TOTALLY SMASHED!
THE MADCHESTER ERA HAD BEGUN—ECSTASY, IBIZA, AND HOUSE. ENGLAND'S HOOLIGANS HAD DISCOVERED THE LOVE DRUG.
IN EARLY 1990, NEW ORDER DID ONE BETTER BY COMPOSING THE ENGLISH "ANTHEM" FOR THE SOCCER WORLD CUP.
"It was the last straw for Joy Division fans," BARNEY JOKED TO NME.
THE ORIGINAL TITLE WAS "E FOR ENGLAND"... WE'RE SINGING FOR ENGLAND!
WE'RE SINGING FOR ENGLAND!
E FOR ENGLAND!
OFFICIALS ONLY REALIZED THE PLAY ON WORDS AT THE LAST MINUTE AND CHANGED THE TITLE TO "WORLD IN MOTION"!
THE ENGLISH TEAM EVENTUALLY LOST IN THE SEMIFINALS. MEANWHILE, WE WERE AT ONE OF OUR VERY FIRST RAVES, NEAR PARIS...
THUMP!
BUMP
RAVE AGE
WOOOOW! YOU OK, MAN?
SHIIIIIT! I'M GREAT!
IT'S COOL!
SUPER COOL!
MUSIC'S GREAT, HUH! I DON'T KNOW ANY OF IT, BUT...
REMINDS ME OF N.O.!
TACTAC
IT MUST BE WEIRD TO INVENT A NEW SOUND AND THEN FIND OUT EVERYONE'S DOING THE SAME THING AS YOU!
KLF
BUT WHAT WILL NEW ORDER DO IN THE NINETIES, I WONDER?
TO BE CONTINUED.

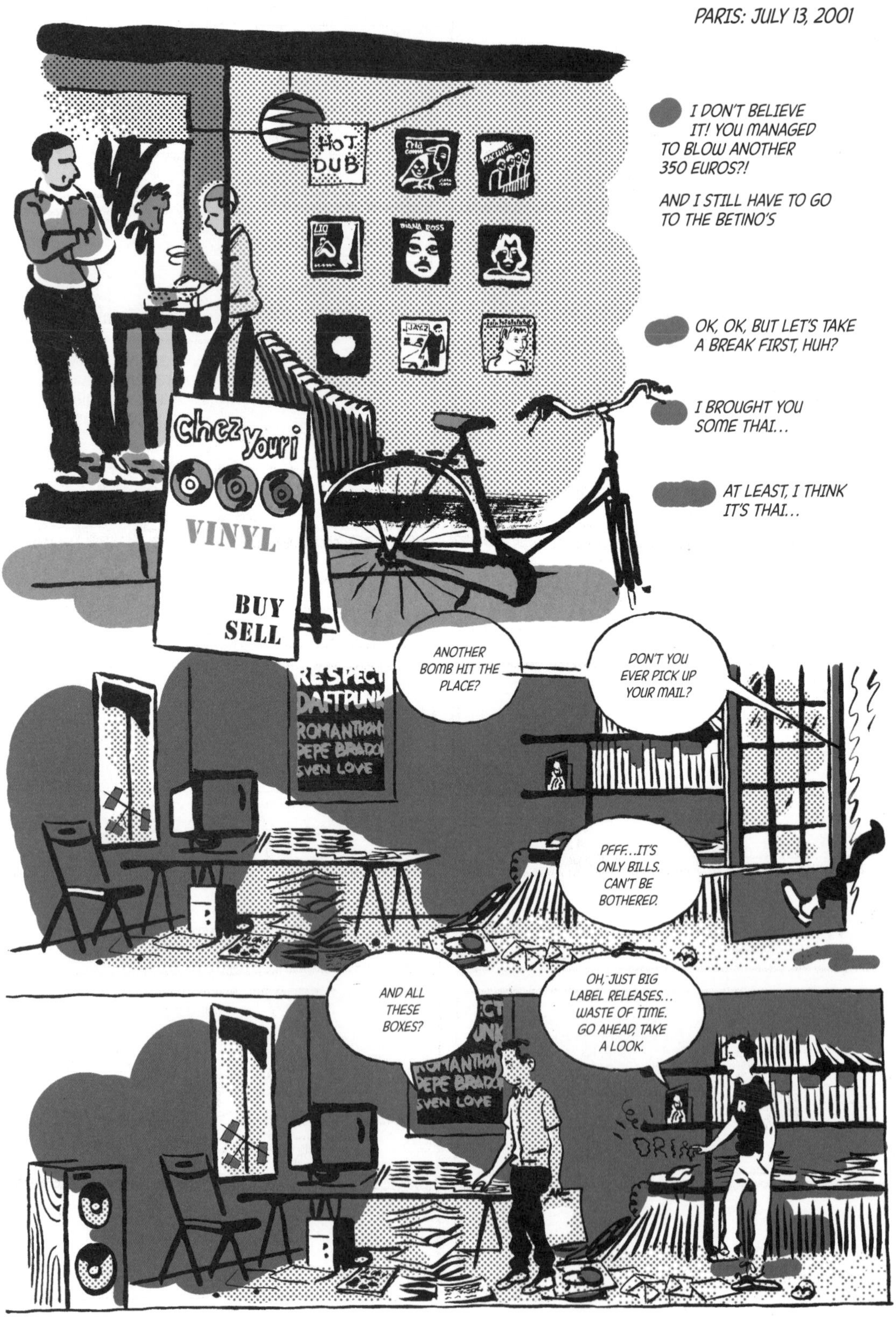
PARIS: JULY 13, 2001
HOT DUB
DIANA ROSS
JAY-Z
I DON'T BELIEVE IT! YOU MANAGED TO BLOW ANOTHER 350 EUROS?!
AND I STILL HAVE TO GO TO THE BETINO'S
OK, OK, BUT LET'S TAKE A BREAK FIRST, HUH?
I BROUGHT YOU SOME THAI...
AT LEAST, I THINK IT'S THAI...
chez youri
VINYL
BUY SELL
ANOTHER BOMB HIT THE PLACE?
DON'T YOU EVER PICK UP YOUR MAIL?
RESPECT
DAFT PUNK
ROMANTHONY
PEPE BRADOCK
SVEN LOVE
PFFF...IT'S ONLY BILLS. CAN'T BE BOTHERED.
AND ALL THESE BOXES?
OH, JUST BIG LABEL RELEASES... WASTE OF TIME. GO AHEAD, TAKE A LOOK.

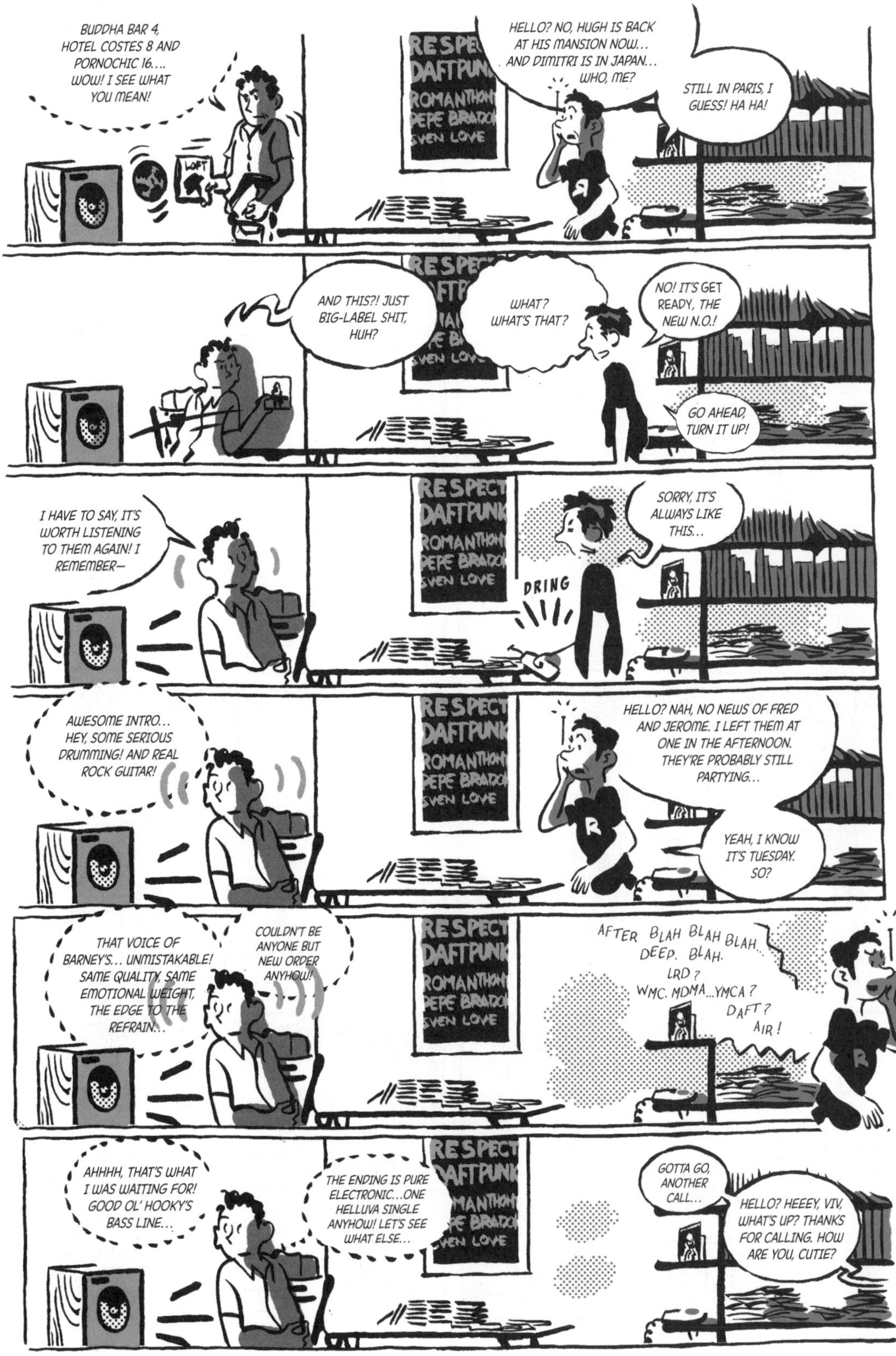
BUDDHA BAR 4, HOTEL COSTES 8 AND PORNOCHIC 16…. WOW! I SEE WHAT YOU MEAN!
LOFT
RESPECT DAFTPUNK ROMANTHONY PEPE BRADOCK SVEN LOVE
HELLO? NO, HUGH IS BACK AT HIS MANSION NOW… AND DIMITRI IS IN JAPAN… WHO, ME?
STILL IN PARIS, I GUESS! HA HA!
AND THIS?! JUST BIG-LABEL SHIT, HUH?
WHAT? WHAT'S THAT?
NO! IT'S GET READY, THE NEW N.O.!
GO AHEAD, TURN IT UP!
I HAVE TO SAY, IT'S WORTH LISTENING TO THEM AGAIN! I REMEMBER—
SORRY, IT'S ALWAYS LIKE THIS…
DRING
AWESOME INTRO… HEY, SOME SERIOUS DRUMMING! AND REAL ROCK GUITAR!
HELLO? NAH, NO NEWS OF FRED AND JEROME. I LEFT THEM AT ONE IN THE AFTERNOON. THEY'RE PROBABLY STILL PARTYING…
YEAH, I KNOW IT'S TUESDAY. SO?
THAT VOICE OF BARNEY'S… UNMISTAKABLE! SAME QUALITY, SAME EMOTIONAL WEIGHT, THE EDGE TO THE REFRAIN…
COULDN'T BE ANYONE BUT NEW ORDER ANYHOW!
AFTER BLAH BLAH BLAH… DEEP. BLAH. LRD? WMC. MDMA…YMCA? DAFT? AIR!
AHHHH, THAT'S WHAT I WAS WAITING FOR! GOOD OL' HOOKY'S BASS LINE…
THE ENDING IS PURE ELECTRONIC…ONE HELLUVA SINGLE ANYHOW! LET'S SEE WHAT ELSE…
GOTTA GO, ANOTHER CALL…
HELLO? HEEEY, VIV, WHAT'S UP? THANKS FOR CALLING. HOW ARE YOU, CUTIE?

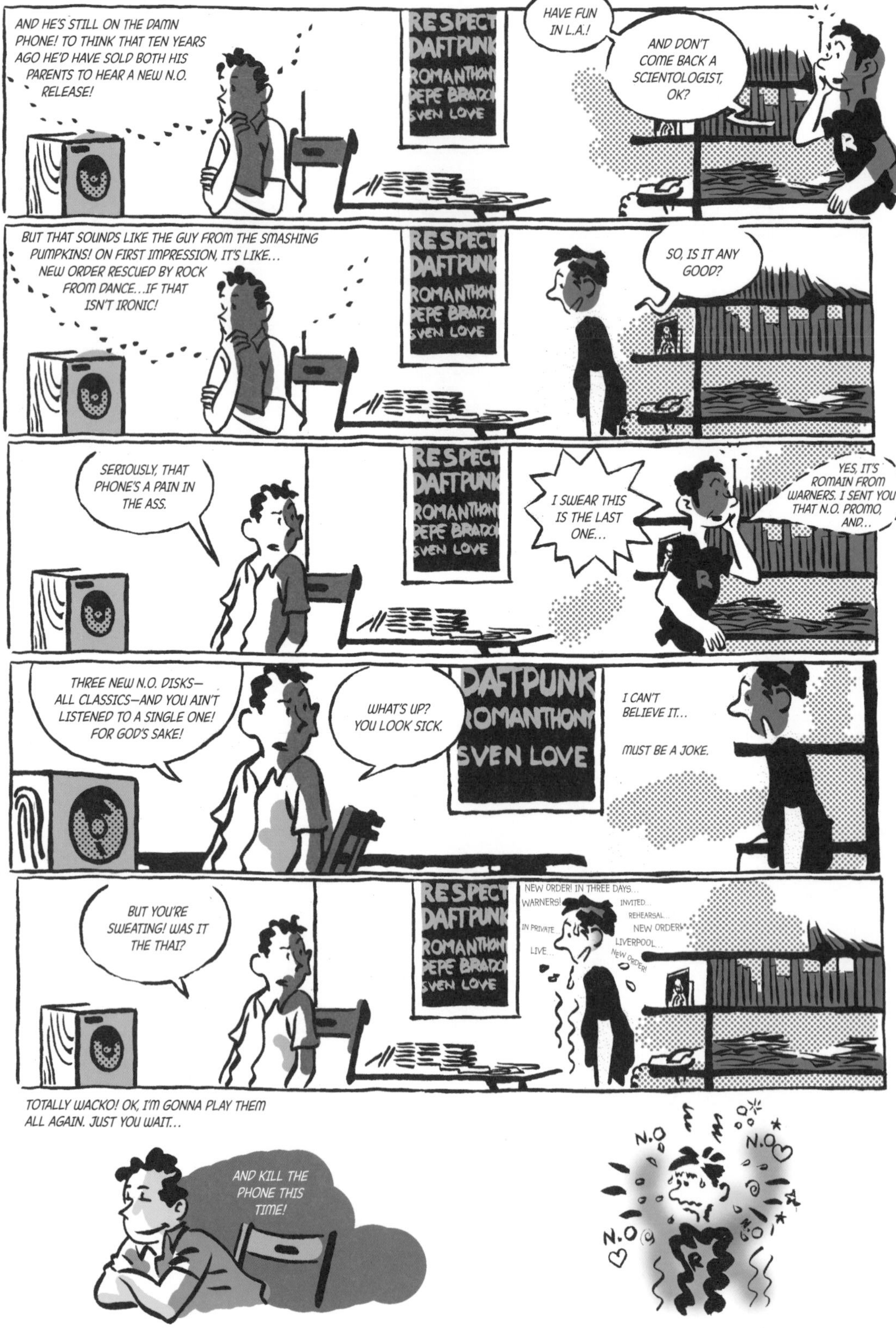
AND HE'S STILL ON THE DAMN PHONE! TO THINK THAT TEN YEARS AGO HE'D HAVE SOLD BOTH HIS PARENTS TO HEAR A NEW N.O. RELEASE!
RESPECT DAFTPUNK ROMANTHONY PEPE BRADOCK SVEN LOVE
HAVE FUN IN L.A.!
AND DON'T COME BACK A SCIENTOLOGIST, OK?
BUT THAT SOUNDS LIKE THE GUY FROM THE SMASHING PUMPKINS! ON FIRST IMPRESSION, IT'S LIKE... NEW ORDER RESCUED BY ROCK FROM DANCE...IF THAT ISN'T IRONIC!
SO, IS IT ANY GOOD?
SERIOUSLY, THAT PHONE'S A PAIN IN THE ASS.
I SWEAR THIS IS THE LAST ONE...
YES, IT'S ROMAIN FROM WARNERS. I SENT YOU THAT N.O. PROMO, AND...
THREE NEW N.O. DISKS—ALL CLASSICS—AND YOU AIN'T LISTENED TO A SINGLE ONE! FOR GOD'S SAKE!
WHAT'S UP? YOU LOOK SICK.
I CAN'T BELIEVE IT...
MUST BE A JOKE.
BUT YOU'RE SWEATING! WAS IT THE THAI?
NEW ORDER! IN THREE DAYS...
WARNERS!
INVITED...
REHEARSAL...
IN PRIVATE...
NEW ORDER!
LIVERPOOL...
LIVE...
NEW ORDER!
TOTALLY WACKO! OK, I'M GONNA PLAY THEM ALL AGAIN. JUST YOU WAIT...
AND KILL THE PHONE THIS TIME!
N.O
N.O
N.O

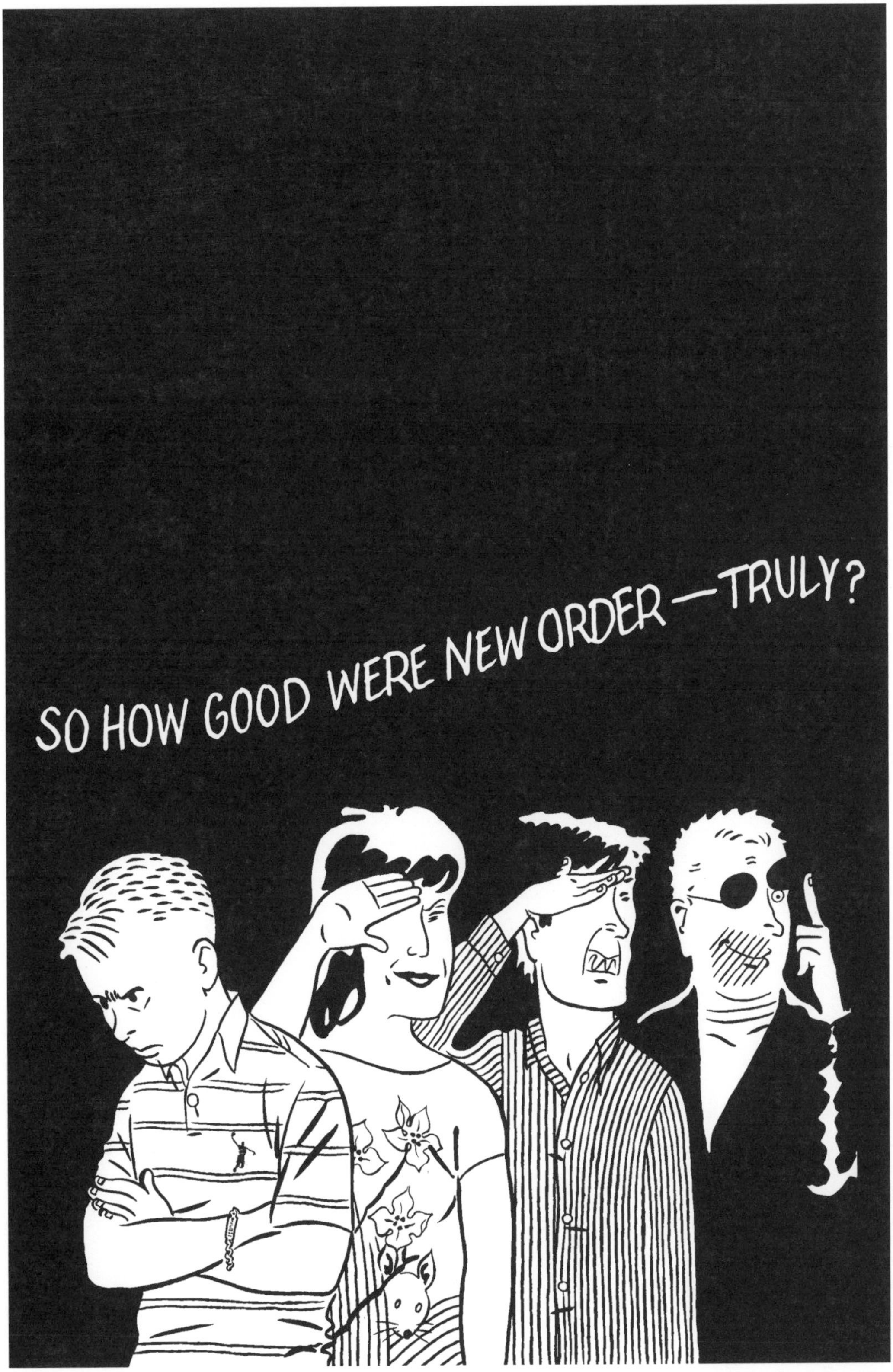
SO HOW GOOD WERE NEW ORDER—TRULY?

SO THAT WAS HOW, ON JULY 17, 2001, MATHIAS AND I FOUND OURSELVES FLYING TO LIVERPOOL, NOT ONLY TO ATTEND NEW ORDER'S FIRST LIVE CONCERT IN THREE YEARS, BUT ALSO—EVEN BETTER—TO WATCH THEM REHEARSE THE DAY BEFORE AS THEIR PRIVATE GUESTS.

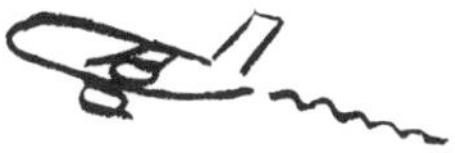

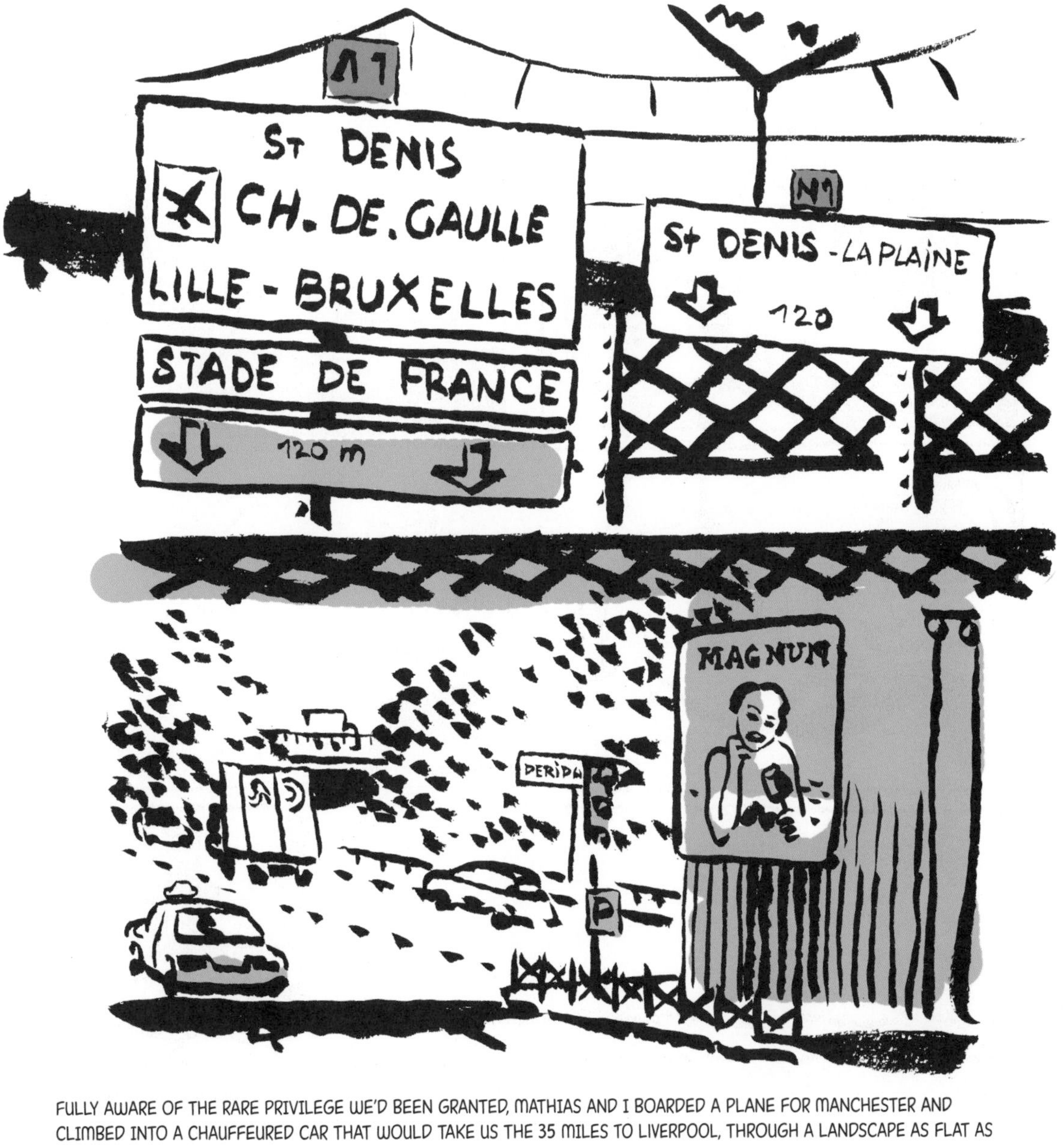
A1
St DENIS
CH. DE. GAULLE
LILLE - BRUXELLES
STADE DE FRANCE
120 m
N1
St DENIS - LA PLAINE
120
MAGNUM
P

FULLY AWARE OF THE RARE PRIVILEGE WE'D BEEN GRANTED, MATHIAS AND I BOARDED A PLANE FOR MANCHESTER AND CLIMBED INTO A CHAUFFEURED CAR THAT WOULD TAKE US THE 35 MILES TO LIVERPOOL, THROUGH A LANDSCAPE AS FLAT AS A RECORD AND BLANKETED AS FAR AS THE EYE COULD SEE BY SMOKE FROM FACTORIES THAT ALL LOOKED EXACTLY LIKE THE ONE ON THE FACTORY RECORDS LABEL.

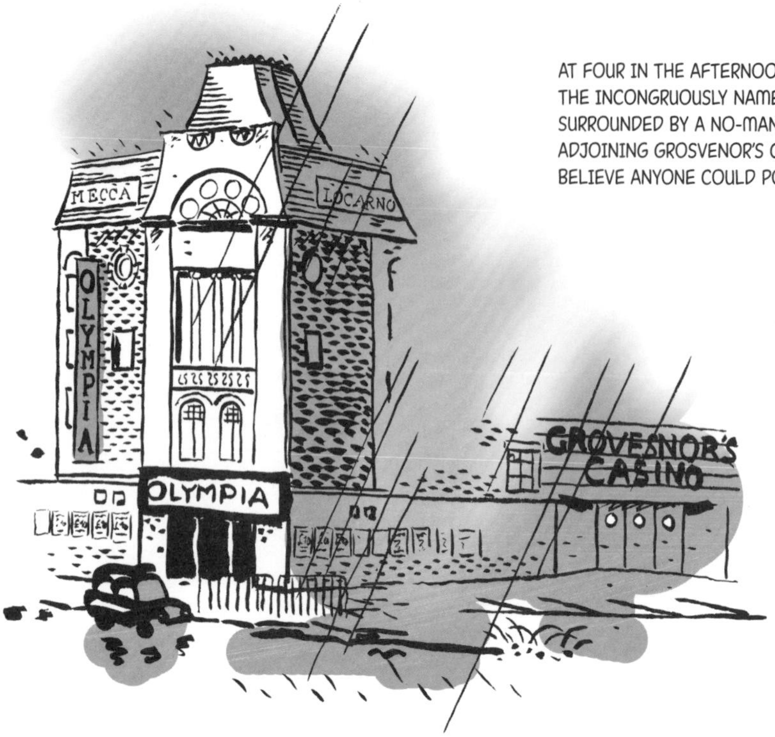
MECCA
LOCARNO
OLYMPIA
OLYMPIA
GROVESNOR'S CASINO

AT FOUR IN THE AFTERNOON, WE MADE OUR WAY TO THE INCONGRUOUSLY NAMED "OLYMPIA," A BINGO HALL SURROUNDED BY A NO-MAN'S-LAND OF EMPTY LOTS, AND ADJOINING GROSVENOR'S CASINO, IN WHICH IT WAS HARD TO BELIEVE ANYONE COULD POSSIBLY MAKE THEIR FORTUNE.

THE HALL, WHICH THE VERY NEXT DAY WOULD BE MOBBED BY 3,000 FANS, WAS DESERTED, BUT AS SOON AS WE STEPPED INTO THE LOBBY AND HEARD THE UNMISTAKABLE OPENING CHORDS OF "REGRET," MATT AND I EXCHANGED DAZED LOOKS. WE WERE LOST IN A DREAM WORLD IN WHICH WE WERE ABOUT TO BE WITH "THE FOUR"—LIVE AND IN THE FLESH.

IN FACT, WHAT WE SAW WAS STEPHEN MORRIS ALONE ONSTAGE WITH HIS DRUM KIT, ACCOMPANYING A RECORDING OF THE REST OF THE BAND! BUT HE WAS STILL IMPRESSIVE—THE ULTIMATE DRUM MACHINE, MANUALLY OPERATED BY TWO WOODEN STICKS: LIKE GUNFIRE ONE MINUTE, FUNKY THE NEXT, AND NEVER MISSING A BEAT.

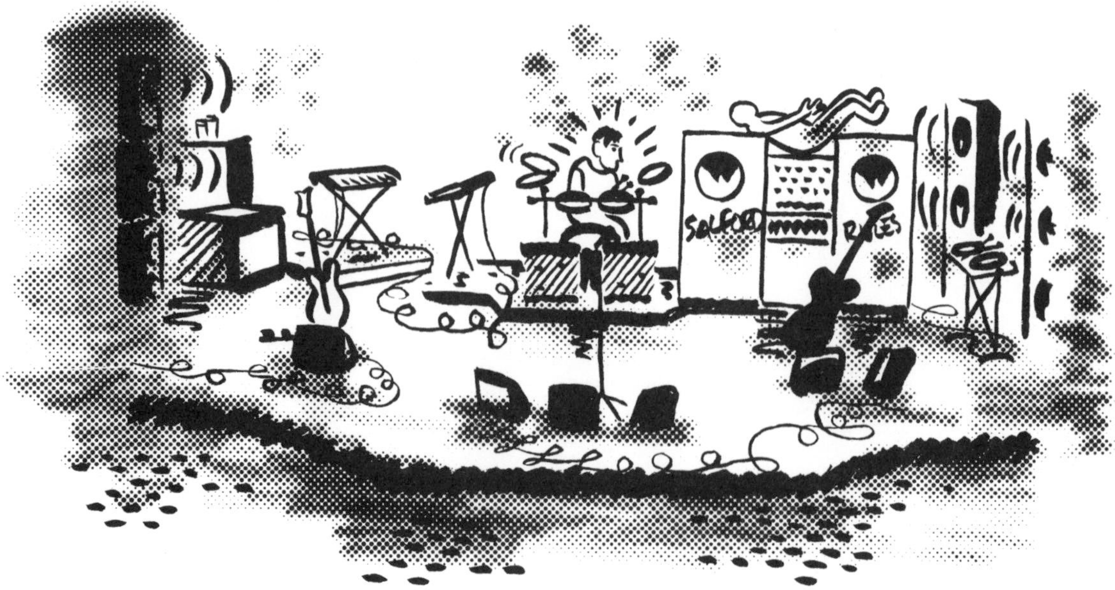
SALFORD
RULES

THE ONLY OTHER PEOPLE THERE WERE A DOZEN OR SO TECHNICIANS, A FEW VENUE STAFF, AND THE GROUP'S MANAGER. IT WAS A MAGNIFICENT HALL, WITH TWO BALCONIES STEPPING UP INTO THE ROOF AND WALLS LIKE A BABYLONIAN TEMPLE. THE LIVERPOOL OLYMPIA HAD PRESTIGE, TOO. SITTING AT A TABLE ON ONE OF THE BALCONIES, WE HAD A PERFECT VIEW, BUT NEEDED OPERA GLASSES TO SEE THE PERFORMERS: WHO *WAS* THAT GUY?

IT WAS BILLY CORGAN OF SMASHING PUMPKINS, GUESTING AS LEAD GUITAR FOR THE NEW TOUR AND ACCOMPANIED ALTERNATELY ON GUITAR AND KEYBOARDS BY PHIL CUNNINGHAM, WHO HAD REPLACED GILLIAN GILBERT. THE TWO OF THEM CAME ONSTAGE AND TOOK THEIR PLACES—ONE STRUMMING THE STRINGS, THE OTHER TICKLING THE IVORIES, WITHOUT SEEMING TO TAKE ANY NOTICE OF EACH OTHER.

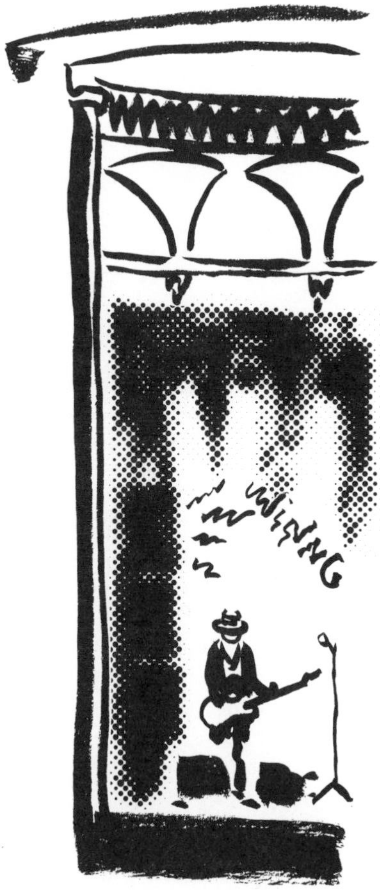

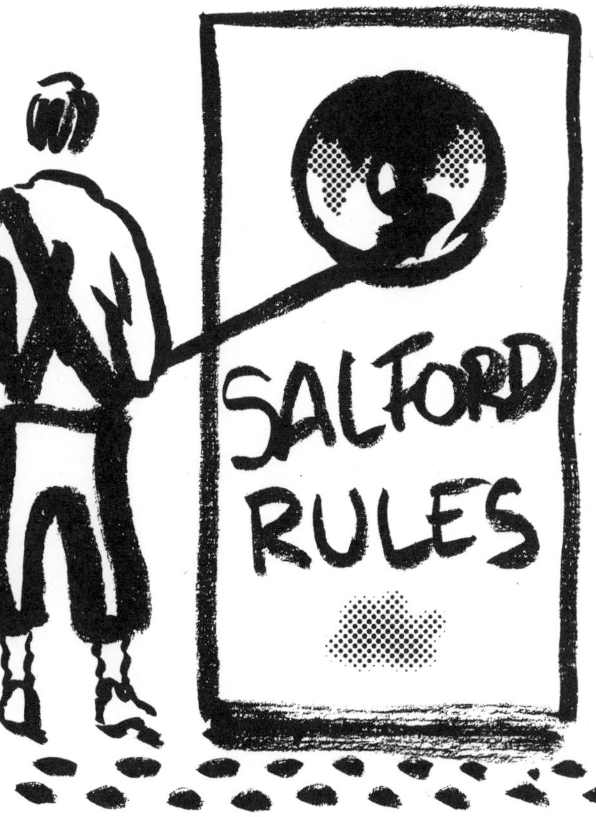
SALFORD RULES

THEN IT WAS PETER HOOK'S TURN TO APPEAR. PRODUCING THE MOST INSTANTLY RECOGNIZABLE BASS SOUNDS IN ROCK, HE STOOD WITH HIS BACK TO THE AUDITORIUM, PLAYING THE CHORDS OF "AGE OF CONSENT" OVER AND OVER UNTIL HE WAS HAPPY—EVEN THOUGH THEY WOULDN'T ACTUALLY PLAY IT THE NEXT DAY.

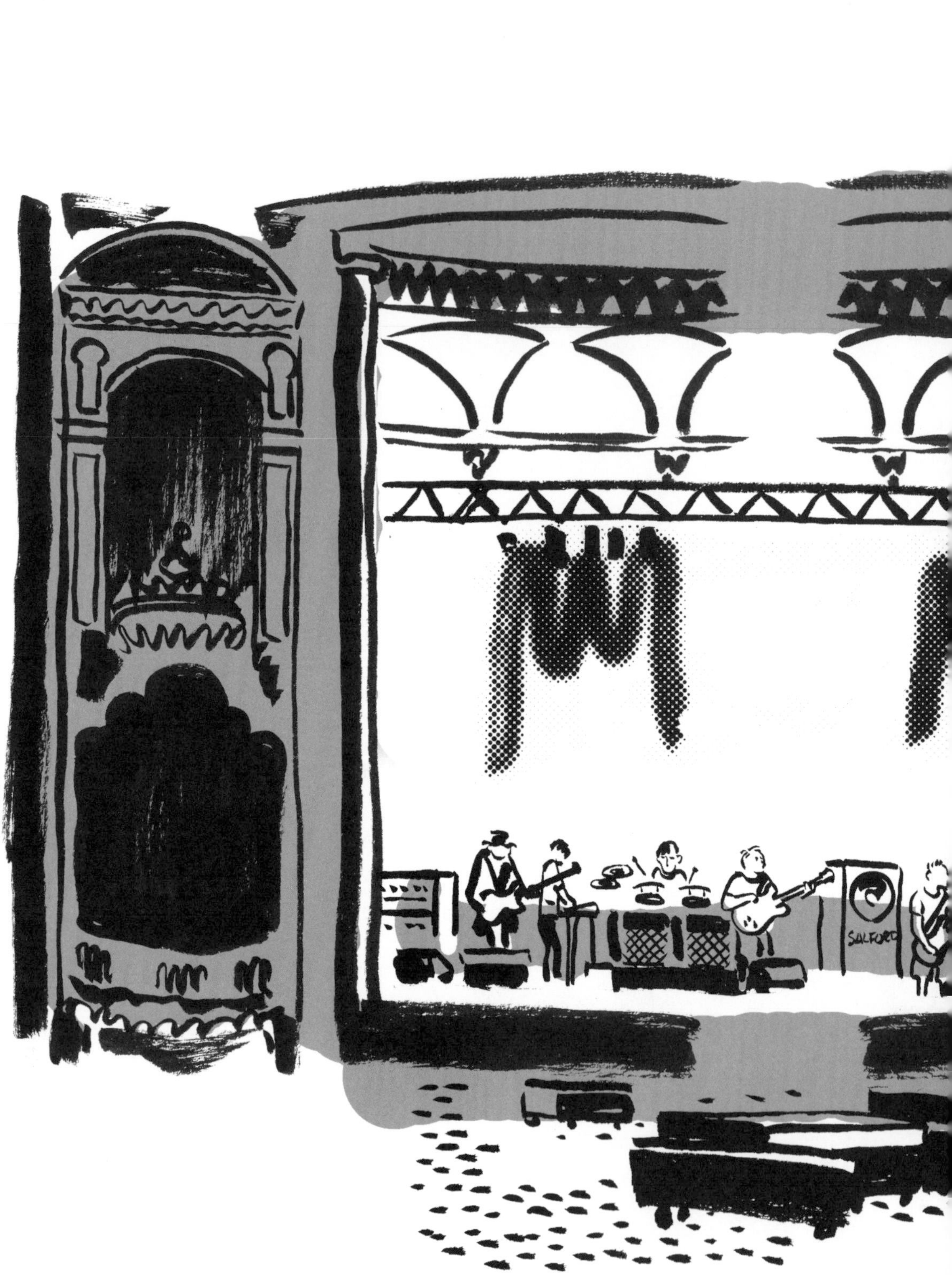
SALFORD

BARNEY SUMNER WAS THE LAST TO ARRIVE, AND AFTER A FEW HELLOS THEY LAUNCHED INTO THE SET—THE WHOLE THING, NUMBER BY NUMBER—PLAYING SOME OF THEM TWICE THROUGH, REPEATING ONLY PARTS OF OTHERS, AND MAKING SURE ALL THREE OF THE GUITARS THEY MIGHT NEED WERE PROPERLY TUNED.

IT WAS 2001, BUT THEY STARTED WITH A SONG BY JOY DIVISION, "ATMOSPHERE," FOLLOWING THAT UP WITH RECENT TRACKS FROM *GET READY* AND SOME OF THEIR ESTABLISHED HITS ("TRUE FAITH," "BLT," "LOVE WILL TEAR US APART," ETC.), MAKING SURE TO INCLUDE A FEW MORE OBSCURE NUMBERS—THE '83 SONG "YOUR SILENT FACE" AND ANOTHER EARLY JOY DIVISION RELEASE, "ISOLATION." THEY FINISHED THE REHEARSAL, LIKE THE PERFORMANCE ITSELF, WITH A PERFECT PERFORMANCE OF "TEMPTATION."

STAGE RIGHT AND ALL IN BLACK—FROM HIS SHOES TO HIS HAT—AMERICAN GUEST STAR BILLY CORGAN BLENDED IN BEAUTIFULLY, SMILING TO HIMSELF AS HE PAID HOMAGE TO THE REVERED BAND.

CENTER STAGE AND CALLING THE TUNE WAS BARNEY, WHO DECIDED WHETHER EACH SONG WOULD BE PLAYED WITH OR WITHOUT REPEATS, THE KIND OF SOUND THE KEYBOARD SHOULD MAKE, AND ABOVE ALL CHECKED THE SPEED OF THE TWO (!) ONSTAGE AUTO-CUE MACHINES, WHICH WERE SCROLLING LYRICS HE HIMSELF HAD WRITTEN AND YET SEEMED UNABLE TO REMEMBER.

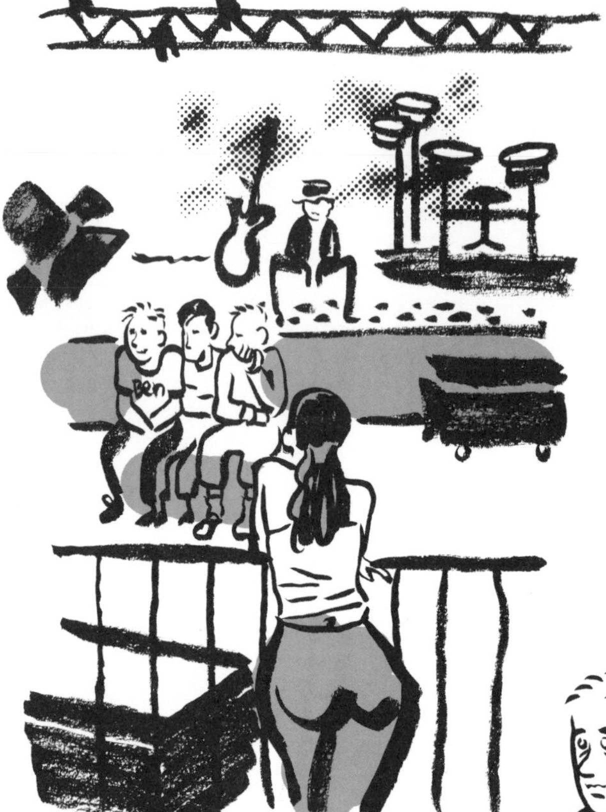
Ben

THE REHEARSAL FINISHES, AND PETER, STEPHEN, AND BARNEY COME DOWN OFFSTAGE, SIT TOGETHER, AND SUBMIT TO A TV INTERVIEW.

THEY'RE ONLY YARDS FROM US, IN THE FULL GLARE OF A BBC SPOTLIGHT. AFTER SOME BRIEF HELLOS, PETER QUIPS, "AS YOU CAN SEE, WE'RE LESS IMPRESSIVE IN THE FLESH THAN IN THE DRAWINGS!"

AND YET I HAVE THE STRIKING IMPRESSION THAT I KNOW THESE THREE FACES—DESPITE THE LINES AROUND THEIR EYES. I TURN TO MATHIAS, WHO IS SCRIBBLING ON HIS SKETCH PAD: "IT'S KINDA WEIRD...THEY HAVE AGED, BUT NOT THAT MUCH..."

BY NINE P.M., THE INTERVIEW'S DONE AND EVERYONE LEAVES THE HALL. WE'LL BE BACK AT THE SAME TIME THE NEXT DAY. IT'S NOT QUITE DARK YET IN LIVERPOOL, AND THE CITY IS EVEN GRAYER THAN BEFORE. NO DOUBT ABOUT IT—WE'RE RIGHT WHERE IT ALL HAPPENS, RIGHT IN THE SHIT...

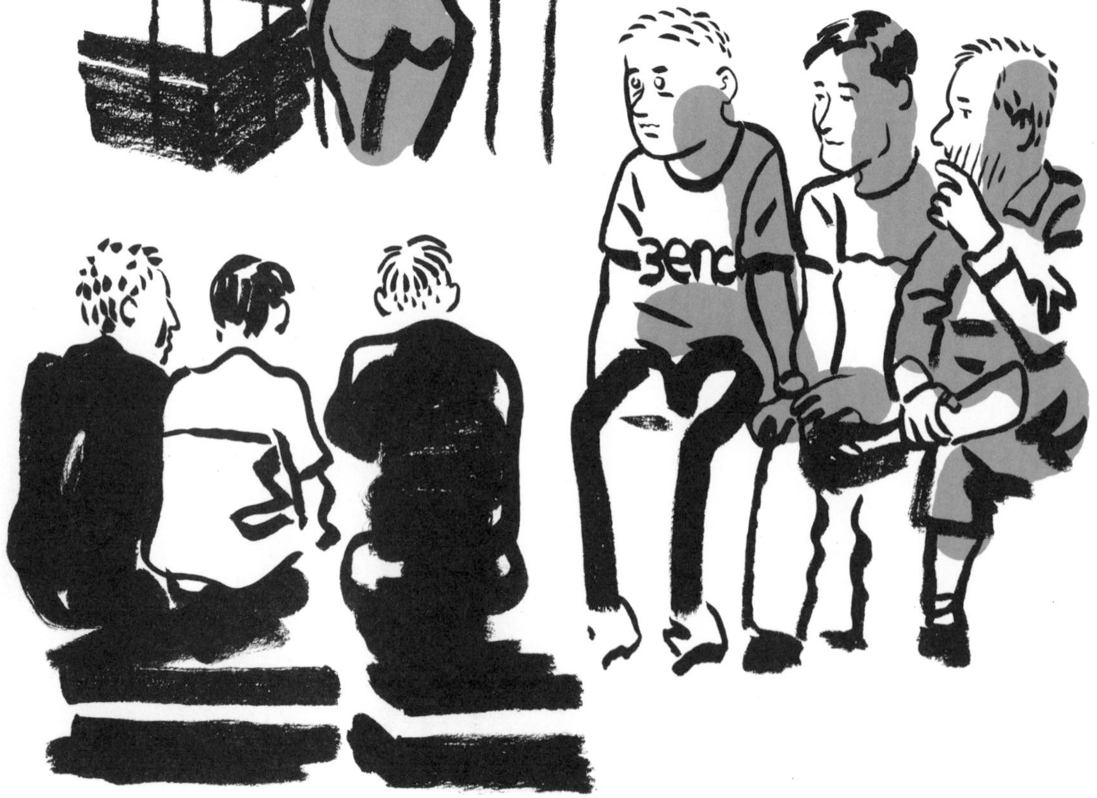

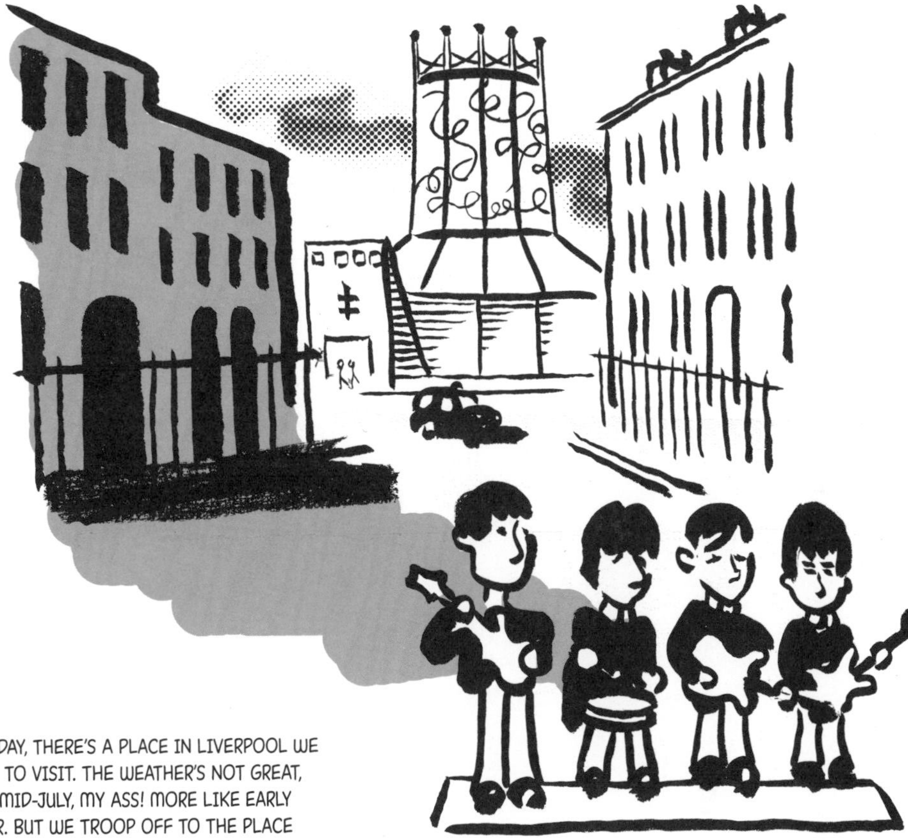

THE NEXT DAY, THERE'S A PLACE IN LIVERPOOL WE JUST HAVE TO VISIT. THE WEATHER'S NOT GREAT, AS USUAL. MID-JULY, MY ASS! MORE LIKE EARLY NOVEMBER. BUT WE TROOP OFF TO THE PLACE CALLED "THE BEATLES STORY." AT FIRST, IT LOOKS DEPRESSINGLY LIKE A WAXWORK MUSEUM, BUT IN THE END WE RATHER ENJOY IT. THE ROOMS ARE LAID OUT CHRONOLOGICALLY AND MANAGE TO CONVEY THE GRADUAL BUILD-UP OF HYSTERIA THE GROUP HAD TO LIVE THROUGH. WE SIT A FEW MOMENTS ON WOODEN CHAIRS IN THE SO, SO TINY RECONSTRUCTED CAVERN BEFORE JETTING OFF TO NYC FOR THE FAB FOUR'S FIRST U.S. TOUR. ALL AROUND US ARE YELLING CROWDS. IT'S PRETTY CONVINCING, EVEN THOUGH IT'S ALL SIXTIES FILM CLIPS... AFTER THAT, WE WANDER AROUND THE STREETS AND, AT THE END OF A PASSAGE COME FACE-TO-FACE WITH SOMETHING THAT LOOKS LIKE A NUCLEAR POWER STATION. BUT IT'S A CATHEDRAL!

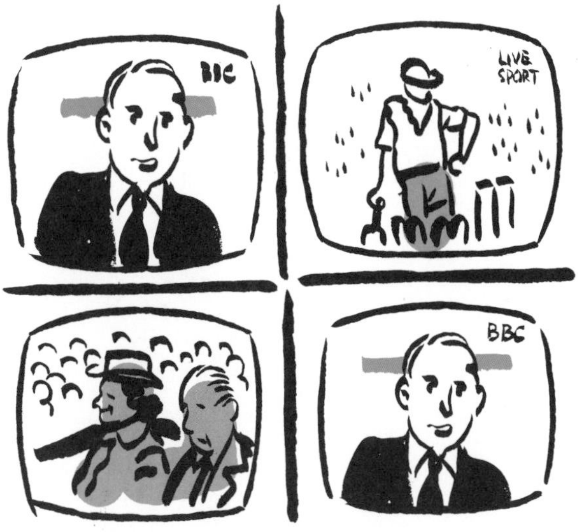
BBC
LIVE SPORT
BBC

ON THE WAY, WE HEAR "TECHNIQUE" BLARING OUT OF AN HMV STORE, AND THE NEW SINGLE "CRYSTAL" ON A RADIO. THE GROUP'S COMEBACK CONCERT IN LIVERPOOL IS ANNOUNCED BY THE BBC...NEW ORDER IS IN THE AIR.

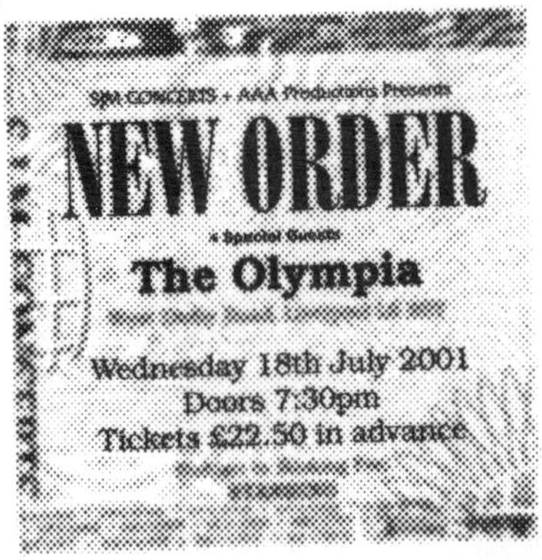
SJM CONCERTS + AAA Productions Presents
NEW ORDER
+ Special Guests
The Olympia
Wednesday 18th July 2001
Doors 7:30pm
Tickets £22.50 in advance

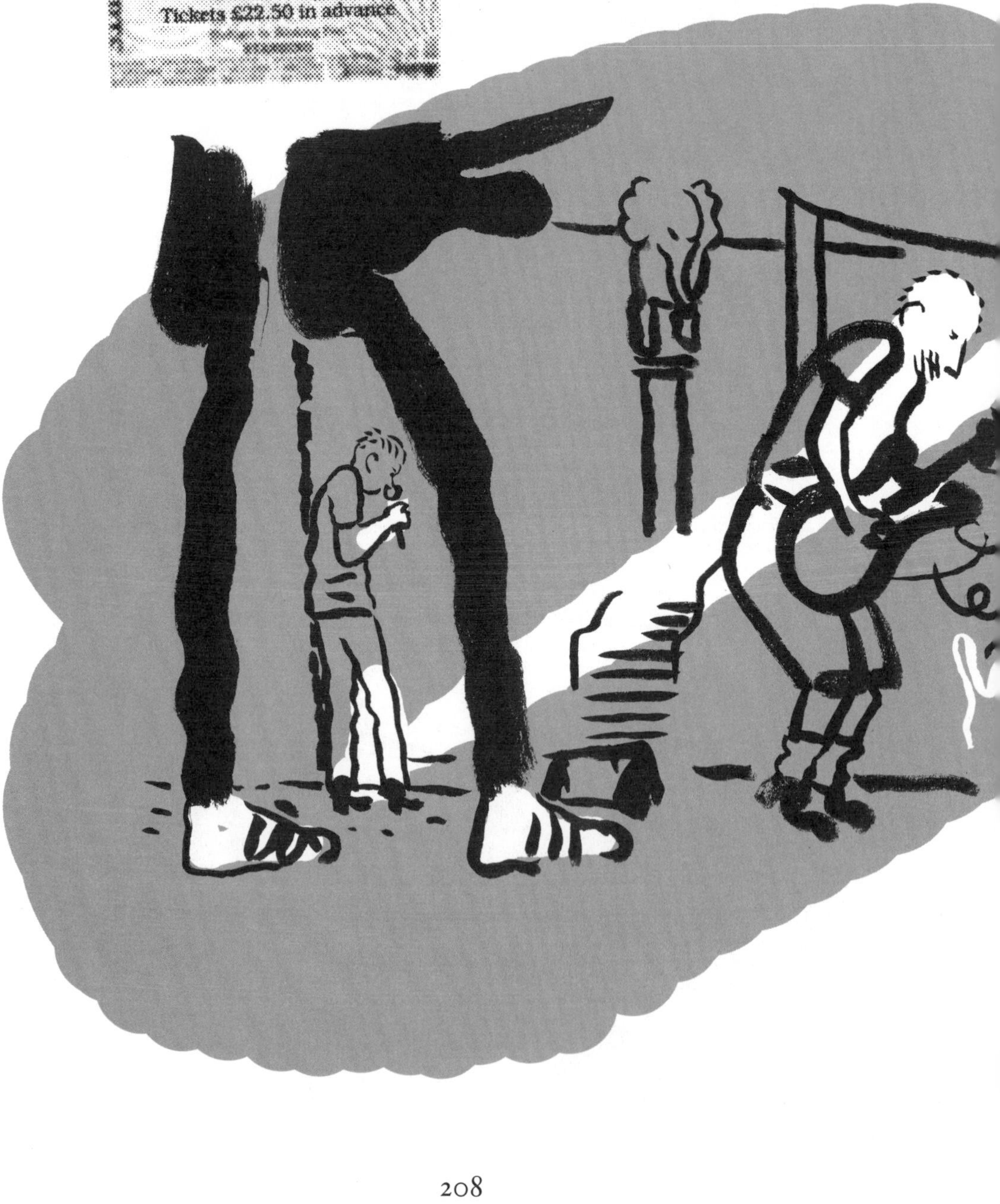

AT TEN P.M. WE'RE BACK AT THE OLYMPIA. NEW ORDER COMES ONSTAGE AND THE FANS ERUPT. THIS TIME, WE AREN'T 20—WE'RE ALMOST 3,000. THE GROUP IS DRESSED EXACTLY AS THEY WERE YESTERDAY, APART FROM BILLY CORGAN, WHO'S DITCHED THE BLACK JACKET TO REVEAL A WHITE SHIRT. THE PERFORMANCE IS ALSO THE SAME AS YESTERDAY, EXCEPT THAT THE GROUP TALK BETWEEN NUMBERS (WE UNDERSTAND ABOUT ONE WORD IN TWELVE) AND PETER HOOK IS MUCH MORE THE SHOWMAN, TWIRLING HIS BASS ON HIS KNEE. BUT HE'S ALWAYS BEEN THE ROCK 'N' ROLL ELEMENT OF THE BAND...THE FANS DON'T NEED AN AUTO-CUE—THEY ALL KNOW THE LYRICS BY HEART. AND HERE'S A PARADOX UNIQUE TO NEW ORDER: IN THE FIRST 20 ROWS OF THE STALLS, EVERYONE'S POGOING LIKE THEY DID IN '77, BUT ON THE FIRST BALCONY WE'RE DANCING LIKE WE DID IN '97—PUNK OR HOUSE DEPENDING ON HOW FAR BACK YOU ARE. THE BAND FINISHES WITH A PERFORMANCE OF "BLUE MONDAY" DEDICATED TO IAN CURTIS. THE CURTAIN COMES DOWN. THIS TIME, LIVERPOOL IS IN PITCH DARKNESS.

AT ONE P.M., IT'S THE AFTER PARTY. THE BAND COMES IN, AND A MOB OF FANS ARE FAWNING ALL OVER BARNEY LIKE HE'S THE GODFATHER OF THE NORTH. WE SEE BEZ FROM THE HAPPY MONDAYS SMOKING JOINT AFTER JOINT. WE DON'T HAVE ANY, SO MATHIAS, LISTENING ONLY TO HIS COURAGE, ASKS HIM FOR SOME WITH HIS TERRIBLE FRENCH ACCENT. "AND SOME SKINS TOO, MAYBE?" BEZ SIGHS, BUT ENDS UP GIVING US QUITE A HUGE ONE. OUTSIDE, IT'S FOUR IN THE MORNING. JUST 35 MILES AWAY IS THE PLACE THAT HAS SO MUCH TO ANSWER FOR: MANCHESTER—IN THE END, A PLACE WE HARDLY SAW. 1977–2001...25 YEARS OF NEW ORDER...AND THE FACTORIES HAVEN'T CHANGED. TO THINK THAT THEY'RE BACK ONSTAGE, AND IN A FEW WEEKS THEY'LL BE IN TOKYO, THEN SAN FRANCISCO, AND SOON PARIS...YOU BETTER GET READY!

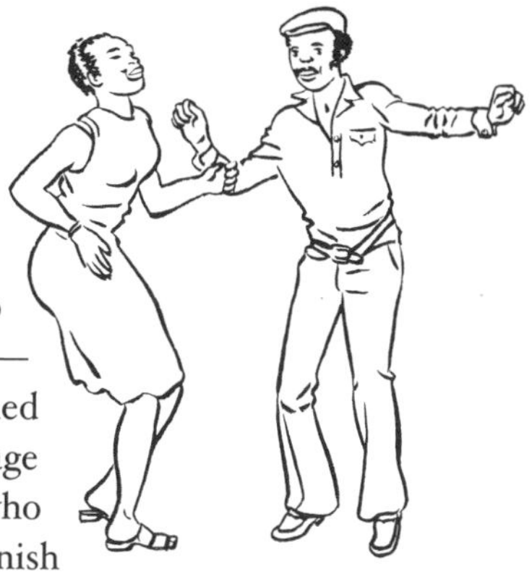

I met Mathias when he was still a kid. I was a friend of his big brother, Laurent. As you know, when you're a teenager, a two-year age gap can seem like the Grand Canyon, so there we were: Mathias (b. 1972) in one corner and us (b. 1970) in another. But eventually he joined our group, which used to hang out near the Cité Universitaire in Paris. We'd talk about comics—*Blueberry* and the early French editions of *Akira*—listen to Prince or New Order, and discuss the latest (in fact, the first) Coen Brothers films. We weren't so much trying to save the world as to find out about it. Mathias got into drawing very early, and he wasn't exactly top of the class in other subjects—not that it mattered much; he got into the ESAG (Graphic Arts School) in central Paris. Matt was gifted. People thought his style had something in common with that of Pierre Le-Tan, a Franco-Vietnamese illustrator of *New Yorker* fame, who was a close friend of the Cousin family. As for me, I quickly abandoned the idea of becoming an artist—but not of telling stories. I remember, when I was about ten, enlisting at least half a dozen classmates to illustrate stories for a comic book I wrote. (It didn't go beyond that afternoon, but the teacher loved it.)

When we were eighteen, a small group of us used to go to a little park in front of the Cousins' flat as soon as night fell and climb over the railings like we did as kids and smoke joints. We talked about doing a story about a superhero robot (we called him Elliott) and we came up with a beginning for it. So Mathias did a few pages of drawings. It went on for a few afternoons, but then the idea was forgotten. A few years later, we started a story about a private detective who hung out at the kind of clubs and rave parties we were going to by then. Our hero—whom we named Bernett, in homage to Jordi Bernet, who illustrated the Spanish *Torpedo* comics—snorted cocaine like a vacuum cleaner (even though we hadn't yet done it ourselves). We did maybe a dozen or so pages and then dropped it.

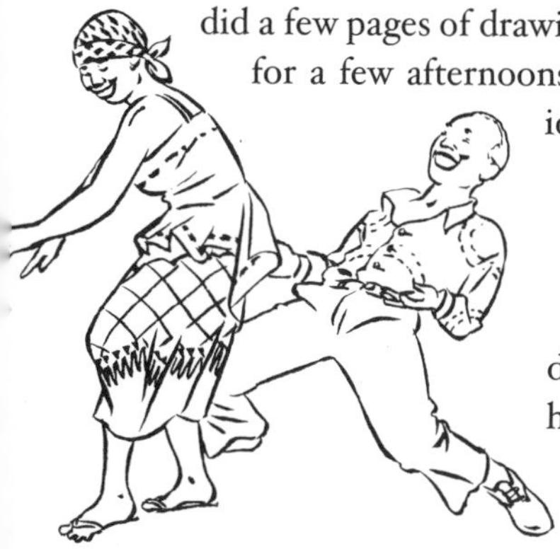

It was probably Mathias who first thought of telling the story of house music in comic form. It must have been around 1995, when he'd just discovered Robert Crumb and probably thought not only that a comic about music would work, but also that the down-and-out bluesmen in Crumb's drawings were a helluva lot like the pioneering DJs of Chicago, who were ripped off by their record labels. I remember us discussing the idea in some detail at the end of a table in a bar called Le Tambour in the Rue du Faubourg Montmartre, where Mathias had recently rented an apartment. (I would soon rent one two stories above him.) One of our friends was Sven Løve, who used to DJ the Cheers parties and was looking for someone to design his weekly flyers. He asked Mathias, who saw it as a great opportunity to establish the outline of what would eventually become *The Song of the Machine*. This also lasted more than an afternoon, but no more than a few weeks. However, the idea was a lot more solid than the robot superhero or the cocaine-snorting PI.

Mathias then went off to look for a publisher. He tried almost all of them, and only Delcourt editions took some interest in it. One of his editors, François Capuron, called Mathias in—as publishers used to do—and looked at his sketches. They asked if he could do an outline of the book and present some finished pages. I was in New York at the time, promoting a Respect Is Burning party

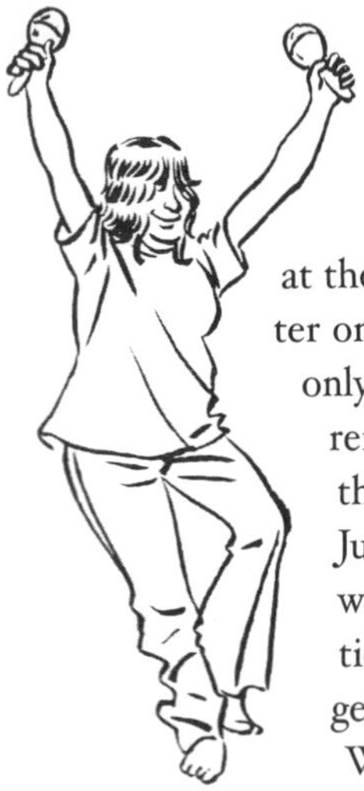

at the Twilo, so I wrote the chapter on New Order, which was the only one I could do without any reference material, and faxed the pages to Mathias. This was June 1998. We had a contract with Delcourt and a publication date, and we needed to get going with it.

We started with some interviews, the first significant one being with Didier Lestrade, the first journalist who wrote about house music in France, who told us all about Le Sept and Le Palace and, most importantly, showed me the proofs of Mel Cheren's book about Paradise Garage and West End, the club and label he'd cofounded. This opened our eyes to everything that had happened before the disco explosion. We also interviewed Daniel Vangarde (real name Bangalter) on a memorable evening at his home on Montmartre looking out over the whole of Paris as night fell but no one thought of switching on the lights—an interview so wide-ranging that by the end we were daunted by the task ahead of us. After our third interview, I started imagining traveling around the world meeting people, Mathias turned to me and said that was enough—we had to make a start. So we did.

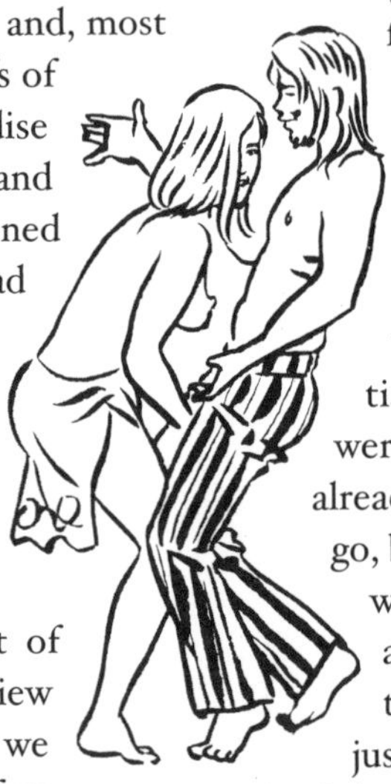

Strangely, I don't remember much about putting the first volume together, except that it happened quickly, without any great problems, and with complete harmony between me and Mathias—even when he would turn whole chapters upside down as he worked on them (in comics, the illustrator always takes the lead). But it always worked out all right, and we managed to fit everything into the first volume without losing our enthusiasm or sense of humor. Volume 1 came out in January 2000. Volume 2, which was supposed to follow immediately, was a whole different ball game. The times had changed, and so had we.

When we'd started planning the book, the "French Touch" phenomenon was just starting to develop. House music was a whole new territory, waiting to be discovered in France and widely derided by the rock magazines, and we were absolutely convinced everyone would get to know about it. And, indeed, by the end of the century, I was running Respect Is Burning parties all around the world, our friends Daft Punk were number 1, and techno was everywhere...In the beginning of the twenty-first century, the inevitable consequence was that house was starting to look its age—jaded, like the pioneers who discovered it initially. Or maybe it was just that we were approaching thirty (in fact, I was already there; Mathias didn't have far to go, but would never make it). So there I was, venting my spleen in hip hotels around the globe, my credit card up to the limit, while Mathias, who was just as broke, wallowed in frustration back home. I promised him pages of text that never materialized, and sometimes we asked, "What's the point?" The first volume had wowed the critics, but sales had hardly gone through the roof, so the publisher wasn't pushing us for the sequel.

In a moment of enthusiasm, we came up with a fictionalization of the whole story, with a single "hero" who somehow manages to be there at all the critical moments in the development of house (convenient for the writer and illustrator). He'd be born in the U.S., then immigrate to England just in time for the first raves, and find himself in France right when the French touch appeared. Two pages of this book (pp. 216–217) were drawn and are published here for the first time. I loved these

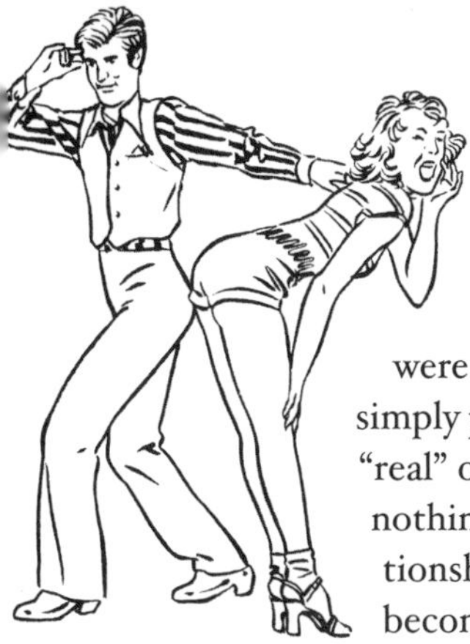

sketches. There was no sense that they were about music; we were simply producing a comic—a "real" one. But it all came to nothing. My working relationship with Mathias was becoming more antagonistic, and he must have gotten fed up with a story that I hadn't even written—incapable as I was of providing a complete scenario, which drove him nuts. (I argued that Stan Lee gave only pitches to Jack Kirby, but...) We dragged our feet; we worked on other things, which appeared in the media but aren't very pretty; Mathias got back in touch with Pierre Le-Tan and worked on the designs for a film by French director Valérie Lemercier; and in the end, we lost sight of *Machine*.

It was at that point that Romain Tassinari of Warner France contacted us and asked us to do a short comic strip about New Order for the release of their new album. So we went to meet them in Manchester and started working on a miniseries that was prepublished in the magazine *Magic*. We had a deadline and a fee, and it could turn into a nice little collectors' comic for New Order fans, with our names on it. What could be better? We were all fired up, and Mathias was at the height of his skills—less Crumb, more "ligne claire." I guess this was what gave us the confidence to make a fresh start on Volume 2.

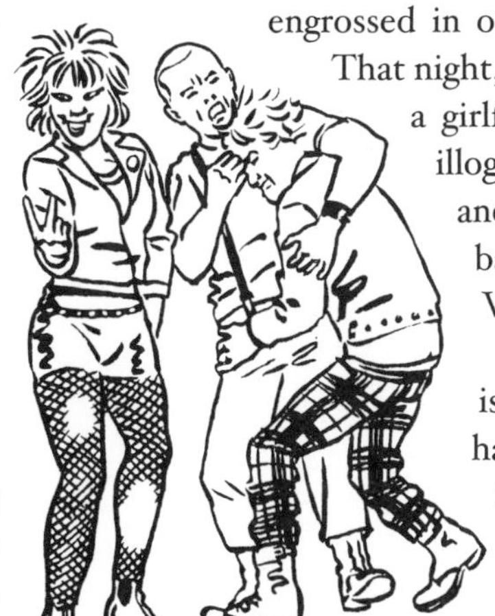

We decided not to try to fit everything into a single imaginary story, but to continue the format of Volume 1, with short chapters focused on key dates and events, each in a different style. What we'd done instinctively in the first volume became the blueprint for the second—with one slight difference: while most of the people in Volume 1 are real, those in Volume 2 are fictional (a small concession to our story idea). Mathias wanted to work quickly. I, as usual, said we should take our time...but I got started. And it went well. Again, I don't remember any particular disagreements or difficulties. Mathias changed his style in every chapter, and every page blew me away. As well as Crumb and ligne claire, his influences included the Japanese printmakers—Hokusai and Hiroshige...

Nevertheless, the work did little to pull us out of the depression that a decade of reckless partying and constant hangovers had dragged us into. One evening, shortly before we completed Volume 2, Mathias announced that he didn't want to work with me anymore, despite the fact that I'd suggested we do a third volume, in which all the characters from the first two would meet up for one night and we'd finally be able to do the fictional story, from start to finish—and in color! But Mathias was somewhere else, miles away, engrossed in other purely graphic projects.

That night, I felt like I'd been ditched by a girlfriend. There was something illogical about Mathias's decision, and I told myself he'd come back to *Machine*—especially if Volume 2 was a hit.

So we worked on and finished the book, as if nothing had happened. I remember, it was early summer, and we were at his flat. Mathias was drawing (flat on the floor!) and I was finishing off the dialogue. The style of the last chapter was totally improvised: the dialogue was so intense, that we'd decided the art should be almost abstract. And I liked the way Mathias was freewheeling through the pages, literally flowing from one to another as he sprawled on the floor. It was probably the first time in comic book history that the writer couldn't

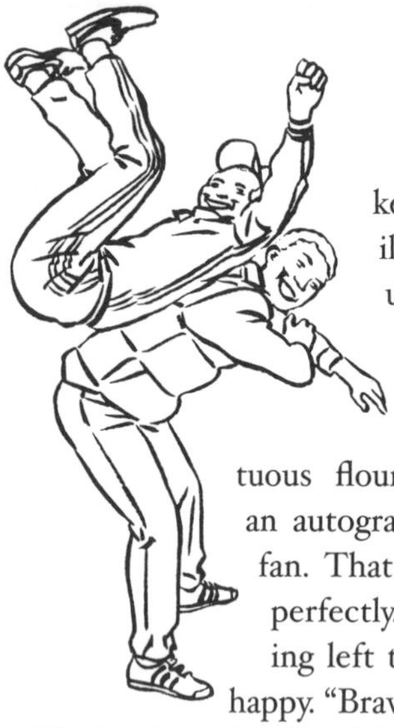

keep up with the illustrator. He got up, grabbed the last page, and scrawled "FIN" (*The End*) with a contemptuous flourish, as if signing an autograph for a groveling fan. That was it. And it fit perfectly. There was nothing left to do. Mathias was happy. "Bravo, Blot! We did it!" He shook my hand with both excitement and relief. Now he could enjoy the summer.

Things didn't go so well a few days later. We had a meeting at Delcourt to discuss the promotional plan, and as we walked up the Rue du Faubourg Poissonnière, our conversation turned sour. Mathias started telling me he couldn't stand "all this" anymore, pointing to people in the street, and I yelled at him, "What the hell do you mean, 'all this'?! What's that about? What exactly can't you stand anymore?" Then, at the meeting, Mathias refused to do anything—the book would just have to be printed; he wasn't going to commit to doing any promotional drawings or anything else.

Two or three days later, I was running the very first "Ete d'Amour" night on a barge on the Seine with my Respect colleagues, DJ Philippe Zdar and Hubert Boombass on samplers—together known as "Cassius"—and soon to be joined by Thomas Bangalter, who was on such a high that night that he went to get his keyboard. While they took care of the dance floor, I went up on deck to find Mathias. We were no longer working together and didn't see each other so much—well, not every day, anyway. I told

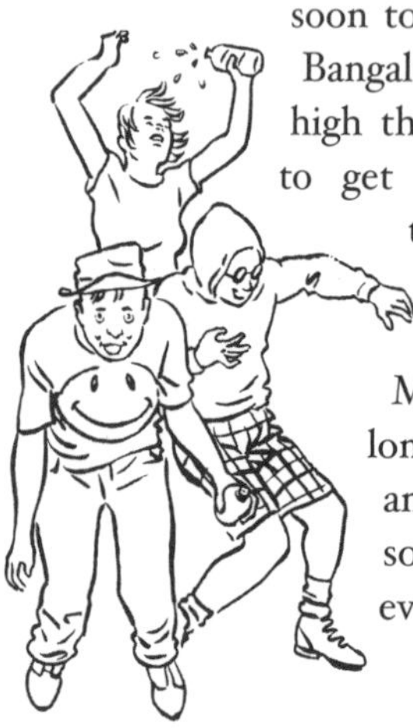

him I'd started writing stuff, not comics... I said I was thinking of writing a dictionary of film, which would take me at least ten years (I never did it). He said he was painting. He seemed calm, and was looking forward to a forthcoming trip to Japan. Except that he never went. He committed suicide on August 3, 2002.

The Song of the Machine 2 came out in September. Mathias wasn't there to see it.

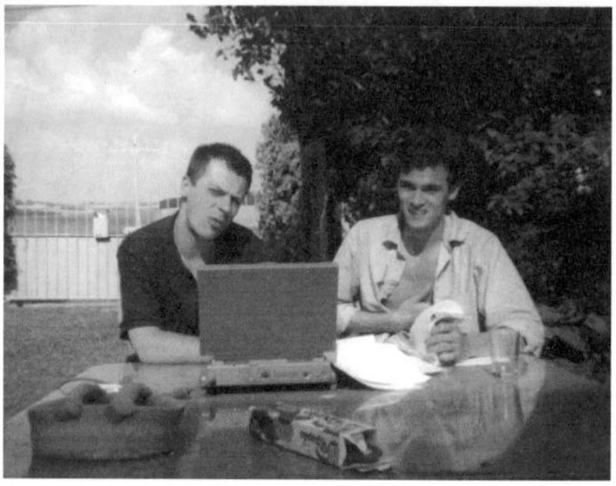

DAVID BLOT & MATHIAS COUSIN IN 1999

Years later, a guy called Benoit Pierre got in contact with me. He told me he'd been working as a bookseller when Volume 1 came out, and even though he knew nothing at all about house or the club scene, he could tell that this book would be a classic, and it absolutely had to be republished. So, with Benoit and Mathias's brother Laurent, I set about trying to find a new publisher for *The Song of the Machine 1*, which was no longer in the Delcourt catalogue.

In 2010, a new edition of *The Song of the Machine* appeared, with a preface by Daft Punk. (Nothing is simple with them—what was supposed to be a few hundred words of text turned into a photo shoot in a Los Angeles studio!) The publishing house, Manolosanctis, was new and enthusiastic, but ultimately short-lived; within a year, *The Song of the Machine* was no longer available. There was, however, also a beautiful Japanese

edition in 2014—thanks to our friend Shoichi Kajino.

The same year saw the release of *Eden*, a movie by Mia Hansen-Løve, which told the story of her brother, Sven Løve—his part in the burgeoning scene of the nineties, its rise, and its post-2001 fall. It was our own story, even though we'd never have told it like that. It was Mia's vision, not ours—nor an adaptation of *The Song of the Machine*. In the film, Mathias is called Cyril and is played by Roman Kolinka, who looks uncannily like him. (I'm called Arnaud and don't look much like Vincent Macaigne, though I confess he plays the hypochondriac just as well as I do.) There are a couple of scenes of us working on Volume 1 of *The Song of the Machine*. They were shot in Mathias's old apartment, which I'd moved into. It was November, and I watched the shooting on a monitor in my bedroom. A few yards away, in my living room, dressed to look like it did in 1999, actors playing Daft Punk, the Respect boys, Sven, Mathias, and me were laughing at the Paul Verhoeven movie *Showgirls*, as we sometimes did at the time…I won't attempt to describe the effect this time travel experience had on me.

Eden is a truthful recollection of that time—but it has to be said that Mathias could be as shadowy a figure as Romain plays him. There was another side to him, though—a crazy, off-the-wall side—that isn't shown in Mia's movie. Despite the tragic end to his life, everything he did—even in his bouts of depression—was full of laughter, joy, music, and carefree abandon.

He was never melodramatic, just morbidly irascible: occasionally at first, more and more frequently later on. Mathias was unpredictable. He could be incredibly funny and totally reckless. We loved watching *Seinfeld*, which had just finished its final season. One night, seeing Kramer slide through Seinfeld's door for the nth time, it was like a light came on, and I said to Mathias, "Shit, man, but that's you! Kramer is you!" And it was true: his hands might have been able to produce incredibly fine drawings, but the rest of his body could get completely out of control and commit the most outrageous blunders, worthy of Cosmo Kramer—and just as funny.

Mathias was handsome but never fit in. He was always elsewhere, or nowhere. There's no doubt he could have become a major illustrator (the increasing refinement and depth of his drawings across the two volumes is striking), but in the end, when all is said and done, so what? "What was the point?" Time to go.

DAVID BLOT, MAY 2016

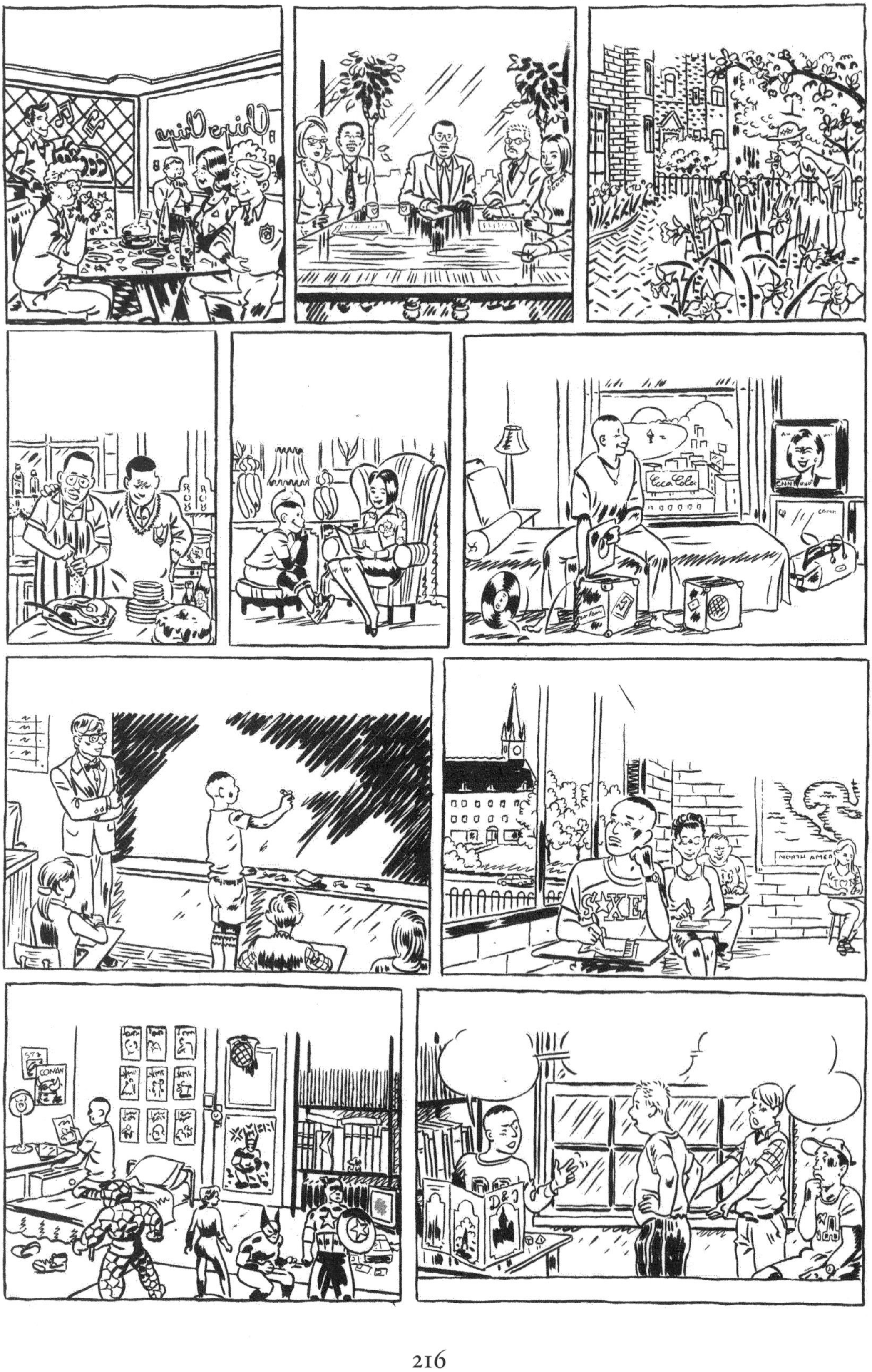
Coca Cola
CNN
CONAN

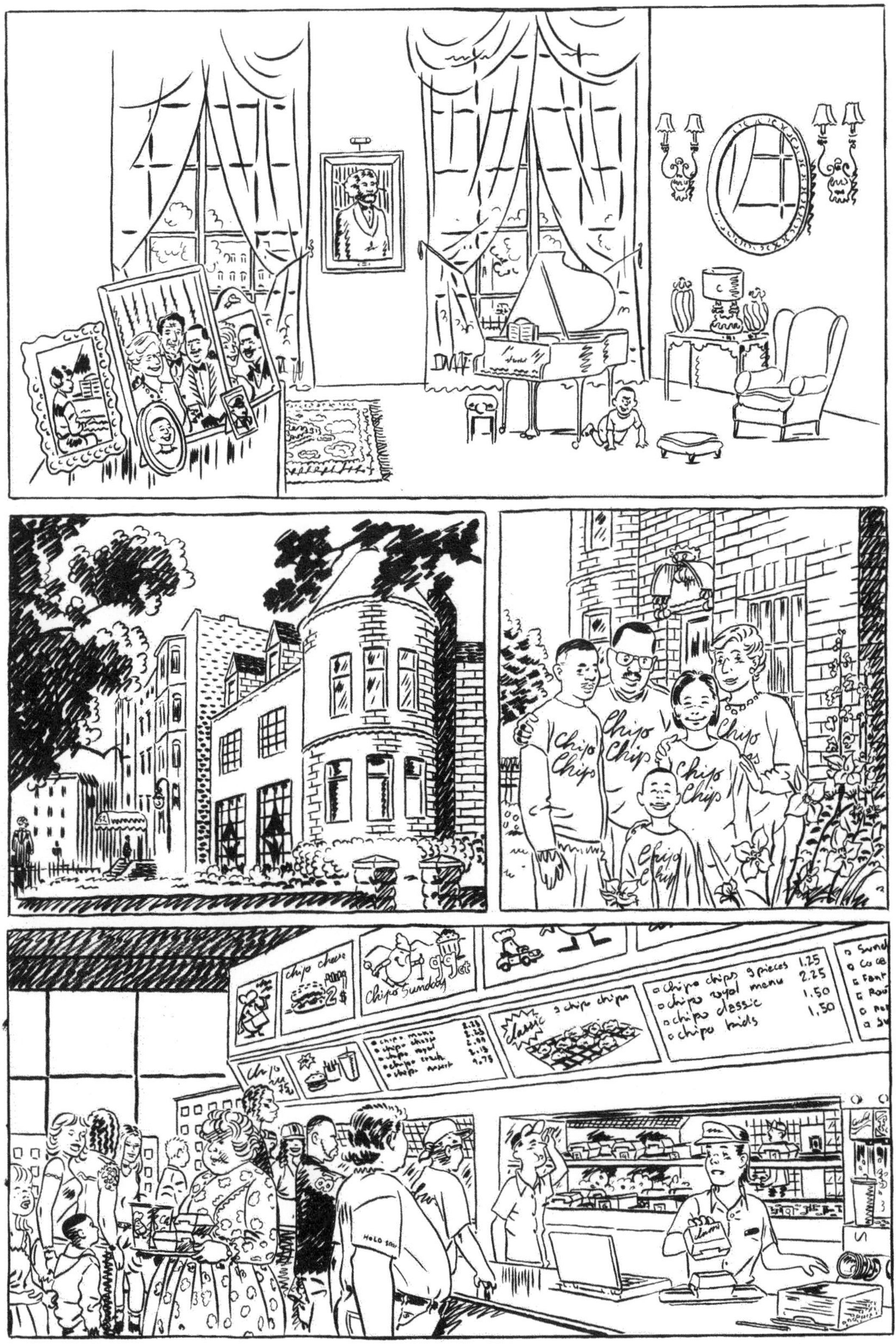
Chipo Chips
Chipo Chips
Chipo Chips
Chipo Chips
Chipo Chips
chipo cheese 2 $
Chipo Sunday
classic
9 chipo chips
chipo chips 9 pieces 1.25
chipo royal menu 2.25
chipo classic 1.50
chipo kids 1.50

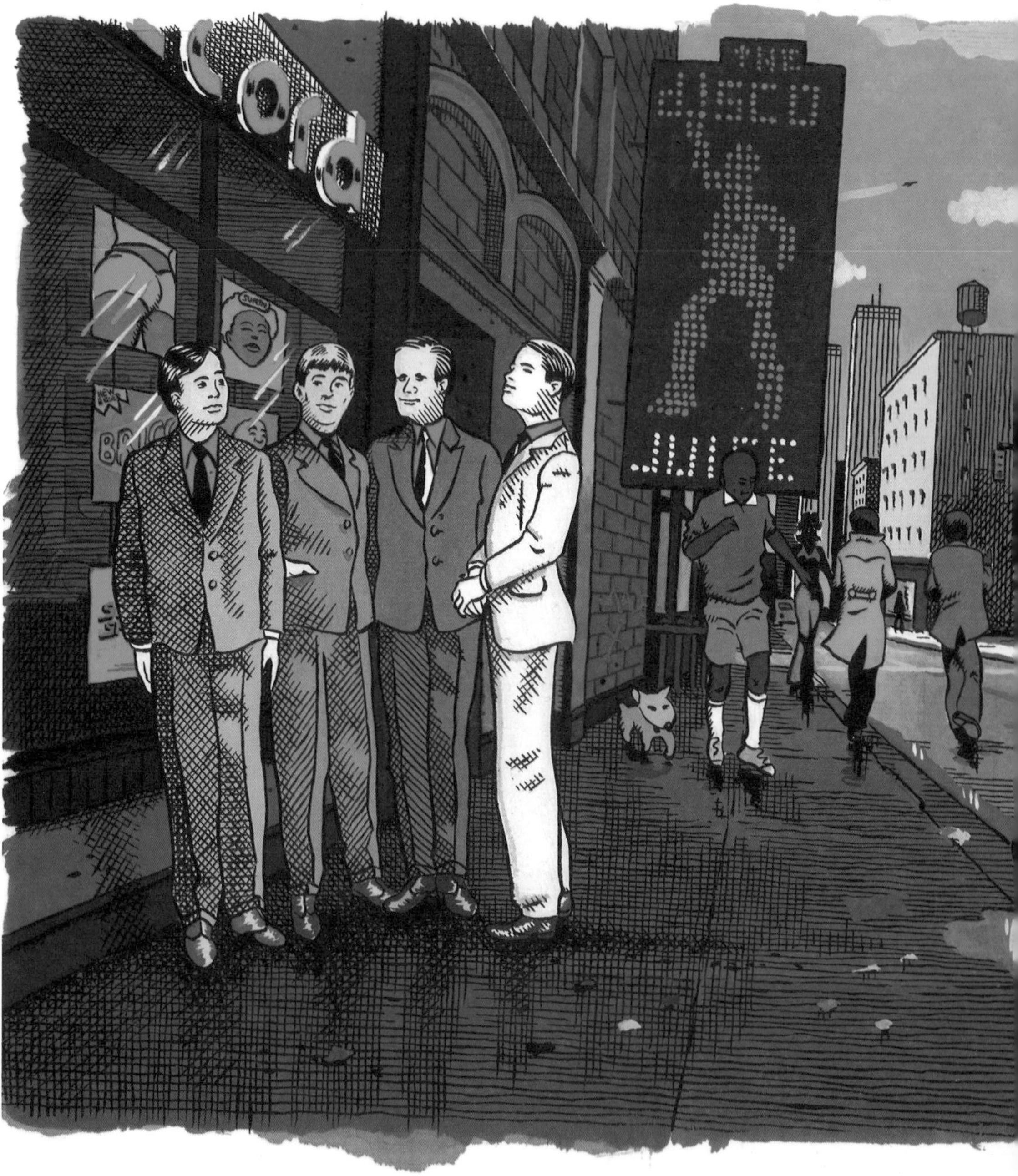
THE
disco

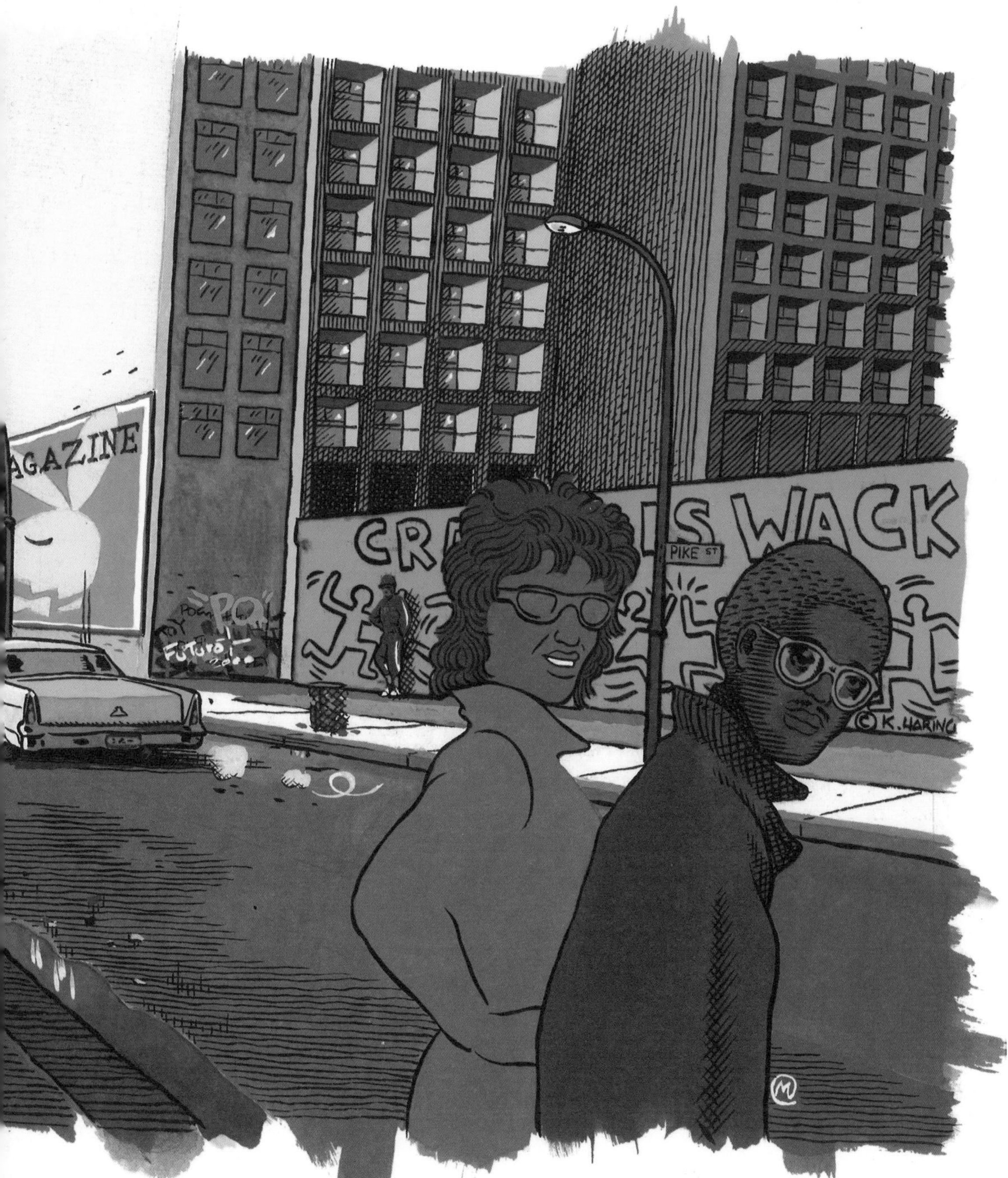
AGAZINE
CR
IS WACK
PIKE ST
© K. HARING

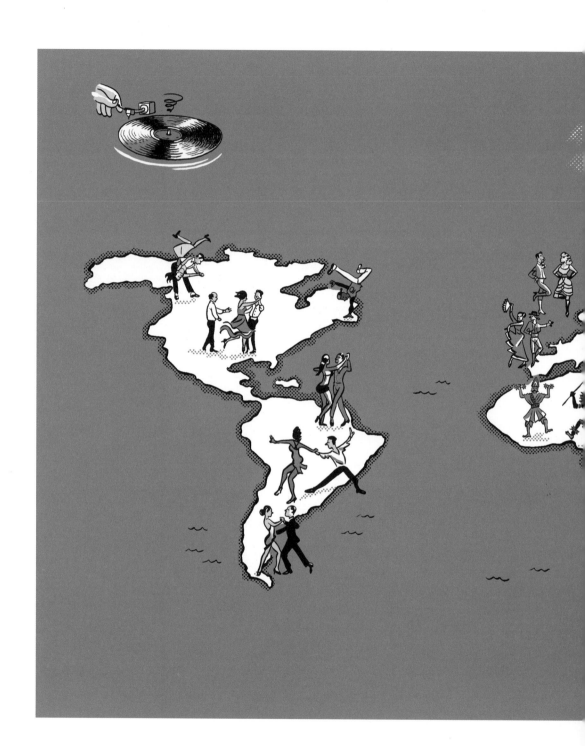

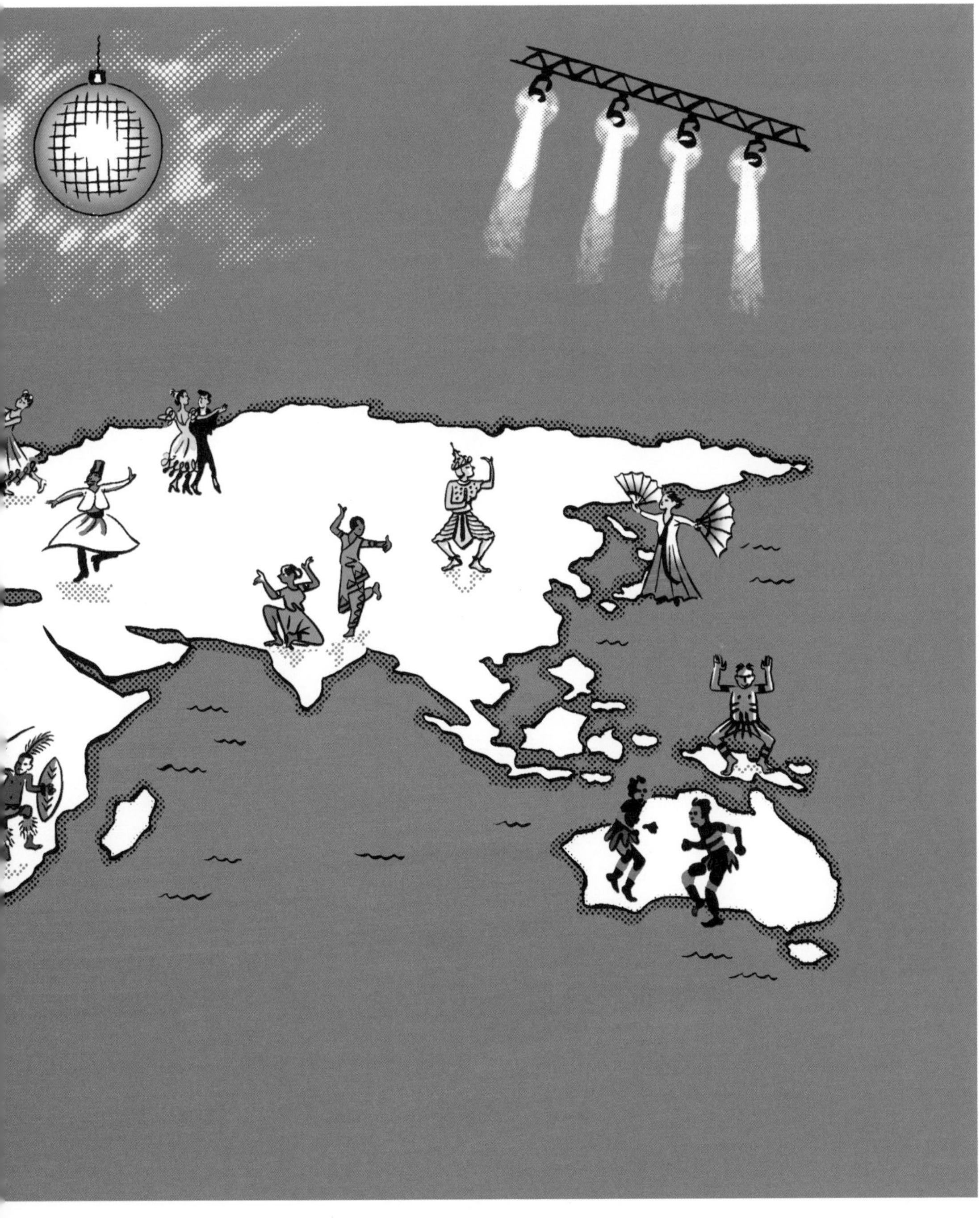

Mathias Cousin
September 7, 1972–August 3, 2002

My father was great friends with Mathias's grandfather. They were both from Vietnam.

The older I get, the more I think I draw like an Asian, even though I'm inspired by Western art. I think Mathias also inherited this Eastern way of using a brush. Still at his parents' house, in the country, are the 15 volumes of Hokusai's *Manga* his grandfather gave him. Mathias never ceased to refer to this encyclopedia of drawing. I remember the little books of rapid sketches he used to make with a brush. He had certainly retained what he'd learned from "the old man mad about art," as Hokusai called himself.

Mathias had, of course, also studied Robert Crumb, and he knew that I admired that strange artist, too. One day, he bought tickets for a jazz concert at an arts center in a sleazy suburb of Paris. It was given by a group that included the man himself, but his skills on the banjo were less convincing than his drawings, and we snuck out halfway through.

I was once commissioned to paint some large backdrops and needed help. I asked Mathias, who was still only a young man, and we spent several long days working together, sometimes without exchanging a single word. That was when I really got to know him and began to admire the boy I'd seen grow up.

In the summer of 2002, I was due to paint a large mural in Jean Cocteau's former apartment. Again, I called Mathias. We discussed how we would tackle the project and agreed to meet two days later. Sadly—very sadly—he never made the meeting.

Pierre Le-Tan, Paris, 2010

DAYS OF FUTURE PAST

2002–2020

LCD Soundsystem
Losing My Edge — 2002

Jay-Z
Dirt Off Your Shoulder — 2003

Octave One feat. Ann Saunderson
Blackwater (String Vocal Mix) — 2002

Ferrer & Sydenham Inc.
Sandcastles — 2003

Wiley
Wot Do U Call It? — 2004

Todd Terje
Eurodans — 2005

The Bug feat. Flowdan and Killa P
Skeng — 2007

DJ Mujava
Township Funk — 2008

Mr Oizo
Cut Dick — 2008

The XX
Basic Space
(Jamie XX Space Bass Remix) — 2009

Kavinsky and Lovefoxxx
Nightcall — 2011

Azealia Banks feat. Lazy Jay
212 — 2012

Cashmere Cat
Secrets + Lies — 2012

Frank Ocean
Thinkin Bout You — 2012

Jeremih feat. Natasha Mosley
Fuck U All the Time — 2012

**Daft Punk feat. Pharrell Williams
and Nile Rodgers**
Get Lucky — 2013

Mssingno
XE2 — 2013

DJ Rashad feat. DJ Phil
Everyday of My Life — 2013

Danny L. Harle
In My Dreams — 2014

Tirzah
Make It Up — 2015

Kanye West feat. The Weeknd
FML — 2016

Prince and the Revolution
Our Destiny / Roadhouse Garden — 2017

And since *Machines Began to Sing?* You've just read the first-ever English edition of *The Song of the Machine*, and we're pretty proud of it. *Le Chant de la Machine* was devised in the mid-1990s, completed at the end of that decade, and published in France, in two volumes, in 2000 and 2002. Now, almost another twenty years have passed, and I'm sure there's a burning question on your lips: what's happened since then? Everything. And nothing.

The story begins in Paris, at my beloved radio station, Radio Nova. It's 2017, and I'm doing one of my favorite things: playing records the old way, without a preconceived plan, but simply riding along from one delight to another—from Aretha Franklin to The Jesus and Mary Chain, from Bohannon to Ennio Morricone, from the latest Omar-S to the earliest Fela Kuti. And then I play a house number (or is it techno? that's debatable...) and a young studio assistant, Malo Williams, only twenty-one, sticks his head around the door and says, "What's that? It's awesome! Is it the latest L.I.E.S.?"

L.I.E.S. is a New York label run by Ron Morelli. Determinedly underground (its releases are vinyl only), L.I.E.S. became a benchmark in house music in the 2010s—one of those labels whose new releases are feverishly snapped up by collectors. Admittedly, the record I was playing sounded rather like a L.I.E.S., but it wasn't a L.I.E.S. And it wasn't anywhere near a new release. It wasn't from 2010, or 2005, or 2002, nor even 1999 or 1995. It was a 1990 track, a classic techno (or house?) twelve-inch by Ron Trent called "Altered States," the kind of cult disk that is totally unknown

outside the clubs but that DJs "in the know" have continued playing year on year—and it hasn't aged a minute. It's an absolute classic—so much so that no one has ever known whether it should be classified as house or techno (that same debate...). Which is why Malo Williams, twenty-one, who has a pretty good ear, genuinely thought a twenty-seven-year-old track was a recent release.

Malo wasn't even born in 1990. It's likely his parents hadn't even met. Not that this particular Ron Trent disk was particularly avant-garde—in 1990, anything techno (or house) was avant-garde. It was simply of its time, part of the continuum of musical development in Chicago. So how come, in 2017, it sounds like a 2017 disk?

Which got me thinking: 1990−27 = 1963. What 1963 disk could I possibly have thought was a 1990 disk if I'd heard it for the first time in 1990? Don't even bother: there isn't one. In 1963, The Beatles have never done a concept album (in fact, they barely have made a proper album, for that matter) Marvin Gaye still dreams of being Nat King Cole, and Kraftwerk were in high school. Psychedelia hadn't even started; nor had disco; punk had yet to take over from prog rock, because prog rock didn't even exist; and as for new wave or hip hop, let alone house (or techno)...all that was way in the future. In musical terms, the planet made forty-five revolutions between 1963 and 1990, between, say, "Love Me Do" and...well, "Altered States."

When I discovered house and techno in the late eighties, I was still in my teens, and people over thirty wouldn't even mention the words. A few condescended to say that it was just "disco," but most of them arrogantly and categorically asserted that "it wasn't even music," since it was produced by machines and not "real" instruments. In France, this attitude persisted for at least ten years. I remember playing "Da Funk," one of Daft Punk's first twelve-inch singles, to the editor of a highly respected rock magazine in 1995 and hearing him say, "This stuff means nothing to me." He was thirty-five and still hopelessly stuck in a world of indie guitar rock, clinging to passé nineties Nirvana or Oasis records and deaf to the great roar of house and deep from New York and Chicago—and soon Paris. He was no more receptive to my music than his uncle would have been when he was enthusing over the first Sex Pistols records and they were still idolizing Yes and prog rock. Or than his uncle's uncle would have been when Elvis was sidelined by a group of long-haired Liverpudlians.

Back then—in fact, right up until 2000—things were simple: pop culture was a teenage phenomenon, and with every generation, new sounds, new styles, new fashions, new ways of speaking, and, of course, new faces would replace those of the previous one, challenging the values and standards of the time. But the fractures were only superficial; whatever the new craze was, its essential elements remained the same: voice, bass, guitar, drums, and a standard pop song format. I remember Keith Richards being interviewed in the late seventies by a journalist who wanted to prove how modern punk was by making him listen to the Sex Pistols, to which Richards replied that it was exactly the same thing as the Rolling Stones—the same format,

the same vocal style, maybe a little faster, but less well played and less well sung. The journalist—who was, of course, young—didn't understand. For him, it was clear that punk had nothing in common with anything that had gone before. Obviously, Richards was right, but it didn't matter; the new generation agreed with the journalist: there was no one over thirty at Sex Pistols concerts.

Although the house revolution appeared to fall into a familiar pattern of conflict—the generation gap—it actually shifted the ground rules. There was a complete change of lexicon. With house, there were no longer "real" basses, guitars, or drums—and not much in the way of voices, either—but machines: synthesizers and rhythm boxes. It was no longer the pop format—three minutes max—but twice that, so that there were intros and outros a DJ could mix with. The idea was the very opposite of compiling a popular CD like those of Dire Straits or Sting, which would sell by the millions; it was back to vinyl—not the pop forty-five or the concept album, but the hybrid twelve-inch single, the maxi-forty-five—at the exact moment when vinyl was being ousted from record store shelves by the all-conquering CD. Soon after that, instead of getting a guitar and an amp for your eighteenth birthday, you'd get turntables and a mixing desk. Plus, it wasn't the kind of music you listened to on the radio or at a concert; you heard it at parties, raves, or clubs. And you no longer applauded the group, but the DJ—though no one wasted much time clapping; they just danced, without really even knowing how the sound was produced. And videos and glossy magazine covers gave way to white labels and no photos—enough to disconcert any thirty-something indie rock fan.

I'm writing this in 2018, and I'm almost fifty. For the last seven years, I've been hosting a daily show in which I play a little of everything—mainly new releases. Nothing scares me, nothing sounds foreign to me, and there's nothing I don't understand—whether it's Jamie xx, Cashmere Cat, Young Thug, PC Music, or Kadhja Bonet. In the last few years, I've happily taken on board everything that seemed new and exciting. I feel in step with my time, and although music obviously no longer excites me the way it did when I was a teenager, I have no difficulty in decoding the sounds kids are listening to now and hearing the same thing they hear. And yet, like my uncles and their uncles before them, I should really "not understand" today's music. Not only do I understand it; I'm familiar with it.

In the early 2000s, the atmosphere was totally different. House had suddenly become archaic, and being a DJ was something mundane and insignificant. True, house was on top of the charts, but it didn't have much left in common with the music we loved. It had been degraded by David Guetta and then a whole army of mass-market EDM hacks. Not easy to get kids excited about a style of music whose hits were mere parodies. People my age, with our DJs and House Nation, were regarded as long in the tooth. But believe me, in 2001, I was far from yearning for nostalgia. When we were working on Volume 2 of *The Song of the Machine*, Mathias and I hardly even listened to house anymore. Besides, the cult Parisian record stores of the nineties (BPM, Rough Trade...) were shutting down,

and even on the other side of the Atlantic, the New York institution Body & Soul was stopping its weekly party nights. My only remaining touchstone was Timbaland—for me the last great producer of our age, which (whether deliberately or accidentally) mixed soul classics with Aphex Twin–style doodling. But that was how it was, and I realized the fight was over; after all, Guetta was number one! All that to wind up here! A sad end.

With my partners Fred and Jérome, I no longer ran Respect nights, but we'd launched an annual "Ete d'Amour" festival on a barge on the Seine, which was pretty successful—especially when we tied in with labels like Ed Banger Records and went right to the limit, with people pushing the envelope and maxing out. But sometimes, we bombed. One of the few opportunities we had to invite our friend David Mancuso, for example, in 2007, only thirty or so people turned up. I remember when the barmaid went round the tables collecting glasses and empty bottles, the trash bag she was dragging behind her made more noise than the handful of dancers. A write-off. David was so shocked, he even left his vinyls behind at the club—which he said he'd never done before. It was the last time he played in Paris, and we took him right back to his hotel so we could round off the night alone—probably in some cramped little bar with a crappy sound system, where the DJs mixed eighties hits on an MP3 player...Oh, yeah, in the 2000s, the reputation of the switched-on city of Paris—and no doubt of London and New York as well—rested on a few small, friendly clubs (like Le Pulp or Le Baron) and some tiny bars offering shitty sound but a guaranteed good time. But what did people listen to in these places? What was the (obligatory) new music, new style, new sound, new trend that was making my Chicago house and Detroit techno things of the past? You won't believe it: it was rock 'n' roll, for chrissake!

In summer 2001, I read about a new band called The Strokes in *NME* (its last gasp before it folded). I went onto Napster (that dates it) and downloaded their first single, "Last Nite." And I couldn't believe my ears. The piece was nothing like any nineties song: there was no synth, no rhythm box (well, there was, but you couldn't tell), and no sampler. It was short, poppy, and breathless, and had a catchy refrain. No doubt about it, it was a great record...but for me, it was "been there, done that." It was somewhere between the Velvet Underground and Television with a melodic outline that seemed to come out of eighties British indie pop. Whether or not you could download it from Napster, you weren't in 2001 but back in 1977. Of course, I could understand the appeal of this short piece: it was a long time since rock had sounded so urgent. You could tell it had been written by twenty-year-old kids: it was simple, straightforward, and direct. Plus, there was the photo of the band...My god—leather jackets, long hair, and skinny jeans. What was this all about? Was it some kind of time warp? I'll get to the answers in a moment, but first let me drive home the point.

A rock spirit took over in the 2000s. At least, it was a type of rock spirit—the (inevitably outlandish) spirit of New York rock, played in CBGB or The Mudd Club, which was somewhere between, say, Johnny Thunders and James Chance..."Electroclash" was an eighties revival sound with a provocative flavor, à la Human League—electro for sure, but written by rockers and a long way from the utopian hymns of house and soul artists such as Joe Smooth or Lil Louis.

Another New York product was James Murphy's LCD Soundsystem, with its incredible debut single "Losing My Edge," in which Murphy, already in his thirties, explains that he was "there" in Paradise Garage and when Daft Punk arrived on the scene, and that he's now "losing [his] edge." The sense of nostalgia in the retro lyrics of this 2000 song are highly symbolic, and DFA Records, Murphy's own label, would be responsible for bringing rock back and combining it with electro. In fact, no one would talk about house or techno anymore; they'd talk about electro. In the 2000s, everyone had forgotten about Kerri Chandler and Chez Damier; they couldn't give a shit about House Nation anymore. So House Nation had to evolve and break with its own past to survive. The ground had already been well prepared by The Chemical Brothers, The Prodigy, and Fatboy Slim. Over in France, Daft Punk's young manager, Pedro Winter, left the duo to start Ed Banger Records, whose headline band would be Justice. Weren't they just Daft Punk clones? But they were also their antithesis. Justice didn't do techno—they'd grown up with that; they did hard rock or prog rock *with* machines and a techno approach. While Daft Punk, like "Mad" Mike Banks, kept a low profile. Justice made sure both their faces and their leather jackets were on the cover of every possible magazine. It was the same, but totally different. Besides, no one really danced anymore; they "headbanged," tapping out the rhythm with their toes.

Rap, which had been so central at the start of the 2000s, with artists like Timbaland and The Neptunes, kept the rhythm going on radio, but also rather lost track of its own rhythm. It had made it; now all it could do was more of the same. Superstars came and went—Jay-Z, Kanye West, Snoop Dogg, and Nas, of course—and when Lil Wayne burst on the scene, the needle turned south; but it wasn't until the 2010s that the Atlanta rappers took over. People were already getting nostalgic for the sounds that had generated house and techno, even though they'd kicked those two old fogeys themselves into the side-lines. Remixes of old singles—with updated tempi—started appearing on Napster, and once lame genres like Italo disco, from the early eighties, became the ultimate in refinement. Amy Winehouse was the new star of soul, but it was all about the soul of the seventies, miles away from the futuristic R & B of Aaliyah in the nineties. Indeed, 2001 was the year of the vintage remake. But the worst was yet to come: the fashion for "mash-ups"—a formless genre in which two totally unrelated songs were mixed together. Once the novelty had worn off, the level of creativity sank to just above zero. So between 2000 and 2010, we were too busy doing collages to be creative…History had skidded to a stop. Would there even be a future?

And yet in 2010, it was all change. Fred and I had moved the Ete d'Amour parties to a little mound by the Seine (it was still an "underground" event, with only a few hundred dancers) and that July we'd invited DJ Mehdi to provide the music. Now thirty, he'd become one of the best DJs in the Ed Banger stable. We were pretty sure the evening would be a success and cautiously anticipated a total attendance of around 1,000 people at any one time. By then, we no longer bothered to print flyers; a Facebook event page seemed to work well enough. Too well, even…By ten p.m., the mound was full, the bar staff couldn't serve the drinks anywhere near fast enough, and the security guys, at full stretch, started calling in "professional" reinforcements. But by eleven o'clock, the event seemed totally out of hand. Not one more person could be let in, the people on the barge were in danger of falling in the river, and those who were being turned away—mostly because they were under eighteen—were simply taking a short walk around the outside of the barriers and finding a place where they could hear the music just as well as those who were inside. So this little stretch of riverbank became a great sea of people, with fifteen-year-old kids all over the place, dancing and staggering around. By 11:30, the party was threatening to implode. I looked up and knew we had to stop it. Hundreds of people were staring down from the street—half of them just onlookers, the other half on their phones telling their friends to come and join in. The steps down from the famous Seine bridges were jammed with interlopers, flooding in to be part of it. 5,000? 10,000? They were coming from all sides. Just as Mehdi was about to put on the first disk, we stopped it—before it became a disaster.

The reason I'm telling you all this is to show that something had happened at the end of the 2000s which no one saw coming. Suddenly, kids wanted to dance again and listen to a DJ, rather than cram into rock bars full of Strokes clones with shit sound and warm beer. That same month, on that same stretch of riverbank, another Parisian club, the Concrete, started its famous "nights," with dancing till the early hours and old-style DJs playing underground techno on vinyl…Exactly what we'd done twenty years earlier when raves started. The electro-rock era had given way to…a return to house and techno! What kind of a timeline is that? *Groundhog Day* meets *Back to the Future*?

So why is house back in fashion? For almost a decade now, techno oldies have been cramming the clubs; Robert Hood, a DJ who epitomizes "the pure Detroit sound," is a star attraction at festivals; Kerri Chandler is idolized (again); and Larry Heard is getting kids on the dance floor who could be his grandchildren. I recently attended one of these techno festivals. There were at least 15,000 people there. When they left, there were riot police vans outside. When the riot police showed up at our raves in the nineties, it was to stop them, seize the gear, and arrest the organizers. This time, they were there just to keep everyone safe and help partygoers—who were all drunk off their asses—into taxis and into buses so they got home. When David Mancuso came to our Ete d'Amour party in 2007, only thirty people turned up; if he was alive today, you'd have to rent L'Olympia to accommodate all the kids who'd want to hear him. Fashions come and go…And the records keep coming. Wherever you look, there's techno,

house, deep, pseudo-deep (or some such derivative). Why should I feel out of touch when kids of twenty are coming up with rhythms Todd Terry produced in 1992? And why wouldn't Malo Williams think Ron Trent's "Altered States" was released last Friday? Having got over the anachronistic "rock revival," we're right back where we were before, in 2001.

So why are we stuck in this groove? Why are kids applauding—and not just politely—DJs in their fifties or even sixties, when even twenty years ago I wouldn't have been caught dead listening to fifty-year-old rockers. No way. Now, don't misunderstand me. I'm not mocking. There are a ton of good pieces out there today, on vinyl, on CD, on Bandcamp and Spotify, not to mention Soundcloud…More new stuff comes out every minute than there are minutes in the day to listen to it all. You don't have to innovate to make a good record. In 2018, there's been good house, (very) good hip-hop, good techno, lots of good rock, and more styles coming from Africa than you can shake a stick at. If you want seventies krautrock, eighties electro, or nineties trip-hop, there's plenty of that, *too*. There's even a Daft Punk album featuring sixty-seven-year-old musicians with their hair tied back. There's a stack of everything. So the problem isn't a lack of quality. It's what comes next…?

There are several theories. Let's start with the dystopian one. In the mid-fifties, "rock and roll" (blues, to be precise, but let's not get into that here…) wiped the popular music slate clean. Everything that had come before was all of a sudden "old people's" music. Until then, kids had been kids, adults had been adults, and for just two or three years of your life you had the misfortune to be an "adolescent." Elvis changed all that. His rock songs signaled a cultural takeover by the baby boomers—or, rather, a takeover of pop culture, which was still "underground" in the fifties, but would gradually come to monopolize everything—from film music to comic series. It was this whole pop culture revolution—essentially a teenage phenomenon—that was responsible for the changes of fashion I talked about earlier. And the pattern continued for forty or fifty years...until 2001, when the system jammed.

There's no longer an "adolescent" period: adolescence takes hold earlier and earlier and never really lets go. Look at the clothes you're wearing. Seriously? At your age? Look at the twenty-first-century explosion of Marvel movies—which came out of those, then, embarrassing sixties comic strips; don't they perfectly symbolize the domination of teenage pop culture? Let's not even mention the endless recycling of the 1977 *Star Wars* movie...All this stuff was conceived in the last century, but is still dominating our lives today. My generation—or, rather, *our generations*, since we're all to blame, whether we're seven or seventy-seven—have been allowed to ooze and seep into the succeeding ones, so that parents (and grandparents) in 2018 are quite happy to watch the umpteenth sequel (or prequel) to *Star Wars* with their (grand)kids, whereas, when I was a kid, my parents would sneer angrily at having to buy me a comic. My father read adult books and led his adult life; he wasn't interested in imposing his own childhood tastes on me. But what was my father's childhood really like? And this is where the story gets murky...It was wartime, the Second World War...a time when kids hid from the bombs and fled from Paris. My father didn't have time for adolescence; he went straight from childhood to adulthood.

Since 1945, the Western world has lived—more or less—in peace (though it's waged war elsewhere, of course). And that's why pop culture spread. Adolescence, the innocence of youth, John Hughes films...they all belong to the realm of peace. Among the first kids to play in the ruins of World War II—literally—were The Beatles, in Liverpool. But the early twenty-first century has been worrying—terrifying, even. I'm writing this in March 2018 for a book that's due to be published in 2019, and sometimes I wonder whether it'll ever appear, the future looks so threatening. It's significant that the debut album by New York band The Strokes came out in October 2001, just a month after the Twin Towers came down. So the twenty-first century began with a reactionary rock revival and the collapse of a symbol of the modern age. The year 2001 took us back in time, as if we were watching a parody of our adolescence. Where was the underground now? What was there left to dominate, now that everything was already dominated? Pop culture was everywhere...

But what if today's teenagers are actually paying attention? What if they themselves realize that humanity's problems can't be resolved by a few songs, as some people naively believed in the seventies—nor even by dancing together after swallowing Ecstasy? Young people today are confused and disturbed; maybe they sense that the future won't be written in music—neither on guitar nor on vinyl. Never has popular music been so downbeat and depressive as in 2018. Today, as I write this, after decades of domination by the particularly foggy, drug-induced sound of Atlanta hip hop, the U.S. charts are topped by the Florida-based XXXTentacion, who a few weeks after I wrote this afterword was found dead in Florida. His music is not exactly revolutionary, but the man (a mere kid of 20, in fact) was a human apocalypse—like a zombie from *The Walking Dead* (and I'll spare you a discourse on the contemporary symbolism of the phenomenal success of that series): I can understand that for a young person today, this is a far more vital question than who, what, and how the future of pop culture might be...

So theory number one is: The teenage king is dead; pop culture is at an end. "The Beatles, Michael Jackson, Prince, Daft Punk...Who cares? A nuclear holocaust, started by a fanatic, is about to descend on us and a fascist militia is preventing us from escaping. In any case, it's 130 degrees outside. This is our reality." That was what my time travel correspondent from 2032 tells me. (I did warn you this was the gloomiest vision!)

The second theory is generally along the same lines as the first, but explains things in more objective terms and allows us a slightly more reassuring outlook. Taking it from that vile curveball in 2001 that messed up our heads and hearts...The twenty-first century had finally arrived, but it hadn't brought us the future any more than the last one. Leastways, not the future we'd imagined, but one that had been hijacked by killer drones, tiny designer screens, and paranoid social media. Where was the "brave new world" we'd been promised? On hold. Or possibly even canceled. And yet the whole

techno revolution—yes, the whole damned thing—had been based on just such a vision. It was already 2001 in 1973, with Herbie Hancock; in '75, with Kraftwerk; in '78, with Moroder; in '82, with Prince ("1999"); in '83, with New Order; and ever since, with Juan Atkins in Detroit. It was 2001 the whole time. We were so conditioned by science fiction, arcade video games, and the advent of the computer, that the Future (with a capital F) had become our collective project. It motivated us. In fact, it drove us. And then...rock came back and the Twin Towers came down. Was that it, 2001? When would the next window of opportunity be? In 3001? Even 2099 is too far away. But how were we to project ourselves into the future without a project? Without a goal, there can be no drive; without drive, no innovation. We're doomed to a retro future—to seeking a refuge from the painful, polluted, and overpopulated present...A future we hinted at in the last chapter of *The Song of the Machine*. Look at the recent resurgence of analog sound—the elitist fashion for electro music that sounds "like it did before." I mean, who wanted things to sound "like they did before" in 1987? No one. Without a horizon beyond 2001, there can be no projection, no future...so we simply press pause. And techno, which was supposed to be the soundtrack to the future, is condemned to run around in circles like a headless chicken. Hmm...I'm not sure this theory is any less gloomy than the first one. Let's move on to number 3...

There's a word I haven't used up to now, and yet it's the keyword underlying all the developments I've been talking about— and that word is "internet." Forgive me for stating the obvious, but the internet changed everything—and not just around the edges, not just the system of record companies that had established itself little by little since the fifties (oh, yes) and suddenly disintegrated at some point in the early 2000s. Today's kids are the first to have grown up with instant access to the whole of music. ALL of it. Oh, sure, the vast majority of them listen to the same few things and stream the same few tracks, by the billions; in fact, the latest research shows that the more there is available, the less wide-ranging people's tastes are. But that paradox applies to the masses, the vast majority, 99 percent of humanity, and the fact that you're reading this means you're in the tiny group of true music lovers—and we music lovers not only have access to, but also *do* access ALL of music. It's an eruption, a seismic shift. Forget all that stuff about apocalypses and even about being stuck in 2001; the reason we're in a period of stagnation is that we're in the process of taking in, stumbling upon, storing up, tracking down, throwing away, sorting through, thinking about, and getting the hang of ALL of music—a mass of music that crosses over from one style to another, from one period to another...

In the nineties—the period of discovery in the clubs—there was no question of mixing styles or of playing a disk that was more than three months old. Programming a house song in the middle of a techno set was risky; a hip-hop track was hard to justify (if you did, it had to be less than five minutes); and a pre-rhythm box disk was totally unthinkable. "Don't screw your crew," as we used to say in the Paris clubs back

then. And it was a case of "each to his own club"—unless you wanted to guest at other clubs to vary the ambience. Today, kids are much more open. Hip-hop and house, rock and techno, salsa and zouk...why not? And there's no current revival—or, rather, there's nothing but revivals, stacking up one on top of the other, without conflicting. There's an eighties revival, a nineties revival, and a seventies revival. So what? If you like new wave, that's fine. You're into country, cool. You only do jazz, no problem. Italo-disco or garage house, right on. In theory, every one of us can have our own little niche. And it happened quickly. Very quickly.

Let me tell you a little story. One night, right at the start of the 2000s, just when The Strokes and skinny jeans were taking off and a whole kindergarten was starting up bands beginning with "The," one of those bands appeared on French TV, and the presenter asked them who'd influenced them the most. One of them piped up, "The Sonics and the whole psyché rock scene from 1966 to '69." That's word for word what he said, and the kid wasn't even eighteen. In 1980 or 1990, it would have taken a Sonics fan in France months to track down all their records, and years to trace the entire ancestry of the precise sub-genre the band belonged to—in this case, psyché rock. To collect everything "from 1966 to '69"...a lifetime. But from 2001—in fact, from the start of Napster everything was available instantaneously. And so this group of baby rockers could go into a little 1966–69 psyché rock bubble and condense a whole lifetime into five minutes. How could they possibly be frustrated enough to want to create anything?

There isn't enough time. Or, rather, it isn't the right time…

We haven't finished eating yet. And after that, we'll need time to digest. And to rethink everything. In the meantime, we're rediscovering things, going back over stuff—even before the baby boom/rock 'n' roll revolution. Hey, just last Thursday, a Thursday in 2018, the English musician Henry Wu appeared at New Morning, Paris's mecca of jazz. Wu, not yet in his thirties, is a worthy representative of the jazz revival, tracing his sound back to the Herbie Hancock of the 1970s while suffusing it with the bass-heavy ambience of London grime. The hall was jammed, and the audience's average age was twenty-two. Twenty-two and listening to jazz…when was the last time that happened? Today, it's possible to worship people like Arthur Russell, Wally Badarou, Harumi Osono, and Lucio Battisti at the click of a mouse. An American, a Benin-born Frenchman, a Japanese, and an Italian—all super obscure at the time they were creating their music, and hardly known at all outside their respective countries. All (re)discovered thanks to the internet. And to Napster babies. What is there to complain about? There are still so many beautiful things to discover, so many records out there, so many forgotten artists and even (or, rather, especially) neglected countries to unearth…Eat, digest, rethink…It'll take a while.

Of course, there *are* new styles, new genres. Plenty. Dubstep, footwork, bass, half-step, gqom, kuduro, reggaeton, beats, trap, lo-fi house, nu disco, cloud, witch house, U.K. funky, grime, chili wave, to mention only a few—some ultra-serious, some ultra-loony. Put any two words together and you've made a new genre. (The ultimate was "tech house," a kind of indeterminate catchall style played in Ibiza.) Take trap, for example—well, it's simply rap with a *t* on the front. Okay, Atlanta trap is different from nineties hip-hop, but nineties hip-hop, which was sampled, was nothing like the eighties sounds of Afrika Bambaataa or Rick Rubin. Most of these "hyphenated" genres are basically rap, house, techno, dub, or one of their variants—drum 'n' bass or ambient house, if you prefer. In other words, they're readily identifiable genres, sometimes combined with others to make them as variegated as possible, but not necessarily more variegated than Masters at Work's 1991 "Nervous Track." Yes, when I listen to one of Dean Blunt's productions or, to be honest, one of my favorite tracks of recent years, "Xe2" by the English artist MssingNo (with around 333,000 views on YouTube, it hasn't exactly gone viral)—a soaring melodic loop that drives you crazy because the rhythm is never really established—when I hear things like that, yes, I can taste the future again, but a future that merely takes existing techniques to the extreme. So the soundtrack to the year 2018 sounds like a limitless concoction of nineties extrapolations. But going back to trap—Atlanta's brand of rap, whose current stars include Future…Now, Future is an excellent example, with his numbed delivery, minimalist melodies, obsessive repetition, and a layer of darkness as black as the smoke from the Detroit factories. In fact, Future's mood and beat are Detroit techno, only slower—much slower, languorous, drained…like Drexciya on Tranxene. Everything about Future sounds underground, niche, minimal...and yet he's number one in the U.S. ("Mask Off," the 2017 classic, has 275 million YouTube views). And there are other hybrids that are even more off-the-wall...

There are three letters I've been avoiding like the plague, but—especially from a U.S. point of view—not mentioning them would be like ignoring the elephant in the room. EDM—electronic dance music. In other words, a white, hetero, redneck, vulgar, noisy, glitzy version of the music we've been celebrating in *The Song of the Machine*. Of course, everything is recycled and reused: the eighties Italo hits I used to love (by Gary Low, Gazebo, Kasso, and all the rest) were in fact nothing but cheap dance music for the masses. Nineties Eurodance was even worse: "recordings" by Corona and Culture Beat and 2 Unlimited were mass-produced in Milan and Amsterdam. But most of those never made it into the U.S. charts—any more than "real" house or techno, which remained hopelessly hidden even in their own country...until EDM came along. Ironically, their European bastard child—with its interchangeable DJs, like Tiesto and Martin Garrix, earning more for a two-hour set than David Mancuso earned in his life (and I'm not exaggerating)—took the U.S. charts by storm. It's too soon to assess the long-term damage EDM did to teenagers worldwide, but at least it allowed the underground to regroup. There was no longer any chance of confusing the two, as there had been at the start of the 2000s, when David Guetta and what was left of the French touch cannibalized house. Now it was "whatever does it for you." "1966–69 psyché rock,"

Kuduro-cum-Bass, or Herbie Hancock revisited for aficionados; EDM for the masses—and good luck to them. But let's be honest, it's all too easy to lapse...Like the night I got totally shit-faced in the VIP area of a scraggy club and climbed onto a bench to sing and dance to The Black Eyed Peas' "I Gotta Feeling"—I had nothing against EDM then...Let's move on.

At the start of the twenty-first century, music was no longer vertical, but horizontal. When it was vertical, it was filtered—first by the record companies, then the radio stations, and sometimes TV channels, with the press waiting more or less eagerly to gift-wrap what got through—and a select few Artists (with a capital A) made it to the top of the pyramid (like David Bowie in his "Low–Heroes–Lodger" period or Prince with "Sign o' the Times") and led us toward the future. It was also vertical in terms of the format it was marketed in: first vinyl, then cassette, then the forced march to CD...and all dictated by the industry. The twenty-first-century explosion made music horizontal in that the different genres rubbed shoulders and tastes became infinitely varied. No one today listens to music in the same way as the guy next door. Streaming? MP3? YouTube? Wav? Vinyl? CD? On your phone or through speakers? At a club or a festival? Free or on subscription?...Whatever your preference, you can have music everywhere, all the time—and ALL of it.

Throughout the fifty-year history of pop culture, the vast majority of the music produced and consumed has been Anglo-Saxon. At the top of the (vertical) tree were the U.S. and the U.K.; then came the rest of the world. Since 2000, the whole thing has opened out horizontally. In terms of electronic music, the French touch has been followed by an assortment of Norwegian producers (Todd Terje, Lindstrøm, Prins Thomas), who put Scandinavia on the electro map; Berlin, of all places, has become the minimal mecca and a musical refuge for young people from all over Europe; Portugal has attracted experimenters in "lo-fi house" (what a name!); and in Romania, people have started dancing to "microhouse" (what a name!). And this time, the revolution isn't restricted to Europe: there's Ricardo Villalobos in Chile and Peggy Gou in Korea, and don't forget the Canadian Kaytranada. And, of course, Africa is exploding (like so many other places at the start of this new century)—from Nigeria to the R.S.A.—and the whole world is dancing to Coupé-Décalé (from Ivory Coast), gqom (South Africa), and Kuduro (Angola), while airwaves across the world have become infused with the Caribbean rhythms of Drake (Canada) and Rihanna (Barbados). Cross-cultural blending and openness seem to be the (unconscious?) antidote to the prevailing musical mindlessness. And the tidal wave continues to travel horizontally, in all directions, around the globe. The internet has made music available, everywhere, to everyone. That's a lot to digest…

The future is fermenting. It's disseminating. We need to adjust our watches: 2001 isn't here yet.

DAVID BLOT, APRIL 17, 2018, PARIS

May 14, 2014: A section of King Street in New York is renamed "Larry Levan Way." François Kevorkian, David DePino, Joey Llanos, and Jocelyn Brown play and sing at a "family" block party in homage to both Larry and Paradise Garage. The video is on YouTube— everyone dancing together: all ages, all genders, all races. It's not an act; it's real. Everyone together. Poignant.

May 5, 2016: Barack and Michelle Obama welcome a number of the "fathers" of Chicago house to the White House: Jesse Saunders, Wayne Williams, Alan King, Terry Hunter, Mike Dunn, and Tony and Andre Hatchett.

November 14, 2016: David Mancuso dies in New York.